ROUTLEDGE LIBRARY EDITIONS:
ECONOMICS AND SOCIETY

Volume 3

AN INTRODUCTION TO URBAN RENEWAL

AN INTRODUCTION TO URBAN RENEWAL

MICHAEL S. GIBSON
AND
MICHAEL J. LANGSTAFF

Routledge
Taylor & Francis Group
LONDON AND NEW YORK

First published in 1982 by Hutchinson & Co. (Publishers) Ltd.

This edition first published in 2026
by Routledge
4 Park Square, Milton Park, Abingdon, Oxon OX14 4RN

and by Routledge
605 Third Avenue, New York, NY 10158

Routledge is an imprint of the Taylor & Francis Group, an informa business

British Library Cataloguing in Publication Data
A catalogue record for this book is available from the British Library

ISBN: 978-1-032-97576-4 (Set)
ISBN: 978-1-041-12751-2 (Volume 3) (hbk)
ISBN: 978-1-041-12754-3 (Volume 3) (pbk)
ISBN: 978-1-003-66641-7 (Volume 3) (ebk)

DOI: 10.4324/9781003666417

Publisher's Note
The publisher has gone to great lengths to ensure the quality of this reprint but points out that some imperfections in the original copies may be apparent.

An Introduction to Urban Renewal

Michael S. Gibson

Principal Lecturer in Urban Planning, City of Birmingham Polytechnic

Michael J. Langstaff

Regional Director, The North British Housing Association Ltd

Hutchinson

London Melbourne Sydney Auckland Johannesburg

Hutchinson & Co. (Publishers) Ltd

An imprint of the Hutchinson Publishing Group

17–21 Conway Street, London W1P 6JD

Hutchinson Group (Australia) Pty Ltd
30–32 Cremorne Street, Richmond South, Victoria 3121
PO Box 151, Broadway, New South Wales 2007

Hutchinson Group (NZ) Ltd
32–34 View Road, PO Box 40–086, Glenfield, Auckland 10

Hutchinson Group (SA) (Pty) Ltd
PO Box 337, Bergvlei 2012, South Africa

First published 1982

Set in Times

Printed in Great Britain by The Anchor Press Ltd
and bound by Wm Brendon & Son Ltd
both of Tiptree, Essex

British Library Cataloguing in Publication Data
Gibson, M. S.
An introduction to urban renewal.
1. Urban renewal
I. Title II. Langstaff, M. J.
711'.5 HT170

ISBN 0 09 147500 7 cased
0 09 147501 5 paper

Contents

Figures and tables

Figures

Tables

Preface

Since the late 1960s we have been involved in urban renewal in a variety of ways – in teaching and research, working in local government, the housing association movement and with community groups. Some years ago this experience brought us to the view that there was a need for an introductory text on this subject. The only available textbook was Wilfred Burns' *New Towns for Old: The Technique of Urban Renewal*, published in 1963, but there had been significant developments by the mid-1970s. The 'inner cities debate' reinforced this view, as the literature on various aspects of renewal expanded rapidly and the future of the older areas of our towns and cities became a central feature of urban policy.

We completed the manuscript as the European Campaign for Urban Renaissance was being launched, an attempt to stimulate progress in renewal through an international exchange of ideas and experience. However, rather than the dawn of a golden age, the immediate prospects in this country herald a return to the Dark Ages. International recession and government economic policy are accelerating the processes of urban decay and reducing the public resources necessary for programmes of renewal.

The aim of this book is to provide a basic text which critically appraises contemporary practice and future prospects within a historical perspective. The book is intended to cater primarily for students on vocationally oriented courses in planning, environmental health, architecture, housing, estate management, community and social work, together with those on courses with an 'urban studies' content, such as geography, sociology, and environmental studies. For such students the book provides a context within which they can develop their particular interests. In addition this overview will be valuable for the variety of professionals working on one aspect or another of urban renewal, for it presents an analysis of the broad process of which their work is a part. Finally, people working with residents' organizations and other voluntary organizations will find that the book helps them to view local issues in a wider context.

This book has been written in our 'spare time'. We are indebted to Mick Bruton and John Ratcliffe and to Rab MacWilliam at Hutchinson for their patience and encouragement during its prolonged gestation. Our thanks also to Martin Morris for assistance with the illustrations and to Geoff Wilkins for compiling the index. The main debt is to our wives and families. Our spare time was also their weekends and holidays, and they objected far less than we had any right to expect. In addition to putting up with a frequently preoccupied and absent husband, Sue Gibson typed several drafts of the manuscript.

Of course, many colleagues and friends have influenced the development of our views over the years, but the responsibility for the text remains ours.

Michael S. Gibson
Michael J. Langstaff
March 1981

1 Introduction

For over a hundred years urban renewal has been an important and controversial public issue. Successive generations have been faced with the problems of decaying urban areas and the consequences of previous attempts to solve them. The impact of urban renewal has been massive. Nearly two million houses, the homes of some five million people, have been demolished since the 1930s through slum clearance. Over three million houses have been improved with the aid of grants since 1949.[1]* This huge state sponsored enterprise has resulted in substantial changes in the physical and social fabric of urban areas.

Yet the mutually reinforcing effects of economic decline, housing decay and environmental degradation are still only too apparent to residents of particular neighbourhoods in our towns and cities. In 1977 Shore, then Secretary of State for the Environment, described the plight of the several million people living in inner urban areas as 'the biggest complex of economic, social and physical problems we face'.[2] Today urban renewal figures prominently in parliamentary debates, discussions in council chambers, and heated exchanges in community centres and school halls when the future of a few Victorian streets is at stake.

The 'inner cities debate' of the mid-1970s marked the end of a transitional decade in the development of urban renewal, during which the major relevant housing and planning policies established in the immediate post-war years were transformed. Since the late 1960s the problem of inner urban areas – poverty, unemployment, poor housing, inadequate schools, hard pressed social services, and deteriorating environmental conditions – have received increasing attention from academics, welfare professionals, politicians and the media. Large-scale comprehensive redevelopment and the dispersal of population and employment have been replaced by policies for the modernization of nineteenth century residential areas and attempts to stem the loss of jobs, particularly in manufacturing industry. There have been increasing efforts to stimulate economic regeneration and integrate this with modified versions of longer established housing, environmental and social policies. Thus the renewal of the older neighbourhoods of our cities and towns has a long history and has recently become a main focus of national urban policy. As we enter the 1980s the momentum of intervention has been lost amidst

*Superior figures refer to the References and notes on pages 319–75.

economic recession and unprecedented cuts in public expenditure, but the problems remain. The need for effective urban renewal features prominently on any agenda of social reform.

Definitions and themes

The term urban renewal is American in origin. It refers there, and in many other countries, to the redevelopment or rehabilitation of the older parts of towns and cities, including their central business areas. In practice, urban renewal, so described, has often meant the displacement of an existing low-income population, creating space for more profitable office, commercial and luxury residential development or the provision of transport facilities.[3]

In this country urban renewal has been closely linked with the issue of housing reform for the urban poor since the late nineteenth century. While the same type of commercial pressures have resulted in the destruction of some housing in city centres, this has been minimal compared with the impact of urban renewal justified and executed as a means of improving housing and environmental conditions. Renewal policies have inevitably been bound up with the issue of housing standards and debate about the scale and nature of state intervention. The origins and continued development of urban renewal are primarily a function of the state's response to the effect of inequality on the standard of mass housing provision. The key issue is the gap between the quality of accommodation which working class households can afford out of income (the effective demand which determines market provision) and some notion of minimum acceptable living conditions.

State intervention to bridge this gap is most obvious when it involves the demolition of slums and their replacement by new, subsidized council housing with associated provision of roads, schools, recreational and community facilities. Over the past ten years intervention has increasingly taken the form of grants to help owners improve older housing, sometimes in conjunction with local authority schemes for modernizing the environment. Urban renewal involves:

> the substitution of new social capital for old . . . in a programme for providing twentieth century amenities in nineteenth century towns.[4]

Until recently, the principal policy instruments have been concerned with renewing housing and (in varying degrees) social infrastructure, increasingly with the participation of residents. However, a revised national urban policy advances the view that it is no longer adequate to treat the symptoms of urban decay – poor housing, environmental and social conditions – and that greater emphasis should be placed on tackling the causes of inner area problems, which are held to lie in the declining economy of the city. Thus urban renewal now incorporates planned intervention in economic regeneration and employment provision, as well as the long established preoccupation with housing and environmental conditions.

The term 'urban renewal' is used in a generic sense to encompass all these aspects of intervention. The main concern is with broad issues of policy rather than detailed aspects of implementation. Thus the book is structured by reference to five main phases in the development of national urban renewal policy, which are treated in broadly chronological order. These phases are: slum clearance and redevelopment, from its nineteenth century origins to its zenith in the late 1960s; the shift of emphasis to housing and environmental improvement in the early 1970s; the emergence of gradual renewal in the mid-1970s, combining selective clearance with improvement; a series of priority area experiments concerned with urban deprivation; and current efforts to evolve a more comprehensive approach incorporating economic renewal. For each phase the debate preceding significant policy changes is analysed, the resultant powers and procedures are outlined, and the physical and social impact is assessed.

Such policies cannot be divorced from the underlying economic and political characteristics of society. At one level this point is immediately apparent. Within a historical analysis of policy it is frequently necessary to refer to political parties, elections or economic crises and their influence on the direction of renewal. Indeed some have witnessed the subservience of technical questions and the dominance of short-term expediency and then been tempted to argue that housing should be 'kept out of politics'. But (sometimes minor) party differences in the perception of renewal problems and the emphasis given to preferred solutions are but the tip of an iceberg. The built environment and social structure of our inner cities are the inherited products of our economic history, while the development of state intervention has been framed within the imperatives of subsequent economic development and dominant political ideology.

Urban renewal is one focus for an examination of the role of the state in a society marked by continuing inequality. In examining and evaluating urban renewal, the book acknowledges the importance of basic structural issues which determine the overall development of social policy. At various points the general theories which underpin explanations of urban change are referred to. In particular, there has been a resurgence of interest in the political economy of the city and the development of an analysis which is concerned with the relationship between the way production is organized and the role of the welfare state in an advanced capitalist society.[5] This introductory text does not explore these complex theoretical issues, but insights derived from this perspective inform an evaluation of the achievements, limitations and potential of urban renewal.

The main purpose of this book is to chart the development of renewal policy within the constraints imposed by wider political and economic influences. As such, it is also necessary to pay more than cursory attention to aspects of implementation, the results of which are always important factors in the periodic reformulation of overall strategy. The book is not a 'how-to-do-it manual', although it provides an outline of the methods and procedures used to secure action on the ground.

National policies are implemented by local authorities operating within the framework of legislation and central government advice. Case studies of renewal policy in two cities, Birmingham and Leeds, explore the extent and nature of local variations, and the degree of local control over the direction and emphasis of renewal programmes within changing national parameters. They examine in more detail the impact of national policy and the compromise and adjustment surrounding its local implementation. The final chapter draws together the main themes of the analysis, assesses the prospects for renewal in the 1980s within the policy framework set by the new Conservative Government, and discusses practical reforms.

National dimension

Chapter 2 begins with the growth of towns and cities in the expansionary phase of industrial capitalism. It traces the development of clearance and redevelopment policies from their origins in the sanitary reform response to the conditions created by rapid urbanization, through the inter-war clearance drive after the Housing Act, 1930, and the post-war struggle for the 'end of the slums'. The complex powers and procedures involved in clearance are outlined and the significance of key elements is drawn out. The effects of clearance and redevelopment policies on the built environment have been drastic. However, it is their social implications which have been the focus of most controversy. The chapter ends by critically reviewing evidence on both the long-term and short-term effects of this method of renewal.

Housing and environmental improvement is then analysed in Chapter 3. Until the 1970s improvement played a subordinate role to clearance but since the Housing Act, 1969 it has become dominant. The chapter outlines the first twenty years of improvement policy from 1949 and examines the reasons for a shift of emphasis in the late 1960s. Grant systems and the area approach to both housing and environmental improvement in General Improvement Areas are discussed and the impact of policy between 1969 and 1974 is evaluated. Improvement is essentially an investment partnership between the state and owners of older housing with diverse attitudes and financial resources. Hence its social implications are explored by reference to the complex housing market of older housing areas.

In Chapter 4 the discussion turns to the contemporary central government policy of gradual renewal, established by the Housing Act, 1974. This approach combines improvement to varying standards with limited clearance and infill building. It was conceived of as a continuous, rather than once-and-for-all, process. It stresses responsiveness to the resources, needs, and wishes of the residents involved, and the importance of an effective corporate approach to the formulation and implementation of local renewal strategies. The chapter outlines the emergence of the concept of gradual renewal in the early 1970s, and the modifications to powers and procedures, including the introduction of Housing Action Areas. A discussion of initial reactions to the policy precedes an analysis of progress and problems as, in the harsh climate of public expenditure cuts, gradual renewal became reduced renewal. Discussion of the 1977 Green Paper on housing and Labour's 1979 Housing Bill revealed growing concern about the failure of current policies to match the rate of obsolescence.

To this point the book is focussed on housing problems and programmes, but Chapter 5 extends the discussion into wider aspects of renewal policy. The chapter examines the 'rediscovery of poverty' in the 1960s and the factors which lay behind the launching of a series of priority area experimental programmes of positive discrimination. It traces the effects of such programmes on the ground and the changing perspectives of those involved.

The conclusions of the two most important poverty programme initiatives, the Community Development Projects and Inner Area Studies, emphasized the underlying economic processes at work in inner urban areas. Chapter 6 relates the problems of older residential areas to the process of industrial change and hence to the development of the economy as a whole. These areas were originally built on green fields to house the workers in a particular set of industries. As investment in both the industry and housing declined, new housing and industry were built in other locations: '. . .it becomes possible to talk meaningfully about the life-span of generations of industry and their associated working-class communities.'[6] Just as the old industrial areas are shifted to the periphery of the economy, their associated housing areas increasingly contain marginal economic groups – the unskilled, the elderly and the immigrant.

The complex problems of inner areas left behind in the wake of economic and social change were the focus of the 1977 White Paper *Policy for the Inner Cities* and the Inner Urban Areas Act, 1978. The new urban policy aims to arrest the decline of inner urban population and employment opportunities by spatial discrimination in the allocation of resources to fund comprehensive inner area programmes. The chapter examines the evolution of this initiative, outlines its key elements, and concludes with an assessment of progress and problems.

Local dimension

One of the main lessons of the discussion of renewal at a national level is that broad policies can have a variable impact in different areas. The inheritance of a particular nineteenth century built environment and a changing local economic base, with its associated housing market, provide the context within which these policies operate. There is some scope for local authorities to interpret national guidelines in different ways. Politics and personalities influence the nature of local strategies and the vigour of their implementation. Since it is now a conventional wisdom that there is not one national housing problem but rather a set of varied local problems, the extent of this discretion merits careful scrutiny.

The book examines the evolution, impact and contemporary problems of renewal policies in two contrasting provincial cities, Birmingham and Leeds. Both chapters are structured so that three key themes can be further developed: the reciprocal but unequal relationship between national policy and local implementation; the significance of geographical variations in urban renewal; and the importance of a historical perspective for an understanding of contemporary issues. Thus the main phases of intervention are discussed in relation to the influence of the housing market, economic and political factors, and the legacy of successive phases of intervention.

Chapter 7 examines urban renewal in Birmingham, a city noted for its massive post-war comprehensive redevelopment programme, and its equally ambitious area improvement programme launched in the early 1970s. Having been the setting for a variety of Poverty Programme experimental projects (including a Community Development Project and an Inner Area Study) it is now one of the Partnership Authorities under the terms of the government's inner city policy. The chapter analyses local action in the context of a hitherto prosperous local economy and high-pressure housing market, action strongly influenced by the city's 'civic gospel' of interventionist local government and independent local initiatives. Now, for the first time in its history, Birmingham is having to attempt to solve the problems of inner city decay despite a stagnating local economy.

Chapter 8 analyses the situation in Leeds, another city which has been prominent in adopting vigorous programmes in the past. The context for the renewal of Leeds has been a built environment dominated by back-to-back housing and a housing market which has often been one of relatively low pressure. Pioneering work in the implementation of area improvement policies in the 1960s left the city with a large proportion of its older housing stock improved to modest standards, but this has not been followed by continuing investment to prevent further decay. Moreover, at a time when its economy is in decline, the city now faces the results of its failure to devise effective housing renewal policies during the 1970s. While national urban policy has accorded Leeds second-class status by designating it only a Programme Authority, the city's inner area problems are considerable and worsening.

Historical perspective and contemporary crisis

In Chapter 9 a historical overview draws together key themes and points to the long history of many current issues. The extent of state intervention and its relationship with the private market, redevelopment versus improvement, the relative roles of central and local government, the validity of area-based policies, and the nature of community participation have all been repeatedly debated, albeit in slightly varying language. This historical perspective provides a basis for defining the problems and challenges facing urban renewal. The relationship between physical obsolescence and the patterns of ownership of older housing are placed in a wider context when urban deprivation is considered in terms of the processes which sustain uneven economic development.

In a 'mixed economy' the capacity to renew an outworn built environment and reduce inequality is ultimately dependent on the allocation of public funds for social programmes. The Conservative Government holds that the requirements for regenerating the national economy preclude the allocation of funds on the scale needed. This view has set the parameters of urban renewal policy for the early 1980s. The dominance of monetarist economics has precipitated the abandonment of the 'middle ground' in social policy. Massive cuts in public expenditure mean that the expectations raised by inner city policy will not be realized. The Housing Act, 1980 marked further withdrawal of support for public sector housing while the Local Government, Planning and Land Act, 1980 will place a straightjacket on overall expenditure by local authorities. A reliance on private sector initiatives, such as the revival of private rental in housing or the launching of Enterprise Zones, will do little for the urban poor.

It is in this immediate context that legislative, administrative and educational changes are suggested, but the limits of reform are acknowledged. Local initiatives can be devised and their lessons more widely applied but it is difficult to be anything other than pessimistic about the level of resources being applied to inner area problems. The chances of making a significant impression on these problems are remote without more fundamental political and economic changes.

2 The bulldozer to clear the slums

Slum clearance and redevelopment are the most visible components of urban renewal. They have changed the face of our towns and cities and profoundly affected the lives of millions of people. This chapter traces the evolution of policy and outlines the powers and procedures involved in its implementation. It then examines the physical impact on the built environment and introduces the debate on the social implications of such fundamental intervention.

The clearance of older houses has been a recognizable part of state intervention in housing for more than a century. Its origins lie in the application of sanitary principles to squalid urban conditions in *laissez-faire* Victorian society. Little was achieved, however, until the large-scale provision of council housing in the inter-war years enabled tenants displaced by slum clearance to be rehoused. The struggle for the 'end of the slums' in post-war years led to the comprehensive redevelopment of vast tracts of inner city land. Redevelopment was firmly established within overall planning strategies for the city–region.

The powers and procedures currently used in the clearance and redevelopment process are the result of this long evolution of policy. Justifying and securing the demolition of houses falling below some defined standard involves a complex series of steps, in which the activities of a local authority are at some points circumscribed by the detailed legislation of central government but at other points are far less constrained.

At any one time clearance has affected particular types of older housing while the form of redevelopment has been conditioned by trends in new council estate provision. The predominant housing and planning ideologies of each period find their expression in the changing built environment which results.

Though the physical consequences of clearance and redevelopment have been the subject of mounting criticism in recent years, it is their social impact which has been the focus of most debate. Comprehensive redevelopment is now out of fashion and a major justification for this change of approach is the argument that it involves 'massive and unacceptable disruption of communities'.[1] The chapter ends by examining the evidence on both the long-term and short-term social consequences of this component of urban renewal.

Industrial capitalism and sanitary reform

Slum housing first became a problem to be officially recognized by the state in the nineteenth century. The sanitary reform movement developed as a response to conditions created during the expansionary phase of industrial capitalism. Although little was achieved by early legislation, the principles established have influenced thinking about older housing ever since.

Urbanization, housing conditions and ownership

In the pre-industrial era the decent cottage had been the exception and the hovel the rule for the great mass of the rural population,[2] but the urban conditions created in this period of rapid industrial growth were of a different dimension altogether. The population of England and Wales rose from 9 million in 1801 to 32 million in 1901. Urbanization went hand in hand with population increase as industrial capitalism, based on large-scale mechanized production and the division of labour, required the concentration of large numbers of the working-class. The new centres of expanding industry all grew with tremendous speed, notwithstanding the complexity of their various characteristics and phases of development.[3] With no mass urban transport system, houses were rapidly built at very high densities, cheek by jowl with the factories where the new industrial workers spent their days.

Much of the housing built in the first half of the century provided slum conditions from the moment it was completed. Both commentators at the time and urban historians since have provided vivid accounts of the ensuing exploitation, squalor, and degradation.[4] By the side of many of their descriptions Engels' report of Little Ireland in Manchester appears restrained:

> In a rather deep hole, in a curve of the Medlock and surrounded on all four sides by tall factories and high embankments covered with buildings, stand two groups of about two hundred cottages, built chiefly back-to-back, in which live about four thousand human beings, most of them Irish. The cottages are old, dirty and of the smallest sort, the streets uneven, fallen into ruts and in part without drains or pavement; masses of refuse, offal and sickening filth lie among standing pools in all directions; the atmosphere is poisoned by the effluence from these, and laden and darkened by the smoke of a dozen tall factory chimneys. A horde of ragged women and children swarm about here, as filthy as the swine that thrive upon the garbage heaps and in the puddles.[5]

The population of this area had to share one privy between 120 persons. The sanitary and moral conditions of slums like this became an increasing focus of debate and intervention during the century.

Some housing was built by large employers and rented to their workers but the dominant system of provision relied on the role of independent private landlords. They borrowed money to finance the building of new houses, managed them and collected the rents, or organized others to carry out these operations. Their capital came in small-scale investment from local businessmen, from trust funds, and from a variety of sources which required a secure return – hence the phrase 'as safe as houses'. The provision of housing for the growing urban population was thus an intricate, but successful, operation of small-scale capitalism, and investment in housing for private rental had its heyday when there were few other comparable forms of investment. This process continued as the standards of new housing rose, but by the end of the century was beginning to lose momentum as changes in company legislation offered the small investor simpler and more profitable opportunities.

Public health

Initial measures to combat the problems of overcrowding, disease and squalor took the form of public health campaigns and the identification of 'nuisances'. Reforms were stimulated by the ravages of cholera epidemics which spread from these festering sores and were no respecter of social class. Fear of criminal activity and the revolutionary potential of the 'undisciplined mob' which resided in the slums also played its part in alerting the establishment, as did the need for a more healthy and productive workforce. These factors, and the activities of reformers and pamphleteers who produced damning evidence of the consequences of unrestrained urban development, forced the problem of the slums onto the political agenda.

All the initial regulations were restrictive and destructive, aimed at the elimination of the worst abuses. The state assumed no direct responsibility for the housing of the working-class, for 'the central belief of the sanitary reformers was that they could improve the living conditions of the poor by reducing epidemic disease, and that by restoring health they could raise earning power sufficiently to allow the renting of decent homes'.[6] While the idea of intervention in public health matters slowly became acceptable, substantial interference in housing was unthinkable for proponents of *laissez-faire* economic and social policies. It would disturb the 'sacred rights' of private property ownership.

There was a slow shift in attitudes throughout the century and state intervention in the interests of public health became increasingly possible. Gradually a pattern of controls was established. It included building regulations for new dwellings, action to improve the supply of water, and limitations on overcrowding. The need to implement these controls was an important element in the development of local government. Legislation for slum clearance was an integral part of this sanitary reform movement.

Pull down and push out

The first slum clearance measure was the Artisans' and Labourers' Dwellings

Act, 1868, known as the Torrens Act after the private member who introduced it. Medical Officers of Health were to report on individual premises which were 'in a condition or state dangerous to health as to be unfit for human habitation', and local authorities with populations of over 10,000 were empowered, but not compelled, to force the owners of such unfit houses to repair them at their own expense or demolish them. The second measure was the Artisans' and Labourers' Dwellings Improvement Act, 1875, known as the Cross Act, which permitted local authorities to formulate schemes for both the clearance and rebuilding of slum areas. These two Acts were the first indications of the two distinct strands of slum clearance legislation which have developed.[7] One strand is confined to individual unfit houses and has been closely related to the sanitary tradition ever since; the other is concerned with wider areas of slum conditions and was the precursor of comprehensive redevelopment.

Actual implementation of these acts was paltry. Procedures for carrying out schemes under the Cross Act were complex and expensive and, without Exchequer subsidies, the finance was available only from reluctant ratepayers. For slum dwellers, it was fortunate that progress was slow, since clearance of homes without an effective rehousing policy could readily increase overcrowding and the intensification of slum conditions in neighbouring areas as 'the people cleared from the destroyed slums sifted away into the interstices of the remaining slum areas'.[8] While the vested interests of landlords, local corruption and political opposition to the financial costs involved played major roles in ensuring inactivity, many Medical Officers of Health were also reluctant to employ this negative solution of 'pull down and push out'.[9] More significant in scale were housing clearance ventures undertaken for commercial profit, and especially those of the railway companies determined to site their termini in city centres.[10] The poor were simply moved on by such 'civic improvements'.

Direct rehousing played no part in early clearance measures. The activities of the '5 per cent philanthropists' provided some indication of future redevelopment possibilities but catered principally for well-to-do artisans.[11] Although the Housing of the Working Classes Act, 1890 empowered local authorities to redevelop cleared areas themselves rather than sell the land to other agencies, few authorities took such action. 'Economic individualism and common civic purpose were difficult to reconcile'[12] and, in the meantime, the poor could neither wait for nor afford any replacement housing which might be provided.

Not only governments, but also the vast majority of reformers, refused to accept two key principles.[13] The first is that improved standards in new housing have to be paid for by somebody, and in the context of widespread poverty this means subsidies. The second is that slum clearance without the simultaneous provision of new dwellings merely shifts and exacerbates the problem. Little by little, some state responsibility for intervention in appalling housing conditions – the concept of 'below this you shall not go' – had been insinuated onto the statute books: real action had to await the acceptance of these two principles in a changed political climate.

Council housing and a slum clearance campaign

The inter-war years were the setting for the introduction of direct state intervention in housing provision. Inevitably, the terms of the debate in the nineteenth century were overtaken as slum clearance became part of wider developments in housing policy.

The need for intervention

In 1918 private landlords provided 90 per cent of all homes. However, the production of new housing to let was declining as alternative avenues for the investment of surplus capital by small merchants and traders opened up in competition to housing. Even before the 1914–18 war there was growing pressure for state subsidies in the system of housing supply: events during the war provided the final impetus.[14] First, there was a virtual halt to new building and maintenance of existing dwellings so that by the end of the war there was an acute absolute shortage of housing as well as continued decay.[15] Second, rent control of privately rented housing had been introduced in 1915 in the face of industrial unrest and rent strikes by the organized labour movement aggrieved by the exploitation of the housing shortage. Rents controlled at the level reached at the outbreak of war were much lower than those needed to make the private building of houses to let profitable, especially since material and building costs were high. Thus, when Lloyd George promised 'homes fit for heroes' at the end of the war, there seemed no other way to provide them, at the scale required and at rents which could be afforded, than by the use of local authorities supported by Exchequer subsidies.

The Housing and Town Planning Act, 1919 provided an Exchequer subsidy for local authority house building for the first time. An extremely generous subsidy, moreover, for it covered losses incurred in excess of a penny rate. The implications of this acceptance of public responsibility, the real beginnings of council housing, have been enormous for the history of housing policy. Not thought to be a permanent commitment at the time but simply an expedient, some kind of subsidy arrangement for council housing has persisted ever since.

The open-ended subsidy of the 1919 Act was abandoned by the Conservative Government in Chamberlain's Housing Act, 1923 in an attempt to prevent local authorities becoming firmly established as the major providers of working-class homes. It was replaced by a flat rate subsidy for houses of a specified standard built by local authorities or private enterprise.

However, the advent of the first Labour Government in 1924 reversed this. The 1924 Wheatley Act increased the subsidy for houses built by local authorities, who were no longer required to demonstrate that private enterprise would not meet local needs before beginning to build themselves. Although this Government soon fell the Act outlasted it, and despite cutbacks in the level of subsidy in 1927, the physical result of these various acts was the construction of nearly half a million council houses in the 1920s out of a total of one and a quarter million new houses.

During the same period slum clearance was minimal, for in a situation of overall shortage the argument was that slum housing was better than no housing at all. Only 11,000 houses were demolished in the 'unhealthy areas' by the archaic procedures still in operation.[16] During the 1920s there were persistent arguments that limited intervention through reconditioning slums, together with piecemeal demolition, would be adequate.[17] But these arguments were eventually discredited as the scale of the problem was exposed. Action to clear the slums became an important issue in the election campaign of 1929 as a spate of pamphlets and books highlighted appalling conditions and appealed to the public conscience.[18] At the same time arguments were introduced about the prospects of a falling population and the inevitability of a continuous easing in the general housing situation which would allow an attack on the slums. A second Labour Government came into power committed to the idea of extending subsidies to provide council houses at rents the poorest slum tenants could afford.

A national slum clearance campaign

The 1919 Act marked a watershed in the history of overall housing policy but Greenwood's 1930 Act which followed from this debate was a key Act in the history of slum clearance. The former can be interpreted as the enabling legislation for effective clearance and rehousing by the state; the latter as the Act which specifically formulated relevant procedures and encouraged a national clearance campaign. The Housing Act, 1930 of the Labour Government introduced the basic powers of local authorities to use clearance area, compulsory purchase and clearance order procedures. Subsidies for clearance were increased and were now to be based on the number of persons displaced and rehoused. The energies of local authorities were concentrated by the need to submit five-year programmes of clearance to the Ministry of Health.

For a while building for the needs of slum clearance displacement and for general needs theoretically continued side by side, though in practice the public finance crisis of 1931–2 meant that little was achieved. In the search for expenditure cuts the National Government abolished all subsidies except for slum clearance. All council housing designed to relieve shortages was stopped and the 1933 Act transformed the 1930 initiative into the corner-stone of public housing policy.

The arguments of the Government were clear. The housing shortage was not over but the way to end the remaining shortage was to abolish subsidies. Prices and interest rates had fallen but private enterprise could not effectively compete with subsidized council housing in providing smaller homes to let. Subsidies would cease, therefore, so that the needs for ordinary housing could be met by private enterprise while council housing met the special needs arising from clearance.[19]

Numerically the policy succeeded. Unsubsidized private building rose dramatically as a combination of building societies' need to lend out the enormous sums they were attracting, their new mortgage schemes, a fall in building costs and low land prices encouraged the first mass movement into owner-occupation – a movement which included some better-off wage-earners. Suburban sprawl developed as families were coaxed to 'take their son and heir to where there is sun and air' into the ever-receding countryside.[20] The peak of the building boom was reached in 1937 when 347,000 houses were completed, of which 275,000 were built by private enterprise. However, the assumption that new private building would be for houses to let proved untenable. Although there was a minor resurgence in the mid-1930s, there was little incentive in comparison with other investments. The overwhelming proportion of this new building was for owner-occupation and home ownership became a new symbol of national stability.

In this context the first slum clearance drive began and the establishment launched a propaganda campaign claiming that the battle against the slums was a great new venture. The returns made by local authorities in 1933 involved the demolition, or closure, of just over a quarter of a million houses, and the rehousing of about one and a quarter million occupants. Successive upward revisions took place so that by 1939 they included 472,000 houses, 347,000 of them in clearance areas.

In the event 273,000 houses were demolished or closed during the 1930s. Far from being abolished, there were still about the same number of slums in programmes in 1939 as in 1933. Despite this backlog, slum clearance in the 1930s was remarkably vigorous (see Figure 1). More people had been rehoused from slum conditions in five years than in all earlier programmes put together. By 1939 the slums were being demolished at a rate never exceeded since.

The start made on a positive slum clearance programme should be seen in a wider context. Clearly, the adoption of a policy of council house building after the First World War provided the subsidies and replacement housing which were absent at the time of the nineteenth century sanitary reform movement. Nevertheless, it could hardly be claimed that the 1919 promise of 'homes fit for heroes' had been fulfilled. No responsibility was admitted for the majority of working-class families; the new sanitary policy was:

limited only to black patches within a vast area of off-white or dark grey. It would

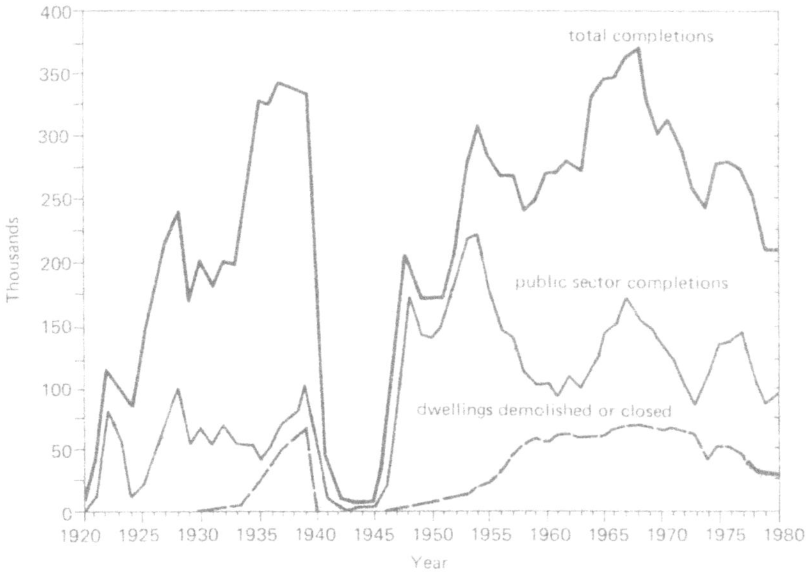

Figure 1 *Housebuilding and clearance (England and Wales) 1920 to 1980*
Notes: Public sector includes local authorities, new towns, housing associations and government departments
1920–45 year ending 31 March
1945 onwards year ending 31 December

Source: 1920–39: Ministry of Health Annual Report, *Housing*; 1939–45: B. R. Mitchell and H. G. Jones, *Second Abstract of British Historical Statistics* (University of Cambridge, 1971); 1945 onwards: *Housing Statistics* and *Housing and Construction Statistics* (HMSO)

make the black patches white by providing housing conforming to modern ideas for the limited number, but it had no concern for achieving this standard for all.[21]

The political battle lines had been redrawn and now divided those arguing for widespread state intervention to satisfy general housing needs and those anxious to restrict intervention to clearance and to promote owner-occupation as the 'normal' tenure. By the end of the inter-war period the latter were in the ascendant.

The end of the slums?

The Second World War not only halted the momentum which had been built up in slum clearance; many houses were destroyed or damaged and new building and maintenance virtually ceased. A pattern similar to that of the inter-war years developed, with an initial concentration on council house-building for general needs being followed by a revived sanitary policy. There was a continuous attack on the slums in the 1960s but in the early 1970s the clearance rate fell.

Planning and the housing drive

According to Donnison, Britain emerged from the war with 200,000 houses destroyed, another 250,000 so badly knocked about that they could not be lived in, and a similar number severely damaged.[22] Housing policy was a major issue in a 1945 election dominated by a vision of a changed society after the sacrifices of war. The new Labour Government pressed ahead with a programme of social reforms and Britain was to be rebuilt as if by a military operation.

The key to post-war rebuilding was seen as planning – both for land-use and for housing production. The former saw the realization of several interlinked philosophies which had been developed by a number of committees on physical planning set up in the mid-1940s and in the various regional strategies of Abercrombie: now they were established in the comprehensive system of control of the Town and Country Planning Act, 1947 and in related legislation for new towns. Central to the system were themes of urban containment; protection of the countryside; the creation of self-contained, balanced overspill communities; and the control of industrial location in the interests of regional balance. The planned dispersal of a large part of the population living in the major conurbations became the strategic setting within which urban renewal would operate. Comprehensive redevelopment at lower densities would depend on effective overspill policies.

Planned production of housing was implemented by controls over the level of construction through building licences and an almost total concentration on the public sector. Just as in 1919, the priority need was for new dwellings and local authorities were the chosen instrument to provide them. Initially, there was a concentration on a crash programme for 'prefabs', requisitioning empty houses and temporary use of other building. The 'housing drive' began in 1946 when subsidies for general needs building were increased. A wider role for local authorities as providers of housing was recognized with the removal of any reference to the working classes in the Housing Act, 1949. However, in contrast with the fundamental reappraisal of many other sectors of the welfare state, the housing programme was quickly assembled and there was no attempt to introduce a comprehensive framework or socialize the means of housing production.

Bevan's 'housing drive' resulted in just over 200,000 completions in 1946, but during the next three years new building remained constant at around 170,000. In housing, as in most other policies, the Labour Government lost its early impetus. Housebuilding was soon affected by government spending cuts when an overwhelming preoccupation with the balance of payments situation and conditions of foreign aid developed.[23] The Conservatives fought the 1951 election partly on the promise to build 300,000 houses a year – a promise they fulfilled by 1953, thanks to an easing of the economic situation and a reduction in standards for new council dwellings.

Operation rescue

Initially the building programme launched by Macmillan, the new Conservative Housing Minister, was implemented by reinforcing the role of local authority building. However, in the period 1954–9 a policy reminiscent of the 1930s developed. Its key elements were:

1 reliance on private building for owner-occupation rather than council housing to satisfy general housing needs;
2 concentration of local authority activity on slum clearance;
3 attempts to increase private investment in older housing by the decontrol of rents, an increase in the level of improvement grants, and the encouragement of low-income owner-occupation.

Restrictions on private building were soon relaxed and there was a progressive disengagement of the state 'from its extensive, though never comprehensively planned, involvement in the housing market'.[24] Council housing would lose its central position in housing policy and private enterprise was again to be the provider of general needs housing. Slum clearance, postponed after the war as an unfortunate consequence of the need to attack the general housing shortage,[25] could thus be resumed. It was portrayed as the remaining finite task necessitating state intervention.

The stage was set for this change of direction with the publication of the 1953 White Paper *Houses – the Next Step*, popularized as 'Operation Rescue'. The Housing (Rent and Repairs) Act, 1954 then established the legal framework for a three-pronged attack on the problems of obsolete and obsolescent housing. The emphasis was on slum clearance; it was complemented by an increase in the level of improvement grants and rent increases for private landlords. Clearance was dominant since 140,000 houses remained from pre-war schemes and hundreds of thousands more had since degenerated into slums. As before, local authorities were required to submit their clearance proposals. They were given new powers of deferred demolition for acquiring and 'patching' houses where they were unable to clear all slums within five years.

Between 1954 and 1959 the change of direction steadily built up. The Housing Subsidies Act, 1956 slashed the subsidy for general needs and ended the obligatory rates fund contribution. Later that year the general needs subsidy was abolished altogether except for one-bedroomed dwellings. Slum clearance subsidies remained. Finally, as discussed in the next chapter, the

Rent Act, 1957 and the House Purchase and Housing Act, 1959 introduced rent decontrol and stimulated owner-occupation in older housing areas linked with housing improvement.

The numbers game and the end of complacency

Once established, the slum clearance campaign continued on the same lines for several years. The Housing Act, 1957 simply consolidated previous legislation. Of most interest was the debate which began about the extent of obsolescent housing and the required scale of the national clearance programme. Attacks were made on the complete inadequacy of the available information about the condition of the nation's older houses, on substantial local anomalies in official estimates and on the pitifully slow progress being made in relation to more realistic estimates of obsolescence.

The returns made by local authorities in 1955 became central in this debate. They indicated that nearly 850,000 houses were unfit out of a total stock of 12.9 million in England and Wales. The programmes planned by local authorities for the first five years were expected to deal with some 375,000 of these, an implied average clearance rate of 75,000 dwellings p.a. The 1955 returns remained the basis of the clearance programme until 1965.

Cullingworth's academic assessment of clearance needs was published in 1960.[26] He concentrated first on local anomalies, concluding that some local authorities had included all unfit properties in their 1955 returns, but others had included just those in their actual clearance programme. Not only were the returns gross underestimates, but the continuing process of obsolescence would itself produce an annual replacement need of 141,000 houses. He argued, therefore, that a demolition rate of 200,000 dwellings p.a. was desirable to deal with this obsolescence and the identified slums. Since this was unattainable, a more extensive complementary programme of modernization was necessary. Needleman reached similar conclusions in 1961[27] and these academic studies were followed by a more biting attack, which cruelly exposed the inadequacy of the 1955 returns.[28] Eventually two official studies confirmed the underestimation of the obsolescence problem.[29]

In the meantime the clearance programme had not reached the 1955 projected rate of action. Initially, there had been a spurt as the annual total of demolitions or closures built up from the 1955 level of 24,000 to 57,500 in 1959. Complacency about slum clearance and housing policy was in harmony with the mood of 'never had it so good' Britain at the 1959 general election. Thereafter, the clearance rate remained constant at around 60,000 dwellings p.a. throughout the early 1960s (see Figure 1).

It was at this point that the Conservative Government's housing policy came under increasing pressure. In its own terms it had successfully reduced direct intervention in housing and further extended the ideology of a 'property-owning democracy' first developed in the 1930s. But changing social and economic conditions were soon to undermine this apparently smooth path. A growing recognition of a housing crisis replaced the complacency which had characterized the late 1950s.[30]

At a national scale demographic changes, including growing numbers of old people and an increasing popularity of early marriage combined to accelerate a growth in housing need. Moreover, the birth rate was rising steadily and quite unexpectedly, with the result that younger households were increasing in size. At the same time the combination of a cessation of council housebuilding for general needs and rent decontrol after the 1957 Rent Act (with its resultant sales for owner-occupation) had reduced the housing opportunities of the less affluent. Council housebuilding had fallen by 1961 to its lowest level since 1947.

Uneven economic development was another important factor in the early 1960s. On the one hand, unemployment persisted in depressed regions. Policies for industrial relocation had not solved the 'regional problem' and urban decay was one result. On the other hand, there were parts of the country, particularly the South-East and West Midlands, where employment and population were growing. Migration from the declining regions and an influx of coloured immigrants as a response to the demand for cheap labour increased pressures on housing in these cities. Growth had been inadequately provided for in policies of urban containment and this was exacerbated by the absence of effective planning machinery for overspill and the development of Green Belt policies by the rural counties to prevent urban encroachment.[31] Several epic planning battles were waged as some major cities pressed for the release of peripheral land for council housebuilding.

The situation in London attracted most attention as a combination of housing and planning policies contributed to a growing crisis tragically manifest in homelessness. The mass media became aware of 'the ruthless battle for space going on in the booming inner areas of London',[32] through the eviction and harassment activities of one of the city's private landlords, Perec Rachman.[33]

The last few years of Conservative rule saw a reappraisal of housing policies in the face of increasing criticism. A 1961 White Paper announced a concentration on the problems of some fifty local authorities where current programmes and progress indicated that they had a long period of clearance ahead of them. The Housing Act, 1961 restored general needs subsidies, albeit on a basis which only rewarded those authorities charging high rents. By 1963 the government had established the National Building Agency to encourage industrialized building techniques and in the next year council housebuilding rose back to its 1957 level. During the 1963 debate on an opposition motion of censure for the impact of the 1957 Rent Act, Sir Keith Joseph announced the commissioning of the Milner Holland inquiry into London's housing. Housing association development was encouraged and the Housing Act, 1964 established the Housing Corporation to stimulate it. However, it was all too little too late and in the 1964 election housing was again a major issue. The Labour Party was returned to power with a slender majority.

The national plan

The new Labour Government took two immediate steps to review clearance policy: both reflected the disquiet felt about inadequate information on the extent of the problem. In the long term, better data were to be provided by the establishment of a subcommittee of the Central Housing Advisory Committee specifically to deal with standards of unfitness. In the short term, local authorities were required to submit returns of all their remaining unfit houses regardless of the time it would take to clear them. The official slums of England and Wales were significantly increased by the replies. Of the unfit houses identified in 1955 some 250,000 remained standing but the 1965 returns gave a total of 824,000 unfit dwellings.

The key elements in Labour's five-year programme emerged later in 1965 with the publication of an overall 'National Plan': its housing proposals were taken up in the White Paper *The Housing Programme 1965–1970*.[34] The central aim was to increase the total housebuilding rate so that by 1970 about half a million houses would be built each year. Within this total programme an increasing share would be allotted to the public sector where industrialized building methods would be used. Replacement of 'about one million houses already classed as slums' and a further 'two million houses not yet slums but not worth improving' provided the main justification for this programme.

Slum clearance action was encouraged by the Housing Subsidies Act, 1967 which attempted to divert more generous subsidies to priority areas identified on the basis of the 1965 returns. Annual clearance rates increased to a new post-war peak of 70,000 by 1967 as council housebuilding rose to just over half the total of 400,000 completions. Regional planning was given a new emphasis and peripheral land released to aid overspill housing programmes around some major cities.

Before the Government could start congratulating itself on this impetus, however, the extent of the problem of older housing was brought into sharp focus by the 1967 Housing Condition Survey. Estimates of unfit housing were based, for the first time, on an independent study carried out for the Ministry by public health inspectors seconded for the task from their local authorities and working to a common brief. The results were disturbing. Unfit dwellings came to 1.8 million compared with the 820,000 identified by local authorities just two years earlier. The consequences of the reappraisal of urban renewal policy which followed this survey are dealt with in Chapter 3. Some comment is made here only on its impact on slum clearance. At the time it was argued that the new concentration on improvement would not reduce the rate of clearance. Ministerial claims were made that the clearance rate would be stepped up by 50 per cent, and Circular 92/69 asked local authorities to define

Table 1 *Clearance progress 1930 to 1979 (England and Wales)*

Years	*Houses demolished in clearance areas*			*'000* *Houses not in clearance areas*			*Total demo-lished or closed*	*Persons moved*
	unfit	*other*	*total*	*demo-lished**	*closed*	*total**		
1930–44	222	7	229	93	16	112	341	1340
1945–54	32	2	33	37	19	56	90	309
1955–9	104	6	110	60	44	104	213	669
1960–4	176	16	192	70	41	112	304	834
1965–9	223	26	249	52	38	90	339	896
1970–4	225	27	252	33	25	57	309	704
1975–9	152†	17†	169	17	27	44	213	378§
Totals	1134	101	1234	362	210	575	1809	5130

*In these columns the figures from 1945 onwards of demolished houses not in clearance areas exclude demolitions of houses previously returned as closed.
†Figures from 1977 onwards do not distinguish between unfit houses and others demolished in clearance areas and those presented are an estimated split within the total.
§Figures from 1977 are only available for families moved and those presented on persons are an estimate for this period.

Source: 1920–39: Ministry of Health Annual Reports, *Housing*; 1939–45: B. R. Mitchell and H. G. Jones, *Second Abstract of British Historical Statistics* (University of Cambridge 1971); 1945 onwards: *Housing Statistics* and *Housing and Construction Statistics*, HMSO.

their programmes for the next four years and steadily increase the pace of clearance.[35]

The actual progress made and the background to this are dealt with in Chapter 4. At first, despite a decline in council housebuilding in the post-devaluation years and a further decline during the 1970–4 Conservative Government, clearance continued at a rate only slightly below the plateau of 70,000 established in 1967. However, between 1973 and 1979 the clearance rate fell by one-half – from 64,000 to 33,000, the lowest annual total since 1955.

Powers, procedures and professionals

The link between national clearance policies and local action to implement them is the framework of legal powers and procedures which governs the various steps in the process. It provides the context, both of opportunities and constraints, within which local authorities can act.

Stages in the clearance process

The first stage in translating national clearance strategies into action at a local level is the definition of a programme. At this point local authorities have complete discretion. Different local authorities vary in the time their programmes look ahead, in the detail by which the areas affected are defined and in the amount of information which is made available to the public. However, the end result of defining a clearance programme is the same: it marks the onset of 'blight' in areas. Once an area is earmarked for clearance it becomes impossible to buy houses with mortgages and often the local authority begins purchasing dwellings by agreement. In many areas the forecast 'lifing' of areas extends in advance of a defined clearance programme so that official neglect begins even earlier.

If the inclusion of older housing in a clearance programme is not tightly defined by legal powers, justifying and securing demolition clearly is. The powers available to local authorities are mainly contained in Parts II and III of the Housing Act, 1957. Part II is concerned with the repair, closure or demolition of individual unfit houses; Part III provides for the clearance of areas of unfit housing. The Part III procedure has formed the basis of large-scale clearance action and will be concentrated on here.[36] The key stages of the clearance process, from representation of a clearance area to the acquisition of property and the settlement of financial compensation are all closely controlled by the imposition of its rules and procedures.[37] Only at the stage of rehousing the displaced population do the controls of central government relax and local discretion becomes more significant.

Figure 2 summarizes the complex series of steps involved in undertaking clearance area action and Figure 3 outlines the key legal definitions used. The first step in the process is for each house in a potential clearance area to be visited to decide whether or not it is 'unfit'. The area is then represented to the council as suitable for clearance, a formal declaration is made and submitted to central government (at present to the Secretary of State for the Environment). The local authority must then secure the clearance of the area by making a Compulsory Purchase Order (CPO) and acquiring the properties.[38]

A CPO has the advantage of enabling a local authority to purchase properties or land surrounded by or adjoining a clearance area as 'added lands' to enable satisfactory redevelopment to take place. By this stage three types of property are identified and a short-hand jargon is often used to identify them, based on their colouring on the statutory maps prepared. In the clearance area are houses unfit for human habitation (pink land) and, less commonly, houses included because of their bad arrangement (pink hatched yellow land). In the CPO a further category is added, land or properties needed for the redevelopment of the cleared area (grey land). During the collection of detailed information on ownership within the CPO area residents may receive their first indication that their area is to be acquired and cleared.

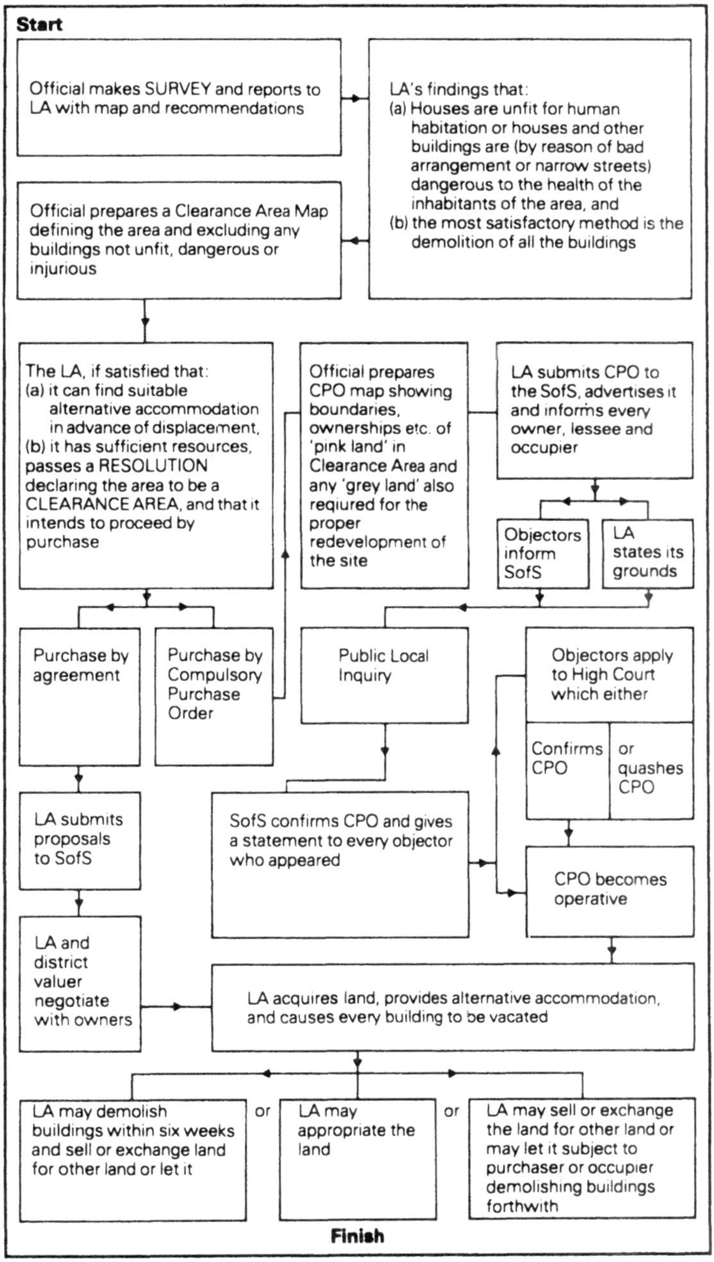

Figure 2 *Steps in the clearance process*

Source: Adapted from *Municipal Engineering*, File Reference 7.10, Unfit Houses Data Sheet (12 March 1976)

1. DEFINITION OF UNFITNESS

The definition of the term *unfit for human habitation* is given in section 4(1) of the Housing Act 1957 as amended by section 71 of the Housing Act 1969.

It is provided that in determining whether a house is unfit for human habitation *regard* shall be had to its condition in respect of the following matters:

repair
stability
freedom from damp
internal arrangement
natural lighting
ventilation
water supply
drainage and sanitary conveniences
facilities for preparation and cooking of food and for the disposal of waste water

A house shall be deemed to be unfit for human habitation if and only if it is so far defective in one or more of the said matters that it is not reasonably suitable for occupation in that condition.

2. CLEARANCE AREAS

The provisions for local authorities using *clearance area procedure* are found in Part Three of the Housing Act 1957. Section 42(1) provides that:

Where a local authority upon consideration of an official representation or other information in their possession are satisfied as respects any area in their district:

a. that the houses in that area unfit for human habitation, or are by reason of their bad arrangement, or the narrowness or bad arrangement of the streets, dangerous or injurious to the health of the inhabitants of the area, and that other buildings, if any, in the area are for a like reason dangerous or injurious to the health of the said inhabitants; and
b. that the most satisfactory method of dealing with the conditions in the area is the demolition of all the buildings in the area;

the authority shall cause the area to be defined . . . a clearance area . . . to be cleared of all buildings . . . .

3. COMPULSORY PURCHASE

Circumstances in which a local authority has powers to purchase land compulsorily for clearance are contained in Section 43 of the Housing Act, 1957. They are as follows:

a. Within a clearance area
b. Land surrounded by the area the acquisition of which is reasonably necessary for the purpose of securing a cleared area of convenient shape and dimensions, and also any adjoining land the acquisition of which is reasonably necessary for the satisfactory development or use of the cleared area.

Before making a CPO the local authority must be *satisfied* that

a. the houses in the Clearance Area(s) are unfit for human habitation and can most satisfactorily be dealt with by demolition.
b. that it can provide or secure the provision by means of other agencies of such rehousing accommodation as may be required in advance of the displacement of persons from the area.
c. that its financial resources are sufficient to carry out the rehousing, demolition and redevelopment.

4. PUBLICITY AND OBJECTIONS

Before submitting a CPO to the Secretary of State the local authority must publicise the order in one or more newspapers circulating in their district. They must also serve a notice on every person with an interest in the land – defined as 'every owner, lessee and occupier (except tenants for a month or less period than a month).

If an objection is made by any person with a recognised interest in the land a public local inquiry or private hearing must be held. After receiving report of his inspector the SOS may confirm the order with or without modifications or reject it. The only appeal is then to the High Court on grounds that the order is not within the terms of the Housing Act, 1957 or that some of the procedural requirements have not been followed.

The Compulsory Purchase Act, 1975 then applies to the purchase and the local authority first serves a 'notice to treat'. They may expedite completion of purchase by a 'general vesting declaration' under S.30 of the Town and County Planning Act, 1968.

5. COMPENSATION

Compensation provisions are found in a number of acts, the chief ones being the Housing Act, 1957; the Land Compensation Act, 1961; and the Land Compensation Act, 1973. The following pattern has built up:

Owner-Occupiers (Fit Houses)	• Full Market Value for interest in the property, including disturbance compensation for other reasonable expenses or losses incurred. • Legal and Valuation Fees • Home Loss Payment (normally payable if living in home for 5 years or more).
Owner-Occupiers (Unfit houses)	• Site Value of land plus disturbance payment to cover removal expenses. • Owner-Occupier's Supplement is payable in most cases, bringing the total up to market value (the property must have been continuously lived in by the owner for at least 2 years). • Well-Maintained Payment is payable to some owner-occupiers if they are not entitled to owner-occupier's supplement. • Legal and Valuation Fees • Home Loss Payment (normally payable if living in house for 5 years or more).
Tenants (Furnished and unfurnished)	• Well-Maintained Payment (either in whole or part) may be paid to some tenants who occupy unfit houses. • Disturbance Payment to cover removal and other reasonable expenses. • Home Loss Payment (normally payable if living in home for 5 years or more).
Landlords (Fit houses)	• Full Market Value for interest in the property. • Legal and Valuation Fees.
Landlords (Unfit Houses)	• Site Value of land. • Well-Maintained Payment may be paid (either in whole or part). • Legal and Valuation Fees.

Figure 3 *The legal basis of clearance*

Residents and owners of properties then become more directly involved. Before submitting a CPO to the Secretary of State the local authority must publicize the order in newspapers and specify where it can be inspected. It must also serve a notice on everyone with a legal interest in the properties and land affected stating that a CPO is about to be submitted. If an objection is made by one of these persons the Secretary of State arranges for a public local inquiry to be held, where his inspector will hear arguments about objections to the order. When an objection is made on the grounds that a house is not unfit the local authority has to serve a notice on the objector stating why it thinks it is unfit (a principal grounds notice). On the basis of the inspector's report after the inquiry the Secretary of State confirms, modifies or rejects the CPO. The local authority advertises the decision and serves notices on all persons with a legal interest in the land.

Procedures for fixing a purchase price for the land and property in the CPO and transferring ownership then begin. Complicated provisions exist for the process of negotiations and the types and amount of compensation paid. The council makes arrangements for taking possession of the properties by serving either a 'General Vesting Order' or 'Notice to Treat'.

At this point rehousing of the residents in the CPO area usually takes place, though it may be delayed by 'deferred demolition'. This is a procedure whereby unfit houses are patched to make living conditions temporarily tolerable prior to rehousing. When rehousing proceeds occupiers are visited and offers of alternative accommodation made to those who require council housing. Empty houses are demolished when convenient blocks become vacant.

Frequently, the cleared land is then used for the redevelopment of council housing. A wide range of legislation, not specifically designed for redevelopment, governs the associated provision of other facilities, such as schools, health centres, shops and open space. Sometimes, the land may be used entirely for another purpose, such as industry. Since 1947 the official framework for the pattern of new uses established by redevelopment has been the land-use zoning of Statutory Development Plans.

Key components

This very brief account of what is in practice a rather more complicated process has been presented without any comment on the origins and contentiousness of its components. Some of the steps mentioned are, in fact, incidental to the process, while others are central. Four key components of the clearance process can be identified:

1 definition of unfitness;
2 rights to object;
3 payment of compensation;
4 rehousing.

Their evolution and the debate surrounding them will now be examined.

The concept of *unfitness* is central to the operation of clearance. Nowhere in legislation which defines the condition of houses suitable for clearance is there a definition of what is a 'slum'. The phrase used from the beginnings of clearance action has been that of 'unfit for human habitation'. The Cross Act of 1875 first introduced the phrase and related it to the extent of a nuisance rendering a house so unfit. The consolidating act of 1890 provided for the representation of Unhealthy Areas to the local authority by the Medical Officer of Health where the dwellings were unfit or where 'bad arrangement' or other environmental evils existed. During the 1930s clearance drive unfitness criteria were used, but depended on the wording and interpretation of local bye-laws and the extent to which, by reason of disrepair or sanitary defects, houses fell short of them.

A government report in 1946[39] identified the need for a more definite standard of fitness and its recommendations were largely embodied in the Housing (Rent and Repairs) Act, 1954. These provisions, repeated in Section 4(1) of the 1957 Act, and still in use today with one slight amendment (see Figure 3), are a direct descendant of early sanitary criteria. They mark an attempt to achieve some uniformity by referring to the matters to be considered in assessing unfitness, but on every one of these a judgement is still required on the seriousness of the defect. In reality the Act merely created a list of items relevant to a judgement of unfitness: it set the scene for any dispute but not the definitive rules. Some further guidance was provided by the Denington Committee in 1966[40] and later recommended to local authorities,[41] but the committee saw no way of specifying more objective criteria.

Two principles established from the start of clearance legislation remain to this day. The first of these is that the criteria for defining unfitness imply a demonstrable connection with health. The definitions used are based on nineteenth century legislation designed to control the menace to health presented by the appalling slums of that era. Meanwhile rising standards of the housing being judged and other public health reforms like smoke control and preventative medicine have weakened this relationship. The second principle is that there is no objective measure: a house is represented as unfit on the subjective assessment of a professional officer. The vagueness of the criteria has provoked such comments as:

> The definition of what constitutes a slum is at any time arbitrary and shifting, depending more upon the vagaries of the English social conscience than upon any precise and identifiable condition.[42]

The dependence on judgement has meant that the standard of unfitness has tended to rise as clearance has progressed, although the 'refereeing' function provided by a national housing inspectorate at local inquiries has allowed some imposition of a common standard on different local authorities at any one time.

Inherent in the clearance and compulsory purchase procedure is the safeguard of an individual's *right to object* to the proposals of a local authority. The procedure incorporates the provision of information to the individual affected and the opportunity for the public discussion of his objection at a local inquiry. At the public local inquiry objectors can seek to have all the houses or particular houses removed from the CPO altogether, or to change the classification of particular houses from 'unfit' to 'fit'.

But which individuals receive information and can have their objection heard? These rights are formally restricted to persons who have a legal interest in the land – landlords and owner-occupiers are included, but almost all tenants are excluded. 'Compulsory purchase procedure can only be understood as a process for expropriating property rights':[43] the law on information provision and the right to object reflects this. It is not concerned with the resident *per se* but with the property owner, as absentee landlord or resident owner-occupier. In practice there has been an increasing but variable trend for local authorities to provide information to all residents, including tenants, and for tenants to be heard at public inquiries as 'non-statutory objectors', but these procedures are discretionary.

A public inquiry is not a court of law but has a quasi-judicial format.[44] The local authority normally opens the proceedings by stating its reasons for seeking the CPO. After it has been cross-examined by objectors (who can be legally represented or call expert witnesses) the objectors can provide a variety of arguments against the CPO. The inspector normally visits the CPO area after the inquiry.

The quasi-judicial nature of the proceedings must be stressed. The central government inspector holding the inquiry and making his recommendations and the minister making a decision are both considering local clearance proposals in relation to national criteria and rules. Though the interests and views of objectors are balanced against the proposals of the local authority, they are evaluated in relation to current central government policy.

The law of *compensation* in the clearance process is consistent with the use of the concept of unfitness to justify compulsory purchase. Houses which are judged to be unfit for human habitation are considered to be worthless as houses, so that their owners are compensated only for 'site value' when they are cleared. In contrast, when houses which are judged to be fit are purchased and cleared as 'added lands', their owners are compensated at 'full market value'.

Having made this basic distinction, important qualifications must be added. Compensation provisions originate from the nineteenth century when virtually all the houses affected by clearance were owned by private landlords. Furthermore, almost all the houses affected by clearance then and in the 1930s were acknowledged as 'slums'. Since the 1930s there has been a history of progressive generosity in compensation provision related to the changing tenure of the houses affected and to rising quality. Modifications and exceptions to the 'site value rule' have weakened the basic distinction between unfit and fit houses.

Modest well-maintained payments for some unfit houses were introduced in 1935 but the real recognition that clearance was increasingly penalizing owner-occupiers was the Slum Clearance (Compensation) Act, 1956. This provided for the payment of supplementary payments to owner-occupiers who had purchased after 1939 to bring their compensation for unfit houses up to full market value. Originally conceived of as a temporary provision, it was extended in 1969 and 1970 so that all owner-occupiers of two years standing get the equivalent of full market value. No similar provisions exist for landlords, who are only eligible for limited well-maintained payments to raise their compensation. A further layer of payments was added in 1973. This was a limited extra payment 'distinct from the value of land and the bricks and mortar' but 'a mark of recognition of the special hardship of compulsory dispossession of a home'.[45] The Home Loss Payment, as it is called, is the only compensation aimed specifically at residents; it can be claimed by both tenants and owner-occupiers of more than five years standing.

The result of all these modifications is a complicated pattern of compensation entitlements related to both house condition and to tenure (see Figure 3). The distinction between 'unfit' and 'fit' still retains some significance, particularly for landlords, explaining a frequent concentration on this issue of public inquiries. Owner-occupiers are more generously treated but the level of 'full market value' in clearance areas still influences their reaction to clearance proposals.

Rehousing of people displaced by clearance into council houses was a crucial issue in the development of clearance policies. Early Acts in the last century laid an obligation on the clearing authority to provide accommodation for the numbers of persons displaced but not to provide directly for the individual families, who simply drifted on to other slums. The subsidies under the 1930 Greenwood Act varied directly with the numbers of people displaced and directly rehoused. Now, when a local authority declares an area to be a clearance area under the 1957 Act, it must consider the availability of housing for those who will be displaced.

However, no clearance legislation gives any resident a legally enforceable right to be rehoused. Local authorities invariably accept a general responsibility for rehousing residents but the Cullingworth Committee of 1969 noted that it had been the practice of successive central governments not to interfere with the way they went about rehousing.[46] Interpretation of the term 'persons' in considering who should be offered council accommodation had almost always excluded lodgers, for instance. 'Suitable alternative accommodation' was claimed to exist by many local authorities for furnished tenants and single people, and, by some, even for owner-occupiers of 'grey' properties. The Committee recommended that local authorities should be required by statute to ensure that every person displaced by public action is satisfactorily rehoused.

The Land Compensation Act, 1973 is now slightly more specific. It imposes a duty on local authorities if 'suitable alternative accommodation on reasonable terms is not otherwise available' to provide accommodation to persons displaced under several procedures, including clearance. However, local interpretation of rehousing obligations is still significant and is complemented by different day-to-day operational procedures.[47] Eligibility rules are applied to ensure that clearance programmes will not become a means of jumping the waiting list queue. Local authorities usually restrict their responsibility to those resident in the CPO area at a particular date, often confirmation, to dissuade households moving in to the area specifically to secure rehousing. Single people can still find themselves excluded from rehousing, or more often 'encouraged' to find their own accommodation, together with transients or former council tenants still in rent arrears.

Rehousing is one aspect of the clearance process which is not tightly defined by central government. Rules and procedures vary significantly between local authorities. The way in which council housing is allocated, what type of house is provided and what degree of choice is presented, are all matters for local discretion.

Professionals

The operation of these powers and procedures is the responsibility of several professional groups within local authorities. During the process there are a variety of powerholders each making decisions within the policy framework provided by national and local political control. The ideologies of these professional groups, their assessment of priorities, interests and power can have a significant impact on the operation of policy.[48]

The key recommendation to a council to include an area within the clearance programme and eventually to represent it as unfit is made by the Environmental Health Officer (EHO), formerly the Public Health Inspector (PHI). The growth of this profession can be directly traced to the sanitary reforms of the nineteenth century when the Medical Officer of Health represented professional training and skills in what were otherwise predominantly amateur and part-time urban governments.[49] Their professional interests led them to play an important role in demanding national standards and legislation to break down local autonomy.

Compared with the relatively straightforward duty of the EHO to inspect dwellings, the long-established nature of his profession and his accumulated local experience of housing conditions, the more recent concern of the planner with comprehensive policy is less clear.[50] Although the planning profession secured some influence over policy through a concern for comprehensive redevelopment, it has been less dominant in practice than might appear on paper.

Rehousing to and management of the replacement dwellings provided has been the concern of the housing management profession since the advent of council housing. A study of local housing allocation procedures in clearance areas has revealed large variations in the implementation of policy.[51] The housing visitor can have a crucial role in judging the eligibility of clearance area families for different types of council accommodation. The use of housekeeping standards for grading tenants – low standards usually resulting in offers of unpopular accommodation – has been criticized.[52] It is subjective, often irrelevant, and can result in families in greatest need being given least help.

With a variety of powerholders involved there are bound to be problems of co-ordination within the clearance and redevelopment process. Muchnick's study of the renewal programme in Liverpool during the 1960s provides an excellent case study of implementation. He concluded:

> . . .although the planning department conceives of renewal in comprehensive terms, although its district plans propose the replacement of facilities other than housing, and although the city council reasserts its intention to pursue such a goal, the corporation's policy is in fact a housing programme coupled with hopes and prayers for ancillary development.[53]

While management tools such as network analysis can go some way towards improving programming and monitoring of the various activities involved,[54] it is inevitable that the local impact of clearance will be closely related to the particular form of organization and departmental styles adopted.

Changes in the built environment

Two types of built environment are involved in clearance and redevelopment policy – the environment replaced and the environment provided. The building cycles of the last century and their characteristic forms of construction have influenced the choice of areas for clearance: in turn, the building cycles of this century can be clearly seen in the replacement housing provided.

The environment replaced

During the early decades of the nineteenth century totally uncontrolled 'jerry-built' working-class housing was provided in great quantity. With virtually no planning or public health regulations and no effective local government, speculative housing was built with poor materials on insecure foundations. Drainage and water supplies for these houses were almost always non-existent. Although locally restrictive powers and the growth of national legislation controlled the worst of such development from the 1840s onwards, minimum standards were still very low. Courtyard dwellings, back-to-backs and tenements were all variations on the same theme – cheap housing at the maximum density possible.

The middle years of the century witnessed a fall in the rate of construction but it then rose again and the peak of the housebuilding boom was reached in 1876.[55] Thereafter the building rate fell, affected partly by more stringently enforced building regulations, but also by the effects of a trade recession discouraging investment and inhibiting lending to developers, and by rising costs. There was a brief resurgence at the end of the century, but by 1914 housebuilding was in decline. The 1875 Act had allowed local authorities to make bye-laws for the layout of new streets, controlling their width and construction, and for the standards of new housing, its space requirements and sanitary provisions. In the latter years of the century the typical 'bye-law' streets were built, characterized by long, monotonous terraces in what were then new suburbs. In select parts of industrial towns and cities more substantial houses were built for middle-class occupation.

The environment provided

Early clearance schemes replaced some of the worst housing built at the start of the last century. Redevelopment by philanthropic trusts was in the form of the tenement block, particularly in London. Municipal authorities followed. As well as being influenced by high land costs, tenements were thought desirable because of the emerging ideas of housing management: they concentrated both control and care of the newly-housed families. Tenement living was often unpopular and the tenements themselves stigmatized as 'barracks' by the population they were meant to house.

During the 1920s new municipal garden suburbs were built with cottage housing on the lines recommended in the 'Tudor Walters' report. When the clearance of the worst nineteenth century housing began in earnest in the 1930s the same principles of design were repeated but standards were lowered and densities increased. Only in London and Liverpool did the tradition of high-density tenement development continue on any substantial scale. However, by the end of the decade other cities had begun experimenting with flats, as they were now called, and subsidies were geared to rebuilding on cleared sites. By 1939 some cities had huge programmes of flat building on inner city estates which would have been completed but for the war.[56]

After 1945 the message from the government was 'plan boldly and comprehensively'.[57] At first this principle was applied to commercial redevelopment, beginning with the rebuilding of the blitzed cities. Later, as large-scale clearance proceeded, it was applied to the rebuilding of residential areas. Comprehensive redevelopment of housing was combined with reshaping road systems: sometimes residential schemes were dominated by a concentration on urban motorways. In some profitable locations it was also combined with the building of new shopping and office areas, although only a small proportion of land freed by slum clearance was diverted from residential use.

High-density redevelopment was one of the prices paid for a preoccupation of planning policies with urban containment. Centres of social activity were swept away together with many back-street workshops. Some attempt was made to replace the former but rarely was a place found for the latter in the new planned environment. Insistence on the need to create a 'total environment' went so far as insulation of the old from the new by a belt of cleared land.[58]

This was also the era of multi-storey blocks, increasingly built by industrialized techniques. Between 1960 and 1968 just over 20 per cent of new council housing was in blocks at least five storeys high.[59] The widely held but mistaken assumption that this was the only way to achieve high densities, and hence savings in agricultural land, was one justification. However, through a process of rationalization and restructuring in the 1950s and 1960s the building industry became increasingly dominated by large firms with the capacity to employ capital intensive and highly profitable system-building technology. With the political need for an accelerated building rate central government became committed to system building. Local councils were encouraged by informal government pressure, increased subsidies for multi-storey flats, the 'hard sell of the package deal', and the influence of architectural fashion.

The decline of multi-storey building in the face of increasing aesthetic and social criticism was given further impetus by the collapse of the Ronan Point flats in 1968. Subsequently, although deck access, 'streets in the sky' flats, were briefly fashionable, the emphasis has been on low-rise, high-density redevelopment schemes. Local authority housing schemes have been influenced by both the minimum standards outlined in the 1961 Parker-Morris report and the constraints introduced in 1967 through the Housing Cost Yardstick.

The standard of replacement housing provided by councils has been affected by a variety of factors. Significant among these, however, is the issue highlighted earlier in this chapter – that of competing ideological views of the purpose of council housing:

> The idea of council housing for all has usually been associated with the building of high-quality houses. By comparison, slum clearance priorities, and the quality of housing associated with them, derive from a narrow sanitary view of the purposes for which council housing is intended.[60]

The contrast is apparent between the immediate post-war housing and the reduced standards of the mid-1950s. During the late 1960s a restricted view of the role of council housing was combined with an emphasis on speed and quantity at the expense of quality: the results are now being felt in repair programmes for system-built developments. The effects of this periodic lowering of standards have been reinforced by housing allocation policies and are now manifest in the growing phenomenon of 'difficult-to-let' estates.

Social effects of clearance and redevelopment

A major focus of argument over clearance and redevelopment has been their impact on the lives of the residents of older housing areas. Conclusions such as, 'what started off as an ameliorative and beneficient policy has taken on the attributes of an inevitable and malevolent process without humanity or compassion',[61] have become increasingly common. Though frequently confused, two separate aspects of the argument can be distinguished: long-term social implications related to the housing aspirations of residents; and more immediate problems of the clearance process.

Threat or promise?

These concerns have always been voiced when discussion of the social effects of clearance has taken place. In earlier periods, however, they were often submerged by explanations of the inevitability of slum housing, couched in terms of the 'slum mentality' of its occupants.[62] In the nineteenth century much of the impetus behind the debate about sanitary reform came from reformers' outrage about moral conditions in the slums. The Victorian establishment launched occasional forays into these areas just as they did into deepest Africa and other outposts of their Empire. Their investigations often concluded that appalling housing conditions were the result of the inherent shiftless nature of the inhabitants, their propensity for breeding and general lack of moral fibre. In the inter-war period the debate widened a little, but similar conclusions were often reached as tenants with a 'slum mind', who would always make a slum wherever they lived, were blamed for the general existence of poor housing conditions. Such arguments have declined further in the post-war years, although in the 1960s a prominent planner could still write '. . .we are dealing with people who have no initiative or civic pride. The task, surely, is to break up such groupings even though the people seem to be satisfied with their miserable environment. . . .'[63]

This offensively patronizing as well as naive discussion about the existence of slums was succeeded by a debate on the wisdom of clearance destroying long-established communities. Studies of residents' attitudes to moving from their existing homes and locality became influential. One summary of research in this field has distinguished two broad categories of studies:[64]

1 early studies begun in the 1950s pursuing a quasi-anthropological methodology, referred to as community studies;
2 sample surveys of slum clearance populations which began in the 1960s.

They differ significantly in style and approach and in the lessons gleaned from their findings.

The most influential of the *community studies* was Wilmott and Young's study of Bethnal Green.[65] As the title *Family and Kinship in East London* implies, they concentrated on the extended family in a stable working-class area. Wilmott and Young concluded that most people did not wish to leave the area because of a deep-rooted attachment to their families and a way of life conditioned by past adversities. While an informal system of 'speaking for' relatives when vacancies occurred in private landlords' houses in the same street ensured continuity of close kinship ties, the system broke down when clearance and rehousing confronted residents with a more bureaucratic system of housing administration.[66]

Other studies found similar supportive relationships based on kinship in older housing areas but were less sure about the relative advantages of maintaining this in comparison with the new opportunities provided by rehousing.[67] On the whole though, the most significant result of these community studies was a growing feeling that there ought to be more questioning of the destructive effects of clearance on old-established communities. The studies have been criticized for failing to place any changes wrought by slum clearance within the context of more important social changes eroding the traditional life-styles described.[68]

The emphasis in these community studies was on the uniform characteristics of the local population to the exclusion of any systematic analysis of the diversity of values and views. In contrast *sample surveys* were designed specifically to identify the range and variety of household requirements, and attitudes to moving, through quantitative techniques. Vereker and Mays' report on the Crown Street area of Liverpool was the first of such studies:[69] many more followed in the 1950s and early 1960s. They initially concentrated on the 'voting' aspect of for and against moving house and locality, but increasingly assembled evidence on the different sectors of the local population holding opposing views and the types of consideration affecting their preferences. Wilkinson and Sigsworth were prominent in the collection of information on these issues.[70] Their various studies in West Yorkshire revealed contrasting evaluations of the costs and benefits of clearance between young, child-centred households, and older households without dependent children. The former were conscious of the potential benefits of clearance and associated rehousing in better housing and environmental conditions. They were less worried by increased housing costs or possible disruption of kinship and friendship ties. The latter were more content to stay in their present house because of low outgoings, and in the area because of its convenient location for friends and family, shopping and work trips. Social surveys pointed to varied reactions and related these to age, stage in the life-cycle and existing tenure.

Only when it is realized that the reaction to clearance will vary from area to area and even from household to household within the same area can some understanding of its social implications be reached. While it is apparent that:

> The people who suffer most by the clearance plans are those who did not envisage any further move in their lifetime. In late middle age, with their children grown up and gone away, they have enjoyed a period of relative affluence, and this money they have poured into their houses. Meticulous and house-proud, they are deeply wounded by the suggestion that their houses are slums, or condemned or unfit – whichever euphemism is currently used in an attempt to make the reality more acceptable. It is an insult to their thrift and cleanliness.[71]

It is also true that substantial support for clearance can be found from those who view rehousing as providing the fulfillment of their aspirations for better housing.[72]

Two myths can be disposed of. The first is that every older housing area contains a cohesive community implacably opposed to clearance and rehousing; the second is that every older housing area contains residents who will universally welcome clearance and rehousing into more modern council housing. Reality is more complex. 'The consumer's attitude to moving is the result of comparing the net gains and losses incurred by remaining in one place with the net gains and losses he expects to incur in the destination of the move', and a variety of 'preference-arrays' can be expected.[73] While the definition of clearance areas depends solely on a judgement of the physical condition of houses, the residents' viewpoint will be influenced by their present tenure[74] and attachment to their house and area. It will also be influenced by the location, standard and costs of the alternative housing provided. Perspectives will vary over time, as the old couple previously opposed to clearance and the change from owner-occupier to the status of a tenant perhaps appreciate the advantages of their new council house, or the young family previously longing for the arrival of the bulldozer may find themselves unable to adjust to higher rents and drift back to cheaper accommodation.

Clearance began by attacking uniformly poor housing, almost all in private rental. A commitment to the idea of comprehensive redevelopment reinforced a blanket approach to older housing. Increasing criticism of clearance and redevelopment has inevitably resulted from a failure to reflect the complexity of older housing areas and their residents' aspirations.

Problems of the process

It is not just the longer-term social implications of clearance and redevelopment which affect residents. More immediate problems of the process are apparent. A Shelter report summarized the undesirable by-products as:

1 the repeated postponement of the date when people are to be rehoused in satisfactory accommodation;

2 the appalling and continually deteriorating living conditions both within the houses themselves and in the surrounding neighbourhood;
3 the despair felt by residents of clearance areas who feel they have little contact with the authorities carrying out the programme.[75]

These interrelated issues have undoubtedly affected the views of residents and in turn influenced changes in the direction of policy.

A basic problem has been inadequate resources for redevelopment programmes. Given the long tradition of false optimism at a national level about ambitious clearance targets followed by subsequent failures in house-building, it is hardly surprising that *delays* have been endemic in the clearance programmes of most towns and cities. A prerequisite of any clearance programme is that there must be enough houses available for people to be satisfactorily rehoused. National fluctuations in housebuilding associated with the use of housing expenditure as an economic regulator and changing political priorities have inevitably had local impact. At a local level such national changes in direction have been matched by councils' own political decisions on building programmes. Cut-backs in building at times of economic crisis not only directly affect rehousing progress in existing clearance areas, they also encourage the postponement of future representations.

Delays are also the result of inadequate detailed management by local authorities and failures to marry demolition with the completion of new dwellings in a location and of a type that will ensure smooth rehousing. The intervening period between representation of a clearance area, rehousing and subsequent redevelopment is to some extent unpredictable because of the lengthy statutory procedures already described, some of which are outside the direct control of the local authority. The problems are compounded by the division of departmental responsibilities for different stages of the process. Areas have sometimes been represented for clearance by public health departments without adequate consultation with the housing departments responsible for eventual rehousing obligations. Lack of attention to the programming of adjacent new housing developments and their dwelling mix in relation to the housing needs of clearance area residents has been common.

Within clearance areas attempts by local authorities to counteract such delays are often made solely in the rehousing period. A lack of rehousing opportunities favoured by clearance area residents sometimes means that, if the redevelopment programming of the area is not to slip, pressures for rehousing in areas where families are reluctant to move to are exerted. Instead of adequate choice, and in particular the availability of local rehousing where desired, rehousing in what may be unpopular overspill estates on the other side of the city, or simply where relets become randomly available, is likely to be offered on a 'take it or leave it' basis.

The appalling *living conditions* found in many clearance areas are often closely related to the delays in programmes. The process of blight referred to earlier also results in lack of attention to repairs and a general run-down of services to what is seen as a doomed area. Once the clearance process begins empty houses become a training ground for vandalism. As the state of repair of occupied houses worsens further, services like water and electricity can even be cut off. Delays prolong the misery experienced by residents of these areas while 'the slow death of a slum' proceeds. When policies of deferred demolition are adopted such conditions can last for many years.

Liverpool was one of the cities where the rate of clearance in the late 1960s and early 1970s outstripped the capacity to rebuild in demolished areas, particularly where sites were earmarked for non-residential purposes, such as public open space, community centres, shops or schools. Areas where the clearance process was operating were often adjacent to vast areas of already cleared, rubble-strewn land. The impact on living conditions was summarized by Stones:

> Life in the new urban deserts is rapidly becoming unbearable for those who remain. Half-demolished houses and broken drains harbour rats, which make their way into still-occupied dwellings. The small number of residents leaves many areas unsupervised and hence subject to vandalism and crime, for which the empty dwellings are ideal. Bricks are thrown through windows by children who find the crumbling ruins a dangerous playground. The wide open spaces have been colonized by gypsies and tinkers, many of whom are running scrap metal businesses. . . . The cleared spaces also double as public lavatories and scrapheaps for old cars and rubbish dumped by suburbanites.[76]

The care that local authorities take in attempting to minimize these problems varies. For instance, some simply leave houses empty for months or years after rehousing their occupants, while others are efficient in boarding or bricking them up. Only a few authorities make properties bought some time before clearance available on licence for short-life use.[77]

Uncertainty and despair have often been caused by lack of *communication*. Four major justifications for improving communication with clearance area residents have been advanced:

1 satisfaction of the felt need of residents;
2 on public relations grounds to reduce hostility and resentment;
3 as a prerequisite of effective choice in rehousing;
4 as an essential basis for participation and greater resident involvement in the redevelopment process.[78]

In 1956 the Housing Management Sub-Committee of the government's Central Housing Advisory Committee reported on the need for residents in clearance areas to receive full and accurate information as early as possible if uncertainty and anxiety were to be reduced.[79] Similar recommendations were repeated in a report in 1969.[80]

Yet when the St. Ann's area of Nottingham was studied:

> The inhabitants had already learned, often through a grapevine in which rumour

> flowed as freely as fact, that the area was about to be flattened. Almost everyone in St. Ann's was torn between two suppositions: that their house would be knocked down next year, or sooner, a belief that was encouraged every time an official-looking stranger walked down the road; and that they would rot another twenty years without being rehoused, an assumption that floated to the top whenever the public authorities made any statement about the progress which was imminently to be expected.[81]

The inadequate transmission of information to residents in clearance programmes has been identified in a number of other studies.[82] A detailed investigation of residents' experience and comprehension of slum clearance procedures reveals a very imperfect understanding of the events involved and their significance. This is especially true of the earlier steps in the process, such as visits by public health inspectors for representation and by the DoE inspector after a public inquiry.[83] Only the housing visitor, who is involved right at the end of the clearance process, was recalled by a substantial number of residents. Bull's study of Manchester's clearance procedures in the 1960s concluded that the alleviation of the problems of people in clearance areas is not primarily a social work issue; it is one of a lack of communication between the local authority and residents.[84] He suggested public meetings; organized trips to new housing estates; local advice centres; information booklets and more comprehensible letters, particularly about such items as possible entitlement to well-maintained payments. Most local authorities did little in response to these suggested reforms.

While problems of delays, living conditions and lack of communication frequently occur during the clearance process, it is also important to recognize that they exist for many years before legal procedures begin. Long-term proposals have often blighted areas by assuming a limited life for older housing to safeguard road widening lines, and reserving sites for new schools, shopping centres and open spaces, to be provided at some unspecified future date. In the all too common situation of such plans lacking the necessary resources, and thus remaining on the shelf for many years, it is no simple matter to establish whether decay is the result of the self-fulfilling prophecy of planning blight, the operation of the housing market, or a combination of both.

Conclusions

The setting for large-scale clearance and redevelopment was the mass housing conditions created by private capital in the industrial towns and cities of the nineteenth century. Fear of revolution and the spread of disease, together with the moral outrage of social reformers, prompted the piecemeal development of sanitary reform measures. Eventually, political expediency in the face of threatened industrial and social unrest and the declining profitability of private rental resulted in the state assuming some responsibility for providing decent housing for the working class. The development of council housing enabled a clearance drive to be launched in the 1930s which began the attack on the worst nineteenth century housing. Although there were periodic and partially successful attempts to reduce state intervention these were now aimed at promoting owner-occupation for general housing needs, while recognizing a residual responsibility for the replacement of slum housing. The end of the slums was promised by successive governments. From the mid-1950s onwards there was considerable continuity in the clearance effort. The replacement of older housing by comprehensively planned new developments was a continuing theme of both housing and planning policy.

One result of these policies has been vastly improved housing and environmental conditions for many families, a gain which is now all too often forgotten when the impact of the bulldozer is discussed. Notwithstanding this, by the early 1970s many of those meant to benefit saw clearance as a threat rather than a promise. Disappointment with the replacement housing provided, an impression that the procedures adopted represented the workings of a machine over which the ordinary citizen had no control, and the disruption involved all played a part in prompting mounting opposition.

Underlying this disaffection were the related issues of inadequate resources, ineffective management of the process and lack of sensitivity. Because the rhetoric of comprehensive redevelopment was not matched by the resources necessary for housebuilding, the slow death of the slums was a painful experience. Moreover, failure to launch legislative and administrative changes, particularly with regard to communication let alone participation in decision making, perpetuated the coercive nature of the process. As comparatively better standard older housing was reached, the prospect of being rehoused in a parsimoniously built and distant estate of the 1930s or 1950s, or in a brutal, high-rise inner city scheme of the 1960s, was often seen as a solution to be avoided. The growth of owner-occupation in older housing areas meant that some residents saw rehousing as the elimination of personal control over their accommodation and loss of their only investment.

This disaffection can be and has been exaggerated. Chapters 3 and 4 trace how comprehensive redevelopment was eventually dismissed as an outmoded form of treatment for older housing. In the shift of emphasis towards gradual renewal the problems of area clearance and redevelopment were portrayed as endemic, rather than an appropriate subject for further reforms. However, the limited impact of improvement in the 1970s has raised the prospect of a further generation of slums. It may well be that this dismissal of redevelopment was premature: a re-examination of its role and reforms of the processes involved are likely to be part of the development of urban renewal policy in the 1980s.

3 Old houses into new homes

During the early 1970s the improvement of older houses and their environment became the dominant component of urban renewal. This chapter first examines the origins and development of this major shift in national policy. The Housing Act, 1969 was the turning point in the evolution of improvement policies, and the framework of powers and procedures it established is outlined. The rapid increase in improvement activity is then analysed in terms of its impact on the built environment and its social and distributional implications.

Reconditioning the slums was a major concern in the 1920s but state intervention to secure the improvement of old but structurally sound housing by subsidizing owners is essentially a post-war phenomenon. It stemmed from government concern that continued decay of better pre-1919 houses would eventually necessitate their clearance before the 'end of the slums' could be reached. Hence, during the 1950s a tandem policy of clearance and grant-aided improvement was established. Although improvement gathered momentum in the 1960s it remained subordinate to slum clearance. The outcome of an appraisal of the housing situation in the late 1960s was a commitment to a reinvigorated tandem policy in 1969, which aimed to accelerate both clearance and improvement. In the following four years there was a spectacular growth in improvement, which increasingly came to be seen as an alternative to clearance.

Implementation of improvement depends on the combined initiatives of local government, private owners and housing associations. The 1969 Act established a comprehensive code of powers and procedures, which gave local authorities considerable discretion. Subsidized improvement involves varying combinations of 'carrots' (e.g. cash grants) and 'sticks' (e.g. the threat of compulsion) increasingly concentrated in small areas.

Improvement policy has a less obvious impact on the built environment than redevelopment as it aims to modernize rather than replace the physical fabric. The nature of improvement work is significantly influenced by variations in the original development. Housing improvement includes both the renovation of individual houses and the conversion of large houses into a number of self-contained units: this work ranges from the installation of an inside toilet to virtual reconstruction. Environmental improvement typically involves work such as landscaping and traffic management.

An unprecedented increase in grant take-up in the early 1970s had a positive effect on the older housing stock, but there was growing concern about its social implications. Some groups and areas benefited, but for others the situation remained unchanged or deteriorated. The chapter ends with an analysis of the socio-economic aspects of improvement policy. It focusses on subsidized improvement as 'an investment partnership' between the state and the owners of older housing: this is the key to an understanding of its distributional consequences and the rapid development of public participation.

Substandard housing and subsidized improvement

For many years improvement was the Cinderella of housing renewal.[1] In the inter-war years reconditioning was originally viewed as an alternative to slum clearance and there was intense debate about its efficacy. It was instrumental in raising basic standards but bitterly opposed as a policy which diverted attention from the need for vigorous clearance. The twenty years from 1949 established the basic framework of the grant system, the concept of area improvement, and the potential and problems of this component of urban renewal, and by 1968 some 1.3 million grants had been approved, compared with the post-war total of 0.8 million houses demolished.[2] This progress was assisted by successive changes in grants and their conditions, which are summarized in Figure 4.

Reconditioning

Compulsory improvement powers have been available since the Torrens Act of 1868, and in the last century, but more significantly during the 1920s, there were examples of locally devised reconditioning schemes. These involved encouragement, backed up by compulsory unfitness notices, of work by private landlords to improve their houses to basic standards, sometimes combined with selective demolition. No grant aid was available and, although the Housing (Rural Workers) Act, 1926 provided rural local authorities with discretionary powers to make grants and loans for reconditioning houses, these were little used. Estimates of the impact of reconditioning schemes vary but Bowley states that about 300,000 houses p.a. were made fit in this way during the 1920s.[3] Reconditioning was an inadequate response to slum housing and after the Housing Act, 1930 clearance became paramount, with the Act's improvement area procedures being largely ignored.[4]

The problem of substandard property outside clearance programmes continued to be considered by a variety of central government committees in the 1930s and 1940s.[5] Despite increasing owner-occupation of older houses, most were still owned by private landlords and had been subject to rent control since 1915. The Moyne Report of 1933 concluded that the inability or

Act	*Renovation grants*	*Area improvement*
Housing Act, 1949	Introduced *Improvement Grants* for houses which would have an estimated life of thirty years or more. At LA discretion and stringent conditions applied.	
Housing (Repairs and Rents) Act, 1954	Increased eligible expense limit and relaxed some of conditions, for example, life qualification to fifteen years.	
House Purchase and Housing Act, 1959	Added a second tier of grant. Discretionary improvement grants were confirmed as being designed to bring older houses into a condition comparable to a modern house, when allowance is made for age and limitations of design, layout and construction. *Standard Grants* were mandatory 'as of right' to make older houses more comfortable for the rest of their (limited) life by the installation of a bath, internal w.c., etc.	
Housing Act, 1964	Increased eligible expense limits for both types of grant, reduced some conditions, and increased landlords' permitted return for their share of costs.	Introduced the *Improvement Area* where comprehensive housing improvement would be encouraged. Compulsory improvement procedures for rented dwellings.
Housing Act, 1969	Substantially increased eligible expense limits and removed most conditions for discretionary and standard grants. Added a third tier of grants – the *Special Grant* for the installation of extra standard amenities in houses in multiple occupation.	Replaced the improvement area with the *General Improvement Area* where concentrated encouragement of voluntary improvement would be assisted by new powers of environmental improvement with exchequer subsidy to LA.
Housing Act, 1971	'Once and for all' higher grant rates and exchequer subsidies to LAs in 'Assisted Areas', for work completed by 1973, to boost improvement in such areas for both housing and employment reasons.	Increased exchequer subsidy for environmental works in GIAs on same criteria and for same reasons as housing improvement.
Housing Act, 1974	Increased eligible expense limits and re-introduced occupancy conditions. Rateable value limit for owner-occupied dwellings eligible for Improvement Grant. Tentative introduction at fourth tier of grant – the *Repair Grant*, only available in HAAs and GIAs.	Confirmed GIAs as areas where voluntary improvement of owner-occupied houses would be encouraged and introduced *Housing Action Areas* where intense activity, including compulsion, was appropriate for areas of stress, with combinations of housing and social problems. *Priority Neighbourhoods* would stop stress 'rippling out' from GIAs and HAAs.

Note: see Appendix for detailed provisions

Figure 4 *Private renovation grants and area improvement – major legislation 1949 to 1974*

unwillingness of many landlords to invest in repair and maintenance was a major cause of continued deterioration, and recommended a move to some form of social ownership. The Housing Act, 1935 provided local authorities with the necessary compulsory purchase powers, but no Exchequer subsidy for subsequent reconditioning work, with the result that little was achieved.[6] At the same time there was opposition, particularly in the Labour Party, to the alternative of subsidizing private owners.[7]

Discretionary grant aid

Improvement of urban housing by private owners first became a subsidized activity in 1949 when a grant system was introduced. The inevitable corollary of concentrating on new housebuilding and suspending clearance in the immediate post-war years was that many older houses had to remain for longer than had been previously envisaged. The Labour Government overruled objections to subsidizing private owners, and the Housing Act, 1949 established improvement grants as a feature of national housing policy. Municipalization was debated during the passage of the Bill, but dismissed as impractical.[8]

In Bevan's words the objective was not 'to rescue slums' or 'to permit landlords to make good arrears of repairs they should themselves have carried out long ago' but to provide 'improvements' in basically sound older housing.[9] Thus the subsidy was for the provision of sanitary facilities with which the houses had not been previously equipped and, in line with the recommendations of the Silkin Committee,[10] for the conversion of one house into two or more self-contained units.

This policy was designed to complement new housing construction. First, additional units created by conversion would help alleviate the housing shortage. Second, and more important, the improvement of single dwellings would help create more houses of a high standard. A housing stock philosophy, emphasizing quality rather than quantity, was established, for it was considered 'much better to secure a smaller number of good houses, than to fritter away the building resources and expenditure on the patching of houses which would remain unsatisfactory in many respects'.[11] At a time when the government's policy was to build council housing to a high standard, improvement was regarded as second best and was not to interfere with housebuilding progress.[12]

The powers provided were consistent with this emphasis. The policy relied on the voluntary take-up of grants by owners, and was oriented to individual houses rather than areas of substandard housing. The main tool was the discretionary grant, so called because it was awarded entirely at the discretion of local authorities. The grant was 50 per cent of the cost of improvement, but was payable only under strict conditions, which reflected both the concern for high standards and a reluctance to subsidize private landlords.

It was clear that a major programme was neither desired nor expected. Local authorities were preoccupied with housing construction and only 6000 grants were approved for the whole country between 1949 and 1953.

The growth of 'the property owning democracy'

Chapter 2 outlined the major shift of emphasis as during the 1950s the Conservative Government's strategy was to move away from state provision towards the promotion of owner-occupation – the building of 'a property owning democracy'. The first step was the launching of 'Operation Rescue' in 1953, which made renewal the focus of housing policy and established a tandem approach. Clearance and redevelopment would deal with the finite problem of the slums. Substandard housing in danger of deteriorating into slums would be tackled by more attractive improvement grants as incentives to private owners, and rent increases intended to stimulate investment in repair and maintenance. Housing improvement was still seen as complementary to the priority task of slum clearance. It would alleviate conditions in older housing areas outside clearance programmes.[13]

Similarly the powers remained essentially the same as in 1949, with a reliance on the voluntary take-up of discretionary grants aimed at high standards of improvement. But the Conservative Government had no doubt as to the legitimacy or desirability of subsidizing private owners. Some grant conditions were relaxed and landlords' returns were increased. Moreover, these measures were backed up by an extensive publicity campaign, and ministerial prodding of the many unenthusiastic authorities. The effect of this action was only modest in relation to the scale of the problem. The take-up of grants increased to 30,000 p.a. but then stabilized at this level. By 1959 some local authorities were still refusing to give grants.

Two interrelated Acts then led to a more dramatic rise in improvement activity which was henceforth bound up with the promotion of owner-occupation. When the policy of rent increases introduced in 1954 failed to secure increased repair and maintenance, the Rent Act, 1957 introduced large-scale decontrol of privately rented accommodation on the assumption that the resultant further rent increases would provide the incentive needed. The legislation did not have this effect, but its implications can only be understood in relation to the House Purchase and Housing Act, 1959.[14] This Act was framed with the dual objectives of extending working-class owner-occupation and boosting private improvement. The Government provided financial incentives for building societies to lend more money for the purchase of cheaper, pre-1919 houses, and added a second tier of improvement grant.

The new standard grant was not discretionary, but available as of right provided that certain conditions were met. The grant could be claimed by owners as a specified sum towards the cost of the provision of five standard amenities (a fixed bath or shower in a bathroom, a wash hand basin, a hot water supply, a w.c., and facilities for food storage), in houses with a life of fifteen years after improvement. The intention was to encourage shorter-term improvements to lower standards in order to make the houses comfortable to live in for their remaining life. The discretionary grant was now restricted to houses with a thirty-year life for improvements to high standards. The government stepped up its publicity campaign and continued to prod recalcitrant local authorities.[15]

The effect of these policy developments was dramatic and immediate (see Figure 5). In 1960 130,000 grants were approved, and the annual total remained at about that level until 1964. During this five-year period nearly 600,000 grants were approved, over twice as many as the total for 1949–59. Some two thirds were standard grants - an eloquent testimony to the popularity of this new measure. However, distribution between different tenures was very skewed with only one fifth of the grants going to private landlords. The major beneficiaries were the new owner-occupiers of older housing. In combination, the Acts of 1957 and 1959 greatly increased both opportunities and incentives for private landlords to sell their property for owner-occupation.[16] The result was a massive transfer of the ownership of older housing from the late 1950s onwards and, initially, an associated increase in investment by owner-occupiers. The relative prosperity of the late 1950s after wartime and immediate post-war austerity encouraged this process.

The area approach and compulsory improvement

Growing evidence of a deteriorating housing situation in the early 1960s led the Conservative Government to modify their strategy. The results of both independent academic analyses and the Government's own research led inexorably to the unpalatable conclusion that the scale of urban renewal did not match the extent of the problem.

A White Paper in 1963 made an explicit distinction between 'slums' defined in public health terms, and depressed and decaying residential areas, increasingly referred to as 'twilight areas'.[17] The main thrust of the White Paper's argument was that the end of the slums really was in sight, and that it was necessary to formulate long term policies for the twilight areas. Urban renewal in future was to involve:

> the enormous task of replacing the older and depressed residential areas; of accommodating the immense traffic increase expected, and of reconciling this with a good living environment.[18]

The twilight areas were destined for the bulldozer: all that remained for the Minister, Sir Keith Joseph, to determine was who would be doing the driving. The White Paper announced that arrangements were in hand for pilot schemes of partnership between the state and large-scale private developers.

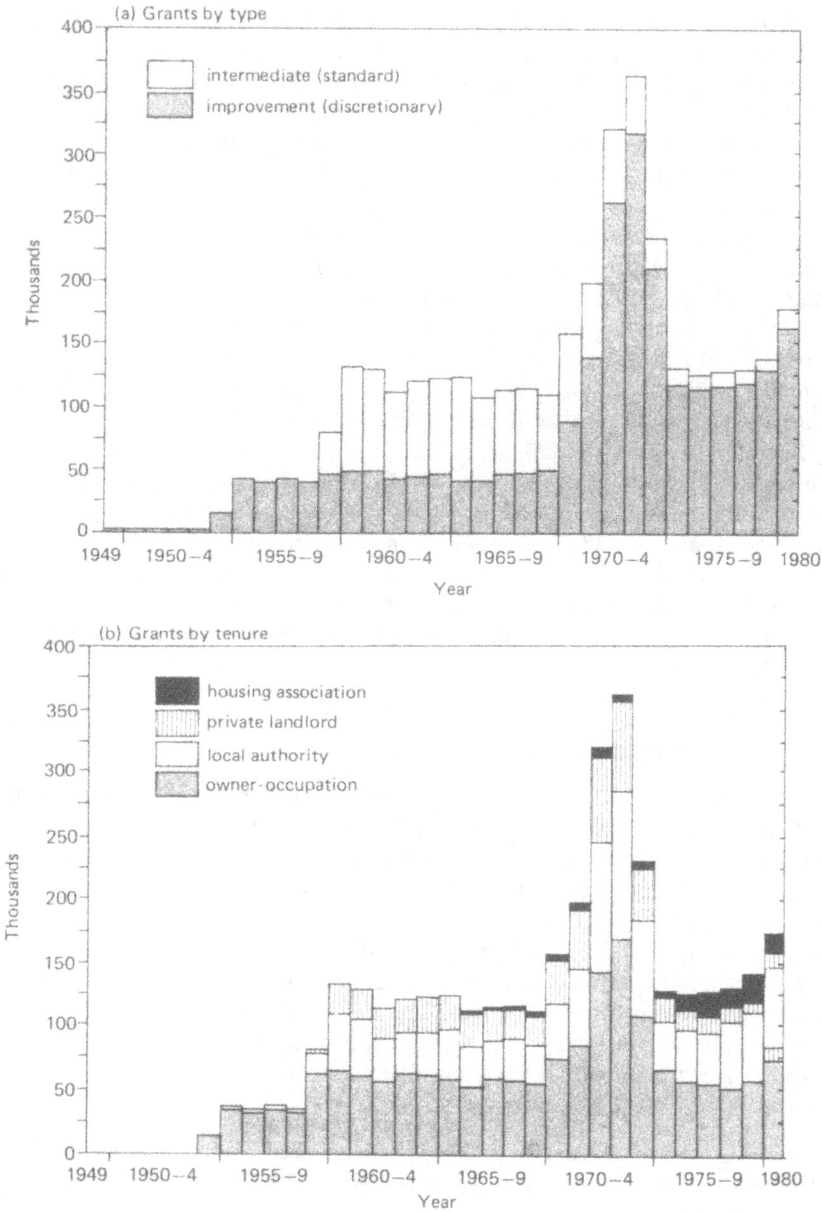

Figure 5 *Renovation grants approved (England and Wales) 1949 to 1980*
Notes: Improvement grants include conversions; intermediate grants include special and repair grants.

Source: Housing Statistics and *Housing Construction Statistics* (HMSO)

Investigations of a possible 'private enterprise solution' were set in motion.

However, given an impending general election, and the furore caused by the Rachman affair only months after the publication of the 1963 White Paper, the Government was forced to take more immediate action. The result was the Housing Act, 1964. For the first time a target was specified, that of improving '. . . within the next ten years most of the 2 million or so improvable older houses which lack amenities and which still have a reasonable life', involving '. . . increasing the present rate of improvement from some 130,000 a year to 200,000 a year as soon as possible'.[19] Now the objective was to secure large numbers of short-term improvements to modest standards, and to achieve this a hitherto exclusive emphasis on voluntary improvement of individual houses was modified by the introduction of an element of compulsion.

The rationale of 'comprehensive improvement' was that the upgrading of all the houses in a given area to a minimum standard would obviate some of the difficulties which had arisen with sporadic improvement. Commitment to comprehensive improvement would enable concentration of local authority effort and reduce uncertainty for owners.[20] But, if there were to be no rotten apples in the Improvement Area barrels, there would have to be powers to enforce improvement. It was well known that take-up of grants by landlords was significantly lower than that by owner-occupiers. This factor, combined with intense political controversy over conditions in the private rented sector, was sufficient to persuade a reluctant Conservative Government to give local authorities 'last resort' powers to compel landlords in Improvement Areas to improve their houses with the aid of grants. There were no powers of compulsion in respect of owner-occupiers.

The 1964 Act also strengthened local authorities' powers regarding multi-occupation, i.e. houses built for one family but occupied by several families without proper conversion. This was a growing phenomenon, particularly in areas where pressure on available accommodation was acute, and resulted in some of the worst forms of exploitation and hardship in the private rented sector. Local authorities were now enabled to use control orders to effect a temporary takeover of houses to improve conditions at the owners' expense.[21] These powers, together with those for compulsory improvement, constituted '. . . a very drastic interference with established property rights and one that would have been unlikely if now downright impossible only a few years previously'.[22]

Circular 53/64 added a broader dimension to the area approach:

> The main point the Minister wishes to emphasize is that area improvement is something more than a means of providing amenities in individual houses. It is part of the process of urban renewal. So, in choosing areas for early action, and in implementing their schemes of improvement, local authorities should consider all the measures which are open to them to fit areas for the requirements of modern living and for improving the quality of the environment – for example, the provision of new street furniture, tree planting, more parking facilities, better open spaces.[23]

Reference was made to the desirability of co-ordinating housing Improvement Areas with smoke control areas, and possible applications of the Buchanan Report's concept of environmental areas designed to improve traffic management.[24] This was the first indication of a serious interest in housing *and* environmental improvement on an area basis, but no Exchequer subsidy was provided for environmental works.

This policy was implemented during the period 1964–9. Its direct impact was minimal. By the end of 1969 only 463 Improvement Areas had been designated, and within these only 5600 dwellings had been improved, less than a quarter of the total eligible houses. The failure of this first attempt at area-based improvement was attributed to the excessive teething troubles of an innovatory approach and cumbersome statutory procedures. Moreover, there was a fall in the overall annual total of grants approved, mainly resulting from a decline in the take-up of standard grants, which the policy had specifically sought to increase. This was considered to be due to a static grant at a time of rapidly increasing building costs.[25] Over and above all these explanations was the uncertainty stemming from the fact that the Labour Government was engaged in a reappraisal of policy.

A shift in emphasis

The unresolved question of the twilight areas was a major issue facing the Labour Government after the 1964 General Election. Within four years there was a substantial change in housing policy aimed at shifting resources from increasing the quantity of the national housing stock by new building, to improving its quality through renewal: both clearance and improvement would be accelerated.

Policy review

The new Minister of Housing, Crossman, held the view that long-term policy should concentrate on the problems of conurbation twilight areas, involving 'comprehensive renewal' and 'large-scale state intervention', although he was ambivalent about the relative merits of comprehensive redevelopment and housing improvement.[26] Ministerial ambivalence reflected growing concern about the inadequate information base of policy making and two important initiatives were taken. A subcommittee of the Central Housing Advisory Committee, known as the Denington Committee,[27] was established to re-examine the question of minimum tolerable standards of housing accommodation, and Crossman commissioned three feasibility studies to help assess the possibilities for housing and environmental improvement.

These initiatives marked the beginning of a major review. A complex array of interrelated factors was involved in the developing debate and subsequent shift of policy, and interpretations of their relative significance vary widely.[28]

At a local level contributory factors were:

1 government sponsored feasibility studies;
2 demonstration projects; and
3 consumer opposition to slum clearance;

while the significant considerations at a national level were:

4 research into the condition of the older housing stock;
5 economic arguments for increasing the relative significance of improvement; and
6 revised demographic projections and the resources of the building industry.

However, the political resolution of the issues raised in the debate was crucially influenced by the deteriorating economic situation.

Several government sponsored *feasibility studies* had been initiated by the Conservatives in 1963 to explore the 'private enterprise solution'. Their briefs required an analysis of the possibilities of comprehensive redevelopment on the basis of a partnership between large-scale commercial developers and local authorities, with the proviso that proposed schemes should allow for the rehousing of the existing population in the new development.

Both the Fulham[29] and the Halliwell[30] studies undertook investigations of the socio-economic characteristics of their areas. The Fulham Study examined an area of high housing market pressure, with high densities, a high proportion of private rented accommodation, and some multi-occupation. In contrast the Halliwell Report analysed a low-pressure area, with lower densities and a 60 per cent level of owner-occupation. Both studies concluded that it was not possible to both rehouse established residents at costs they could afford and secure a high enough rate of return to make investment profitable. The 'verdict of the market'[31] on the possibility of private enterprise undertaking large-scale comprehensive redevelopment was an emphatic 'no'. If the twilight areas were to be redeveloped it would be the responsibility of the state. However, the Halliwell Report did recommend that the practicality of large-scale rehabilitation as an alternative to redevelopment should be examined afresh, i.e. a different kind of partnership, one between government and house owners.

A reappraisal of the potential of rehabilitation was the purpose of the Crossman initiated feasibility studies, of which the Deeplish Study was by far the most influential.[32] The Deeplish area of Rochdale was in many respects similar to the Halliwell area of Bolton. It was an old, stable, working-class community, with relatively low household incomes and housing costs. The study area contained some 1600 houses, mainly 'two up and two down' terraces, three quarters of which were owner-occupied and nearly half lacked basic amenities. The area was chosen because 'it was felt to be reasonably typical of older neighbourhoods which have not yet reached the stage of slumdom'.[33]

Factors which favoured rehabilitation included the structural soundness of the majority of houses, the reluctance of residents to leave the district, and the willingness of a significant proportion of them to pay more for better housing standards. Moreover, an appraisal of renewal priorities in Rochdale as a whole indicated that redevelopment would not be possible for many years, yet there was a clear need to check deterioration. On the other hand, the study indicated that the majority of landlords and some of the elderly and poor owner-occupiers were unable or unwilling to bear the costs of improvement, particularly to high standards. The conclusion was that an appropriate policy would be housing improvement to modest standards, together with environmental improvement aimed at boosting private investment by owners, particularly owner-occupiers. A pilot environmental improvement scheme was suggested and subsequently implemented in four streets.[34]

The Deeplish pilot scheme was one of five *demonstration projects* initiated by local authorities and supported by central government between 1967 and 1969. The four others were in Exeter,[35] Whitworth,[36] Skelmersdale,[37] and Leeds.[38] With the exception of the last, these projects were completed in 1969, and represented the experience of area-based improvement as the 1969 Act came into force.[39] Clearly this was a limited basis on which to judge the practicality of this approach.

The demonstration projects took further ideas that had been discussed in the early 1960s, particularly the issue of Exchequer subsidies for environmental works. Although they showed that area improvement was technically feasible, the projects were all very small scale, the houses involved were predominantly owner-occupied or in public ownership, implementation of the schemes had been resource intensive, and no demonstration project was located in an area of market pressure. Moreover, little of this work had been completed by the time the Government made its major policy decision in late 1967. Thus, while the feasibility studies were significant in mobilizing professional and political support for rehabilitation, the role of the demonstration projects was largely that of legitimating a prior decision.[40]

Chapter 2 outlined the arguments about the social impact of clearance during this period. While it had yet to become effectively organized on an area basis, growing *consumer opposition* to clearance was related to the often lengthy, insensitive and disruptive nature of the process, to disenchantment with the replacement accommodation provided and, crucially, to increasing levels of owner-occupation in clearance areas. Cullingworth's study of Lancaster had already shown that:

> the problem is no longer one of old insanitary courts, of back-to-back houses, of dangers to the public health, or of abject poverty. Rather it is one of sound old houses needing improvement and continued maintenance. The political problem is also changing: in the phraseology of stereotypes, the unpitying and unpitied landlord is being replaced by the upstanding owner-occupier. Dispossession of owner-occupiers for the sake of redevelopment is quite a different matter from the dispossession of landlords in the interests of public health. . . . The problem is now one of raising the

quality of housing in the city. This calls for a policy of improvement, rehabilitation and conservation – of the neighbourhood as well of individual houses.[41]

Unfitness criteria and compensation provisions were becoming difficult to justify, particularly outside the major conurbations.

In addition there was the growing popularity of the notion of retaining the community: 'increasingly improvement was seen as a physical means of preserving the sort of community attributes which seemed to disappear on redevelopment'.[42] The prospective benefits of improvement were viewed uncritically, while little effort was devoted to reforming the clearance process.

However, while the local dimension was a significant element in the reappraisal, a more important factor was a changing perception of the national housing situation.

A concern for more accurate information on the *condition of the older housing stock* emerged from the Denington Committee.[43] Its report concluded that both clearance and improvement policies were inadequate in view of the then known scale of the problems, and that there was an urgent need for more effective action on both fronts. Furthermore, the Committee emphasized the continuous nature of obsolescence and advocated the adoption of a more comprehensive approach necessitating local authorities taking responsibility for all older housing, effectively co-ordinating clearance, repair and improvement action. In the light of an appraisal of the older housing stock, areas should be identified for early clearance, short-term improvement, and longer-term full improvement. The need for an area-based approach was re-emphasized, and attention was drawn to the pioneering work in Leeds.

The Committee identified two particular fields where research was needed in order to implement a comprehensive programme: housing condition and the economics of renewal. The former suggestion met with an immediate government response. In 1967 the first National House Condition Survey was undertaken on a sample basis. It revealed that 1.8m houses were unfit, and 4.5m either required substantial repairs or lacked one or more basic amenities. These findings made uncomfortably clear the effects of continued neglect of the twilight areas, substantiated previous academic criticism of national policy, and reinforced the views of the Denington Committee. The results of the survey could not be ignored and a renewal policy initiative became imperative.

Little attention had previously been paid to the latter area of research – the *economic arguments* surrounding renewal. They had been implicitly acknowledged in the tandem policy first adopted in 1954, in that improvement of basically sound older houses was seen as a means of slowing down the rate at which houses became unfit and required expensive replacement. However, while most local authorities had defined area-based clearance and redevelopment programmes, very few had developed formal improvement strategies. The implementation of a comprehensive area-based approach required answers to three related questions. At what point is it more worthwhile to replace a house rather than improve it? How could areas be identified for the three-pronged approach advocated by the Denington Committee? What criteria should be used to determine the most economic balance between redevelopment and improvement at both local and national levels?

From the mid-1960s onwards there was a significant increase in academic research directed to these questions, stimulated initially by Needleman. He argued that, in economic terms:

> ... whether it is cheaper to renovate old properties, or demolish and rebuild them will depend on three factors: the rate of interest; the future length of life of the renovated property; and the difference between the running costs of the modernized property and the rebuilt one.[44]

The relationship was expressed as a mathematical formula, the application of which was intended as a guide for decision making.

Although challenged on several important points,[45] this research contributed to a developing climate of opinion which favoured an increase in the relative significance of improvement. The research findings suggested that improvement became more economic as interest rates rose, and this coincided with an escalation in interest rates which continued into the 1970s. The work was taken to indicate that it would be economic to invest more money in lower-quality houses than had previously been thought appropriate.

However, there was no clearly established view of the balance between redevelopment and improvement at the national level. Indeed some academic research into the economics of urban renewal suggested a different perspective. The arguments of Lewis which linked renewal policy to *demographic projections and the resources of the building industry*, were that simple 'better value for money' criteria might be inappropriate if they accentuated fluctuations in building activity.[46] The starting point of Lewis' argument was that demand for new houses stems principally from the need to relieve shortages (the shortfall of dwellings when compared with existing households needing separate accommodation), to cater for the growth of new households, and to replace houses demolished. He forecast a decline in net household formation in the early 1970s, followed by another sustained boom. He concluded that to avoid peaks and troughs of demand in the building industry the early 1970s should be seen as 'the last golden opportunity for a well directed rehousing drive',[47] i.e. an emphasis on redevelopment, followed by a switch to improvement in the late 1970s when demographic demand for new building increased. As will be seen later, this long-term perspective was not adopted. Instead demographic projections were used to justify a switch of resources from housebuilding to improvement.

Housing policy 'blown off course'

During 1967 the threads of the debate were drawn together, but their policy implications were evaluated in a political climate dominated by an economic crisis. The Labour Government had come to power in 1964 in the belief that, with more effective management, the economy could be modernized and restructured, and that resultant economic growth would generate the resources required for implementation of its social programmes. The National Plan of 1965 committed the Government to a rapid expansion of housing production, primarily to sustain an accelerated slum clearance programme. However, there was a serious underestimation of the structural weakness of the economy, and the extent to which the economic tide was ebbing. This weakness was reflected in an inherited balance of payments deficit and the recurring financial crises of the years 1965–7. The growth premises of the National Plan were seriously undermined before its publication, and during 1965 and 1966 deflationary policies were incrementally introduced, involving modest spending cuts and increasing interest rates.[48]

At this stage Crossman successfully defended public sector housing from the cuts the Treasury wanted to impose for the sake of the foreign trade balance.[49] However, during 1967 the Government found itself on the horns of a dilemma. On the one hand, the National House Condition Survey had demonstrated the need for an increase in both clearance and improvement. On the other hand, the Fulham and Halliwell studies had made it clear that private capital would not be forthcoming for socially acceptable large-scale redevelopment, and growing Treasury pressure on social spending indicated the likelihood of a reduction in the planned level of public resources for housing.

Three ministerial conference speeches in 1967 indicated the emerging political resolution of these contradictions. In April, Mellish argued that the end of the housing shortage was in sight 'in all but a very few of our big urban centres', and that quality rather than quantity would become a major preoccupation in the 1970s and beyond.[50] In July, MacColl outlined the progress which had been made in a comprehensive review which aimed 'to find out clearly what should be the balance of priorities as between . . . redevelopment and rehabilitation'. He announced that the Government was framing new legislation for housing and environmental improvement, but made it clear that the emphasis would be on voluntary improvement.[51] In September, the debate on the future of the housebuilding programme took a dramatic turn when Greenwood, the new Minister of Housing, claimed that by the early 1970s houses should outnumber households by more than one million and that many local authorities could give more attention to urban renewal.[52]

This view of the changing national housing situation reflected the forecasts of a decline in household formation during the early 1970s. However, although Lewis' conclusion was that fluctuations in the building industry should be minimized, this was precluded by the exigencies of the immediate economic situation. Far from minimizing fluctuations housing policy was once more to be used as an economic regulator.

In November 1967 the balance of payments problem reached crisis proportions, the pound was devalued, the Government introduced a series of deflationary budgets. In 'the agonized review' of housing policy which followed, the argument focussed on the £700m it was costing to build 200,000 council houses p.a. and the £900m it would cost to expand the programme to the National Plan's target of 250,000 out of the total of 500,000 houses promised.[53] Greenwood attempted to hold the building programme at the 1967 level and divert whatever could be retained of this £200m difference to improvement. In January 1968 he announced both the completion of 400,000 houses in a year for the first time, and the abandonment of the National Plan target, explaining that 'housing had had to make its contribution to economic recovery along with other social services . . . the Government do not now expect 500,000 houses in 1970 to be completed'.[54] He claimed that this meant that the public sector programme would merely expand more slowly. Referring again to the decline in household formation he suggested that a new emphasis on improvement would reduce future needs for new building.[55]

At the beginning of the policy review in 1965, after a visit to Rochdale, Crossman had written:

> I was shocked and surprised when I actually walked round Deeplish. This so-called improvement area and its houses have been given thirty more years of life; yet they are little dwellings, each with a tiny courtyard behind. . . . It's a primitive and dismal life in Deeplish.[56]

At the official opening of the Deeplish pilot scheme (which had cost only £10,555), the week after the announcement of expenditure cuts, Greenwood said:

> If the future of older housing is to be assured, most towns in Britain will have to do a Deeplish in the next few years.[57]

The Housing Act, 1969

The shift of emphasis to improvement was presented as a tandem policy, in that both clearance and improvement were to be accelerated. It was generally welcomed, but some significant doubts were expressed. In the event, the role of improvement changed dramatically as it became the dominant component of renewal. However, an unprecedented increase in housing improvement was accompanied by the emergence of problems which raised further policy issues. The Housing Act, 1969 was the watershed in the transition from comprehensive redevelopment to gradual renewal.

Voluntary improvement and the area approach

The change in government policy was outlined in the 1968 White Paper *Old*

Houses into New Homes,[58] given legislation backing by the 1969 Act and further explained in a series of ministerial speeches and circulars. The White Paper stated that:

> . . . as a result of the very large increase in housebuilding in the last few years it is possible to plan for a shift in emphasis of the housing effort. The need for large new housebuilding programmes will remain for many years ahead. But the balance of need between new housebuilding and improvement is now changing, so there must be a corresponding change in the emphasis of local authority housing programmes. The Government intend that *within a total of public investment in housing at about the level it has now reached, a greater share should go to the improvement of older houses.*[59] (authors' emphasis)

It claimed that 'the policy behind the legislative changes now put forward is simply that much more should now be done year by year to improve and repair houses that can be improved, and to get rid of the unfit ones'.[60] Greenwood stated that he wanted 'to step up the rate of slum clearance by at least 50 per cent over the next few years. . .' and 'to see the number of grants doubled in the early 1970s'.[61] A subsequent circular stressed that 'it is necessary always to keep in mind that area improvement is not an alternative to clearance'.[62]

An increase in grant take-up was to be achieved by changes in the emphasis of improvement policy. Since the 'voluntary principle' was to guide action, public participation would be crucial for success. Considerable importance was attached to the promotion of long-term comprehensive improvement of houses to a uniformly high standard on an area basis, and related environmental upgrading.

This change of emphasis was reflected in modifications to provide more 'carrots' and fewer 'sticks' (see Figure 4). The grant system was extended and made more flexible. A third tier was added by the introduction of the special grant for the provision of amenities in multi-occupied houses. The maximum amounts for both standard and discretionary grant-aided expenditure were increased, but subsidy remained at 50 per cent. Grant conditions related to the life expectancy and resale of dwellings after improvement was relaxed, and provision was made for the conversion, after improvement, of controlled tenancies to regulated tenancies, with phased rent increases. General compulsory improvement powers were replaced, and the limited ones remaining were to be used only as a 'last resort'. The replacement of the Improvement Area by the General Improvement Area (GIA) was designed to stimulate area-based improvement. For the first time Exchequer subsidies were made available for environmental works. The rationale for the GIA was basically that which had been established in the early 1960s, i.e. environmental improvement was both intrinsically desirable and would induce owners to invest in their homes.

Initial reactions

There was a generally favourable initial reaction to the change of policy, particularly to economic and social justifications for an increased emphasis on improvement.[63] This was predictable, given the tenor of the preceding debate. However, significant reservations were expressed about the new emphasis on renewal, and the likely effectiveness of changed improvement powers.

Considerable controversy surrounded the Government's assessment of overall housing needs and its implications for housebuilding. During the passage of the Housing Bill in 1969, Robinson, Minister for Land and Planning, reinforced the 'end of the housing shortage' argument by announcing that there would be a crude national surplus of a million houses by 1973. Apart from scepticism about the accuracy of the forecast, critics argued that the prospect of an overall surplus merely signified that the nature of the problem was changing. In many parts of the country shortages had been overcome and renewal of the existing stock was the major issue, but there was no room for complacency in some conurbations where continuing shortages were combined with a substantial backlog of slums and substandard housing.[64]

Council housebuilding declined steadily during 1968 and 1969. The Government and some commentators attributed this to newly elected Conservative councils cutting back programmes for ideological reasons.[65] While this was a factor, the decline was mainly the result of government policy. In the post-devaluation review of public expenditure, Greenwood had failed in his attempt to switch resources earmarked for an expansion of the housebuilding programme to improvement. Instead, additional resources for improvement had to come from a redirection of resources pegged at the 1967 level. This was stated in the 1968 White Paper, but it was not at all clear at the time that an emphasis on improvement would mean a reduction in council housebuilding, not merely a slowdown in its rate of increase.[66] This confusion and the *post facto* 'end of the housing shortage' rationalization of expenditure cuts, together with Conservative support for a policy of improving housing conditions with a minimum interference in property rights, were all factors which explain the favourable reaction to the 1969 Act.

Another important factor was the Government's commitment to boosting both clearance and improvement. However, uncertainty about council housebuilding raised doubts about the viability of this strategy. A considerable body of opinion still regarded improvement as 'second best' and viewed the Government's enthusiasm for it as too ready acceptance of short-term economic arguments.[67] There was a suspicion that reductions in council housebuilding and an increase in improvement could readily be combined in decisions to abandon redevelopment proposals. This suggestion was contested by government spokesmen who stressed that top priority would be given to council housebuilding to replace slums. But the Government could not ensure that local authorities stepped up their clearance programmes.

Indeed, there was some evidence to suggest that the Ministry was less ready to confirm CPOs, which contributed to a developing view that improvement was 'in' while clearance was on its way out.[68] By the time the Labour Government lost office in 1970, the ambiguity of its urban renewal policy was becoming apparent. A shift in emphasis from housebuilding to improvement had also become a shift from clearance to improvement.

In addition to doubts about the overall policy, there were criticisms of the likely effectiveness of improvement powers. Incentives to owners would clearly be crucial to the success of a voluntary approach, yet the possibility of raising the level of subsidy above 50 per cent was not discussed, and some argued that the raising of the maximum limits for grant-aided expenditure would be inadequate.[69] Paradoxically, possible adverse consequences of the main incentive to owners – the abolition of occupancy conditions – were not widely discussed. The provisions relating to the private rented sector provoked some debate. The Conservative opposition and landlords' associations argued that phased rent increases allowable after decontrol were insufficient to induce landlords to invest. In contrast, the Labour left were opposed to the scale of rent increases, the fact that landlords who had failed to improve would now have first place in the queue for decontrol if they improved their properties, and the emasculation of compulsory powers.[70]

The argument was raised that a voluntary policy would mean that those in greatest need, particularly low-income owner-occupiers and private tenants, would not benefit. Blair, for example, commented that in the pressurized housing market of inner London:

> . . . rehabilitation is not the panacea it is claimed to be. All past attempts at rehabilitation lead to the same result: 'gentrification' (the displacement of existing residents by high income groups), high rents, overspill and nomadism for as much as 20 to 30 per cent of the residents. . . . For the lower paid, the immigrant, the aged and families under stress, rehabilitation is one big 'notice to quit'.[71]

This concern was shared by many community activists working in housing stress areas. However, the Housing Centre Trust expressed prevailing attitudes to the inability of many families to meet the costs of improvement: 'we must not forget this problem, but there is plenty we can get on with straightaway'.[72]

While the introduction of the GIA was generally welcomed, some critics argued that the absence of effective compulsory powers would preclude comprehensive improvement and that the environmental subsidy was too low to achieve improvements which would stimulate private investment. Others argued that even modest environmental improvement would be more difficult to implement than was commonly supposed.[73] In contrast, several academics criticized the concept of comprehensive improvement, arguing that a piecemeal approach was more appropriate to the diverse physical and social conditions in twilight areas.[74]

Progress and problems

The 1969 Act had an immediate impact. The total of 156,000 grants approved in 1970 was the highest since the introduction of subsidized improvement. However, there was a marked regional imbalance, in that the rate of increase in the Development and Intermediate Areas was only just over half that for England and Wales overall. The Housing Act, 1971 raised the level of subsidy in these areas exclusively from 50 to 75 per cent, for work carried out by June 1974.[75] This supplementary measure had a dramatic effect. Grant approvals soared in the Assisted Areas, remained relatively constant elsewhere, and in 1973 reached a massive total of 361,000. This demonstrated the crucial importance of the level of subsidy. The overall standard of improvement increased as discretionary grants rose from 43 per cent of the total in 1969 to 86 per cent in 1973. During the same period annual grant-aided investment grew from £66m to £751m, an increase in real terms of 460 per cent.[76] In 1971 the second National House Condition survey revealed a fall of 1.1m in the number of houses lacking basic amenities – of which 0.65m was accounted for by improvement rather than clearance – a trend which continued during the early 1970s.

All this had very little to do with the major innovation in 1969, the GIA. By the end of 1973 there were approximately a quarter of a million houses in declared GIAs in which some 27,000 grant-aided improvements had been completed. In the peak year of 1973 only 32,600 grants were approved in GIAs, less than 10 per cent of the total. Comprehensive area-based improvement to high standards had simply not happened. Nonetheless, the target in 1969 had been to double the annual total of grants and by 1973 it had trebled – an unprecedented event in the 'numbers game' of housing politics.

Table 2 *Grant approvals 1949 to 1979 (England and Wales)*

	'000		
Years	*Discretionary/improvement (including conversions)*	*Standard/intermediate (including repair and specials)*	*Total*
1949–58	160	—	160
1959–64	271	418	689
1965–9	222	345	567
1970–4	1009	257	1266
1975–9*	592	50	642
Total	2254	1070	3324

*From 1978 figures are not available for grants approved, the totals include from then works completed for local authorities and grants paid for private owners. Figures for Welsh local authorities' improvements are not available from 1976 onwards and are not included.

Source: *Housing Statistics* and *Housing and Construction Statistics*, HMSO

The shift of emphasis to improvement was by no means an unqualified success. In the late 1960s the political spotlight had been on the pre-1919 stock yet the proportion of such dwellings lacking amenities which had them installed was lower than that for inter-war houses.[77] This was in large measure due to the 1971 Act stimulating local authorities to improve their inter-war estates and, in part, to private sector improvement of inter-war houses and flats. Although investment in inter-war council housing was badly needed, it meant that the overall increase in improvement activity had less impact at the lower end of the quality scale than aggregate statistics of progress suggested. Similarly, owner-occupiers accounted for 70 per cent of grant approvals in 1973 despite the fact that privately rented property was in most need of improvement. Thus the improvement drive was not getting to the worst houses capable of improvement. However, with this important qualification, progress in the early 1970s realized the prime objective of the 1969 policy change – an acceleration in the rate of improvement of the nation's existing stock of houses.

The social objectives and consequences of improvement – who benefits and who loses – were very much a secondary concern, but it gradually became clear that the better-housed and better-off sections of the community were deriving most benefit. This was particularly the case in the private sector where it was more than simply the dominance of owner-occupier improvement. Over half the owner-occupiers of improved houses were in professional or managerial occupations and a mere 13 per cent were semi-skilled or unskilled workers. Even in the private rented sector less than half the tenants of improved dwellings were semi-skilled or unskilled, and a quarter were in the professional and managerial groups.[78] Within these broad trends the incidence of costs and benefits varied with local housing market conditions: in attractive rural areas grants were used to renovate cottages as second homes for affluent city dwellers, pricing local residents out of the market; in many poorer neighbourhoods of northern industrial towns there was little impact; as some housing stress areas of inner London became fashionable working-class residents were squeezed out; other stress areas in London and the provincial conurbations were little affected. In social terms the effects of the improvement boom were largely regressive: most of those in greatest need were either deriving no benefit at all, or even paying the price of improvement enjoyed by others.

While the rate of improvement had exceeded all expectations the clearance rate, far from increasing, had initially remained constant and then declined. Many local authorities, with DoE encouragement, had adopted an improvement policy for areas which a few years previously would have been considered suitable only for clearance. Improvement came to be viewed as an alternative to clearance, and the tandem strategy of 1969 could be more appropriately characterized as a penny farthing strategy by 1973.

However, before moving to an analysis of a further shift in national policy, discussion turns to a closer examination of certain key aspects of improvement. This is necessary not only to understand the spectacular growth and associated problems of improvement in the early 1970s, but also because improvement has since become the main plank of housing renewal policy.

Powers, procedures and professionals

As with slum clearance and redevelopment, the statutory framework of legal powers and procedures, together with related central government advice, is the link between national policy and action on the ground. In contrast to redevelopment, implementation of national policy is dependent on the combined initiatives of three main agents: local government, the private owners of older housing, and (more recently) housing associations. A major characteristic of subsidized improvement is its discretionary nature.

The statutory framework evolved over many years, but it was not until 1969 that a comprehensive code was established. Parts of this code have been modified, but the basic principles remain unaltered. To understand the progress of improvement to 1973, the problems which emerged and the policy debate which developed, it is necessary to outline the basic elements of this framework and the procedures adopted by local authorities. These are discussed under the following headings:

1 local strategies;
2 the private improvement grant system;
3 public sector housing improvement;
4 General Improvement Areas; and
5 professionals.

Local strategies

As one commentator has observed, 'although central government may provide the tools, and establish certain requirements, it is up to the local authority, ultimately, to put the pieces together'.[79] A tandem approach of clearing slums and improving the best older houses was established in 1954, but before 1969 few local authorities had an improvement programme. Rather, the major strategic decision was a negative one. Clearance programmes identified areas where the anticipated life of property was less than fifteen years in which applications for grants would be refused – another aspect of the 'planning blight' referred to in Chapter 2.[80] Although there was more variation in the policies for the award of grants outside these excluded areas (with some councils approving only standard grants) local authorities commonly adopted a passive approach.

The key to this variation was attitudes to the principle of grant subsidy, the powers available, and the priority given to improvement. For a long time many authorities were opposed to subsidizing owners, particularly landlords, and saw it as putting public money into private pockets, although this attitude gradually changed from the late 1950s with the emergence of low-income owner-occupation.[81] The majority of authorities, particularly those with a lukewarm approach to improvement generally, felt that the powers and procedures for area improvement were cumbersome, time-consuming and costly and were reluctant to use compulsory powers. A survey in 1968 showed that only 10 per cent of urban authorities had prepared major reports on Improvement Area policy, although this activity was increasing.[82] However, the major factor was the low priority given to improvement compared with slum clearance.

In 1969 the Government specified three key requirements for the formulation of local renewal strategies:[83]

1 *A comprehensive review of older housing.* Local authorities were placed under a statutory duty to periodically survey unsatisfactory conditions in their older housing areas. However, no guidelines were established, and there was no requirement to submit information to the Ministry.
2 *A consideration of the balance between redevelopment and improvement.* No statutory conditions were imposed but authorities were helpfully advised to 'clear the areas that should obviously be cleared and improve areas which would obviously repay attention of that kind'.[84] Areas where the physical condition of the housing made the choice difficult should be tackled at a later stage when more experience had been gained of improvement work. A method for selecting areas on economic grounds (using a version of Needleman's formula) was incorporated in the advice.
3 *The development of area-based improvement.* No statutory limitations were placed on the condition, character, or size of a GIA, other than it must be predominantly residential and must not include a clearance area, although it could include individual unfit houses. The importance of gaining experience, and the need for the first scheme to succeed and show results quickly were stressed. Selection criteria suggested for early GIAs included: a secure planning future; the physical potential of the houses; and residents' and owners' attitudes. However, the first and second eliminated very few areas, and the third is very difficult to ascertain at the selection stage. Finally, areas of 300–500 dwellings were suggested as a norm.

This discretion encouraged different responses. During the early 1970s many authorities continued their existing clearance programmes, some re-examined areas formerly earmarked for medium- or long-term clearance and began evolving new policies based on improvement, and a minority virtually abandoned redevelopment in favour of improvement.[85] Additionally, many previously 'passive' authorities developed a more 'active' attitude to improvement. The start of GIA work was instrumental in this as many authorities, conscious of the political problems of concentrating effort in small areas, began widespread promotion of grants. By 1971 most had at least one GIA 'in the pipeline'. Some formulated a rolling programme of declarations but the majority opted for a more cautious approach by declaring only one or two. Thus, in contrast with the Improvement Area of the 1964 Act, the GIA was widely accepted as a means of promoting improvement programmes.

Diverse interpretations of the role of GIAs were reflected in three categories of objectives:[86]

1 *housing stock objectives* concerned with lengthening life of properties;
2 *planning objectives* e.g. traffic management and conservation;
3 *social objectives* e.g. preserving communities and a pool of relatively cheap housing.

Some authorities explicitly considered these, others either did not have clear objectives, or tended to identify several without specifying priorities. Roberts' 'on the spot' investigation confirmed the dominance of physical objectives (housing stock and planning) and revealed the 'lip service' paid to social objectives.[87]

Three types of selection criteria can be identified:[88]

1 *Ownership.* Local authorities were faced with the dilemma of improving their own housing or subsidizing private owners – many compromised and selected a GIA of each type.
2 *Quality of housing.* Some authorities, following government advice, first chose 'safe' or 'easy' areas in relatively attractive neighbourhoods with high levels of owner-occupation. However, others chose potential clearance areas, on the grounds that these would soon be beyond reclaim.
3 *Other criteria* e.g. pressure from residents or councillors.

During the early 1970s it became clear that the relationship between redevelopment and improvement was changing, and that GIAs were being declared in a variety of areas with varying degrees of success.

The private improvement grant system

The analysis of the evolution of national policy has illustrated how the terms of subsidized improvement have varied over time (Figure 4). Variations in types of grants, conditions and allowable costs have reflected the objectives of the policy adopted, and influenced the nature and scale of its impact. By 1969 the grant system in operation for private owners had developed six key features:

1 eligible works;
2 grant contributions;
3 types of grant;
4 grant conditions;
5 compulsory improvement;
6 local administration;

A key question is the extent of *eligible works* for grant aid. The dividing line between grant-aided work and informal processes of sporadic investment in repair, maintenance and modernization has changed over time. Before 1969 grants covered only improvement – not ordinary repair and maintenance. Thus work which provided facilities for the first time was grant-aided, e.g. the installation of a bath. Work which represented 'holding one's own' was not, e.g. replacing a bath. Moreover the house had to be brought up to a reasonable standard of repair before grant-aided improvements could be undertaken. This was justified in terms of preventing the decay of houses improved with grant aid, but was nonetheless a considerable disincentive to owners. As Cullingworth pointed out 'the line is obviously a difficult one to draw, but it must be drawn if every house owner is not to have a statutory right to public assistance for normal repair and maintenance'.[89] The Denington Committee took the view that improvement and repair should be regarded as part of the same effort to preserve the national asset represented by the existing stock of houses. It recommended additional powers for the enforcement of repair, but concluded that the principle of grant aid for such work could not be conceded as this would 'put a premium on neglect'.[90] The 1969 Act moved the dividing line. Compulsory repair powers were extended and for the first time certain repairs could be grant-aided, but only as part and parcel of improvement work. Up to half the total amount of a discretionary grant could relate to repairs if the local council considered that such work would make the improvement work fully effective.[91]

Grant contributions are such that owners receive a cash grant covering a proportion of the cost of approved works, subject to specified limits. The principle of a 50 per cent, 'pound for pound' subsidy was established in 1926, although the 1971 Act increased it to 75 per cent in Assisted Areas for a temporary three-year period. Exchequer contributions are paid to the local authority at 75 per cent of annual loan charges for a twenty-year period to cover the major proportion of the grant payment. Loans can be made by a local authority to cover the owner's share of the cost of works, and the 1969 Act introduced maturity loans which are repayable on the death of the owner or when the property is sold. Loans are provided in effect as a mortgage with similar eligibility checks on applicants' repayment potential.

By 1969 there were three *types of grant* in operation. Their provisions are outlined in Figure 4.

1 Discretionary grants were originally introduced in 1949 for long-term improvements. The required life after improvement was normally thirty years, but the 1969 Act allowed local authorities to reduce this to ten. Their objective was to bring houses up to a defined standard, which was why an owner could not 'half improve'. Twelve points had to be met until 1969 when authorities were given discretion to relax some requirements.
2 Standard grants were introduced in 1959 and were available as of right until 1969 when their use in GIAs became discretionary. The grant was available as a specified sum towards the cost of installing five basic

amenities. Before 1969 the use of this grant was restricted to dwellings with a fifteen-year life and all the requirements of a five-point standard had to be met. The 1969 Act gave authorities additional powers to award grants for social reasons for shorter-life property, and on a partial basis where the owner could afford to put in only one amenity at a time.[92]

3 Special grants were introduced by the 1969 Act, and were made at the discretion of the local authorities towards the cost of installing standard amenities in multi-occupied houses.

In addition to *grant conditions* attached to particular types of grant, there are those which generally apply. Owners must be freeholders or leaseholders with at least five years of the lease unexpired. Occupancy conditions have been a variable feature of the grant system. They specify that a landlord has to keep his property available for letting and an owner-occupier (or member of his family) remain in occupance for a specified period of time after grant aid. This condition was progressively reduced from twenty years in 1949 until it was abolished in 1969 (to be re-introduced in 1974). Conditions are also imposed on the maximum amount of a landlord's rate of return. Until 1969 this was in the form of rent increases as a specified percentage of the landlord's share of the cost of works. In 1969, the grant system was linked to the decontrol of privately rented property. Improved properties could be converted from controlled rents to regulated rents with increases for existing tenants phased over five years.

Compulsory improvement is another variable element. Should improvement be undertaken by volunteers or should conscript owners also be involved? The voluntary principle was the basis of policy until the 1964 Act gave local authorities the power to compel landlords in Improvement Areas (and elsewhere at the request of the tenant). The Denington Committee argued that the scale of voluntary improvement was inadequate and that compulsory powers should be strengthened and extended to encompass owner-occupiers. Cullingworth dissented and argued that while compulsory repair was justifiable in preventing the decay of the nation's housing stock, this justification could not support compulsory improvement to increase standards. He felt that persuasion should stop short of coercion except where tenants of unwilling landlords requested improvements, and argued that more could be done to increase the scale of voluntary improvement.[93] This view prevailed and the 1969 Act empowered local authorities to compel repairs, and standard amenity improvements where tenants wanted them, but repealed more general compulsory powers.

Each council is responsible for the *local administration* of grants. There are usually six basic steps in the process:

1 the owner decides to improve and contacts the local authority;
2 an officer inspects the property, draws up a schedule of works and determines what is eligible for grant aid, including the repairs element;
3 the owner gets plans, estimates of the cost, building regulations approval

and, if appropriate, planning permission. He then submits a grant application, and possibly an application for a loan;

4 the local authority approves the application and determines the allowable expense;
5 the owner arranges for a contractor to do the work; and
6 on completion of the work the local authority pays the grant (and loan) to the owner who then pays the contractor.

The complexity of grant procedures had been a cause of concern since 1949. While cumulative relaxation of conditions had somewhat simplified procedures, an increased emphasis on improvement prompted attempts to further speed up the process. These included delegation of grant approvals to officers and the appointment of additional staff. While the 1969 Act gave local authorities agency powers (i.e. taking responsibility for the last four steps), a more common means of assisting owners was the compilation of a list of approved builders. During the period 1969–73 most local authorities complemented national publicity with local campaigns including advertising, posters and leaflets, show-houses and mobile exhibitions.

Public sector housing improvement

Local authorities have powers to improve houses in their ownership, and this work is subsidized by Exchequer contributions. In 1969 the subsidies were increased. The 'standard contribution' was paid for basic amenity improvements, and the 'improvement contribution' was paid in all other cases and included (for the first time) a subsidy for acquisition costs. The same cost limits as for private owners applied but with a small additional allowance for acquisition. The most important element of local authority improvement activity was the improvement of purpose-built council housing, especially after increases in the Exchequer contribution brought in by the Housing Act, 1971.

Although *housing associations* have a long history, their role in the acquisition, improvement, and conversion of older housing only became significant from the late 1960s onwards.[94] They were heavily dependent on local authorities for finance, either in terms of loans for acquisition and grants for improvement in the same way as private owners, or contributions in the same way as a local authority. Housing association involvement was entirely at the discretion of the local authority. Some authorities were enthusiastic, but many regarded associations with scepticism, being doubtful of their technical capacity or the motives of the people involved. Other authorities were downright hostile, seeing the very existence of associations as an implied criticism of their own work. The 1969 Act and government advice gave an impetus to housing associations' activity, but it was the 1974 Act which significantly increased their role.

General Improvement Areas

The first widespread attempt to implement area improvement took place between 1969 and 1973. It is useful to outline the relevant powers and procedures in relation to three aspects of GIA work.

1 *The establishment of a GIA.* There were minimal statutory procedures for the declaration of a GIA. After considering a report prepared by 'a suitably qualified person or persons' a local authority could resolve that an area should be declared. This resolution had to be advertised in the local press, and further publicized in the declared area. A copy of the report, resolution and a map of the area had to be sent to the Secretary of State, but until 1974 this was for information only. Residents must be informed of the grants available, and of any environmental improvements proposed. Beyond this it was the responsibility of the local authority to determine procedures. The Government advised that the report could be prepared by local authority officers, or by a civic society or residents' organization with the necessary expertise. Authorities were exhorted to make every effort to gain public confidence and co-operation. Not surprisingly a wide range of procedures was adopted, but the typical stages are summarized in Figure 6.

2 *Environmental improvement.* Similarly the content of an area improvement scheme is not closely prescribed. Local authorities were empowered by the 1969 Act to carry out amenity improvements and to acquire land for this purpose, either by negotiation or through compulsory purchase. The Government suggested appropriate types of improvement, e.g. tree planting, providing play spaces, grass or paved areas. This type of work would be eligible for the new government subsidy and was seen as complementary to normal neighbourhood maintenance (such as the resurfacing of streets) which would not be eligible. A maximum amount was fixed for grant-aided environmental improvements. This was 50 per cent of the sum arrived at by multiplying the number of houses in a GIA by £100 (raised to £200 in 1972[95]). Thus the subsidy for a GIA of 300 houses would be 50 per cent of £30,000 (£60,000 after 1972). This subsidy ceiling indicated what the Government thought would be reasonable to spend.

3 *Housing improvement.* Under the 1969 Act the grant system was the same within GIAs as elsewhere with two main exceptions. First, there was greater intensity of publicity and promotion. Second, the Government emphasized comprehensive improvement to high standards. Thus local authorities were not obliged to give standard grants in GIAs and government pressed the use of discretionary grants. While most authorities tried to secure improvement to the full twelve-point standard, others were not so single-minded.

Stage	Local authority involvement		Outside involvement		Possible causes of delay
	1 Committee	2 Directorate and division	3 Other authorities	4 Residents	
Declaration	Committee meetings held monthly or six weekly Housing Environmental health Technical services Policy and resources	GIA working party meetings held fortnightly or as required Housing Environmental health Architecture and planning Engineering Leisure and amenities Chief executive Treasurer	DoE for informal consultation and approval to proceed to full declaration	House-to-house surveys and investigation of public attitudes Formation of Residents Association from street or other community groups	(a) More than one committee involved (b) Submissions to Committee not ready (c) Lack of co-ordination within the Steering Group
Consultation and planning Promotional work Design proposals	As above	As above	DoE for loan sanction and grant approval County and Area Authorities for: Planning Highways Social Services Fire services Education Water and sewage Police Statutory undertakers for: GPO, gas and electricity Specials: e.g. Ministry of Agriculture Port Authorities	Street groups and Residents Association for agreement on joint proposals Meetings Newletters Exhibitions Show house and area office Commercial and industrial firms for support for proposals	As (a), (b) and (c) above. Also: (d) Inadequate information to DoE (e) Unresolved issues involving Highways Authority (f) Lack of co-ordination with Service Authorities (g) Residents fail to agree on basic objectives (h) Acquisition and improvement of show house (j) Negotiations with non-conforming users
Detailed design and implementation	Committee meetings held monthly or six weekly Housing Environmental health Technical services Policy and resources	Working level in individual departments: Planner Architect Engineer Landscape architect Environmental health	DoE for grant aid County and other authorities as above	Residents for continuing consultation and active help Public inquiries on e.g. road closures and CPOs House grant processing	(k) Lack of departmental co-ordination at working level (l) Orders for road closures (m) Highway Authority's standards for road design (n) Public inquiries into pedestrianization or CPOs (o) Modifications to design necessitated by costs or residents requests
Work on site	As above	Working level supervision of direct labour force and/or private contractors	DoE for grant aid County for highway works Statutory undertakers for underground services	Reactions with work force Vandalism	(p) Contractors or direct labour organization not available when required (q) Lack of co-ordination on site between contractors and service authorities (r) Residents complaints about work on site (s) Replacement of materials, planting, etc. due to vandalism

Figure 6 *Stages in GIA implementation*

Source: DoE, *Environment Improvements: A Report on a Study of the Problems and Progress in a Sample of General Improvements Areas*, Improvement Note 1-76, p. 8. (1976)

Professionals

As with redevelopment, the operation of powers and procedures is the responsibility of several professional groups.

Environmental Health Officers have traditionally been responsible for the exercise of powers to maintain and improve private housing. Prior to the 1969 Act the Health Committee was usually responsible for the grant system and action in respect of multiple-occupation. In many authorities this arrangement had continued. Of all local government officers EHOs had the most detailed knowledge of conditions in private older housing areas, and during the early 1970s they were often responsible for GIAs. Their experience 'on the ground' of the private rented sector was the basis of their long-standing commitment to an area approach backed by compulsory powers and of scepticism about the return to the voluntary principle in 1969.

Housing officers' traditional responsibility is for council-owned houses. As such they were the prime movers in the development of improvement programmes for inter-war council estates and are responsible for older houses purchased and improved by the council. Their involvement in the private sector is more recent than that of EHOs, and stems in part from central government exhortations since the mid-1960s for local authorities to take a wider view of their housing responsibilities, embracing both public and private sectors. During the early 1970s Housing Departments became increasingly influential in overall renewal strategies and in some authorities assumed responsibility for the administration of the grant system.

Planners were not significantly involved in improvement until the development of an area approach. In the formulation of renewal strategies, planners were prominent in the development of techniques for establishing zonal variations in housing conditions, part of the process of defining areas for clearance, short-term improvement, and long-term improvement.[96] In implementation they are centrally concerned with local plans which may provide the context for GIA work and, together with architects, the preparation of environmental schemes. Other groups with particularly important roles are treasurers responsible for grants, loans and mortgages; engineers responsible for road works and traffic management; and community workers assisting residents groups.

With this diversity of inputs, the shift of emphasis to improvement posed significant organizational problems.[97] GIAs in private housing areas made the most exacting demands for three main reasons:[98]

1 the number of departments and agencies involved;
2 in contrast to clearance and redevelopment where the involvement of the participants is broadly sequential, GIAs require simultaneous involvement of the majority of participants; and
3 the need to generate widespread public support and involvement.

This hitherto unique combination of demands was recognized by central government, and circulars advised local authorities to make special arrangements to secure effective co-ordination, i.e. centralizing the direction of work under a committee or subcommittee serviced by officers, including a principal officer with specific responsibilty for the improvement programme. However, very few responded in this way, as it would have encroached on the responsibilities of existing committees and departments. Interdepartmental politics resulted in a diversity of attempts to secure co-ordination without, or with very little, centralization of responsibility or executive powers. In most authorities each element of housing and environmental improvement had to be approved by the appropriate committee – a major factor in the delays in implementing environmental works (see Figure 6). The allocations of overall responsibility for GIAs to one committee only eased the process of referrals, for executive powers remained with established functional committees. At officer level the usual co-ordinating mechanism was an interdepartmental working party, reliant for success on the quality of personal working relationships between key officers:

> The nature of GIA work is such that co-ordination consists of trouble shooting rather than simply controlling a smooth running machine. This function is very much one performed by individuals rather than by committee or working parties. The task demands competence, commitment and authority. Although informal co-ordination structures can help, informal contact and commitment among staff in key departments are crucial. An atmosphere conducive to co-ordination is the key, rather than any particular bureaucratic structure.[99]

To the extent that the GIAs of the early 1970s failed it was partly the result of inadequate management.

Changes in the built environment

The physical impact of improvement is obviously less dramatic than redevelopment but is similarly influenced by previous building cycles and their characteristic forms of construction. Although the 'before' and 'after' relationship illustrated in Figure 7 was in the minds of many politicians and professionals in 1969, there was a considerable gulf between image and reality. During the early 1970s very few schemes made such an impact, and even now it is the exception rather than the rule.

Before improvement

As a result of widespread availability of grants under lax conditions and varied objectives and selection criteria adopted in choosing GIAs, the improvement drive of the early 1970s had an impact on diverse types of built environment which can be divided into five main categories:[100]

Before

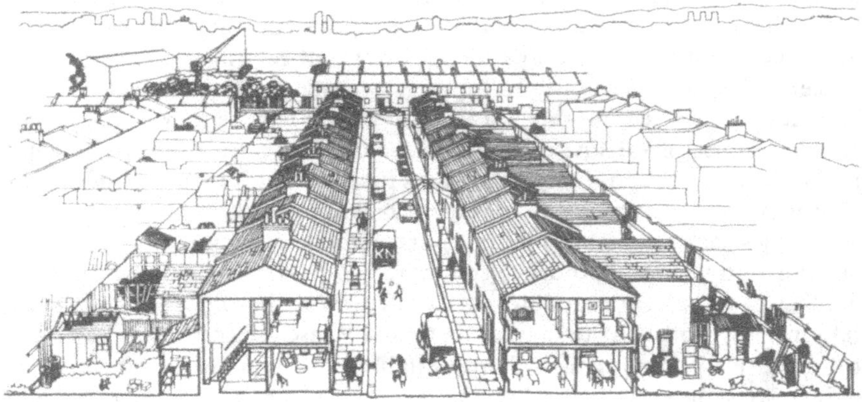

After

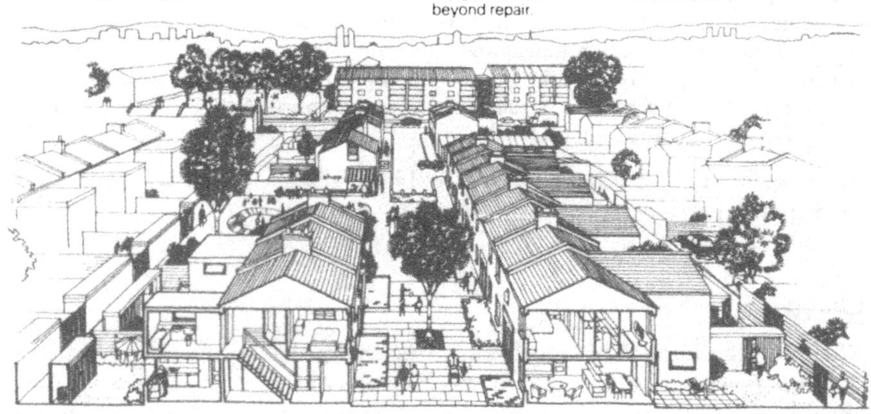

Figure 7 *GIA improvement – before and after images*

Source: National Building Agency, *Improvement Areas* (1971)

1 *Bye-law areas of small terraced houses*, mainly in single family occupation, built between the 1870s and 1914 to house skilled artisan tenants moving out into what were then new suburbs. A combination of the rent-paying capacity of these workers and building bye-laws resulted in sturdily built houses, but by the late 1960s many of them (particularly those still owned by private landlords) were suffering from a backlog of repairs and still lacked basic amenities. The houses had narrow frontages, two storeys, often with a rear extension, provided 750–800 square feet of floor space and were built at high densities in a monotonous rectilinear street pattern. Within these basic characteristics there were significant variations in house types and layout, particularly in garden provision. These areas, typified by the Deeplish and Newtown demonstration projects, had a generally run-down appearance, the schools were obsolete, streets badly lit and maintained, and community facilities, play areas and parking facilities were virtually non-existent.

2 *Areas of large pre-1919 houses* built in either imposing terraces or in semi-detached form for middle-class owner-occupiers and their servants, but by the late 1960s largely privately rented and multi-occupied. This change in housing function had accelerated physical decay by increasing the intensity of usage – amenities were now shared by several families – and had been accompanied by a virtual cessation of repairs. They were built at low densities, often with spacious rear gardens, and set in tree-lined streets, but were now characterized by poor environmental maintenance and inadequate social infrastructure. This was the predominant physical environment of the housing stress areas.

3 *Villages or engulfed villages* were smaller groupings of old houses, often in informal layouts, and included the historic cores of small towns and villages where the conservation motive for improvement was dominant, and old industrial (particularly mining) villages.

4 *Inter-war council housing estates*. The 1969 Act was passed just half a century after the beginning of large-scale council housing and many of the 1.1m council houses of the inter-war period were badly in need of investment, a point not widely recognized at the time.[101] This was particularly the case with those built in the 1930s to rehouse families displaced by clearance, when standards of layout, room sizes and fittings were cut to the bone: by 1935 the size of a three-bedroomed non-parlour house was only 723 sq. ft. Many houses and flats had only an outside w.c., no bathroom or wash hand basin; in many cases the bath was installed in the kitchen, which itself was small and primitively equipped. Electricity supply was minimal – often only one point was provided, and fire-places and hot water systems were obsolete. Estates often lacked any provision for car parking and planning of play spaces and other community facilities had not got beyond the reservation of sites, now disused and derelict.

5 *Mixed areas*. The most common combination was that of bye-law terraces

and large Victorian villas where the local authority owned some of the houses.

After improvement

The physical impact of improvement can be discussed by reference to the type of work involved in individual house improvement and the area approach.[102] In housing improvement, kitchens, bathrooms and bedrooms are provided or enlarged, either by *extensions* (in about one third of improvements) or more commonly by *adaptations* such as converting a bedroom into a bathroom.[103] The provision of baths, sinks, inside w.c.s and a hot and cold water supply accounts for half the work done to reach the twelve-point standard; the rest is to ensure freedom from damp, adequate natural lighting, renewing drainage fittings, and rewiring. *Conversions* usually involve more structural work – in extreme cases all that remains of the original house is the shell. In the peak year of 1973 the net 'housing gain' from conversion was about 50,000 units. Major items of grant-aided *repair* are roof coverings, chimney stacks, gutters and downpipes, plastering and renewing floors – in many cases 'repair' necessitates replacement.

Although the volume of discretionary grant approvals and extent of associated work meant that improvement in the early 1970s had a more significant impact on the built environment than at any other time previously, several important qualifications must be made. First, there is some doubt about the quality of the work, and in many cases houses brought up to the twelve-point standard will need remedial work long before thirty years has elapsed. Although professionals (architects, surveyors, etc.) became increasingly involved, private house improvement work remained predominantly in the hands of the small jobbing builder, who acted as adviser to the applicant and undertook the work. Many such firms did work to a high standard, but the improvement boom overstretched the local building industry. This led to an influx of 'cowboys' who also took advantage of the inability of the local authority to ensure effective quality control, and made substantial profits on substandard work.[104] Second, although the distribution of improvement grants between the five broad types of built environment mentioned is not known in detail, the majority of local authority improvements were to inter-war stock, and 20 per cent of private grant approvals were for post-1919 houses. Thus in 1973 approximately 40 per cent of total grant approvals were for post-1919 houses. The fact that in the private sector overall half the improvement items provided to meet the twelve-point standard were replacements, not first-time installations, was a further indication that much of the effort was directed towards better quality housing and that the impact was least where it was most needed. Moreover, as experience of conditions in older housing areas developed, it became clear that there was a growing backlog of repairs in houses which had either been improved earlier or the local authority and/or owner did not want to improve. Without improvement such repairs were not eligible for grant aid, and decay continued. Third, there was a general 'pepper-pot' pattern of improvement because of reliance on the voluntary principle and the very limited impact of GIAs.

Almost a third of GIA declarations in 1969–73 were in council-owned areas (mainly inter-war estates), and most of the rest were in predominantly privately-owned bye-law areas. It was only in the inter-war council estates that comprehensive housing improvement to high standard accompanied by modest environmental improvements were achieved. Council ownership of houses and land enabled systematic improvement on a block contract basis, achieving the scale economies and efficiency objectives of the area approach. In contrast, private sector GIAs made little more contribution to housing improvement than the Improvement Area programme of 1964–9. By 1973 18 per cent of total houses in private sector GIAs that needed improvement had in fact been improved, a rate which was no more than the national average. In 1973 'only a comparatively few GIAs could be significantly distinguished from surrounding areas as a result of environmental schemes'.[105] The reasons for long delays and the limited scale of environmental works, varied significantly from one area to another, but a few common elements will serve to illustrate the problems.[106]

First, the formulation of proposals properly involved lengthy consultation with residents. Second, it frequently became apparent that the improvements which residents would most like to see were beyond the budget for GIA works, e.g. the removal of a 'non-conforming use' such as scrapyard. Third, improvements such as more efficient and regular street cleaning and refuse disposal involved changing priorities of the relevant departments, and the limited interdepartmental organization for GIAs was inadequate to achieve this. Fourth, many preconceived ideas about appropriate environmental improvements were not implemented either because residents did not want them, or because suitable sites were not available.

In many GIAs the only space available was in the streets, or land which residents could be persuaded to sell. Even where there were vacant sites, land acquisition often took years to complete. Moreover, an apparently simple matter such as the siting of a playground could cause considerable controversy because of its impact on adjacent houses. More complex proposals involving the purchase and demolition of houses to create space were often impractical: very few GIAs had small groups of houses in substantially worse condition than the rest. Finally, it soon became apparent that early implementation of on-street works was impractical, as house improvements necessitated the renewal of drainage and water supply services.

Several important conclusions can be drawn from the experience of the early GIAs: limited improvements took a long time to implement (three to seven years) and accelerating this required improved local authority management; modest environmental schemes based on consultation with residents were generally welcomed, but significant improvements required a more substantial Exchequer subsidy; even in GIAs nearing completion there was little evidence that environmental improvement had more than a marginal impact on grant take-up. The propensity of owners to improve is affected by more fundamental factors than environmental cosmetics, and it is to these issues that the discussion now turns.

Improvement: an investment partnership

The increased scale of the improvement programme was accompanied by growing concern about its social consequences. During the early 1970s attention became focussed on the variable way in which different social groups and housing areas were affected. This was a very different perspective from which to view a policy designed primarily to improve the quality of the housing stock.

Redevelopment is predominantly a state responsibility, reliant on public finance, and resulting in the abolition of the private housing market in the areas affected. Improvement by private owners is very different, for it is an investment partnership reliant on a combination of public and private capital. Not only is partnership potentially cheaper for the state, but in general the availability of private capital is a precondition for the release of public funds. Implementation involves intervention in the highly complex market conditions of older housing areas. Diversity at a local level was particularly important as GIAs were envisaged as achieving comprehensive improvement on the basis of the participation of 'the community' engaged in collective self-preservation and enhancement. The volume of improvement investment, its social and geographical distribution, are all dependent on the ability and willingness of private owners to invest.

Ownership and finance

Criticism of improvement policy stemmed from growing concern that those in greatest housing need, particularly poor tenants and low-income owner-occupiers, were deriving least benefit and in extreme cases found their housing situation worsening. It became clear that this was largely the result of implementing policies in older areas without an adequate understanding of their housing market function:

> . . . It is necessary to know *who* we are talking about: the *young en route* for suburbia? The *elderly* trapped by institutional constraints such as the policies of building societies? The *coloured immigrant* seeking a place where he can live without being ostracized? The *settled* who have been overtaken by decay? The *poor* who have no alternative open to them? Or the *mobile* who have no long term interest in the area? And what will be the effect of 'improvement' on the area? Will it change its function: if so how are the displaced needs to be met?[107]

Improvement policies are significantly influenced by varying political attitudes to different forms of tenure and the range of related fiscal and housing policies. Within tenures there are considerable variations in the circumstances of ownership and rental, financial resources, and resultant attitudes to repair and improvement.

Private landlords

Virtually all the housing built before the First World War was originally owned by private landlords. This situation remained largely unchanged until the 1950s and 1960s when a significant proportion of the remaining pre-1919 stock was sold for owner-occupation. The private rented sector is subject to central government regulation which has a two-fold aim. First, it aims to arrest physical deterioration by ensuring proper maintenance, and wherever possible grant-aided improvement. Second, it aims to equitably reconcile the landlord's need for profit with the tenant's need for security and rents within available means – this is the basis of measures to provide security of tenure (i.e. protecting tenants from arbitrary eviction and harassment) and of rent control.

This intervention has been both a response to and one cause of the decline of the private rented sector. Decline has been dramatic in terms of the proportion of total accommodation provided by private landlords – from 90 per cent in 1914 to 19 per cent in 1971. The fall in the number of tenancies has been a less dramatic but more recent and rapid phenomenon. The combination of losses through demolition and sales to owner-occupiers, together with the virtual cessation of private building to rent, halved the number of tenancies between 1947 and 1971, but there were still 3.1m compared with 8.1m in 1914. The decline is not only quantitative but qualitative. In 1971 three quarters of all private tenancies were in houses built before 1914. Almost a quarter of them were unfit (over half the national total of unfit houses), 40 per cent lacked one or more basic amenities and 30 per cent were in substantial disrepair. Thus the picture is of a shrinking sector which contains an increasing proportion of the worst housing, but which is still the only option open to many households.[108]

'Landlords in Britain have been frequently vilified, but seldom studied':[109] policies have been based on inadequate knowledge and resultant stereotype images.[110] It was not until the mid-1960s that research began to shed light on the constraints affecting landlords, and the diversity of landlords.

The three main constraints are:

1 rent control;
2 tax system;
3 grant conditions.

Rent control is the factor most commonly blamed for deterioration of the housing stock in private rental. Since 1915 a variety of Acts have imposed, partially lifted, and re-imposed limitations on rents by reference to types of lettings and rateable values. Controls after both wars were initially severe but were relaxed in the 1930s and 1950s. A concentration on rent control ignores other factors, such as the competition of other forms of investment and encouragement of other tenures. Nevertheless, rent control (or the threat of further control) has been a disincentive to improve – and has only been marginally affected by periodic upward revisions in the rent increases allowed after improvement.

The *tax system* is another crucial factor. The Inland Revenue assumes that a house lasts for ever, and landlords are not allowed to deduct sums from their taxable income to set aside for the replacement of their capital asset, the house.[111] Furthermore, the landlord receives no tax relief on his costs of acquisition and improvement. Both these factors decrease the attraction of subsidized improvement.

Moreover the operation of *grant conditions* compounds these problems. Until 1969 repair work was not subsidized, but a house had to be brought into good repair if an improvement grant was to be paid. This meant that a landlord considering grant-aided improvement could be faced with a large bill for repairs. Many landlords did not have the necessary available capital, and the loans system was only a limited incentive as the payment of interest on the loans would further reduce their rate of return. The importance of this constraint was recognized in 1969 when the repairs element was introduced for the Discretionary Grant, an innovation which contributed to some increased investment.

Thus these basic constraints, stemming from the interrelationship of the landlords' tax position (a derivative of fiscal policy) rent control and the grants system (aspects of housing policy), are fundamental to an understanding of landlords' attitudes to improvement. Moreover, the large difference between the *capital value* of previously rented property and its investment value if it remains tenanted has ensured that many landlords regard their holdings as a possible source of capital gain rather than as an asset to be improved while still tenanted. A house or flat can be improved once vacant possession is obtained or be sold unimproved: private rental is often viewed not as a long-term commitment by landlords but rather as a temporary phase until the death or rehousing of a tenant allows sale.

However, a further aspect of considerable significance is the variety of landlords. Research since the mid-1960s has revealed a complex diversity of individuals, organizations and institutions:[112]

1 *Individual landlords* can be considered as four broad subgroups:

(a) Small landlords owning one or a few properties, acquired by inheritance. The majority are elderly, including many widows, with low incomes and no capital. Over the years their rented property, originally seen as a source of security, has become an encumbrance. This group declined in the 1950s and 1960s as a result of demolitions and sales to sitting tenants. The remainder continued to let old, small, unfurnished

terraced houses, often at low controlled rents, to long-standing tenants. The majority have neither the inclination nor the resources to improve.
(b) Small landlords who have acquired one or more properties as an investment, and are concerned to maximize their returns. Many have bought their property relatively recently and include immigrant landlords for whom the status of ownership is often also significant. Much of this property is rented furnished to a mixed group of shorter-term tenants and is multi-occupied as a means of maximizing rental income. Repairs are neglected, and there is no incentive to improve as this would reduce the number of rooms available for letting and hence the rental income.
(c) Owner-occupier landlords who let part of the house in which they themselves live, in order to pay off the mortgages or loans (often secured at high rates of interest) taken out to finance purchase. Many lack the capital to improve.
(d) Individuals with inherited large holdings who are more likely to use estate agents for management. This group have in the past, and particularly since the 1969 Act, improved their houses with the aid of grants. They are more likely to have the necessary capital resources.

2 *Company landlords* can be considered in two groups:
(a) Property companies whose activities are concerned not just with the renting of housing, but with the full range of acquisition, management and sales. They are concerned to maximize profitability, in the main operating at the top end of the market, owning better-quality purpose-built (often inter-war) flats. Such companies were prominent in the take-up of improvement grants in the early 1970s, having the capital resources and tenants who were able to pay increased rents. Moreover some, taking advantage of the relaxation of occupancy conditions attached to grants, bought older property in poor condition, improved with the aid of grants and then either sold to owner-occupiers in much higher income groups than the former tenants, or let to high-income tenants. Some are large London-based property companies who also own property in other towns and cities. Local companies are often part of a set of linked interests comprising estate agents, builders, owners, solicitors, etc.
(b) A mixed group of corporate owners not primarily engaged in the property business, either renting accommodation to employees, or investing some of the surplus capital of another small business in rented accommodation, usually at the top end of the market.

Private tenants

Three quarters of private tenants live in pre-1919 housing. Until the introduction of rent allowances in 1972 they were the only regularly employed group in society who received no state aid in meeting their housing costs. Improvement grants subsidize owners not tenants – for the latter increased rents had to be met from income. It is useful to consider two subtypes – unfurnished and furnished tenancies.

1 *Unfurnished tenancies*. This is the traditional form of private rental, and while it is declining, it is four times the size of the furnished sector. Over two thirds of these tenancies are in pre-1919 terraced houses, the majority of which are in poor repair and lack basic amenities. The accommodation is let at modest (sometimes still controlled) rents, but the average income of unfurnished tenants is lower than that of any other tenure group, so rent can be a substantial proportion of disposable income. Two thirds are manual workers and most of the rest are retired. This sector houses a large proportion of the country's smaller and poorer households in two main groups:

(a) Small elderly households. The largest group of all private tenants, many of whom have been tenants all their lives, frequently in the same house, never having had the opportunity, resources or desire to purchase. The majority are retired and, while they may not be satisfied with their accommodation, many are tolerant of poor conditions and lack of amenities. Some could not afford higher rents, or face the upheaval of improvement work.

(b) Small younger households. This is a less numerous group with the majority of wage earners in unskilled or semi-skilled manual occupations. For some, unfurnished rental is a stepping-stone to owner-occupation, and improvement of their houses with resultant rent increases would simply reduce their capacity to save. For others it is temporary, pending an eventual council tenancy. For those who fail to accumulate sufficient capital to buy a house, or to qualify for a council tenancy, their only prospect of better housing conditions is the repair and improvement of their existing homes.

2 *Furnished tenancies*. This sector was relatively insignificant until the early 1960s, but since then has increased in size both relatively and numerically. Most of the units are small flats or bedsitters, often in large subdivided houses. The absence of basic facilities is less marked than in the unfurnished sector, but a much higher proportion of furnished tenants share the use of a bath and w.c. Rents are considerably higher than in the unfurnished sector. Furnished tenants are much more mobile, and more heterogeneous in terms of income and social class. Again there are two main groups:

(a) Many are young people, often single, and for some (particularly middle-income groups and students) this type of accommodation is tolerable, even desirable, on a temporary basis.

(b) Young poor families with children, for whom furnished lettings are the only available form of shelter within their means. During the mid-1960s this group grew in number and by the early 1970s were a third of the total of furnished tenants. Following the Rent Act, 1965, landlords tended

Table 3 *Changing ownership of older housing (England and Wales)*

	(Millions of dwellings built pre-1914)				
Ownership	*1914*	*1938*	*1960*	*1971*	*1975*
Private landlords	7.1	5.7	3.9	2.5	2.2
Owner-occupied	0.8	1.9	2.9	3.3	3.4
Local authorities	—	—	0.2	0.3	0.3
Total	7.9	7.6	7.0	6.1	5.9

Source: Adapted from DoE, *Housing Policy* (1977), Technical Volume, Part 1, p. 38, Table 1.23.

to change to furnished rental to achieve higher rents and less protection for tenants. In stress areas many furnished tenants of this type were coloured immigrants informally denied access to other forms of tenure. For families, cramped conditions, shared facilities and high rents constitute oppressive living conditions. Mobility for them means moving from one inadequate letting to another. Their plight was analysed by the Milner Holland Committee in 1965, and dramatized two years later in the television play *Cathy Come Home*. Landlords of these properties are generally not interested in improvement for existing tenants.

Owner-occupiers

The number of formerly privately rented dwellings sold either to sitting tenants, or with vacant possession, has been massive, and the majority of older houses are now owner-occupied. A significant proportion of these owner-occupiers have low incomes and many are elderly. Few households can afford to purchase outright and the majority have to borrow the necessary funds. Building societies are the major source of finance for home ownership. However, they are not philanthropic but commercial institutions which have to secure an adequate return on investment in order to attract funds. They have to be sure that the property on which they lend will retain its value, and that borrowers are able to maintain repayments. Older property often sought by low-income buyers is not viewed favourably, and societies are reluctant to lend in many areas of pre-1919 housing.[113] Attempts by local authorities to persuade them to liberalize their lending policy, especially in GIAs after the 1969 Act, met with very little success.

This problem has been recognized for some time, and since 1958 local authorities have been empowered to lend money to marginal buyers and in more marginal areas. Local authorities were seen as 'lenders of last resort', and many linked mortgages with improvement grants in package transactions. However, the fulfilment of this role has been limited by the fluctuating availability of funds and the varying attitudes of local councils, with the result that the flow of investment has not matched needs.

There are a variety of other sources of finance for purchase, including loans from other family members, but increasingly finance companies became 'lenders of last resort', loaning money at higher rates of interest, often 20–30 per cent. The activities of these 'fringe finance' organizations are concentrated in poorer-quality areas where the ability of buyers to qualify for more orthodox loans is least. Clearly people entering owner-occupation on this basis are unlikely to be able to afford the cost of adequate repair and maintenance, let alone improvement.

Rapid growth in the owner-occupation of older housing took place in the late 1950s and the 1960s. The houses were relatively cheap, and as the backlog of repairs was not too substantial, large numbers of the new owner-occupiers improved their property with the aid of a standard grant. However, many did not have the disposable income to improve at the time of purchase. Improvement became increasingly difficult as the repairs backlog mounted, grants remained static, and building costs rose. For some the 1969 changes were a real incentive and they were finally able to improve their property. However, for a substantial proportion of poor or elderly owner-occupiers improvement is either a low priority or beyond their means.

During the late 1960s, the drift into owner-occupation slowed down. Sitting tenants who had wanted and been able to buy had done so, and the 1965 Rent Act had restored security of tenure in the unfurnished sector, reducing opportunities for sales with vacant possession. Much of the remaining property was in poorer areas and less likely to attract a mortgage. Sales for owner-occupation tended to polarize. In stable areas or those going 'up market' the demand was from middle-income young families, priced out of the market for new housing. They were able to secure mortgages from a building society or their local authority, and many had the resources to finance improvement. In poorer areas, often characterized by immigrant settlement, low-income owner-occupation became increasingly financed from fringe sources. In these areas the 1969 Act's incentives were of little help.

The geographical dimension

Substantial local variations in market conditions result in older housing having a different function in different areas. The social and physical conditions in the older housing areas of Lancaster and Lambeth are as alike as chalk and cheese. In the policy debate of the late 1960s the distinction was drawn between *low-pressure areas* where there were no housing shortages but massive problems of obsolescence, and *high-pressure areas* where shortages compounded problems of continuing decay. This distinction was made in identifying areas where resources could be shifted from new building to improvement. However, there was little recognition of the relationship between demand, different types of twilight areas and the likely impact of improvement.

Moreover, within towns and cities different neighbourhoods can fulfil different functions in the housing market. A general distinction is commonly drawn between two broad categories of twilight areas.[114] *Residual settlement areas* consisting of substandard small terraced houses in poor environments – traditional working-class areas with relatively stable populations of elderly households and younger families living in cheap unfurnished rented and owner-occupied dwellings. Deeplish and Halliwell epitomized these neighbourhoods, which were envisaged as the prime targets for improvement. *Transitional areas* containing large, often multi-occupied, houses, accommodating a nomadic and mixed population of predominantly furnished tenants, and serving as a reception area for immigrants – these types of areas are commonly referred to as 'housing stress areas'. The significance of these geographical variations was not adequately recognized in 1969, but they soon became apparent and can be illustrated by reference to contrasting situations in London and the North.

In inner London continued high demand resulted in a large number of furnished tenancies (about a third of the national total in 1971) which were concentrated in transitional areas. In the less attractive of these neighbourhoods scarcity was exploited by small landlords able to charge high rents for poor accommodation. Improvement would have reduced rather than increased profitability. Moreover, pressure in these areas was intensified by the displacement of low-income tenants from other transitional areas such as North Kensington, which became more fashionable. Here, growing middle-class demand was catered for by property developers who took advantage of the abolition of occupancy conditions in 1969, and made huge profits by the grant-aided conversion of large multi-occupied houses into small self-contained flats which were sold or let to high-income groups.[115] Similarly, some residual areas of smaller terraced housing in attractive locations changed their social composition. Landlords sold vacant properties to middle-class families in areas which went 'up market'.[116]

Thus in London the majority of grants went to landlords and property developers (it varied between 40 and 70 per cent in different boroughs), and most of this formerly privately rented property was sold for owner-occupation. It was for low-income tenants in these areas that improvement meant 'one big notice to quit'. Few existing tenants benefited and there was mounting evidence of harassment and 'winkling out' in this process of 'gentrification'.[117]

The voluntary improvement policies of the 1969 Act accentuated rather than initiated these changes, which were a function of increasing house prices and changes in the employment structure of Central London as office development resulted in an influx of young professionals. Moreover, the situation in other parts of inner London was quite different. Some residual areas changed little and grant take-up was low, as they continued in predominantly private unfurnished rental. Other residual areas gradually changed their social composition as landlords sold to low-income owner-occupiers, many of them squeezed out of rented accommodation elsewhere, and funding purchase through 'fringe finance'. These changes were not accompanied by substantial housing improvement.

In transitional areas of large towns and cities in the North the 1969 Act had little impact. These areas continued to house low-income furnished tenants, often in multi-occupied 'investment properties'. There was no middle-class demand for conversion and hence no 'gentrification'. Local authority intervention was minimal and few GIAs were declared. While the Rye Hill experience in Newcastle in the late 1960s had shown the pitfalls of attempting comprehensive improvement using compulsory powers,[118] the Shelter Neighbourhood Action Project (SNAP) indicated the difficulties of a reliance on a voluntary approach.[119] These areas continued to deteriorate.

The problems of implementing improvement policy in residual areas where demand was low were epitomized by North East Lancashire, but again the key factor was diversity in local conditions.[120] Generally, improvement was undertaken by young families who were relatively affluent owner-occupiers in better-quality areas. Some residual neighbourhoods were in the Deeplish mould. These were the more attractive stable areas with a reasonable balance of age groups. Younger owner-occupiers were prepared to invest (especially after grant aid went up to 75 per cent in 1971), and in so doing encouraged initially more reluctant older owner-occupiers.

However, in other less attractive neighbourhoods conditions were very different. These residual areas were declining rapidly as young families moved out leaving behind an ageing and poor community. Parts of Nelson and Rawtenstall typified these conditions.[121] Here 'improvement potential' was very low as up to three quarters of the houses were owned by poor middle-aged or elderly owner-occupiers who had neither the inclination nor the resources to invest. The rest were owned by small landlords letting at rents of £1 per week, and the majority of tenants did not want rent increases.[122] Even after improvement rent levels would still be low. While most landlords wanted to sell there was little opportunity because of lack of demand in comparison with suburban housing, which does not impose significant travel to work difficulties or costs in these smaller towns. In this type of declining residual area few owners were interested in financing an improvement partnership.[123]

Participation

The shift of emphasis to improvement took place during a developing debate about public participation in local decision making, initially focussed on environmental planning. The Town and Country Planning Act, 1968 made public participation a statutory requirement in the preparation of development plans, and techniques of participation were investigated by the Skeffington Committee which reported in 1969. The 'investment partnership' characteristics of post-1969 improvement policy generated two imperatives for the encouragement of public participation. First, the emphasis on voluntary improvement meant that substantial financial participation by individual owners was a prerequisite for success. Second, a commitment to an area approach resulted in local authorities negotiating with residents on a collective basis about environmental works in GIAs. The importance of participation was stressed in government circulars:

> The improvement proposals for the area must certainly include some definite areas, but these must be capable of adjustment in the light of people's response. . . . Local authorities should make every effort to gain the confidence of residents and owners and secure their co-operation. There should be public meetings at the important stages to explain objectives, to test reaction and to seek ideas. Personal visits to discuss house improvements and repairs, grants, loans and rents will play a vital part; and it would be helpful too if demonstration houses could be provided. The formation of residents' associations should also be encouraged. This would focus the various interests of residents and open another door of communication.[124]

and the Government provided an illustrated folder explaining area improvement and grant provisions, to which local authorities could add information about a particular area and circulate to GIA residents.[125]

It is important to recognize just how much of a tall order this was for local authorities. Public participation was in its infancy and in many areas, for local authorities and residents alike, GIAs were the first experience of it. It is not surprising that participation varied considerably with both the attitudes of local authority and the characteristics of declared areas.

The range of local authorities' responses to central government exhortations was very wide. At one end of the spectrum efforts were perfunctory: a formal letter was sent to residents informing them that their area had been, or was about to be, declared a GIA, and inviting them to a public meeting where the grant system and environmental proposals were explained. After often lengthy and occasionally confusing speeches from the platform, occupied by chief officers and councillors, there was an opportunity for questions from the floor which often elicited uninformative replies. The meeting ended with the assumption that the plans were approved by the public, subject to one or two minor amendments, and that was that. The local authority waited for residents to come forward with grant applications and residents waited for the local authority to begin the environmental improvements. Although this was the lowest common denominator in GIA participation, it was by no means an infrequent occurrence and it was often two years or more before there was any further initiative.

At the other end of the spectrum local authorities identified a potential GIA, undertook a social survey to give an indication of residents' attitudes and used this information to draw up draft plans. The survey itself stimulated local interest, and imaginative publicity, using newsletters and the local press attracted residents to an exhibition of draft proposals which were exhibited and discussed at a public meeting. This was conducted as informally as possible, the questions from the floor being supplemented by an opportunity to discuss problems and issues with officers who knew the area well, and ended with the formation of a residents' organization. A local office, ideally in a showhouse, was quickly established to promote grants. This was followed by individual visits to prospective improvers, and efforts to identify landlords and persuade them to improve their properties. The office also acted as an advice centre and a base for the residents' group. The initial nucleus of this group expanded and developed a system of street representation. Informal meetings between residents' organizations and officers thrashed out environmental proposals and problems about housing improvement, for example difficulties with local builders. Regular newsletters produced by the residents' group and/or the local authority officers kept people informed about progress, or reasons for delays. A further public meeting, this time jointly organized by the residents and the local authority, finalized the proposals, which were then approved by the council. Within eighteen months of the initial survey environmental works were started, and at the end of three years or so a modest scheme was completed and a substantial proportion of houses had been improved. This level of participation was very much the exception.

During the early 1970s most local authorities moved from the lowest common denominator, but many had still a long way to go.[126] Although the general attitudes of officers and councillors were clearly important factors in the development of participation, the reactions of residents were crucial, and often not understood. The 'community' was bureaucratically defined, primarily by reference to 'natural boundaries' such as main roads, railways, marked changes in land use, etc. A degree of physical uniformity often obscured social heterogeneity, and as Davies pointedly remarked, there is no reason to assume that 'an area drawn on a map by some junior doodler in a planning department should suddenly become a substantive community'.[127]

This process of GIA definition had important consequences. The proportion of owners willing and able to invest in improvement in a given GIA was largely a matter of chance. There was often the mistaken assumption that intensified promotion and publicity would substantially increase grant take-up, and frustration when the efforts involved yielded only marginal returns. The basic constraints on the voluntary approach were the same in GIAs as elsewhere: the pattern of ownership and the availability of private capital. Furthermore, the differential benefits of improvement influenced involvement in resident organizations. Owner-occupiers tended to be prominent, whereas tenants, having either no long-term interest in the area, or little real prospect of having their houses improved were, understandably, less likely to be interested. In some areas there was marked conflict between residents, for example where private tenants saw themselves being squeezed out by incoming owner-occupiers, who quickly formed residents' organizations which had nothing to offer tenants.[128]

Even where levels of owner-occupation were relatively high, participation was not necessarily harmonious. Residents' groups frequently came into conflict with the local authority over issues such as delays in implementing environmental works, or the reluctance to implement obvious, but expensive, improvements. There were often conflicts within residents' groups, over issues such as the location of play spaces, which street should be pedestrianized and which should have resultant increases in traffic. In other areas a combination of local authority inactivity, diverse tenure pattern and social composition, absence of local leadership, or scepticism born of previous encounters with the local authority resulted in little collective action of any kind.

In sum, participation in GIAs varied significantly, but the rapid growth of community action in many cities and towns had its initial stimulus from GIA proposals, or demand for them. During the early 1970s many residents of inner areas came to understand the workings of the local authority, became better organized and able to put forward their views forcefully, and were no longer to be the docile recipients of renewal policies.[129]

Conclusions

Before 1969, the underlying principles of a grant system were periodically debated and its basic elements cumulatively established. A reorientation of housing policy made improvement more significant as part of a tandem policy, ostensibly aimed at accelerating both the clearance of slums and the improvement of other substandard housing. The improvement policy of 1969 relied on incentives to stimulate the voluntary take-up of grants and stressed an area approach aimed at achieving comprehensive improvement to high standards, on the basis of changes in the grant system plus Exchequer subsidized environmental improvements in GIAs. A significant supplementary measure in 1971 raised the level of grant aid from 50 to 75 per cent in the Assisted Areas.

The paramount concern in the early 1970s was to arrest the deterioration of the older housing stock. In crude numerical terms the policy was successful, producing a unique relationship between expectation and achievement. However, even in terms of housing stock objectives, a series of problems emerged:

1 only a limited amount of effort was going where it was most needed – to improvable houses at the lower end of the quality scale;
2 the failure to achieve comprehensive improvement to high standards in GIAs highlighted the limitations of an area approach based on the voluntary principle;
3 the limitations of environmental improvement, both in terms of what

could be achieved within the Exchequer subsidy and its marginal impact on grant take-up;

4 it was apparent that in areas of poorer housing, particularly where private rental was significant, GIAs were not often successful; and

5 a growing awareness of the continuing decay of houses which were not being improved nor were likely to be cleared.

The improvement boom highlighted the ambiguities inherent in a policy with primary and explicit housing stock objectives, and secondary but largely implicit social objectives of preserving communities and improving the housing conditions of those in greatest need. The regressive consequences of virtually unrestrained subsidized improvement by private owners became increasingly obvious and further problems emerged:

6 poorer tenants and owner-occupiers were achieving least benefit;

7 housing stress areas were either changing their market function as existing residents were displaced or, where there was no middle-class demand, continuing to deteriorate;

8 other areas either saw a less dramatic change in their social composition as the level of owner-occupation increased and new owners took up grants or, in areas of very low demand, there was little improvement by either owner-occupiers or landlords.

These social consequences and 'abuses' of the grant system by speculators taking advantage of lax grant conditions, raised an obvious dilemma:

> The basic question is: do we regard older housing as a wasting national asset, to be managed, improved, conserved etc. in the long-term interests of society; or as a special kind of consumer durable, to be fashioned and managed in the way in which the existing population requires and can afford?[130]

Social objectives increasingly became the focus of debate in the evaluation of improvement policies.

A further issue of crucial importance was the changing relationship between clearance and improvement. The ambiguity of the Labour Government's renewal policy was becoming apparent by the time of the 1970 General Election. The change from regarding improvement as complementary to viewing it as an alternative developed within the framework of Conservative housing policy. Both the problems of improvement policy and the changing balance between clearance and improvement were key issues in a further reappraisal of policy in 1973–4. The next chapter examines this reappraisal and its outcome – gradual renewal.

4 Gradual renewal

Legislation introduced in 1974 gave official blessing to gradual renewal. This chapter outlines the development of arguments in favour of this changed approach, the legislative changes and local strategies which ensued, the progress made and the framework of overall housing policy within which it was implemented during the late 1970s.

The concept of gradual renewal is imprecise. Its official version encompasses a greater emphasis on physical change being responsive to social needs; on combining improvement with limited clearance in a continuous manner with the participation of those affected; and on effective corporate planning within a comprehensive strategy. But its origins lie in academic debate about the need to retain low-cost, poor-quality housing. Moreover, the circumstances surrounding its introduction lend weight to the argument that it was primarily a rationalization of financial expediency.

The new approach emerged from debate about the implications of both comprehensive redevelopment and comprehensive improvement discussed in Chapters 2 and 3. This raised policy questions which were taken up in the early 1970s as the housing situation deteriorated. An inflationary boom exacerbated the consequences of a voluntary approach to improvement, particularly in stress areas. It also compounded the problems of an unreformed clearance process and provided further legitimation for declining clearance programmes. Community activists argued for more responsive policies, while academics stressed the functional virtues of older housing.

This debate culminated in the Housing Act, 1974 and its associated circulars. New area improvement powers were introduced in Housing Action Areas and the renovation grant system was amended. Improvement was now viewed as an alternative to redevelopment. Initial reactions to the policy change focussed on scepticism about the real intentions of the Government and on the competence of local authorities to use the new powers.

Reduced activity was soon apparent. Despite the progress made by local authorities in formulating comprehensive renewal strategies, both clearance and improvement declined. The key factor was a climate of economic stringency and cumulative cuts in public expenditure.

At the same time the Labour Government was undertaking an overall review of housing policy and finance. Although started with the aim of 'slaughtering sacred cows', this review baulked at radically altering the subsidy system for owner-occupied and council housing. Complacency about residual housing problems resulted in only minor reforms. The most important changes for urban renewal were the creation of Housing Investment Programmes and attempts to improve the effectiveness of the grant system, but doubts about the efficacy of gradual renewal grew.

The lessons of the early 1970s

The experience of the early 1970s indicated that the legislative framework for urban renewal was inadequate in certain crucial aspects. Earlier chapters have indicated the problems of comprehensive redevelopment and improvement. This section outlines the policy issues which arose from the exposure of these problems during the Conservative Government of 1970–4.

Housing trends

The combined effect of the 1969 and 1971 Housing Acts was a massive increase in the rate of housing improvement. This was the one success story of the Conservative Government's housing policy, for:

> The early 1970s saw the collapse of both public and private sector building programmes, runaway inflation in house prices, rising mortgage interest rates followed by a mortgage famine, a static slum clearance programme and a deepening crisis in the inner city rented housing market.[1]

Pressures for change and the development of arguments in favour of specific reforms can only be understood in the context of these trends.

One factor was constant over these years: the encouragement of owner-occupation and the discouragement of council housing.[2] The broad objectives of the Heath Government's housing policy were expressed in the 1971 White Paper *Fair Deal for Housing*.[3] The Housing Finance Act, 1972 intended to shift the balance of advantages between renting and buying.[4] Additional measures to promote owner-occupation included lifting restrictions on council house sales and increased local authority mortgage lending. However, other factors were not constant. In particular, the Government's economic policy, which was geared towards increasing consumption and boosting the money supply, engendered an inflationary boom which then severely distorted the housing market. Three phases can be distinguished in the impact of housing market changes on urban renewal.

At first, the overspill problems of the large cities appeared to be evaporating.[5] Private housebuilding increased and this coincided with rent rises. Since there was evidence of a growing number of families in clearance areas rehousing themselves and relets of existing council houses were sharply rising, a decline in council housebuilding did not produce significant pressures on either clearance rehousing or waiting lists. Indeed there was speculation about a public sector housing surplus by the late 1970s.

At this point, however, a surge in demand for private housing, fuelled by the increasing availability of building society mortgages at a time when the supply of houses increased slowly, precipitated a house price spiral. The average price of new dwellings nearly doubled between 1971 and 1973. One response of land owners was to engage in speculation rather than release greater amounts of land for building.[6] House prices rose far more rapidly than earnings, with the uncontrolled flooding of large amounts of money into a situation of inelastic supply. By 1973 there was increasing concern about 'land hoarding' and some government response.[7] The same period also witnessed a considerable commercial 'property boom' which committed much of the resources of the building industry to office development.[8]

The last phase in this cycle was marked by the end of the boom as the Government's 'dash for growth' failed. Interest rates rose and the availability of credit contracted. Mortgages were difficult to secure and builders and developers were under increasing pressures. Several prominent firms went bankrupt.

In the meantime these inflationary trends had affected urban renewal in several ways. First, costs of council housebuilding rose and many councils found it impossible to persuade private builders to tender. The Conservative Government was disinclined to promote council housing and failed to adequately increase the cost yardstick in this period. Council housebuilding declined from 135,000 completions in 1970 to 79,000 in 1973. Many cities were demolishing more houses than they were building and delays stimulated further reaction against comprehensive redevelopment. Second, as many families were priced out of home ownership, council relets fell and waiting lists were swollen. Third, the property boom stimulated gentrification in some inner areas. Pressures in stress areas were increased by these trends and doubts about the social impact of both clearance and improvement were reinforced. Although the 'Barber cuts' at the end of the boom in late 1973 specifically excluded housing, it was apparent by then that any reformulation of policies towards older housing would be strongly influenced by public expenditure constraints. The 'dash for growth' created the climate for a policy review, but its failure determined much of the outcome.

Voluntary improvement and stress areas

Policy questions were raised about the redirection of resources within the improvement programme as it became a focus of academic and journalistic comment. In particular, priorities among the older housing stock became a key issue. As the tandem policy of 1969 collapsed and improvement became dominant, the line between housing fit only for clearance and that suitable for improvement was blurred. More specifically, changes in grant arrangements to discriminate in favour of the worst areas and to provide further aid for repair work were debated. Policy questions about housing stock objectives were brought together in 1973 when an Expenditure Committee of the House of Commons evaluated the cost effectiveness of the operation of the 1969 Act. It received a mass of written and oral evidence from the civil service, local authorities, contractors and other bodies.[9]

The social impact of improvement also raised policy questions. As the Expenditure Review commented:

> In retrospect, it is clear that objectives other than purely housing ones have been attributed to the 1969 Act. It has come to be realized by local communities, and now by planners, that improvement is a housing technique which attempts to meet the needs of existing residents of an area and prevents the blight of a neighbourhood while a redevelopment is being planned, as well as the social disruption of communities caused by eventual clearance. Social objectives were not made clear during the passing of the Act, but they have figured prominently in discussions of the effects of the legislation.[10]

The 'side-effects' of improvement policy led to calls for the reintroduction of more stringent grant conditions, stronger compulsory powers and the reformulation of area improvement powers.

The problems of housing stress areas received most attention for here the social implications of the voluntary approach were particularly apparent. Advice after the 1969 Act had been ambivalent about GIA declaration in these areas[11] and they were often ignored by both clearance and area improvement initiatives.[12] It was increasingly argued that local authorities needed stronger powers if they were to tackle such areas more effectively.[13] The insecurity of furnished tenants in stress areas was recognized but the Francis Report recommended that they should not be given security of tenure, fearing that this might restrict the availability of lettings.[14]

Municipalization was seen by some as one solution to the problems of such areas but was not viewed favourably by the Government. A CPO for eighteen tenanted houses was confirmed with some reluctance in the SNAP area of Granby, Liverpool in 1971 to secure improvement and several London boroughs began acquiring private housing by agreement. Although Part V of the Housing Act, 1957 provided possible powers for more active intervention, councils were discouraged from using them to meet social objectives as part of their improvement policies.[15]

The problems of housing stress areas reawakened the Labour Opposition's interest in the principles and mechanisms of municipalization. Widespread acquisition of the private rented sector had been raised as an alternative to encouraging voluntary improvement by landlords in the 1950s.[16] The Labour Party was committed to a proposal that all tenanted, rent-controlled property would be taken into municipal ownership, but this was dropped in 1961. In the early 1970s the need for systematic acquisition of privately rented houses was argued on the grounds of retaining a supply of good standard rented housing and reducing insecurity.[17] Significantly, Labour now referred to its policy as 'social ownership', having widened its definition to include housing associations, previously regarded as just another type of private landlord.[18]

The need for the definition of special areas where voluntary action was insufficient was also taken up. The Milner Holland report had earlier suggested 'areas of special control' where an extension of statutory powers over private landlords was necessary. Similar proposals were made at the Greater London Development Plan Inquiry.[19] Faced with the rehousing of homeless families displaced by the activities of speculators, some London boroughs began using their discretion to refuse grant aid to absentee landlords.

Comprehensive redevelopment – reform or rejection?

Chapter 2 commented on increasing opposition to clearance programmes in the late 1960s. The image of a cosy secure community ravaged by the 'planners' replaced that of the miserable slum fit only for the bulldozer. As well as opposition to the principle of clearance this reaction was partly a result of a lack of attention to the process.

In the early 1970s there were pioneering attempts to reform the redevelopment process which could have altered the debate on the relative advantages of clearance and improvement. The refinements proposed can be summarized under the general heading of *community-based redevelopment* with three main elements:

1 a commitment to rehouse on site all those residents who wish to remain;
2 redevelopment in small phases to reduce the impact of demolition allowing rehousing on site from one phase to the next; and
3 an ongoing and thorough programme of public involvement.[20]

The major argument in favour of community-based redevelopment is its potential for preserving the social continuity of an area. A large area can be divided into subareas so that each becomes one phase to be demolished and redeveloped in turn. Such an approach was suggested by Barnes in the 1930s. After discussing opposition to clearance stimulated by old-established habits and community ties, he proposed the simultaneous initiation of many clearance schemes and commented on one major problem – how to rehouse locally from phase one if there is no vacant land in the immediate area:

> . . . the main part of any slum clearance scheme is first to find a 'decant' on which to house the people first displaced. It is like the vacant hole on the solitaire board, it must be there before you can play the game.[21]

Yet a report on the Meadows area of Nottingham by a local residents group analysed how, some forty years later, the detailed planning of clearance and redevelopment frustrated the chances of residents to be rehoused locally.[22] It claimed that large CPOs were delaying the whole clearance programme of the city.

Two well-publicized examples of community-based redevelopment in the early 1970s were undertaken in Byker, Newcastle and the Swinbrook area of North Kensington in London. Byker was composed of Tyneside flats in which lived some 12,000 people. A long process of consultation between the architects and local residents was undertaken in the context of phased CPOs, preallocation of dwellings and feedback from those initially rehoused. The brief was to translate the political aim of 'Byker for Byker people' into a coherent plan.[23] Swinbrook displayed much more severe social problems. A 'perpetual slum' almost from the time it was built, it was the focus of community action in the 1960s and in 1971 this resulted in the election of a neighbourhood council. A 'community rehousing census' by the GLC was followed by an attempt at on-site rehousing during the redevelopment process.[24]

However, such examples were rare. Criticisms of comprehensive redevelopment gathered force as local authorities pursued demolition in one area, while in nearby areas they were increasingly involving residents in GIAs. A lack of DoE advice on the implementation of clearance contrasted sharply with a burgeoning literature on survey techniques, organizational patterns and participation in improvement. In 1973 mounting journalistic comment about the hardships endured during the clearance process was added to by criticism of authorities demolishing more houses than they were building. Legitimation for a further shift of emphasis towards improvement could be sought in popular reaction against unreformed clearance procedures.

Reaction against clearance fed, and in turn was fed by, the growth of community action groups as the coercive aspect of compulsory purchase was contrasted with the virtues of improvement. The many groups which blossomed at this time can be seen as a reaction against a system of 'ossified and unresponsive local government'.[25] Representative local politics was failing to discuss the key issues which concerned local people. Without effective grassroots membership and a viable ward party system the Labour Party, in particular, was no longer an effective vehicle for the articulation of concern about renewal policies.[26]

Consumer opposition to clearance was evident at the time of the 1969 Act: in the early 1970s it became more organized as proposals increasingly blighted areas with significant owner-occupation. Community groups established to contest clearance programmes were aided by disquiet about compensation and the standard of replacement housing offered, by the increasing difficulty of justifying standards of unfitness and by the presentation of what has been summarized as the 'community case for improvement'.[27] The preservation of established communities was claimed to be a major advantage when improvement was promoted as an alternative to clearance. Often local residents were assisted by independent professionals in presenting their case. Opposition by a federation of residents' groups in Manchester was one element in the abandonment of the later phases of the city's massive post-war clearance drive.[28]

Most groups adopted an uncritical attitude to the benefits of improvement and sought to influence the speed of implementation or type of improvements. Official encouragement of participation provided a ripe field for action groups seeking to promote change at a local level. As the journal *Community Action* stressed, groups could use the opportunities presented to challenge local authorities on wider issues. An obvious issue like housing and environmental improvement could assist in providing an initial focus for discussion, though groups should 'remember that a lick of paint on a house is not going to cover the fundamental problems that caused the house to deteriorate in the first place'.[29]

Evangelistic researchers and cellular renewal

Discontent about established renewal policies was underpinned by a developing academic critique of their consequences. This critique (with differing emphasis) could, paradoxically, be found in the arguments of both 'radical sociologists' and 'market economists'. Their conclusions stressed the way in which comprehensive improvement, and more strikingly comprehensive redevelopment, subordinated the immediate housing preferences of the existing community in the interests of futuristic ideals. Conventional renewal policies were derived from a philosophy of housing affluence, 'the belief that housing standards ought to rise in step with gross national product because we are members of a rich and technologically advanced society',[30] but in reality imposed immense hardships on those they were meant to benefit. They ignored the functional need for low-cost housing and relied on outmoded and inflexible concepts of unfitness and comprehensiveness. An alternative approach was put forward on economic, social and aesthetic grounds: cellular renewal would combine housing improvement matched to demand and social changes, with piecemeal redevelopment over an extended period of time.

Two influential sociological studies were carried out in the North-East.[31] Dennis traced the decision-making process of Sunderland council which led to the definition of areas for comprehensive redevelopment. He examined the supposedly scientific basis of these decisions and found them lacking in any objective rationality. Furthermore, the sense of loss that many residents experienced by the demolition of their homes was not taken into account in official deliberations. The protection of their rights through attempts at participation was thwarted by their lack of power and the failure of the council to perceive any requirement to reconsider and justify decisions. Davies' study was of an attempted scheme of improvement to high standards in the Rye Hill area of Newcastle. He too focussed on planners' spurious professionalism and argued that an ideology of planning appealing to vague future interests of the general community is regressive, 'it complements and reflects the class structure, giving most to those who already have a lot and giving least to those who need most'.[32] Both authors were partisan. They provided virulent and often entertaining evidence of the activities of the 'evangelistic bureaucrats'.

In questioning the implications of renewal policies these two studies emphasized the diversity of social and personal ends pursued in older housing areas. This issue was also taken up by McKie who stressed the economic function of twilight areas in providing a reservoir of accommodation for those with low income. This functional view of older housing depends upon a filtering process – a housing ladder with a queue of households trying to climb it.

If the bottom rungs of the ladder are cut away suddenly and completely by redevelopment or even by over-improvement, some households will never be able to climb at all because the base from which they can start has been destroyed.[33]

The imposition of statutory standards of unfitness is derived from Victorian health criteria, which are now almost completely irrelevant and ignore the fact that many older houses are not functionally obsolete. Once the relativity of standards for different households is accepted:

The only guide to the need for redevelopment over and above the sanitarian level would seem to be the effective demand for redevelopment as expressed through the market or, since the market in twilight zones has been distorted by rent controls and the range of consumer choice is restricted by local housing shortages, by the application of market research techniques to establish satisfactions, preferences and capacity to pay.[34]

For McKie the same arguments apply to the definition of 'first-class improvements' and to the confused notion of 'lifing'.

The alternative to comprehensive policies put forward was the management of a continuous process of small-scale change in older housing areas. This alternative has been given a variety of titles but is best described as *cellular renewal.* Like many modern ideas its basic principles were set out in the writings of Geddes, who described the process as 'conservative surgery'.[35] More recently the concept was suggested in plans for Peterborough in 1967[36] and then taken up in the early 1970s.[37] The operation of cellular renewal would involve the establishment of neighbourhood-based staff teams working with local residents to establish functionally 'soft' cells where redevelopment is appropriate and 'hard' cells where varying levels of improvement should take place. A continuous sequence of change would occur within a flexible framework, generally by agreement, so that the phased infiltration of new housing would enable the maintenance of an existing social fabric. Aesthetically, cellular renewal would create a variety of architectural styles and ages of buildings similar to those found on the high streets of small towns and villages as a result of piecemeal decisions about adaptation or rebuilding over the years. Economically, it would establish the conditions necessary for the re-emergence of the small, local developer-builder.

From 1966 onwards Oxford City Council had adopted a policy on these lines in the Jericho area of the city.[38] Aided by the fashionable location of the area and its partial gentrification, housing improvement to varying standards was combined with the purchase of small blocks of the worst houses for demolition by the council. Pockets of land were then used for infill redevelopment to the existing street pattern (usually council housing but also some private housing) and for environmental improvements.

The concept of improvement, repair, clearance and new building occurring organically – at a pace determined by the wishes of local residents – had obvious attractions. It ran counter to the principle of large-scale comprehensive policies at a time when their effects were increasingly criticized. A critique of cellular renewal will be pursued later in this chapter: for the moment it is only necessary to acknowledge the influence of these emerging ideas as renewal policies were being reappraised.

The emergence of a new approach

Changes in national policy introduced by the 1974 Housing Act were preceded by several indications of intent by the Conservative Government. Before the Act could be introduced a Labour Government was elected, but the major elements of the previous administration's proposals were carried through.

Comprehensive strategy

A commitment to the idea of introducing comprehensive strategies, by bringing together the elements of clearance and improvement, was expressed in Circular 50/72.[39] This circular called on all local authorities to join the Government in '. . . a concerted and decisive drive on the problems of slums and older housing',[40] and to deal with this problem by 1980. Having assessed housing conditions and needs in their area, 'in particular the needs and wishes of those now living in slums and older houses', each local authority was to draw up a renewal strategy and to inform the Minister of any practical constraints standing in the way of its implementation.

The Minister for Housing's speech which accompanied the Circular was characterized by gratuitous self-congratulation, as Amery joined a long list of previous ministers who felt that we could 'beat the problem of slums and unsatisfactory houses within a measurable time'.[41] He could see light at the end of the tunnel and felt we must strike out for it. His comments on improvement showed no sign of reaction to criticisms about the social impact of the voluntary approach.[42]

In the same year the DoE launched a policy review on older housing, stimulated by the loss of momentum expected in housing improvement once the temporary provisions of the Housing Act, 1971 expired and the need to devise a further stimulus for grant take-up.

Housing stress and housing associations

The first outcome of this review was the 1973 White Paper *Better Homes: The Next Priorities*, which outlined the Government's response to mounting criticism of its improvement policy in areas of housing stress.[43] Publicity about the unacceptable face of the grant system had produced a change of attitude. Now, it was proclaimed that the time had come to 'grasp the nettle' of housing stress areas, and revise the improvement process. The concept of the *Housing Action Area* (HAA) was revealed, with its array of 'carrots and sticks' designed to both encourage and control housing improvement. Housing associations were seen as agencies which could resolve the Government's dilemma about the role of private landlords in stress areas. Acutely conscious of criticisms of many landlords, but with a traditional dislike of an 'unhealthy municipal monopoly' of rented housing, the White Paper shied away from municipalization. While hoping that private landlords would co-operate, the Government looked to associations to acquire and manage properties in HAAs and suggested a new power requiring landlords to give them first refusal of properties for sale in these areas. An earlier White Paper in 1973, *Widening the Choice: The Next Steps in Housing*, had included proposals 'to widen the range and choice of rented accommodation by the expansion of the voluntary housing movement'.[44]

At the same time opposition to clearance was recognized and *Better Homes: The Next Priorities* presaged the endorsement of gradual renewal in preference to comprehensive redevelopment:

> The Government believes that, in the majority of cases, it is no longer preferable to attempt to solve the problems arising from bad housing by schemes of widespread, comprehensive redevelopment. Such an approach often involves massive and unacceptable disruption of communities and leaves vast areas of our cities standing derelict and devastated for far too long. Regardless of the financial compensation they receive, many people suffer distress when their homes are compulsorily acquired. Increasing local opposition to redevelopment proposals is largely attributable to people's understandable preference for the familiar and, in many ways, more convenient environment in which they have lived for years. Large-scale redevelopment frequently diminishes rather than widens the choice available in terms of the style of houses, their form of tenure, and their price.[45]

There was no indication of how a more sensitive approach could be combined with the 'decisive drive on slums' referred to only a year before.

In January 1974 the Government introduced the Housing and Planning Bill. It included measures designed to eradicate 'abuses' of the improvement grant system, to encourage housing associations and to strengthen powers in stress areas by the introduction of HAAs. However, debate within the Conservative Party between publication of the White Paper and the drafting of the Bill resulted in the deletion of three of the more radical proposals for HAAs. Landlords selling tenanted property would not be required to offer the property first to a housing association or local authority; local authorities would not be given the right to nominate tenants for empty houses or flats where a landlord appeared to have made no effort to find any; and a statutory duty on local authorities to rehouse any tenant displaced by improvement disappeared. By this time overall cuts in public expenditure at a time of rising inflation had led to Treasury pressure to limit expenditure on improvement once the 1971 Act's provisions ended. To compensate for the increased expenditure flowing from some of the Bill's proposals, e.g. preferential grants in HAAs and GIAs, there would also be restrictions on the general availability of grants in the private sector, e.g. Rateable Value limits, and new powers for regulating the volume of public sector improvement.

A new government

The Conservative Government fell before their Bill completed its passage through all the necessary Parliamentary stages. The incoming Labour administration was faced with a rapidly deteriorating housing situation. Housing was a priority issue, and, in addition to freezing rents and pegging mortgage rates, the Chancellor permitted local authorities to borrow an extra £350m in 1974–5 for housebuilding, buying up unsold private houses, and making a start on '. . . a programme of social ownership for rented housing in the worst areas of housing stress'.[46] The new Government also introduced the Rent Act, 1974 which extended the same security of tenure to furnished tenants of non-resident landlords.[47] These measures had important implications for renewal, particularly in stress areas.

After these apparently substantial changes, the Labour Government took on board the renewal legislation of the previous administration. With broad all-party support the Housing Bill was reintroduced by Crosland, the new Secretary of State, despite his protestations when in opposition about its inadequacy.[48] Some minor changes were made, including the introduction of 'safeguard areas' or *Priority Neighbourhoods*, as they came to be called; the replacement of the earlier requirement for landlords to offer first refusal to local authorities when selling properties in an HAA by a 'notification procedure'; the extension of the period of time which must elapse before the owner of an improved house could sell without having to repay the grant; and finally the removal of the discretion of the Secretary of State to direct local authorities to sell land or houses acquired in an HAA. However, in almost all its major provisions, the 1974 Act was the same as the Bill introduced by the previous Conservative Government.

The Housing Act, 1974

The Housing Act, 1974 and its associated circulars provided some new tools and modified existing ones. It also greatly strengthened the role of housing associations. However, the change of direction was more than simply a reformulation of detailed legislation: it involved a new emphasis on comprehensive strategies; the social objectives of renewal; housing stress areas; corporate working; and the concept of gradual renewal. Initial reactions concentrated on two interrelated questions: did the new approach provide the framework for a vigorous but sensitive attack on the problems faced or was it just 'buying time' – a new version of deferred demolition; were the new tools adequate and did local authorities have the administrative capacity to use them?

The dimensions of gradual renewal

The legislation ushered in a different approach to housing renewal, the major characteristics of which were encapsulated in Circular 13/75:

> . . . the local authorities should . . . place at the centre of their policy a commitment to flexible, co-ordinated and continuous renewal – using that term in its widest sense to cover the building of new homes, the renovation of existing dwellings to a variety of standards, environmental improvements and, where necessary, the clearance of individual properties – in ways which avoid the disruption of, indeed provide for the enhancement of, established communities.[49]

Central government's advice to local authorities on the implementation of this approach consisted of three elements:

1 the need for a comprehensive strategy;
2 an emphasis on gradual renewal; and
3 implementation by a corporate approach.

A *comprehensive strategy* was regarded as an essential precondition of an effective renewal programme. By this the DoE did not mean that the statutory planning framework of structure plans and local plans would determine renewal policy. Rather, local authorities were expected to develop an assessment of overall needs, priorities and resources for housing. Within these parameters, local renewal strategies were to be formulated including the declaration of special areas: GIAs, HAAs, Priority Neighbourhoods and clearance areas. Specific factors to be taken into account in devising such strategies were itemized:[50]

1 *social stress* – areas of stress to be identified by detailed survey work focussing on '. . . the worst conditions in terms of overcrowding, multiple occupation, insecurity, or other forms of hardship';
2 *local attitudes* – the views of residents and owners to be ascertained through 'impartial canvassing', street meetings, etc. This could be important in determining whether compulsory powers were necessary and hence whether HAA or GIA declaration was more appropriate;
3 *physical condition of the housing stock* – to be reviewed in terms of both its present condition and its potential for improvement;

4 *environmental factors* – the potential for the enhancement of the physical environment at reasonable cost to be assessed, in view of the decisive effect that this could have on an area's medium- to long-term potential for rehabilitation;
5 *displacement* – the availability of temporary or permanent rehousing to be established if areas being considered were characterized by very high densities;
6 *resources* – a thorough assessment of available resources was required, in terms of finance, the capacity of the construction industry, and the local authority's own capability for planning, executing, and monitoring of its strategy. It was pointed out that some schemes, in particular HAAs, would be very demanding on staff resources. Local authorities were advised to consider utilizing housing associations and local residents;
7 *prevailing trends in the local housing market* – the importance of identifying pressures for change in local areas was identified as a crucial element.

The new approach emphasized the concept of *gradual renewal*, defined as:

> . . . a continuous process of minor rebuilding and renovation which sustains and reinforces the vitality of a neighbourhood in ways responsive to social and physical needs as they develop and change.[51]

Large-scale clearance was seen to be coming to an end. Only those houses beyond renovation should be demolished, and replacement housing built in small pockets over an extended period of time. House improvement should be carried out to varying standards, and some low-standard housing maintained to meet the need for cheap accommodation. HAAs were seen as *either* a short-term 'holding operation' pending clearance *or* eventually leading to longer-term GIA treatment.

Finally, the Circular drew attention to the potential of a *corporate approach* to renewal strategies. In special areas, the main emphasis was on housing powers, but local authorities were pointed to the opportunity to relate social programmes to their strategy by redirecting other services.

The specification of these three elements of the new conventional wisdom marked the end of a period of policy development which had begun in the late 1960s.

The new tools

Changes in powers and procedures are briefly described under the following headings:

1 area improvement;
2 types of renovation grants;
3 stringent grant conditions;
4 compulsory powers; and
5 public sector acquisition and improvement subsidies.

All related to improvement – there were no revisions to clearance powers.

The new and revised powers for *area improvement* were set out in Circular 14/75.[52] They confirmed an emphasis on HAAs for tackling the worst housing conditions, with GIAs reserved for better areas. Their main provisions are outlined below.

Housing Action Areas were to be in '. . . areas of housing stress where bad physical and social conditions interact and where intense activity will follow declaration'.[53] Their objectives were to secure:

1 improvement of the housing accommodation in the area as a whole;
2 the well-being of existing residents; and
3 the proper management and use of the accommodation.[54]

Illustrations of the kind of conditions likely to justify HAA declaration included: a high incidence of multi-occupation and shared amenities; low-income areas with disrepair; areas where clearance is impossible with local rehousing; areas where private rental means that improvement is unlikely to take place except to the disadvantage of residents; and low-demand areas with unattractive surroundings leading to houses being abandoned.[55] HAAs were designed to deal with 'that 3–4 per cent of the nation's housing stock . . . where no other housing powers will serve to ensure progress in eradicating stress'.[56] Their size would depend on particular local circumstances, but should not be so large that significant progress could not be secured within the first five years. The DoE's view was that GIAs had shown that management problems could arise when they were larger than 300 houses. Given the more intensive nature of action, it would be inappropriate for HAAs to exceed this size. Action programmes should take account of the existing housing function of each area and include regular monitoring. Preferential grant rates (75 and 90 per cent in cases of hardship), compulsory powers and grant conditions are described later. A notification procedure for landlords selling tenanted properties or serving notices to quit on tenants was introduced, but with no statutory responsibility to follow up such notifications with action. Environmental grants were for modest works only, on land in private ownership and to a level of £50 per unit for subsidy.

Priority Neighbourhoods were designed to prevent housing conditions in and around stress areas from deteriorating further, and to stop stress from rippling out from areas which are the subject of concentrated action. No special powers were available for the physical improvement of the housing stock but the notification system and CPOs provided in HAAs were applicable. A Priority Neighbourhood must abut an HAA or GIA and would normally pave the way for later declaration as one of these areas.

General Improvement Areas remained substantially the same but were more firmly defined as being only suitable for areas with a relatively long life, without much private rental, and where improvement would result from voluntary action. A preferential rate of improvement grant (60 per cent) was made payable but the maximum amount for environmental works remained at £200 per dwelling for subsidy.

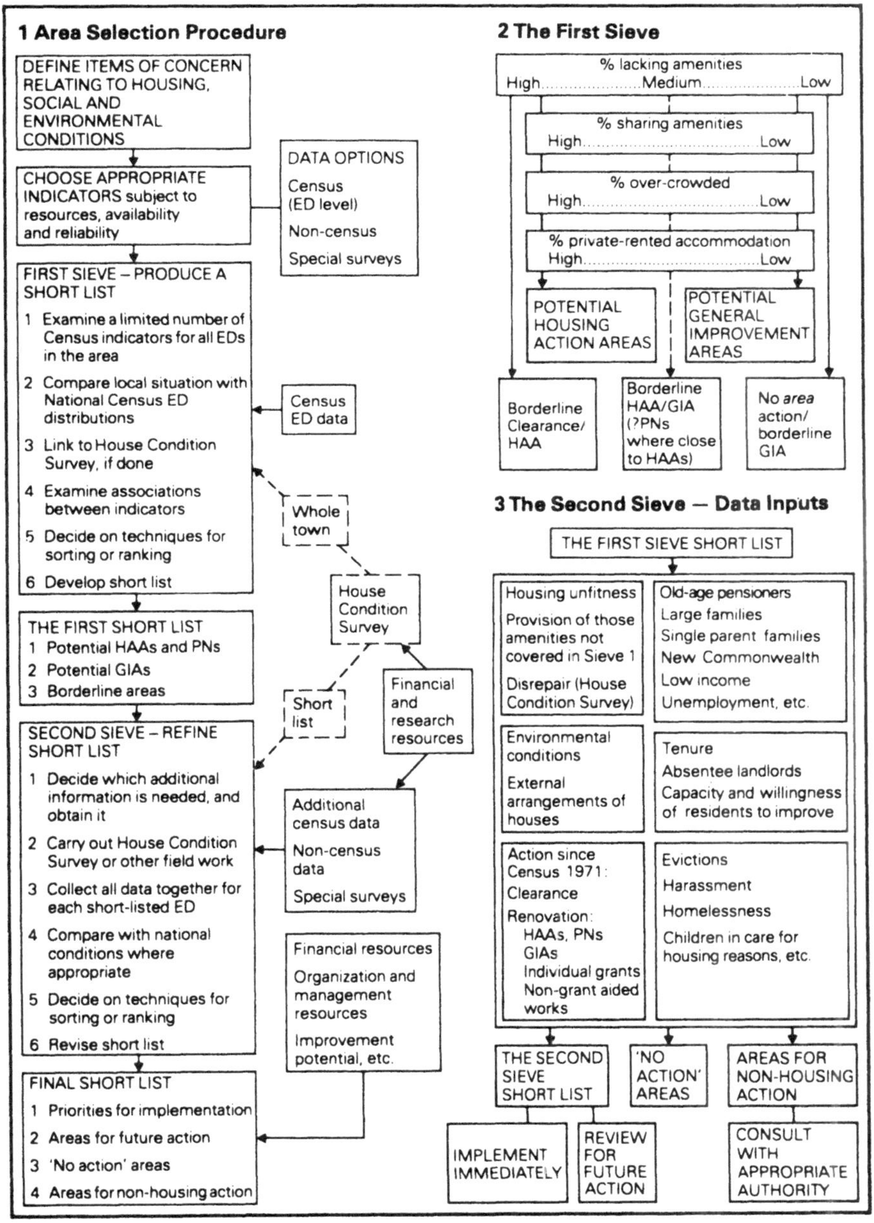

Figure 8 *Selection of areas for special action*

Source: DoE, *The Use of Indicators for Area Action: Housing Act, 1974*, Area Improvement Note 10, pp. 21, 23 and 27 (HMSO 1975)

Figure 8 illustrates the process by which a local authority could identify and declare these special areas. The DoE suggested the use of 1971 Census material, wherever possible linked to a house condition survey, to sift out areas for more detailed investigation. Academic interest in translating concepts of housing and social stress into numerical terms through the use of indicators found its way into government advice.[57] Significantly, criticisms of a somewhat random selection process for GIAs in the 1970s were reflected in a modification to the declaration procedure: DoE approval was now required. Furthermore, HAA declarations could be rescinded by the DoE.

The revised *types of renovation grants* were described in Circular 160/74[58] and are summarized for the different areas in Figure 4, on page 52. Four types of grants now operated though repair grants were only available in HAAs and GIAs. The three major revisions were:

1 preferential levels of grant aid in special areas;
2 grants for repairs only, though only in certain circumstances; and
3 'means-tested' provisions for 90 per cent grants in HAAs and for repairs-only grants in HAAs and GIAs.

Maximum grant levels were raised but then remained constant until 1977.

These new grant arrangements were accompanied by *more stringent grant conditions*, the most important of which are listed below:

1 none of the four types of grant could be given for post-1961 houses;
2 improvement grants could not be given for houses which had previously had one, or for conversion of premises not previously used as a dwelling (e.g. barns), or for second homes;
3 certificates of future occupation: an owner-occupier had to keep the dwelling as his main residence and a landlord to let for 5 years after receiving a grant (7 years in HAA). Local authorities could require all or part of the grant to be repaid (with interest) if this condition was broken;
4 rateable value limit: improvement grants could not be given for owner-occupied houses above a specified rateable value. Until 1977 this was £175, (£300 in Central London) when it was then raised to £225 (£400 in Central London);
5 in an HAA or GIA the local authority had tc ensure that any dwelling tenanted after a grant was let at a registered rent.

In special areas there were revised *compulsory powers*. Procedures for compulsory improvement were strengthened in HAAs and GIAs to enable the local authority to initiate such action for both rented and owner-occupied houses (see Figure 9). Additional powers of compulsory purchase to satisfy one or more of the objectives of HAA declaration were introduced. Authorities were advised to use these in an incremental manner where conditions justified a significant amount of acquisition. While clearance areas were still incompatible with GIA declarations, their use to secure pockets of demolition within HAAs was not precluded.

Changes *in public sector acquisition and improvement subsidies* accompanied

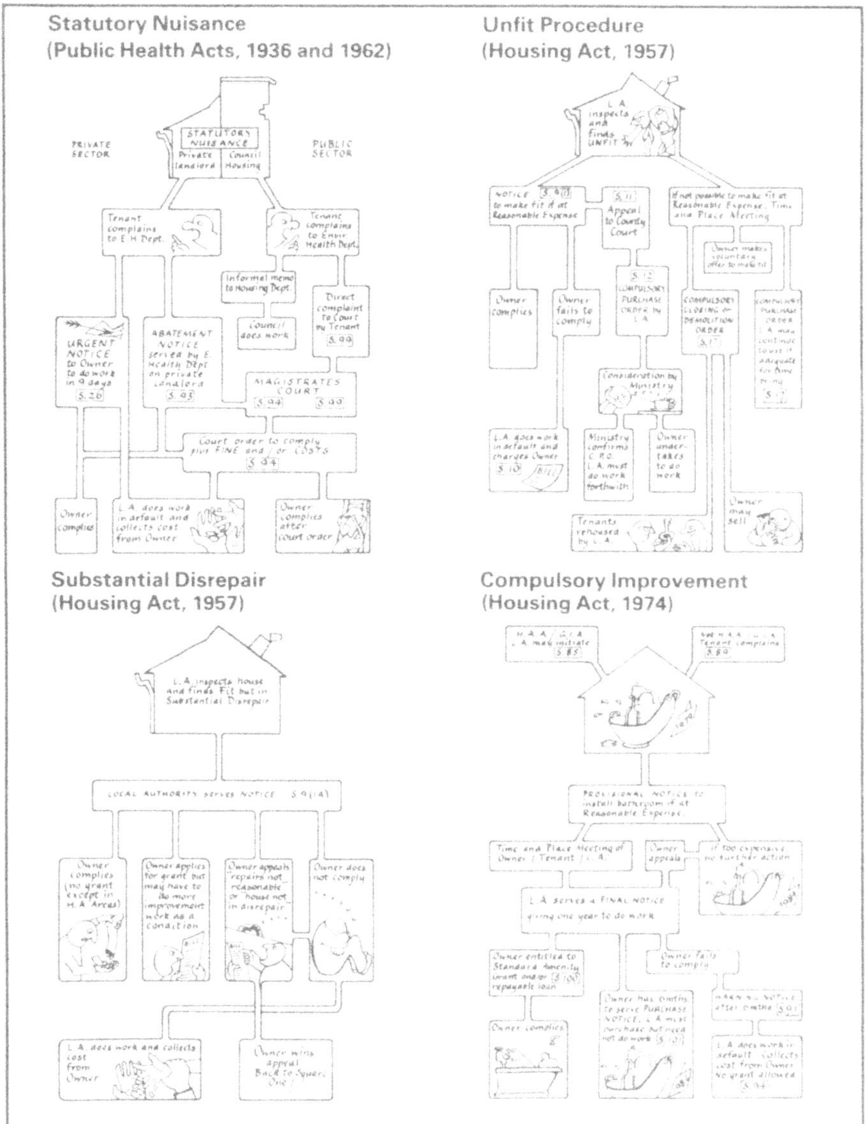

Note: The disrepair procedure for fit houses above has been extended by S. 149 of the Housing Act, 1980. Now there is also an S. 9(1B) procedure which can be initiated if the condition of the property materially interferes with the personal comfort of a tenant.

Figure 9 ***Steps in compulsory repair and improvement***

Source: T. Hadden, *Housing: Repairs and Improvements* (Sweet and Maxwell 1979)

the emphasis on social ownership and were introduced by the Housing Rents and Subsidies Act, 1975 which provided the same proportionate assistance to all forms of local authority housing investment. Local authorities were also given delegated authority to approve their own improvement schemes, provided that they fell within a cost limit system differentiated by region and size of dwelling.

The 1974 Act established the framework for a considerably increased role for housing associations. The Housing Corporation became their controlling body and only registered associations were allowed to borrow money from the Corporation or local authorities and receive government subsidies.[59] With a considerably enhanced budget, it also became their main funding agency. A new system of Housing Association Grant (HAG) replaced all existing subsidies both for new build and improvement – a subsidy which bridges the gap between 'fair rent' income (net of defined management and maintenance costs) and expenditure on repaying loans. The new provisions were accompanied by advice directing associations to stress areas. Although as yet numerically insignificant, housing co-operatives are another form of social ownership.[60] These were encouraged by amendments made to the 1975 Act and, after a government working party report,[61] by the launching of a Co-operative Housing Agency.

Initial reactions

Initial reactions centred on the relative importance of two major issues. First, some critics were concerned with the ambiguity surrounding a further shift of emphasis to improvement at a time of economic stringency, questioning whether this would lead to a vigorous but sensitive renewal or whether it was simply the result of financial expediency. In this debate the scale of the problem and the resources to tackle it were crucial. Second, there was some concern about the adequacy of new powers and, even more, about the capacity of local authorities and other agencies to employ them in an imaginative way.

The first issue was illustrated in an exchange between McKie and Fleetwood. For McKie the advent of gradual renewal was a long overdue and much needed refinement to the process of improving the living conditions of millions of people living in old neighbourhoods.[62] He argued that the new approach had a sound theoretical basis and welcomed the rejection of the simplistic solution of comprehensive redevelopment as the rediscovery of common sense. He approved of the fact that Circular 13/75 'quietly puts down the sacred cow of standards'[63] in favour of a much more flexible approach. On the other hand, the development of official enthusiasm for gradual renewal during an economic recession understandably generated scepticism. As Fleetwood pointed out,[64] while the English Circular 13/75 was not explicit about the way financial constraints modified policy objectives, the parallel circular for Wales was more blunt:

> In the current housing crisis, where there is evidence to suggest that waiting lists . . . are longer than they have been since the war, it will not normally be acceptable to permit houses which are still capable of performing a limited life function to be closed or demolished. Houses must not be abandoned to the bulldozer, unless there is no alternative, while there are families without homes.[65]

It admitted that local authorities must 'buy time' by the maximum use of the existing stock 'bad as much of it is' until thriving building programmes were resurrected. Fleetwood argued that gradual renewal should not become the means of obscuring the extent of the problem and the resources needed to tackle it.

Others voiced the suspicion that the new approach would amount to re-direction of reduced resources.[66] Clearance would be avoided with the result that a backlog of immense proportions would develop. Improvement of better quality dwellings would be cut back, particularly on inter-war council estates with increased central government control over local expenditure. New powers of refusing or vetoing GIA and HAA declarations caused some disquiet. The White Paper preceding the 1974 Act had been described as 'vague and vacuous' on the issue of resources.[67] The circulars which followed it were in a similar vein with references to the possible redirection of spending programmes and staff.

The second issue was the effective use of resources. Would the new tools for area improvement work, were they relevant to the problem faced and would they be used effectively? One argument was that reliance on area-based policies such as HAAs is itself inappropriate. It can lead to the existence of stress areas being attributed to the nature of their residents rather than to the operation of a wider housing market.[68] With limited declarations, all efforts would be devoted to 'privileged' small areas, particularly in London, for whose problems many of the new provisions seemed to have been devised. Yet there are heterogeneous housing functions within areas as well as between them. Many of the worst conditions would inevitably be outside special areas, where there would be a continued reliance on voluntary improvement without higher grant levels (at a time when 75 per cent grants in assisted areas were ending) or repair grants. The worst 3–4 per cent of the nation's housing stock was not conveniently located in identifiable pockets of 200–300 houses. Both within and outside special areas there was little confidence in the use of compulsory improvement powers and there was suspicion about the effectiveness of new CPO powers in HAAs.[69]

Reservations were also expressed about the capacity of local authorities and other agencies to meet the demands of the new approach. McKie claimed that 'the most serious doubt . . . must be whether local authorities are sufficiently sophisticated to match a package demanding detailed and sensitive survey work, resident participation, and corporate planning at the local level'.[70] Others questioned the capacity and desirability of housing associations acting as an arm of local authorities in urban renewal, thereby losing some of their independence and capacity for innovation.[71]

Progress and problems

These related issues of resources and management provide a useful focus for a discussion of the implementation of gradual renewal. At a national level reduced activity soon became apparent. Progress in redirecting priorities and implementing local strategies varied, particularly in HAAs. Nevertheless, overriding all local initiatives was the effect of a deepening economic crisis on both private investment and public expenditure.

Reduced activity

In 'numbers game' terms the 1974–9 period was dismal. As Figure 1 on page 25 indicates, the clearance rate showed a sharp fall in 1974 and, although it rose again briefly, by 1979 it had dropped to 33,000, the lowest total since 1955. Initially this was the result of reductions or postponements in representation programmes when council building rates fell during 1971–3. Subsequently the effect of decisions made since 1974 became apparent in demolition figures and the number of houses in confirmed clearance CPOs fell to 23,000 by 1979. Although housebuilding performance initially improved, by 1979 completions had fallen to 212,000 (93,000 public) while starts were well below this at 198,000 (72,000 public).

Figure 5 on page 56 shows the collapse of the improvement programme. Renovation grants plummetted from their 1973 peak of 361,000 to 127,000 in 1975 to rise again slightly to 136,000 by 1979. Grants to private owners slumped from 238,000 to 66,000 within these totals. The trend towards higher unit standards of improvement continued (by 1979 only 7 per cent of all grant approvals were for intermediate or special grants) but the decline in grant approvals resulted in a massive decrease in the volume of grant-aided investment. Between 1973 and 1975 alone it fell by 60 per cent in real terms[72] and this downward trend continued.

Initially, the policies introduced by the new Government had a marked impact on the rate of municipalization. In 1974–5 local authorities purchased 26,000 houses from the private sector (although some were under the temporary provisions enabling them to buy new unsold houses). Acquisitions then fell to 10,000 by 1977–8. The encouragement given to housing associations had a more sustained effect and their acquisition and improvement activity expanded rapidly. By 1979 grant approvals were 19,000 (four times their 1973 level). At first, this activity was concentrated in London and some other large cities where associations had established themselves in the early 1970s: subsequently it became much more widespread.

HAAs were the major innovation in area improvement powers. As might be

Table 4 *GIA and HAA declarations 1969 to 1979 (England and Wales)*

Year	*GIAs*			*HAAs*		
	Areas	*Houses*	*Total grants completed*	*Areas*	*Houses*	*Total grants completed*
1969	30	8,235	27			
1970	108	33,982	1,119			
1971	194	57,648	2,300			
1972	274	89,028	7,271			
1973	233	60,174	15,143			
1974	67	30,152	12,968			
1969–74	906	279,220	38,828			
1975	54	17,865	11,011	78	26,316	189
1976	114	29,217	7,255	119	41,537	1,346
1977	71	23,779	5,359*	75	23,652	4,320*
1978	78	22,626	10,850*	112	35,793	8,545*
1979	70	30,188	10,856*	65	26,406	7,289*
1975–9	387	123,675	45,331	449	153,704	21,689
Totals	1,293	410,006	84,159	449	153,704	21,689

Sources: *Housing and Construction Statistics* (HMSO) and **Local Housing Statistics* (HMSO).

expected, most were in the major conurbations, but an examination of declaration reports reveals that a diverse range of conditions were accepted by central government as justifying declaration.[73] They were not restricted to the high-pressure areas of London and other large cities. Significantly, over two thirds of the first HAAs were areas which had previously been affected by blight.[74] Both national statistics and detailed progress reports reveal that progress in private improvement was minimal, particularly in London.[75] Very few privately rented houses were improved. Action on compulsory improvement or compulsory purchase was not significant, while delays in improving houses actually acquired by local authorities was heavily criticized. As Table 4 indicates, GIA declarations fell markedly. GIAs were more significant in smaller towns outside the major conurbations. Nearly 60 per cent of houses needing improvement in GIAs remained unimproved, and in many areas environmental works showed little sign of being completed.

Local strategies

The 1974 Act marked the major turning point in the preparation of local renewal strategies and the documents which emerged can be examined with reference to the three key elements of the new approach.[76]

At this stage renewal strategies were not usually set within a framework of *comprehensive housing policies* but concentrated on programmes of special area declarations. The 1971 Census was invariably used as the basic data source for an initial quantitative assessment of conditions. Choice of indices generally followed the statutory requirements for information to be presented in declaration reports with variations in the degree of sophistication claimed for the house condition surveys which complemented them. Little use was made of data generated by past renewal activity or by the day-to-day functions of service departments. These sources exist for a wide variety of operations (e.g. renovation grants, homelessness cases, social services clients or rent allowances) but are often difficult to analyse on an area basis. Local authorities usually deferred incorporating a systematic analysis of residents' views until implementation began, when it was claimed that adjustments could be made to reflect the results of both detailed local survey work and the development of public involvement. The common element in renewal strategies was a phased programme of GIA and HAA declarations. Priority Neighbourhoods, with their lack of improvement 'teeth', were almost totally ignored. The variation lay in the way in which different local authorities coped with uncertainty about future levels of resources and courses of action once experience developed.

Most local strategies accepted an emphasis on *gradual renewal* in so far as improvement proposals were seen as the backbone of the area approach. Advice that only houses beyond renovation should be redeveloped was reflected in reduced clearance: limited short-term programmes (five to eight years) were the only firm commitments, and the individual areas involved were usually small, representing the residue of earlier programmes. Local strategies were decidedly less specific about 'continuous minor rebuilding' in the medium term: open-ended 'as the need arises' statements being commonplace with later clearance to be related to the impact of improvement programmes. There was often an uncritical acceptance of selective clearance and infill redevelopment, without an adequate analysis of its applicability to different nineteenth century built environments.

Local authorities were encouraged to treat clearance in this manner by DoE interpretations of the new approach. Apart from the limited use of temporary provisions in the 1974 Act to allow councils to change their mind after CPOs had been made and instead pursue rehabilitation orders, the changed climate had its major impact on the initiation of action in new areas. With the dismissal of large-scale clearance as an outmoded form of treatment and the encouragement of HAAs as alternative, local authorities reduced representations. Action groups and anti-clearance councillors often sharply reminded them that 'in declaring a clearance area . . . local authorities will have to establish . . . that a housing action declaration is not more appropriate'.[77]

Reliance on intuitive assessments of the need for clearance was under challenge at public inquiries and, although official DoE advice on economic techniques for the evaluation of renewal options was lengthily delayed,[78] local authorities were aware that more rigorous cases would have to be made.[79]

There was some evidence of progress in the direction of a *corporate approach*. Strategy documents implicitly recognized the extent to which entrenched departmentalism and lack of co-ordination bedevilled past activity. A variety of formal organizational structures was established, ranging from full-time area renewal teams with a diversity of skills to small core groups backed up by permanent or temporary secondment from relevant departments. The need for a presence in special areas was emphasized, the development of widespread public involvement proposed, and continuous monitoring promised. Local authorities frequently recognized the importance of relating housing intervention to planning briefs, but there was little sign of more ambitious area management approaches.

Implementation

It was within a common framework of opportunities and constraints provided by the 1974 legislation that local authorities reformulated their local strategies. Perhaps differences in style of implementation and in the vigour with which it pursued justified doubts about managerial competence? As implementation developed some aspects of these local strategies were adapted in the light of experience.

Relatively little attention was given to refining the clearance process. Ironically, national policy guidelines dismissing clearance meant that pioneering initiatives in community-based redevelopment had less influence than would otherwise have been the case.

GIA implementation benefited from the criticisms raised about organizational requirements in the early 1970s and the advice given on establishing priorities and realistic programming.[80] However, at the same time problems of co-ordinating environmental work increased. The reorganization of local government in 1974 into a two-tier system meant a division of responsibilities between District and County Councils, with the former being responsible for GIA implementation but the latter being highway authorities. Particularly in those district authorities without agency agreements for GIA highway works, there was ample scope for frustrating duplication of effort, disagreements over priorities and endless consultation. The establishment of Regional Water Authorities had a similar effect.

However, it is in HAAs that the managerial capacity of local authorities is being most severely tested. By 1979 pessimism was rife about HAAs as a focus of intense activity. This pessimism was not universal. Implementation in some areas indicates that an energetic approach can produce results.[81] Five key issues can be identified.

First, HAAs are staff intensive. A DoE sponsored study of one of the first London HAAs identified the need for a large staff input into the multi-disciplinary project team for just one area.[82] Experience in all areas shows that the clear definition of responsibilities in staff organization and the injection of a local presence with area offices means that action is likely to be accelerated and more related to the wishes of residents.[83]

Second, action in relation to the privately rented sector is crucial. Use of compulsory improvement powers is unlikely to achieve either speedy or significant results for these powers are lengthy, time-consuming and hazardous. In the relatively low-pressure HAAs of Newcastle the local authority were successful in using the Repair Notices of the 1957 Act, combined with offers of grant aid or 'voluntary' sale to the council or a housing association.[84] In a high-pressure HAA in the London Borough of Islington CPO powers against landlords who failed to improve their properties and harassed tenants were used with marked success soon after declaration.[85]

Third, innovation in assisting low-income owner-occupiers can have some impact. A generous interpretation of eligibility for 90 per cent grants in cases of financial hardship; packages combining grants, mortgages and improvement loans; and the provision of comprehensible information (including where appropriate translation into Asian languages) were used to some effect by particular authorities. Agency schemes for handling private owners' improvements, and thereby reducing administrative burdens and strengthening building contract supervision, were further developed by a limited number of councils.[86]

Fourth, the capabilities of the housing associations nominated for particular HAAs and the relationship between them and local authorities are important. In an increasing number of authorities HAAs became the focus of intense rehabilitation work by associations and sophisticated programming for decanting and the letting of building contracts, a local presence and clear lines of communication with the council and residents all became essential. In Liverpool, for instance, associations became the main implementation agency for the HAA programme, with an agreed zoning system between them and transfer of unimproved properties to their ownership after compulsory purchase by the City Council. The integration of buying, rehabilitation and housing management on an area basis here and in other cities provided a responsive service that few local authorities could match, although progress was slowed by an irritating system of dual technical scrutiny of individual schemes by both the DoE and the Housing Corporation. As the role of housing associations increased their accountability became a central issue.[87]

Fifth, HAAs can succeed in involving local residents if effective action is combined with an open approach. Almost all local authorities improved their basic publicity measures with leaflets, meetings, exhibitions, show houses of typical improvements and local newspapers playing their part. Others went much further. Islington, for instance, created joint committees between local residents and the council, and, despite some major disagreements, their meetings have been invaluable in sharing information, monitoring progress and tackling delays.[88] In some areas, notably Islington again and Liverpool, tenants have been brought together in co-operatives.[89]

Resource problems

While local initiative and managerial competence is obviously an important factor in the effective use of resources, the impact of local renewal strategies has been more significantly affected by the level of resources available. In essence, this stems from the intrinsic character of local strategies as improvement partnerships, involving intervention in the complexity of the private housing market. Chapter 3 analysed the operation of the housing market in older housing areas and the constraints on any policy concentrating on area improvement. These constraints were reinforced by severe resource problems, and the vulnerability of the new approach became fully apparent.

The strategies depended on a substantial level of both private resources invested in older housing and of public resources made available by central government. 1974–9 was characterized by a decline in both these inputs[90] which can usefully be assessed by reference to:

1 social ownership;
2 private investment;
3 clearance and housebuilding; and
4 environmental and social programmes.

Social ownership was a key element of the policy. The Expenditure Review Committee had earlier commented that all the evidence submitted suggested that the introduction of the 1974 Act's proposals would result in only limited voluntary improvement by landlords.[91] Yet, after a brief flurry of activity, municipalization lost its momentum. The crucial factor was the imposition of cash limits and restrictive spending criteria by central government. The use of Section 105 of the Housing Act, 1974 was the first illustration of the contradiction between declared policies and the resources made available to carry them out. It introduced a requirement for local authorities to have central government approval for any expenditure on improvement to their own housing stock, both purpose-built and acquired. The use of this new power in 1975–6 resulted in a one-third cut in expenditure in real terms. Overall expenditure has been tightly controlled ever since.

The smoke-screen created around this measure was the need to shift resources from the improvement of inter-war council estates, where many houses already have basic amenities, to private houses acquired by councils and in a worse condition.[92] But, while redirection of effort may well have been desirable, in some areas low allocations under Section 105 had very serious implications. Most obviously, continued neglect of obsolescent council estates threatened to store up a massive problem for the next decade.[93] The deterioration of such estates had long been evident, but there was also a growing realization of the need for significant expenditure on more recent council housing, particularly some of the 'system-built failures' of the 1960s. Moreover, it was not just a question of redirection but of reduced resources being redirected in what seemed to many local authorities to be an arbitrary way. There was little evidence of initial DoE allocations being directed to authorities with substantial acquisition programmes. The fate of widespread municipalization was sealed as the improvement of acquired houses was delayed and the Government restricted acquisions to HAAs, GIAs and Priority Neighbourhoods, and houses which had stood empty for more than six months.[94] Cash limits were imposed on the scale of purchases undertaken. In this situation housing association acquisition became more important.

Private investment in older housing areas is a concrete expression of the improvement partnership and was highlighted as a key element in many local strategies. That such investment would be forthcoming was always doubtful. To expect rehabilitation to be funded from the private resources of those living in the worst housing conditions is itself hardly a recipe for success. When the selection of areas for intensive action, HAAs in particular, rests on indices of poor housing conditions and social stress, the question of whether or not low-income owner-occupiers can afford improvement is critical.

The difficulty of grant take-up was compounded by stagnating or falling real incomes, rising unemployment and escalating improvement costs in these years. Between 1975 and 1977 average total costs per improved unit rose by over 50 per cent from £2350 to £3610, with the share devoted to repairs and replacements rising most,[95] but maximum grant levels remained static.

A further contradiction in some areas was the £175 rateable value limit. A special allowance of £300 was made for London, but the implication was that 'everywhere else north of Watford is very much the same'. As Chapter 7 shows, houses in renewal programmes and occupied by low-income owners were excluded in some cities. In 1977 both eligible expense and rateable value limits were increased but the real value of the former had been eroded again by continuing inflation in costs by 1979. While studies have shown that there is still considerable scope for achieving some results in increasing grant take-up by minimizing 'red-tape' and maximizing promotional activity,[96] the central problem of low incomes and high costs in areas most in need of investment is less amenable to local action.

The availability of mortgages is also important in encouraging private investment and creating confidence in older housing areas. During the mid-1970s there was mounting evidence of building societies operating 'red-lining' practices in a formal or informal way. They excluded whole areas from normal lending, aggravating housing stress and frustrating improvement policies.[97] Their commercial role, particularly 'the need to retain investors' confidence' meant a self-fulfilling prophecy ensuring decay.[98] At the same time local authorities' role as 'lenders of last resort' was further undermined by central government restrictions.[99] These cuts were accompanied by nebulous government agreements with the building society movement and the claim that the area of overlap between local authority and building society lending was considerable. Notwithstanding some local success stories with the hastily established 'support scheme', societies did not substantially increase their overall commitment to older areas and low-income applicants.

Clearance and housebuilding. Chapter 2 has shown how the existence of a vigorous clearance drive was dependent on the provision of replacement housing. Building by councils has for many years been a test of Labour Governments' political virility in housing policy. Controls over the council housebuilding rate were the final piece in a dismal jigsaw of expenditure cuts when in 1976 an immediate freeze was announced on all letting of contracts.[100] This short-term measure was then followed by a new form of control designed to concentrate new building in 'stress areas' identified by the Government.

Environmental and social programmes were from the outset portrayed as essential complements to housing measures. No formal cuts were made in subsidy limits for environmental schemes in GIAs and HAAs, but neither were they increased to take account of inflation: to maintain their real value GIA environmental grants should have been about £600 per dwelling by 1979. A wider perspective is more significant since a series of rate support grant settlements reduced expenditure on the capital programmes associated with environmental improvement, e.g. traffic management. Restraints on staffing levels and revenue budgets not only discouraged innovation in establishing social programmes in stress areas, they also meant the reduction of normal 'civic housekeeping', e.g. street cleansing.

Housing policy between 1974 and 1977 was dominated by these confusing *ad hoc* cuts in spending and an extension of central government control. Table 5 indicates the changes in the various components of public expenditure on housing. What were the overall implications for the renewal strategies of local authorities?

First, government by 'circular, telephone and leak' not only restricted resources, it diverted effort from implementation.[101] As alterations in the rules of the game were made virtually on a monthly basis, staff resources were eaten up by continuous adjustments to programmes, attempts to find ways around a particular measure, or making appeals to central government for a change of heart because of local circumstances. Cuts were especially resented when they led to the abandonment of a policy, only to be followed by a minor reinstatement of finance to aid the beleaguered construction industry, on the assumption that action could immediately be resumed.

Second, they led to increased resentment about the regional distribution of

Table 5 *Public expenditure on housing 1974–5, 1976–7 and 1979–80*

	£m at 1979 survey prices		
	1974–5	*1976–7*	*1979–80*
Current expenditure			
Mortgage interest tax relief	1322	1411	1450
Option mortgage subsidy	150	196	193
Public sector subsidies			
Central government subsidies to local authorities, new towns and SSHA	1250	1522	1619
Rate fund contribution to local authority housing	350	264	349
Housing association revenue deficit grants	14	21	22
Rent rebates and allowances	492	526	560
Administration	68	80	85
Total	2175	2413	2635
Total current expenditure	3647	4020	4278
Capital expenditure			
Local authorities			
Land and new dwellings	1655	1995	1076
Acquisitions	450	141	51
Improvement	644	509	720
Other	102	109	69
Total	2851	2754	1916
New towns and SSHA	264	318	197
Housing associations			
Loans and grants from local authorities	201	276	154
Loans and grants from Housing Corporation	185	360	416
Total	386	636	570
Assistance to private sector			
Improvement grants	313	102	130
Lending for house purchase and improvement	1096	281	265
Total	1409	383	395
Sales and repayments	-312	-433	-530
Other	231	-4	-3
Total capital expenditure	4829	3653	2544
Total current and capital	8476	7673	6822

Source: Adapted from *The Government's Expenditure Plans 1980–1 to 1983–4* Cmnd. 7841, Table 2.7, pp. 66–8 and p. 184. Mortgage interest tax relief figures for 1974–5 and 1976–7 are taken from Cmnd. 7439, revalued to 1979 survey prices in accordance with p. 198, para. 31.

spending allocations. Despite a government study group's recommendation that the North, North-West and Yorkshire and Humberside regions should receive more of the money allocated for improvement,[102] the political influence of London boroughs appeared to ensure that those local authorities furthest from London got least.[103]

Third, the cuts were accompanied by claims from councils that the new approach was designed to rescue houses from the bulldozer but that the necessary funds to do this were being denied. The giving of powers on the one (DoE) hand and the witholding of resources on the other (Treasury) hand spawned scepticism about the Government's intentions. In Manchester, for instance, shortly after announcing the end of clearance and the start of a massive area improvement programme, the Chairman of the Housing Committee was forecasting that the 'bulldozer must come back'.[104] The policy initiative of 1974 was now obviously one of reduced renewal. Comments such as:

> The end of the 1970s will probably see as many people living in slums as at the beginning. The difference is that they will be in 'improvement areas' and surrounded by derelict sites that local authorities have cleared but can't afford to build on.[105]

were not restricted to radical critics.

Housing policy review

The backcloth to this day-to-day juggling of finance was a prolonged exercise in reviewing the general direction of housing policy. The conclusions of this review were the basis of a further debate on the future of housing renewal.

The need for reform

Until the mid-1970s central government's role in determining the local pattern of housing expenditure was largely through indirect controls. By adjusting or refusing to adjust rates of subsidy or more specific controls such as the housing cost yardstick, it could accelerate or slow down activity.

Even before the 1974 Government the trend was for expenditure on subsidies to rise with no comparable growth in investment.[106] Subsidies towards households had become the implicit priority rather than capital expenditure on additional housing. The 1974–7 period exacerbated this trend as capital programmes were hardest hit by cuts.

Between the two general elections of 1974 the Labour Government's 'honeymoon period' saw a sharp rise in total subsidies from £2700m in 1973–4 to £3500m in 1974–5. Council housebuilding and municipalization both increased, but the main reasons for this expenditure were rapid inflation and, to some extent, financial measures designed to ameliorate its effects. Council housing subsidies rose dramatically because of the effect that a high rate of inflation has on the time pattern of loan repayments for existing debts. Increased building costs and the effects of the temporary rent freeze also played a part.[107]

The outcome was that while local government struggled with the implications of hastily imposed cuts, central government portrayed the situation as one of curbs on overspending. Ministers were making 'I see no cuts' statements not just because their telescopes were put to blind eyes but because, initially at least, overall public expenditure on housing had dramatically increased.

This trend was one major outcome of a muddled system of housing finance. Its other obvious outcome was the way in which subsidies went in greatest proportion to those who needed them least. The clearest example of this is mortgage tax relief which increases with the size of the mortgage and encourages 'over-consumption': it disproportionately benefits the richest households. Subsidies to council housing did not adequately reflect differences in costs between local authorities, while the proportion of council housing costs covered by rent income at a national level fell from 72 per cent in 1972–3 to 55 per cent in 1975–6. Equity in housing finance, both between the two main sectors and within them, was conspicuous by its absence.[108]

This was the background to the housing policy review. Crosland had argued for some time that the system of housing finance was riddled with anomalies and inconsistencies.[109] The 'dog's breakfast' it had become was in need of radical reform. During his period in office he maintained his insistence on the need for coherent policies and set up a review of housing finance (later to be housing policy) in 1974. The review was designed to answer three key questions:

1 how much housing do we need and how can our resources best be used to get it?
2 how much should individuals pay for their housing?
3 what are the wider social implications of the way in which we organize our housing?[110]

The overriding aim would be to create a rational housing policy.

An earlier review of housing finance had been started by Crossman under the previous Labour Government but when they lost office the outcome was the Conservative's Housing Finance Act, 1972. Its central feature was provision for determining council rents by reference to the 'fair rents' concept previously confined to the private rented sector. Local authorities lost their freedom to set their own rents and the higher rents which ensued would be offset for those on low incomes by rent rebates. This reform left untouched the system of subsidy to owner-occupiers through tax relief and was bitterly contested, not just because of the actual measure introduced, but also in terms of the ideology of housing it represented.[111] The Housing Rents and Subsidies Act, 1975 was a temporary measure designed to fulfil the Labour Government's commitment to abolishing the 1972 Act and enable local authorities to maintain a higher rate of investment. Any more fundamental reform would await this overall review: it would deal with all tenures, not just council housing.

The system of housing finance is obviously critical for urban renewal policies. Rates of subsidy closely influence the nature and scale of its component elements.

The Green Paper

A wealth of evidence was submitted by interested organizations during the preparation of the review.[112] But, by the time it was completed in 1977, Shore, Crosland's successor, was in no mood for radical reform, not wanting to repeat the one-sided 1972 Housing Finance Act and wary of upsetting the owner-occupier and aspiring purchaser.

The basic assumption underlying the Green Paper was that housing problems are residual and of manageable proportions. A crude overall shortage of housing no longer exists and present arrangements are broadly satisfactory:

> We and our colleagues believe that we should adopt a more selective and discerning approach to housing policy – one which will ensure that the most pressing housing needs of individuals and areas are tackled effectively and urgently, while at the same time making it easier for more people . . . to get the kind of home they want. But we certainly do not believe that the household budgets of millions of families – which had been planned in good faith in the reasonable expectation that present arrangements would broadly continue – should be overturned in the pursuit of some theoretical or academic dogma.[113]

It was in this context that the Green Paper answered Crosland's three key questions.[114]

The first question on *housing needs and resources* was largely ignored. Hidden away in a technical annexe were forecasts which 'are not policy statements of any kind'.[115] They suggested that a 1976 estimate of 2.8m households in unsatisfactory housing might be reduced to 720,000 by 1986. Projections were based on an average total building rate of 175,000 houses p.a. while demolitions were expected to average 40,000 p.a. in 1977–81, thereafter falling to 35,000. Given the lack of targets for housing production it is not surprising that future levels of investment were also ignored. The central issue of an inability to meet both high existing subsidies to households and increased investment to create better standards was thus conveniently obscured.

It had to be obscured because of Shore's answer to the second question on the *level of subsidies to housing and their distribution*. The paper concluded that any attempt to compare the subsidies received by owner-occupiers and tenants is sterile. More radical solutions were excluded[116] and the structural weaknesses of housing finance perpetuated. The present system of tax relief remained for owner-occupiers (and was even endorsed as a counter to a progressive tax system). The only change quickly put into legislation was a limited scheme of assistance for first-time buyers. In the council sector a new deficit subsidy was proposed, to be linked to the principle that rents would rise roughly in line with average earnings.

Crosland's third question on *the social implications of the way housing is organized* received the fullest treatment. A host of recommendations were made about reforms of management and allocation policies in the public sector, co-operatives and intermediate forms of tenure. However, the virtues of owner-occupation as the 'natural' form of tenure were strongly endorsed and the public sector referred to almost apologetically, chiefly as catering for special needs. While reinforcing the Labour Party's move away from a belief in the positive values of council housing, little comment was made about the control of financial institutions engaged in private housing, e.g. building societies' lending in the inner city.

Housing investment programmes

Although the main thrust of future housing programmes was not to be based on the public sector, local authorities were given a new strategic responsibility for housing. The new role was provided by the introduction of Housing Investment Programmes (HIPs) which had been debated during the preparation of this review. Cullingworth, for instance, had suggested that:

> The duties of local authorities should be redefined to require them to produce comprehensive housing strategies. They would submit to central government annually a review of their housing situation, the steps they propose to take to meet identified needs, and the resources necessary to enable them to do so.[117]

In the early 1970s the argument that local authorities should have a wider role than simply building and administering council houses had gained credence. The concept of a comprehensive approach, utilizing a variety of agencies and powers, was promulgated. Moreover, the discovery of a crude housing surplus rendered more attractive the view that we no longer have a national housing problem but rather a series of local problems.

HIPs grew out of such arguments. They were also the culmination of the pattern of *ad hoc* cash limits on individual programmes introduced in the 1974–7 period. In essence, they are a much more sophisticated form of control over total public expenditure on housing, while at the same time giving local authorities more flexibility in determining their own priorities. Compartmentalized arrangements were replaced with the stated aim to '. . . increase the freedom of local authorities to do the job as they think best within parameters agreed with central government; and . . . end the distortions and niggling interferences of the present financial régime.'[118]

The idea of HIPs is that each local authority should make a comprehensive assessment of its housing needs and then formulate proposals to deal with them by a rolling programme of expenditure under various categories.[119] An embryonic version was introduced for 1977–8[120] and then a more fully developed system for succeeding years.[121] Submissions were required in three parts:

1 the local strategy statement;
2 an appraisal form containing data on housing needs; and
3 the local 'bid' – an investment programme.

The HIP system now encouraged more effective capital programming and focussed attention on the resource requirements of renewal policies within a comprehensive housing strategy.

In practice, local authorities overbid by about 50 per cent for 1978–9 (that is in relation to the total spending to be allowed, not necessarily in relation to local needs),[122] and although allocations for 1979–80 were partly diverted to inner city areas, initial criticism of the system focussed on its generation of 'more and more freedom to spend less and less'. While the introduction of HIPs marked the end of *ad hoc* cuts in spending programmes, many categories of investment continued to fall. A reduction in new housebuilding was only partly offset by a switch of emphasis back to the improvement of local authority housing in these years. The teething problems of the new system, delays in making allocations, and the lack of continuity inherent in annual rather than multi-year allocations, combined with Conservative control of many cities in the late 1970s to ensure underspending.

Housing Bill

Other proposals in the Green Paper were further developed in a series of consultation papers during 1978 and then appeared in a Housing Bill introduced by Labour in 1979. This contained a package of legal rights for public sector tenants including greater security, rights to carry out improvements and receive grants, and become involved in management. It also required local authorities to publish their allocation schemes and introduced measures to assist mobility. Further measures were designed to enable local authorities to encourage owner-occupation; to introduce a new system of subsidies for council housing; to provide revised arrangements for housing association rents; and to amend the law relating to leasehold houses. 'The Tenants Charter lies at the heart of the Bill' claimed the Labour Government[123] and it was this package which formed the focus of most public debate:[124] in the general election campaign of 1979 it was in competition with Conservative proposals for massive council house sales.

This Bill fell with the Labour Government but many of its provisions, with the addition of the 'right to buy', reappeared in the Conservative Bill later in the year (for discussion see Chapter 9). Labour's proposals for the renovation grant system prompted a resumed debate about the requirements of an effective housing renewal policy: they emanated from the 1976 Housing Condition Surveys' findings, were outlined in the Green Paper and detailed in a later consultation paper.[125] The surveys indicated that the number of unfit houses had fallen from 1.2m in 1971 to 900,000. There had been a parallel downward trend in the number of houses which, while fit, lack one or more of the basic amenities, from 1.8m in 1971 to 980,000. However, they also revealed a substantial increase in the number of houses requiring extensive repairs. In 1971 some 720,000 needed repair work exceeding a cost of £1000; five years later nearly half as many again needed an equivalent amount of expenditure (£2350).[126] Most of the houses in severe disrepair were in private ownership almost equally divided between owner-occupiers and private landlords. The Green Paper commented: 'without effective measures we shall see the growth of a new generation of slums'[127] and raised possible changes.

The consultation paper stated the case for a change of emphasis 'in order to direct a greater proportion of the available resources to bring the worst of the improvable houses up to a decent standard of amenity and a sound state of repair'.[128] The official view was that major changes in improvement powers would be premature: the proposals were not 'intended to take the place of a full examination of present improvement policies and programmes. Such an examination must, of necessity, wait until the area improvement programmes introduced by the 1974 Act have had sufficient time to make an impact.'[129]

Detailed measures presented in Labour's Bill were essentially a consolidation of the 1974 approach. They included: the extension of repair grants; making grants available to public and private tenants; increased flexibility in the grant system; improvement for sale by local authorities; and increasing the scope of environmental works qualifying for grant in HAAs and contributions to GIA environmental works. Most measures reflected increasing concern with the lack of progress among owner-occupiers – an important departure from the original conception that privately rented properties in stress areas was the key issue.

There was a widespread view that the proposals would not take us far fast enough – cleaning the plugs is not much help when a new engine is needed.[130] The absence of firm proposals to substantially increase grants, simplify compulsory improvement procedures and overhaul grant administration generated criticism. In the most forceful statement the Association of Metropolitan Authorities (AMA) advocated 'bold new measures'.[131] Many organizations came together to submit joint views on the inadequacy of the proposals.[132] This detailed debate about powers and procedures reflected growing unease about the impact of improvement-dominated renewal strategies.

Shifting views

The late 1970s saw a widening gulf between the continuing complacency of central government and the declining credibility of its policies.[133] Criticism became increasingly pointed, and concern is now reflected in shifting views about three key propositions which have been prominent in policy debates since the mid-1960s:

1 *Improvement is quicker and cheaper than redevelopment.* In practice, not only has the overall level of improvement slumped, but the comprehensive improvement of significant areas is taking far longer than initially anticipated. It is now a decade since the introduction of GIAs, but the number 'completed' is miniscule. Since 1974 mean street after mean street has been withdrawn from clearance programmes and included in HAAs. Less reliant on voluntary improvement, HAAs are providing a more appropriate device for comprehensive action and have had considerable impact in some areas, but more commonly progress has been patchy. In virtually all HAAs and many GIAs the housing has remained in unchanged and outworn environments. By 1979 it was clear that few HAAs would be completed within the five- to seven-year period specified.[134] Moreover, in accordance with government advice, most local authorities had used GIAs and HAAs selectively, although problems are widespread. A low rate of declaration means that many areas in need of positive action have yet to get into the pipeline.

   In crude unit cost terms improvement is still usually cheaper than redevelopment. This sways the balance of economic advantage in its favour, particularly when interest rates remain high. But these factors are beginning to be countered by the incorporation of more realistic repair and maintenance costs and doubts about the assumption of a thirty-year life. Few now believe that improvement is the cheap alternative it was once thought to be, particularly if environmental work is taken into account. In recent years analytical techniques for determining the best value for money on an area basis have been refined, but have had little influence on local renewal strategies. Elaborate exercises to determine appropriate levels of investment for a particular area have appeared decreasingly relevant, when the mechanisms for deriving the finance have imposed severe limitations on achievement. The fact that many owners cannot afford their share of the costs has meant that improvement relying on an investment partnership has obviously been much cheaper for the state. The comment by CDP that 'it has to be cheaper primarily because it is cheaper to improve a few houses than redevelop a whole area'[135] reflects the way in which gradual renewal has been condemned to reduced renewal: it is cheaper because it is ineffective. Gradual renewal has not been approached with the same vigour as comprehensive redevelopment was a decade ago.

2 *Improved houses are an adequate alternative to new build.* While slogans such as 'old houses into new homes' and 'as good as new' have never been taken literally, there has always been the implication that the quality difference is insignificant. The surging tide of opinion in favour of a shift

to improvement swept aside the concern, voiced by a dissenting minority in the late 1960s, that this would result in second-class homes. This concern has re-emerged, influenced by failures to adequately increase cost limits for grants in both the private and public sectors, the consequent erosion of standards[136] and the perpetuation of second-class environments. Moreover, improvement was compared with high-rise schemes in the 1960s: it is now contrasted with more imaginative infill schemes built by local authorities and housing associations. The limitations imposed by the built form of older housing – be it back-to-backs, Tyneside flats, byelaw terraces, or large villas which may be difficult to 'naturally' convert – are increasingly recognized.

3 *Improvement is more sensitive to the needs and wishes of residents.* A central theme has been that much reduced relocation, uncertainty, delay and blight would 'preserve the community'. The simplistic assumption of tightly-knit stable communities in all older housing areas still persists in some quarters, but the complexities of changing neighbourhood social structures are now more often acknowledged. Moreover, to the extent that there are localities where attachment to an area is strong and should be taken into account, improvement in practice is not as straightforward as it appeared in prospect. Many areas where there has been significant improvement have seen substantial changes in tenure patterns, as private rented property has passed into owner-occupation or social ownership. While change of ownership does not necessarily mean change of occupant, it is likely that there has been an increase in the rate of population turnover. Many will have welcomed moving, but new neighbours may be viewed less than enthusiastically by those who remain and the proportion of unwilling movers is simply not known. The sensitive management of such change is far more demanding than was often assumed at the outset.[137] Many of those who improved their houses found the process stressful, as they had to cope with complex bureaucratic procedures and difficulties with builders. In the common situation of piecemeal improvement in areas of poor-quality houses, this anxiety may be fuelled by the absence of environmental improvement, an impression that the local authority is keeping its options open, and the blighting effect of building society lending policies. Decisions to declare areas without a commitment of adequate resources is tantamount to a policy of benign neglect reminiscent of the early stages of comprehensive redevelopment, and may have similar consequences, as those who have the opportunity to leave the area do so.

Another aspect of 'giving the people what they want' was that, in contrast to the unacceptable financial costs imposed by redevelopment, improvement could be tailored to residents' means by the use of flexible standards. However, given the present pattern of income inequality, subsidy arrangements and legislation, second-class homes and environments are a continuing reality for 'second-class people'. Avoiding the removal of a low-rent neighbourhood which 'performs a vital function in the social fabric and economy' or the implementation of environmental improvements, 'which often seem designed to implant middle-class conceptions of "amenity" on working-class populations that do not see the need for it', may meet the current aspirations of some of the 'housing poor'.[138] Yet such approaches are not far removed from the *laissez-faire* concepts of the last century: they relate to residents' means but not necessarily to their needs.

The first two of these propositions relate to physical (housing stock) objectives while the latter is based on social objectives: the last ten years have seen growing recognition of the conflict between these criteria. The 1974 Act signalled the formal abandonment of large-scale clearance and an attempt to direct improvement to those in greatest need by a more interventionist approach. Subsequent cuts in public expenditure emasculated this policy and increased the relative importance of private improvement at a time when economic circumstances could scarcely be less favourable. The disparity between the rate of decay and the rate of investment has become increasingly pronounced and the extent to which housing stock objectives are being met has decreased. At the same time social objectives are not being met – only a small proportion of those in greatest need are benefitting from current policies. Not surprisingly, there is a growing feeling that during the past decade housing renewal has jumped out of the frying pan into the fire.

Alternative prescriptions

What solutions are proferred to this dilemma? This question can be explored by examining the four major components of area renewal:

1 Comprehensive improvement to basic standards;
2 Cellular renewal;
3 Comprehensive improvement to high standards; and
4 Area clearance and redevelopment.

Gradual renewal means all things to all men. While the local strategies which immediately followed the 1974 Act were similar in many respects, subsequent implementation and debate demonstrates competing interpretations of the effectiveness of these components.

Comprehensive improvement to basic standards. A widely held view, enshrined in the 1977 Green Paper, is that more flexibility is required – a euphemism for reducing standards. Many authorities have already taken the line that 'improvement as a holding operation' is most appropriate. Particularly in areas of uniform, poorer-quality housing the only way to achieve comprehensive improvement is by lowering standards so that more private owners can afford to improve and the cost of residual social ownership is minimized. A reappraisal after ten to fifteen years could lead to further upgrading or redevelopment or a combination of the two.[139] While this might seem a practical response to meeting social objectives in areas of low-income owner-occupation, it may well generate more problems than many advocates envisage. The aphorism that 'the best should not be the enemy of the good' has been often quoted in discussions of housing standards. The 'good' can be attractive to government as a given level of resources could in theory yield larger numbers of improvements: minimum housing stock objectives could be met and more of those households in greatest need would benefit. However, the reality is that owners and building societies want long-term security and are unconvinced by algebraic arguments for the investment of significant capital sums in an uncertain future. To the extent that the requisite increase in private improvement is not forthcoming, public ownership will be necessary. Yet few local authorities or housing associations are enthusiastic about low-standard improvement on a large scale with the management difficulties implied. In addition, it is difficult to justify any significant environmental work. Even 'success' would result in housing standards being primarily determined by the financial resources of owners: it will store up physical problems for the future and reinforce social inequality.

Cellular renewal. Some critics argue that the pursuit of comprehensive improvement is misguided, as it ignores the diversity of needs and resources among owners and variations in physical conditions. The imposition of uniform action, even at the lowest acceptable standard, would result in hardship for some existing residents and destroy the vital housing market function of low-cost housing areas. Cellular renewal, however, would enable incremental action giving priority to the immediate requirements of all residents. In the longer term this fine-grained approach might result in the replacement of a significant proportion of the older housing stock in a given area.

Circulars following the 1974 Act gave cellular renewal official blessing. It has not been generally implemented. In some areas, particularly HAAs previously in clearance programmes, improvement has been combined with the selective demolition of blocks of properties but with a more coarse-grained approach. Moreover, while there has been variation in improvement standards, this has tended to be by default: a mix of high and modest standards within an HAA results from compromises where individual households cannot afford the cost.

The paradox of the non-implementation of cellular renewal despite central government exhortation requires some explanation. For one of its proponents 'the logical coherence of the promised renewal policy which was to relate local action to local needs in the context of a continuous process is beginning to evaporate in a familiar muddle of expediency and compromise'.[140] Some argue resistance to its adoption betrays the entrenched attitudes of narrow-minded bureaucrats (whose defective vision is compound by mediocre technical ability) and dyed-in-the-wool politicians (whose preoccupation with numbers keep them wedded to the apparent simplicity of a comprehensive approach). There is more than a grain of truth in the charge of prejudice – professional ideologies and local political elites often exert a conservative influence – but criticisms of the practicalities of cellular renewal are as substantial as some attempts to refute them are unconvincing.[141]

The nub of the issue is that the available resources, powers and procedures are not adequate for the task of applying individualized solutions to mass housing problems, while still producing sufficiently speedy action to close the gap between the rate of investment and the rate of decay. Detailed schemes for individual houses and continuous implementation require intensive inputs over an extended period of time. Most local authorities could only staff a few projects and such a concentration of resources would be difficult to justify, not least to residents of the many similar areas condemned to minimal attention. Any attempt to skimp on resources would be fraught with danger: there is a fine dividing line between steady, cumulative progress and the depressed environment of a perpetual building site. The problems of co-ordinating clearance, housebuilding, housing improvement, environmental works and the renewal of main services would be even more demanding than action in contemporary GIAs and HAAs.

The feasibility of incremental clearance of small groups of houses depends on the pattern of house type and condition. Organic renewal may well be possible in neighbourhoods which were developed organically: acquisition of houses which are in significantly worse condition than the majority could be justified under present CPO powers, although central government procedures would have to be streamlined to avoid blight. However, in most industrial towns the housing is so uniform that selective clearance could not be justified in physical terms. Allowing some houses to deteriorate to the point of clearance is hardly a recipe for confidence in an area, and it is far from clear how in the process of cellular renewal room could be made available to provide desirable infrastructural improvements, such as school playing fields. With such constraints on implementation under present circumstances, the view that cellular renewal 'requires considerably more thought and practical testing before it can be relied upon as a means of urban renewal'[142] is a more accurate assessment of the state of the art than that offered by some of its evangelists.

Comprehensive improvement to high standards. This approach emphasizes the importance of long-term housing stock objectives. As the failings of some earlier phases of council housebuilding graphically illustrate, 'low-quality housing is always an expensive mistake':[143] if a new generation of slums is to be avoided, housing renewal must take place to high standards. Since the 1974 Act there have been a few examples of comprehensive improvement. But, apart from local success stories, compromises have been necessary to keep costs within owners' means. Hence the case for 'improving improvement', such as that the AMA advocated, involving subsidies for local authorities to undertake extensive repair work to the external fabric of private houses on a block-by-block basis or an emphasis on public sector acquisition in some authorities. Certainly, if the single-minded pursuit of housing stock objectives is not to be regressive, massive public subsidy to private owners, a better resourced programme of social ownership, or a combination of both, is essential.

Area clearance and redevelopment. This is an alternative response to the need for high standards. For its proponents, a significant increase in major disrepair is the first fruit of a misguided policy of turning our back on redevelopment. Since area improvement has been an 'unmitigated flop' it is time to 'bring back the bulldozer'.[144] A small minority of local authorities maintained substantial area clearance programmes in the late 1970s against the tenor of central government advice, and frequently in the teeth of opposition from community groups. Others have begun to reformulate such programmes, particularly where experience of area improvement has been visibly disappointing and where there is clear evidence of a housing surplus. Acknowledgement of the need to reform the clearance process is now more common; but community-based redevelopment is vulnerable to fluctuations in housebuilding programmes. Furthermore, there remains the vexed question of opposition in principle from many owner-occupiers.

Clearly, each of these components has a number of advantages and disadvantages. Within a comprehensive strategy geared to local conditions they are not necessarily mutually exclusive. But, at the moment, expediency induced by variable constraints on implementation prevents local authorities choosing that combination which minimizes the conflict between housing stock and social objectives.

Conclusions

The 1974 Act marked a consolidation of the shift to improvement. The bulldozer was 'pensioned off' in terms of large-scale comprehensive redevelopment and an attempt was made to direct improvement to stress areas, primarily as a response to the problems of the private rented sector.

The paradox has been that more sophisticated policies have been accompanied by declining resources and political commitment. The complexities of older housing areas have been increasingly recognized; public participation in proposals to tackle their problems has been encouraged; and a greater variety of powers and procedures introduced. In principle, HIPs enable local authorities to tune their policies to meet local needs more effectively. However, these trends have coincided with decreasing investment in the housing stock and the encouragement of a climate of complacency about what are portrayed as residual problems.

The ambiguity of the 1974 approach is now all too clear. On the one hand, gradual renewal can be viewed as a much needed refinement to the process of improving living conditions in older areas. Both improvement and selective clearance could theoretically be pursued and many areas tackled concurrently. On the other hand, the line between gradual and reduced renewal was potentially very thin in 1974. One theme behind its introduction was that of expediency – 'buying time' in a housing crisis. A reduced level of activity and investment can also be rationalized in terms of meeting 'effective consumer demand', undermining the case for intervention to raise standards for those least able to afford them in the market-place.

The policies of 1974–9 have undoubtedly seen more effective action in some housing stress areas through the implementation of HAAs. However, the same period saw an inexorable rise in the number of houses in severe disrepair, a recognition that home ownership does not by itself guarantee adequate investment in older housing, and concern about limited achievement in environmental improvement. The great mass of older houses has largely been unaffected by both improvement and much reduced clearance programmes. Moreover, an appropriate epitaph for much of the improvement in the 1970s is:

> Small-scale, incremental, sensitive – the appeal of rehab was intoxicating: the reality is not. A mean rehab replaced a mean high-rise.[145]

Soon after the initiatives of the 1974 Act were launched the Labour Government's housing policy was shackled by economic events.[146] By 1979 the opportunity to reform housing finance had been missed and the prospects for significantly remedying the resource problems of local renewal strategies remained bleak.

5 The Poverty Programme

The transition from comprehensive redevelopment and the problems of gradual renewal are key issues in an understanding of inner urban policy. However, parallel and related innovations, in the form of a series of priority area experimental projects, added a spatial dimension to social policy.

During the mid-1960s inner areas became the focus of a debate on social problems and policies. Academic research demonstrated the continued existence of poverty and offered competing explanations. A series of official inquiries prompted the development of a priority area approach. In the politics of policy making poverty was assumed to be a problem of small minority who had fallen through the welfare state net and who were geographically concentrated in small pockets. These assumptions underpinned the Government's response: the Poverty Programme. A variety of experimental projects were launched, notably the Community Development Projects (CDP) and the Inner Area Studies (IAS), and their work ranged across the full spectrum of urban problems. The analyses and prescriptions which emerged in the mid-1970s rejected the initial assumptions and established the basic economic causes of inner area decline.

The rediscovery of poverty

For two decades after the war it was generally assumed that the problem of material poverty had been substantially eradicated by the social reforms of the immediate post-war years and the elimination of mass unemployment. Poverty was regarded as a 'slight social hangover' from the pre-war years.[1] But by the mid-1960s, after more than a decade of controversial work, academic research had re-established (for the non-poor) the continued existence of widespread poverty. The evidence demonstrated that several million people were living in poverty and that the structure of inequality was little altered. This research, and the debate it engendered, was concerned with the characteristics of the poor – their numbers, who and where they were – and explanations of the persistence of poverty.[2]

Poverty and urban deprivation

A traditional subsistence definition was rejected in favour of the concept that poverty is both relative, i.e. related to prevailing living standards, and movable, i.e. sensitive to changes in these standards. In these terms the poor are those:

individuals and families, whose resources over time fall seriously short of the resources commanded by the average individual or family in the community in which they live.[3]

Many studies took the supplementary benefit scale rate (approximately 40 per cent of average net earnings) as their 'poverty line'.[4] The most influential was *The Poor and the Poorest* by Abel-Smith and Townsend, which estimated that in 1960 some 7 m people in the UK (over 14 per cent of the population) were living in poverty – nearly double the proportion in 1953.[5] Five groups were identified: 3 m people living in households headed by a full-time wage-earner – 'the working poor'; 2½ m pensioners; ¾ m in 'fatherless families'; ¾ m in families with one parent disabled or sick; and ½ m in families where the father was unemployed. These findings implied that the largest group of the poor earned their poverty through low wages, and that the remainder were poor because of inadequate state benefits.

While this relative approach is principally used to compare a poor minority with the average, it can show that a majority of the population are poor when compared with a privileged minority. Research on the distribution of personal incomes after direct taxation challenged the assumption of increasing equality. Whereas in 1949 the richest 5 per cent received 17 per cent of total incomes, by 1967 their share had only fallen to 15 per cent – a larger share than that received by the poorest 30 per cent. Furthermore, after adjustment to allow for factors such as benefits in kind and untaxed property income, the privileged 5 per cent received roughly the same share as the millions in the bottom half of the population.[6] Similarly the concentration of wealth in the hands of a tiny minority had only marginally reduced. The top 5 per cent owned 87 per cent of private wealth in 1911–13; half a century later this had fallen to 75 per cent. Large wealth holdings were primarily the result of inheritance rather than lifetime accumulation.[7]

Much research examined poverty in terms of income levels and undermined the myth of redistributive taxation and effective income maintenance policies, while other studies began to identify the gaps between the conditions experienced by a minority and the standards which social policies were designed to secure, e.g. that no family should live in an unfit house. Such 'gaps' are measures of *social deprivation*, and it was argued that definitions of the poor should not be restricted to income but should include people suffering these kinds of deprivation. Finally, research indicated that a group of the poor suffered more than one form of deprivation – they were victims of *multiple deprivation*.[8]

In contrast, the 1960s generated 'depressingly little evidence about the geographical concentration of the poor'.[9] A few localized studies led researchers to the conclusion that there were concentrations of deprived people living within small areas characterized by inferior housing; higher than average proportions of unskilled workers, large and one-parent families; a lack of play and recreational facilities; a high incidence of delinquency; and poorer health than found in the population as a whole. Such areas existed in both the inner cities and outlying council estates. Those who lived in these areas suffered by living among concentrations of the deprived in a deprived physical environment.[10] This additional, geographical dimension came to be known as down-town poverty, and later as *urban deprivation*. However, there was no evidence to suggest that majority, or even a significant proportion of the millions in poverty, lived in these small areas, or that all of the most deprived lived there.

Blaming the victim[11]

Research into the facts of poverty prompted the resumption of a long-standing debate about its causes. Academic exchanges centred on the relative importance of two sets of explanations: those emphasizing the failings of the poor, and those which argued that poverty stems from circumstances beyond their control, that it is rooted in the unequal structure of society.[12]

In the Victorian era there was a widespread belief that the poor had only themselves to blame: people could escape poverty if they tried hard enough and failure to do so was because the poor were workshy and feckless. Such explanations re-emerged in modified form during the early post-war years: with a return to full employment and with extensive welfare provision, 'normal' people could avoid poverty if they chose. Failure to do so reflected personal, mental or physical inadequacy – such as inability to manage household budgets, lack of effort to improve earnings, or not making full use of welfare benefits.

Explanations which rested on the concepts of a 'culture of poverty' and a 'cycle of deprivation' were variants on this social pathology theme which emerged in the USA during the 1960s, and rapidly gained currency in this country. It was asserted that the poor are a distinct social group sharing the same patterns of behaviour which combine to keep them impoverished. They adapt to financial hardship and squalid living conditions by living from day to day, rather than trying to secure a better future. Their negative attitudes to education result in such values being passed on from one generation to the next. The poor are habituated to poverty and this condemns their children to the same fate.

Although these explanations, or popular versions of them, constituted the most widely held view of the causes of poverty in this country, many social scientists considered them unsatisfactory. The characteristics of the poor could not explain the scale of poverty and the groups mainly affected. Why did many work hard only to earn poverty? Why could the poor who wanted to work not find employment? Why were so many of the retired impoverished?

Why were those wanting to leave 'culturally deprived areas' unable to do so? These questions emphasized the need to look at poverty by examining the distribution of resources throughout society, rather than the behaviour of the poor. It was argued that poverty is primarily determined by the structure of income distribution – the poor are those who can command only low or irregular wages in the labour market. Poverty is therefore a function of basic economic inequalities, and will not be reduced by a general improvement in living standards which is equally shared by all groups, but only by relatively greater increments to lower incomes at the expense of higher incomes. The distribution of income through the labour market clearly precluded this: between 1913 and 1960 there was no change in the relation of wages of unskilled men to average national earnings, and there was little evidence of a reduction in the enormous differential between the highest-paid and the poorest-paid occupations.[13]

The continued existence of poverty in a welfare state pointed to the basic inadequacy of redistributive mechanisms. Taxation policies were, at best, having only a marginal impact, and many argued that their effects were regressive. Social policies for redistributing resources can be summarized by reference to the different dimensions of poverty. Income maintenance measures (e.g. sickness benefits) are intended to offset the effects of crisis poverty, i.e. the hardship resulting from injury, illness or unemployment, while other measures (e.g. free medical care) aim to reduce its incidence. Long-term dependency of people who never recover from these crises or are permanently handicapped from birth is the subject of income security measures. Measures to alleviate these two types of poverty, together with those attempting to improve wages, provide free education and subsidized housing, constitute 'half the traditional package of social democratic policies': the other half is geared to life-cycle poverty, which affects people in childhood, early parenthood, and old age, and mainly comprises family allowances and old age pensions.[14]

The extent of continued financial hardship and social deprivation was a reflection of two basic and related limitations of the welfare state as it had developed since the early post-war years. First, because the real value of universal, 'as of right', income maintenance benefits had been allowed to fall, more people needed to claim supplementary, selective, means-tested benefits, but many were not doing so because of the associated stigma. Second, not only were the major social services failing to benefit those in greatest need, it was also clear that the more affluent were gaining most from education, housing and health provision. It was argued that this necessitated fundamental changes to achieve greater selectivity within a more adequately resourced system of universal benefits and services, i.e. an effective safety net would still be provided for the many, while positive discrimination would provide extra help for those in greatest need. However, others argued for further means-tested provisions for the most needy, i.e. positive discrimination should be a substitute for, rather than an addition to, universal services – an argument which leads towards potentially massive reductions in social spending. The balance of the academic debate was that poverty was a large-scale rather than residual problem, was not the fault of its victims, and its alleviation depended on a basic change in social policy.

Urban deprivation and positive discrimination

Mainstream social policy is directed at social groups not geographical areas. Inter-regional inequalities had long been recognized and were the targets of regional economic planning policies. Growing awareness of the interlinked problems of deprived urban areas tended to be combined with concern about the failure of social policies in meeting the needs of the poor. It constituted the case for a new approach: positive discrimination in the allocation of resources through co-ordinated neighbourhood-based programmes. This section examines the major influences which contributed to the emergence of priority area policies.[15]

Administrative pressure

Increasing disquiet about a wide range of social problems generated administrative pressure for reform. A series of government reports added to the evidence that major social services were failing to reach many of those in greatest need and that some areas were deprived across the board. All made recommendations for policy and organization changes.

The Plowden Report on primary education focussed attention on the educational deprivation of children in neighbourhoods which 'have for generations been starved of new schools, new houses and new investment of every kind'.[16] It argued that the handicaps of a poor home and environment were reinforced by inadequate schools: low educational achievement resulted in low earnings and adult life in a similar poor neighbourhood – 'a vicious circle' which 'may turn from generation to generation'.[17] Therefore schools with large numbers of socially handicapped children needed extra resources to compensate for the disadvantages of home and environment. The Report recommended more parental and community involvement in schools and positive discrimination, seen as the redirection of existing resources to areas of greatest need.[18]

The Seebohm Report identified inadequacies in the personal social services (child care, provision for the aged, care of the handicapped) together with problems of co-ordination within them and between them and other services, and difficulties of access to services experienced by clients.[19] Shortage of resources was identified as the underlying cause of these shortcomings, together with inadequate knowledge of problems and divided responsibilities.

The Committee recommended a unified, community-oriented family service: 'the family and community are seen as the contexts in which problems arise and in which most of them have to be resolved or contained'.[20] Particular concern was expressed about recognized problem areas lacking a sense of community and 'characterised by rapid population turnover, high delinquency, child deprivation and mental illness rates and other indices of social pathology'.[21] Restoring this sense of community and its concomitant 'strong social control over behaviour' was to be the task of community development defined as:

> a process whereby local groups are assisted to clarify and express their needs and objectives and to take collective action in an attempt to meet them. It emphasizes the involvement of the people themselves in determining and meeting their own needs.[22]

This was seen as complementary, not alternative, to conventional social services provision, requiring the allocation of additional resources to 'social development areas', in contrast to the Plowden concept of diverting resources from other areas.[23]

At about the same time the Planning Advisory Group reviewed land-use planning and advocated a more comprehensive approach with structure plans to deal with strategic issues and local plans for co-ordinated implementation.[24] Its proposals for increased public participation in planning were developed in the Skeffington Report[25] which recommended the appointment of community development officers and the establishment of community fora. The Milner Holland Report on London's housing problems, discussed earlier, had recommended both 'areas of special control' and more effective co-ordination of housing and other services.[26]

Although each of these reports focussed on specific services, they all reflected a growing awareness of local government's limited capability to respond in a co-ordinated way to the interrelated needs of local areas. The limitations of the traditional approach of providing services directed to what were seen as essentially discrete problems were highlighted by the Maud Report on local government management.[27] Departmentalism and fragmentation of effort resulted in a lack of co-ordination between services and little assessment of their effectiveness, particularly their impact on problems which involved the activities of several departments: the management of comprehensive redevelopment was a case in point. The late 1960s saw the beginnings of a move towards a corporate approach which has been defined as:

> taking an overall view of a local authority's activities and the way they relate to the changing needs and problems of its area. More specifically it involves the local authorities' development management *and* political processes and structures which will enable it to plan, control and review its activities as a whole to satisfy the needs of the people in its area to the maximum extent consistent with available resources.[28]

The Maud Committee stressed the importance of breaking down departmental and professional barriers. It recommended the adoption of an authority-wide approach to identifying needs, setting objectives, devising and evaluating policy options, monitoring implementation and policy review.

Race and immigration

Problems facing ethnic minorities were one dimension of changing needs which figured in most of these official reports and became an intensely controversial political issue. The National Committee for Commonwealth Immigrants argued that the difficulties faced by local authorities with a high concentration of coloured immigrants should be recognized and accepted as a national responsibility with the designation of priority areas within which housing and all other social services should be co-ordinated.[29] Debate about race and immigration came to a head in the late 1960s and coloured immigrants became scapegoats for shortfalls in housing provision and other services. The discussion of poverty, inequality and positive discrimination became associated with the multi-racial and multi-cultural dimension of inner urban areas, often with the implication that immigrants caused problems rather than experienced them. In political terms the corollary of restrictive immigration policies was the need for positive measures to assist existing immigrant communities.

War on poverty

In the USA reaction to deteriorating urban conditions and racial inequality had found an expression in both the Civil Rights Movement and ghetto riots. This was a major factor prompting the American 'war on poverty' and attempts to resolve urban problems there generated ideas which spread among academics, welfare professionals and politicians here. Management techniques borrowed from industry, community development, and citizen participation, together with the notion of positive discrimination, were all prominent features of the area-based American poverty programme. Many such ideas were incorporated in policy development in this country often with insufficient regard for the lessons painfully learned during their application in the USA.[30]

Official perceptions

Policy was developed within the framework of a restricted perception of poverty and the resources which could be devoted to social expenditure. Academic research had exposed the myth of increasing equality but its fundamental implications were ignored. Instead, official thinking established a view of poverty as the problem of a minority who had fallen through the welfare state safety net and were heavily concentrated in small pockets. Attention was focussed on the social and environmental problems of small geographical areas, rather than an examination of underlying economic processes and the inadequacies of redistributive social policies. In government reports explanations of the persistence of poverty were couched in terms of a culture of poverty and a cycle of deprivation, 'but the analysis stopped firmly short of any fundamental questioning of the social structure within which these "pockets" of poverty were thought to persist'.[31] Poverty was viewed as the result of inefficient local authority management – unco-ordinated services and insensitivity to local needs – combined with the inadequacies of the poor who were not fully utilizing existing services. For Morrell, a civil servant who played a key role in the work of the Seebohm Committee and the conception of the Urban Programme and CDP, ideas about the re-creation of 'community' took on a mystical significance. Crossman, then Secretary of State for the Social Services, recounted a discussion of 'this extraordinary community experiment idea' (CDP) in which Morrell 'made a curiously Buchmanite kind of religious speech about action changing lives'.[32]

Certain common themes emerged from this perception of the problem which pointed to an area selective approach: management reform to increase the overall efficiency of local government and improve its capacity for co-ordinated responses to particularly needy areas; community development and public participation to help define needs, determine priorities and stimulate self-help; and positive discrimination in the allocation of resources to fund these innovations.

Pressures for policy innovation emerged at a time of acute economic difficulties and resultant cuts in major services in the aftermath of the 1967 devaluation crisis. A restricted perception of problems and available resources – the political and bureaucratic metamorphosis of poverty and inequality into urban deprivation – was fundamental in shaping the policy response.

Urban Experiments Ltd

The Labour Government's resolution of the political problems posed by demands for more resources for priority areas at a time of economic stringency was the launching of what is commonly referred to as the Poverty Programme. There were two main elements; first, the allocation of very limited 'topping-up' central government funds to areas of special need; second, a series of low-cost, high-visibility, area-specific experimental projects to determine the most effective ways of operationalizing positive discrimination. The 'poverty business' boomed as successive governments initiated essentially similar but unco-ordinated projects, sponsored by different departments in partnership with various local authorities (see Figure 10).

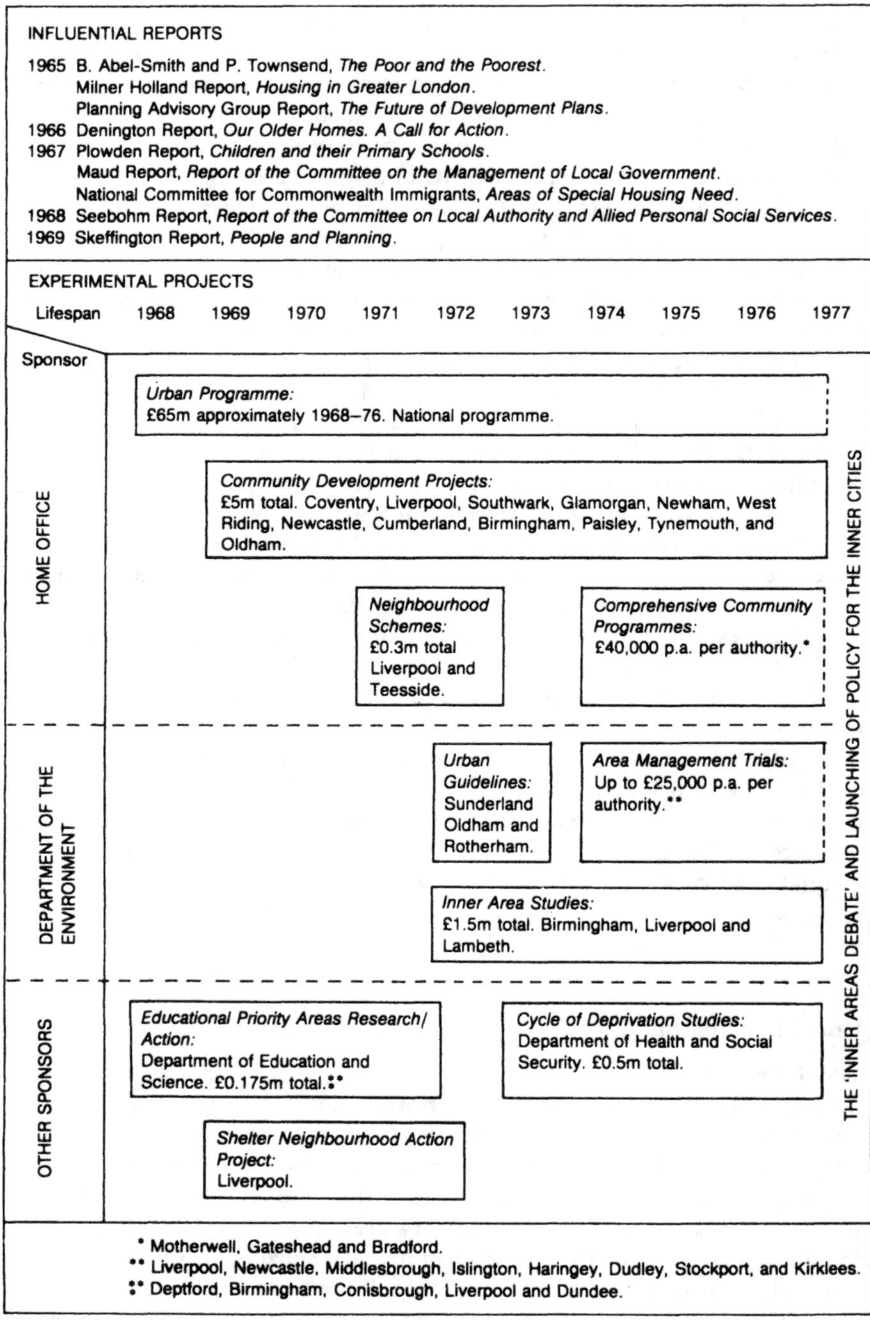

Figure 10 *Accumulating urban experiments*

Urban Programme

The immigration issue precipitated the major innovation when, in the charged atmosphere generated by Powell's inflammatory 'rivers of blood' speech in 1968, the *Urban Programme* was launched.[33] Announced by Wilson in May 1968, it was an immediate political response which catalysed developing arguments about priority area programmes. While indicating concern for problems associated with coloured immigrant settlement, it was deliberately aimed at all deprived areas. An interdepartmental working party, led by the Home Office, translated the Prime Minister's statement into a quickly formulated programme.[34] The Local Government Grants (Social Need) Act, 1969 provided the legislative basis for financial support.

The then Home Secretary, Callaghan, outlined its objectives thus:

> There remain areas of severe social deprivation in a number of our cities and towns – often scattered in relatively small pockets. They require special help to meet their social needs and to bring their services to an adequate level. . . . The purpose is to supplement the Government's other social and legislative measures to ensure as far as we can that all our citizens have an equal opportunity in life.[35]

Subsequent government circulars did not specify precisely how the programme was to meet its objectives. Areas of special social need were described as 'districts which bear the marks of multiple deprivation',[36] such as poor housing and environmental conditions (particularly overcrowding), large families, unemployment, children in trouble or in need of care, and concentrations of immigrant settlement. It was stressed that the programme would not do the work of the major social services but fill in 'gaps' by encouraging projects which would not otherwise have started, and would have a 'reasonably quick effect and which go directly to the roots of special social need'[37] (e.g. nursery schools, family advice and community centres and language classes for immigrants).

The programme's 'topping-up' funds were limited to £25m for the first four years to 1972 and a further allocation of £40m for the remaining four years. After Treasury pressure in 1971 these funds ceased to be extra resources but were diverted from the existing Rate Support Grant (RSG). The programme was the responsibility of the Home Office which issued annual circulars providing (varying) guidelines within which local authorities submitted individual projects. There was provision for voluntary organizations to secure funds but, as a result of pressure from local authority organizations, their applications had to be channelled through, and approved by, the local authority. Projects approved by the Home Office received a 75 per cent grant, the remaining 25 per cent had to be found from rate funds. This procedure for allocating supplementary resources to deprived areas became known as *Urban Aid*. It was the most extensive and expensive of all the poverty initiatives and by the end of 1975 some 3750 projects had been approved at a cost of £34m.

Community Development Projects

In 1969 the Home Office announced that some Urban Programme funds were to be used to finance the Community Development Project, described as 'a neighbourhood-based experiment aimed at finding new ways of meeting the needs of people living in areas of high social deprivation'.[38] Heralded as 'government opening campaign against urban poverty',[39] the CDP was to identify needs in deprived areas, encourage local residents to participate in this analysis 'and take some initiative and responsibility in what follows'; propose solutions both 'to plug immediate gaps' and test new methods, with a 'special emphasis' on improved co-ordination between relevant social welfare agencies and communication between them and local people; and, finally, identify 'solutions which are beyond immediate local action but merit feeding back to wherever policy is formed'.[40] This was the task of twelve projects using an extension of the action-research methods being followed in the already established Educational Priority Area Projects (EPAs).[41] Each CDP had a neighbourhood-based action team employed jointly by the Home Office and local authority on a 75–25 per cent funding. Action teams were linked to Home Office funded research teams based in universities and polytechnics, responsible for diagnosing local problems and evaluating experimental work. The projects were to run for five years at a total cost of £5m, but they had a staggered start and were not all established until 1972. The basic assumptions underlying the CDPs clearly reflected the prevailing official view that the causes of urban deprivation were essentially local in origin, and that improved area-based action would significantly ameliorate social problems in inner areas.

By 1972 the Urban Programme was coming under fire.[42] The validity of the priority area approach had been questioned from the outset: small areas with the highest incidence of poverty were unlikely to contain a high proportion of the poor so that action there would not significantly attack poverty. Even within its own terms of reference it was vulnerable to criticism. First, Urban Aid funding developed a 'grapeshot approach'. Neither central government in setting guidelines nor local authorities preparing bids defined small target areas and there was no effective co-ordination at either level between different services. Local authority participation was discretionary: some authorities ignored it, others became masters of 'grantsmanship' (the art of submitting successful bids) and the distribution of funding was haphazard. The CDP areas were specifically defined for Urban Programme funding, but their action budgets were small, about £40,000 p.a. per project. Second, the inadequacy of the programme's resources became only too apparent: 'gaps' were highlighted but could not be plugged. The volume of bids grew as awareness of Urban Aid increased, especially among voluntary groups, and in 1972 the available funds were only one tenth of what would have been necessary to approve all projects submitted to the Home Office. Finally, scarcity of resources focussed attention on their allocation. The very low proportion of successful bids by voluntary groups became a bone of contention, particularly as some authorities were using Urban Aid for projects which should have been funded from normal expenditure.

Shelter Neighbourhood Action Project

These criticisms were extended by the highly publicized report of the Liverpool Shelter Neighbourhood Action Project (SNAP), the first broadly based neighbourhood action-research project to be completed in this country. In 1969 the SNAP team 'was given three years to go into one of the most deprived areas of Merseyside, to experience problems, provide assistance, demonstrate improvement and promote more effective policies for the future'.[43] As discussed in Chapter 3, the shift to improvement was accompanied by the development of an area-selective approach to housing and environmental action and this was the initial focus of the project: by 1972 the Granby GIA was one of the most successful in the country. However, 'success' served to underline the limitations of such intervention in the face of the acute deprivation revealed by the team's work with both the local authority and residents. The people of Granby were clearly not to blame for their predicament – SNAP explicitly rejected social pathology explanations of urban deprivation, arguing that the problems could neither be understood nor resolved until inner areas were seen as part of the urban economy in its regional context. The root cause was structural change in employment and housing markets which had caused selective decentralization of jobs and people, a process which had been reinforced by dispersal policies subsidizing suburbanization.

SNAP argued that these processes caused both increasing demands on welfare services and declining rate revenue. Cities with a greater than average share of problems were not receiving a commensurately higher proportion of government resources through RSG. Liverpool lacked the resources to halt inner area decline. The relevance of co-ordinated intervention across a wide range of services at the neighbourhood level soon became apparent, as did the political powerlessness of the poor. Despite pressure by the project team, continued dominance of departmentalism at the local level was reinforced by fragmented central government budgets and procedures. Liverpool lacked the political will and management capability for effective intervention.

SNAP concluded that a new national urban programme was required. Its central purpose would be the renewal of the economic base of the major cities in order to improve real incomes. A defined proportion of the RSG, as a new key sector urban renewal grant, would be channelled to clearly defined inner city priority areas via local authority bids based on comprehensive policies and programmes prepared at district level. Area management and budgeting would weld together housing, health, social services, education and employment policies under a single executive. These bids would be co-ordinated by consolidated Whitehall regional machinery, responsible to a 'task force' under the Cabinet office forging links between government departments. The case for the development of such a programme on a pilot basis with significant resources was presented as both a challenge and an opportunity to Peter Walker, Secretary of State responsible for the newly created DoE.

Inner Area Studies

The response was the Six Towns Studies, which included the three Inner Area Studies (IAS), the most influential of the second wave of experimental projects launched by the Conservative Government of 1970–4. With the customary ministerial flourish, Walker announced his intentions during the 1972 budget debate:

> I believe that the next most important step for my department is to bring about a total approach to the urban problem. In the past the attitude has been a series of fragmented decisions not properly co-ordinated. . . . I intend in the next few weeks, with the co-operation of local authorities, to designate six towns and inner city areas where a group from my department and local government will examine the total resources needed to completely transform such areas.[44]

During the ensuing hectic months in Whitehall the 'total approach' was significantly trimmed to bring the scope of the proposed studies into line with the responsibilities of the DoE. It was decided to commission professional consultants and the brief given for the IAS was:

> to discover by study a better definition of inner areas and their problems;
> to investigate by experiments on the ground the actions affecting the physical environment of these areas which could usefully be undertaken for social and environmental purposes;
> to examine whether the concept of area management can usefully be developed and what the practical implications would be for the local authority;
> to provide the base for general conclusions on statutory powers, finance and resource questions, and techniques.[45]

After preliminary investigations, the consultants for each of the studies in Liverpool, Birmingham and Lambeth began work in late 1973. Their three-year contracts costing £1½m (including an 'action budget' of approximately £100,000 p.a. per study) were funded 75–25 per cent by the DoE and the local authorities involved. The objectives and methods prescribed were very similar to those of CDP, although there was less emphasis on community involvement and more on local authority management. Conspicuous by its absence was any reference to the economic causes of urban deprivation highlighted by SNAP. An emphasis on localized research and experimental action reflected the official view of the causes of poverty.

Accumulating projects

Prevailing government assumptions about the nature of poverty and appropriate solutions were evidenced in other projects initiated by the Heath Government. They included: Urban Guidelines Studies (the other half of the Six Towns Studies) concerned with how management structures of the new (post-reorganization) local authorities could deal with urban problems; experimental Neighbourhood Schemes (Home Office) to assess the impact of a capital injection of £150,000 into each of two small areas; and research studies into 'transmitted deprivation' sponsored by Sir Keith Joseph at the Department of Health and Social Security to examine how more people could be helped to break out of the 'cycle of deprivation'. Finally, in an attempt to co-ordinate some of these proliferating projects, the Home Office established the Urban Deprivation Unit, whose work the Home Secretary announced as 'the key to providing a better life for those who live in the cities and as a way of improving community relations'.[46]

Soon after the return of a Labour administration in 1974, two further projects were announced; Area Management Trials run jointly by the DoE and selected local authorities, and Comprehensive Community Programmes (CCPs), organized on a similar basis by the Home Office and concerned with authority-wide co-ordination of services to tackle urban deprivation. In the event, these marked the end of almost a decade of *ad hoc* experiments. Announcements about CCPs stated that rather than further supplementary, small-scale community and environmental projects, 'huge resources' would have to be channelled into deprived areas, necessitating the direction of 'the major programmes and policies of government to those most in need'.[47]

Action on the ground and changing perspectives

The most influential of the Poverty Programme projects in the development of urban renewal policy were the CDP and the IAS. As these projects evolved their scope widened significantly from the localized social welfare and environmental problems emphasized in their initial remit. A developing understanding of the underlying economic processes and national policies shaping urban and industrial change in the project areas led the teams to reject initial assumptions about the causes of poverty and deprivation, and shift to perspectives which emphasized structural explanations.

From neighbourhood action to structural explanations

The work of CDP, as it had developed by 1973–4, is illustrated by Figure 11, an extract from the *Inter-Project Report*,[48] the publication of which marked the turning point of the projects. In the early years the 12 CDPs developed in relative isolation, establishing work programmes and methods in response to

Project	*Employment*	*Income maintenance welfare rights*	*Housing*	*Education*	*Information and advice*	*Research*
Birmingham Policy strategy	Consultant employed to investigate economic structure of surrounding industrial belt and history of local trade union activity.	Analysis of rate revaluation effects on the project area.	(a) Leasehold issue (b) Environmental team (Planner, Public Health Inspector).		(a) Project office serves as information/advice centre. Information and priorities of callers fed into action programme. 75% of callers came about leasehold. Urban renewal, Pakistan Act. (b) Support for community groups	(a) Household survey. (b) Race-relations research. (c) Nature of leasehold problem; effects of legislative change. (d) Employment position in the surrounding industrial area.
Neighbourhood strategy		Worker appointed to process collective rate appeals.	Servicing resident groups concerned with short leases and urban renewal.			
Coventry Policy strategy	Research and Consultant's report on role of schools, youth employment service and industry in assisting young people in transition from school life to work life.	(a) Research on knowledge of rights and extent of unmet need. (b) Research into income maintenance for elderly.	(a) Study of the wider interests which have influenced the investment in urban revewal since the war. (b) Research and Consultant's report on city's general improvement policy.	Community education programme in 13 schools involving nursery annexes curriculum development and home–school relations.	(a) Community worker appointed to specially formed independent body. (b) Annual grant to umbrella community association to support local groups and initiatives. (c) Hard skills and advocacy from community lawyer, and community planner.	(a) Status and needs of the elderly. (b) Structure of interests and ideologies which influence allocation of resources (land and housing) in city.
Neighbourhood strategy	Possibility of co-operative improvement industry.	(a) Resident controlled information centre and advocacy for claimants. (b) Community lawyer. (c) Collaboration with Trade Union groups in campaign for legal and income rights.	(a) Community planner offers consultancy and hard skills to resident groups campaigning for GIA investment. (b) Appointment of consultant to set up resident controlled housing co-operative.	Adult education work with informal groups in pubs and clubs and with Asian immigrants in homes, temples and factory floor.		
Liverpool Policy strategy	Study of employment conditions and levels of unemployment locally.	Appointment of DHSS liaison officer, at multi-service centre.		(a) Community education programme. Home–school relations. (b) Educational resources centre. (c) Experimental reading scheme.	(a) Resident run information centre. (b) Neighbourhood newspaper. (c) Support for community groups and federation into neighbourhood council (d) Multi-service centre.	(a) Local authority management structures for participation. (b) Local community organizations. (c) School to work and early job experience. (d) Development of multi-service centre.
Neighbourhood strategy	Study groups on unemployment. Contact with work group over issues of local redundancy and closure.	(a) Resident run Information Centre. (b) Old people's welfare council.	Servicing tenants groups in implementation of improvement schemes with planner and architect as consultants	Adult education programmes. Playscheme. Adventure Playground		

Figure 11 *Community Development Project activities*

Source: Extract from National Community Development Project, *Inter-Project Report*, CDP Information and Intelligence Unit, pp. 40–7 (1974)

diverse local conditions – some were located in older areas characterized by declining populations and traditional industries, others in the inner areas of more prosperous towns and cities. Initially the teams concentrated on neighbourhood work. They established a base in the area and gathered information about local conditions and residents' attitudes. Generally they identified key issues, such as housing, education, and welfare rights, around which residents could organize. They fostered community involvement in two ways: by deploying their limited action budgets to fund small-scale, community controlled, projects to help meet identified needs, e.g. play facilities and advice centres; and by assisting residents' groups to secure additional local authority investment in the area, e.g. by campaigning for a GIA. This work, oriented towards self-help, participation, and improved communication objectives, frequently generated conflict with the host local authorities – three CDPs closed before the end of their scheduled five-year term.

The inherent limitations of work solely within project areas soon became apparent: problems could not be solved by better co-ordination of social services provision when there were basic inadequacies which required policy changes. Using analyses of the impact of local authority policy, and supported by local residents, the teams opened a dialogue with officers and politicians to promote changes. While some improvements were secured, this work did not achieve policy and resource allocation changes in any way commensurate with the problems identified: the failure of Coventry and Southwark CDPs to bring about changes in the redevelopment process was a case in point. This experience, similar to that of SNAP, revealed both bureaucratic inertia and political constraints on positive discrimination at the local authority level. It also demonstrated the effects of limited local authority resources, prompting research into the RSG system. Most importantly, it became clear that local authorities lacked both the powers and resources to effectively intervene in income maintenance and employment issues.

By 1973 the Coventry team:

> . . . had become increasingly aware of the extent to which the fortunes of an area like Hillfields are influenced by forces operating largely outside local democratic control (changing land-values, interest rates in the money markets, the operations of private landlords and speculators, the pattern of central government expenditure and the employment and investment policies of industry).[49]

As one of the earliest established, it was at a more advanced stage than many of the others, but at about this time the CDPs realized that the issues they faced locally were not diverse isolated problems, but symptoms of essentially similar underlying processes. Wider issues of urban population movements, employment and housing changes were seen to be more relevant to the development of policies to combat inner area problems than the concerns engendered by the original emphasis on the inadequacies of the poor and administrative inefficiencies. The project areas were no longer to be seen as isolated pockets suffering an unfortunate local combination of circumstances. Instead, the spatial dimension of inequality represented by conditions in these and many other similar areas was the product of external forces. The teams decided to pool their experiences and develop analyses through collaborative and comparative studies. The *Inter-Project Report* concluded:

> the problems in these areas are not going to be solved by marginal rearrangements to take account of their special minority needs. From its small area base, CDP can map the points at which private and public policies are having negative and unequal effects. We can also aim to explore strategies for developing local awareness of these points and for raising them to greater public attention. But the major response must come from central and local government, with substantial changes in policy and the allocation of new resources.[50]

This credo was adopted, in varying degrees, by the teams and shaped the scope and nature of their subsequent work. There was a significant shift of effort to a historical analysis of the changing structure of industrial investment (which involved developing links with trades councils and shop stewards' organizations), the operation of the private housing market, and the limitations of national policies. The work was documented in a series of national reports aimed at a wide audience. Neighbourhood work continued, but some teams attempted to change its nature by using it to 'raise political consciousness', i.e. developing residents' understanding of the market and political processes which denied them opportunities for an improved quality of life.[51]

Although the action-research methodology was part of their brief, the shorter time-scale of IAS (three years) made it more difficult to establish, monitor and evaluate projects involving residents, as did the consultancy style of work. Generally such projects were 'low-profile', far less advocacy-oriented and controversial than CDP. Some of the most productive experiments were concerned with local authority management structures, such as pilot local renewal project teams in Birmingham and area management in Liverpool. Oriented to conventional research methods from the outset, the teams expanded their brief to include income maintenance policies and contracting job opportunities. This development was clearly influenced by the shifting perspective of CDP, widely debated within the 'poverty business'. By early 1975 the Birmingham consultants, for example, were arguing that area-based studies would also have to evaluate 'what may *not* be changed through area action, the necessity for wider ranging policies and more fundamental structural changes in our political and economic system'.[52]

Declining credibility

By this time perspectives on the Poverty Programme were changing on a wider front as criticism of the apparently endless stream of *ad hoc* experiments mounted. The final report of the Coventry CDP concentrated on the need for radical changes in national policies, including more public ownership and control of industry and housing, together with substantial changes in income maintenance provision and public sector finance.[53] The emerging CCPs appeared to be the Government's response to the prospective end of CDP and reaction was, at best, lukewarm: having listed the accumulation of experiments on Merseyside 'all without any recognizable improvements even at the very local level' one commentator posed the question 'does it now need a massive injection of new resources, or a CCP in the Wirral '. . . without the first it is doubtful if the second will have any impact at all'.[54]

This reaction reflected the declining credibility of the Poverty Programme. Critics pointed to two related contradictions: the continuity of the restricted official view of poverty in the face of overwhelming evidence which discredited it; and the fact that the ministerial rhetoric accompanying each initiative had implied that it was a necessary prelude to substantial policy changes, yet with each new round of experiments the prospects of such changes apparently receded. It was argued that the Poverty Programme was a sham – a series of token gestures in the face of sudden pressures, which fulfilled the important political function of maintaining the view of poverty as a limited problem about which something was being done.[55]

A sustained and co-ordinated anti-deprivation strategy was increasingly conspicuous by its absence. Positive discrimination had become a fashionable concept, but its credibility was reaching crisis point: 'either the spillover into wider social reform is acknowledged and grasped, or PD is exposed as the facade it largely is at present'. It was '. . . perhaps the best technique of social egalitarianism not yet seriously tried'.[56]

Conclusions

Throughout the Poverty Programme the concept of area-selective positive discrimination remained ambiguous. It was frequently pointed out that positive discrimination in favour of deprived areas cannot be the principal means of dealing with poverty. It does not reach the majority of deprived people because most of them do not live in the areas defined.[57] A crude, and at worst token, gesture to such areas obscures the necessity for more fundamental action at national level through policies to minimize unemployment, provide adequate state benefits and develop a tax system which redistributes wealth more equitably. While accepting much of this criticism, others pointed to the need to pull together a variety of policies to achieve effective action in defined localities.[58] Similarly the extent of the programme was questioned. For some, the way forward was to develop positive discrimination as part of a more substantial redistribution from the rich to the poor, channelling some of the additional resources to the poor on an area basis. For others, positive discrimination was a way of adjusting policies within the existing parameters of redistribution – in effect this meant redistribution from the less poor to the very poor.[59] The previous chapter has shown the application of the latter version of the concept in the housing programme as the increasing emphasis on an area approach had been accompanied by the redirection of reduced resources to the stress areas. This approach was to become the hallmark of a revised national urban policy.

6 Saving cities

The debate on urban deprivation prompted increasing awareness of the social consequences of spatial planning and this merged with a questioning of growth oriented policies in a no growth situation. During the mid-1970s these concerns were given impetus and a specific inner area focus by the reports emerging from the most influential of the Poverty Programme experiments, CDP and IAS. In 1976 a major speech by Shore, the then Secretary of State, precipitated what became known as the 'inner areas debate'. This centred on the economic causes of inner area decline, the extent to which public policy was to blame, and the relative merits of different courses of action.

The 1977 White Paper *Policy for the Inner Cities*[1] established a revised national urban policy, outlining the official view of the urban crisis and the Government's response. In essence, the policy aimed to arrest the decline of inner area population and employment opportunities by spatial discrimination in resource allocation to fund comprehensive renewal programmes. The Inner Urban Areas Act, 1978 extended local authority powers to assist industry, but the implementation of the new policy relied mainly on the modified use of existing powers.

This reformulation of national urban policy gave a higher priority to urban renewal. Thus the problems posed by inner area decline are the subject of more broadly-based intervention, incorporating economic measures, directed particularly at stemming the loss of jobs in manufacturing industry. Comprehensive Inner Area Programmes (IAPs) have been developed within new political and administrative arrangements to co-ordinate economic initiatives with modified versions of longer-established housing, planning and social policies.

A balanced assessment of the potential and limitations of IAPs suggests that while they are in step in the right direction, the revised policy needs strengthening significantly if it is to have more than a marginal impact.

A memorable speech

In September 1976 the new Secretary of State for the Environment, Shore, was appointed chairman of a cabinet committee to co-ordinate and review government urban policy. The DoE seized the initiative from the Home Office, and Shore made a major policy speech on 'the inner urban problem'.[2]

Pointing to the scale and rapidity of population decline – e.g. 40 per cent in fifteen years in Liverpool – he emphasized the significance of migration to the suburbs and beyond of mainly skilled workers and younger people. This unbalanced population loss left inner areas with disproportionate numbers of unskilled and semi-skilled workers, old people, and concentrations of immigrant communities. Housing conditions were inadequate, social and community facilities inferior, and environmental decay continued unabated. A rapid decline of jobs in manufacturing industry had been inadequately compensated for by the growth of city centre office jobs which were mostly taken by suburban commuters. Unemployment in inner areas was well above the national average, even in the more prosperous cities. Acknowledging the pressure for urgent shifts in policy Shore stated that these trends necessitated 'powerful countervailing action'.[3]

He argued that over the previous decade central government had become increasingly aware of the special needs of inner urban areas and that considerable effort had gone into tackling environmental and social problems. Modifications in the allocation of Rate Support Grant in favour of metropolitan districts together with developments in housing policy, particularly the move to gradual renewal and the introduction of housing investment programmes, were cited as changes made with their needs very much in mind. Similarly, he pointed out that the priority area projects were primarily concerned with the problems of older urban areas. However, the kernel of the speech was the statement that:

> Crucial though all these programmes have been they have to some extent dealt only with the *symptoms* and not the *causes* of the decline of the inner areas. The causes lie primarily in their relative economic decline, in a major migration of people, often the most skilled, and in a massive reduction in the number of jobs which are left. . . . We shall need to see what can be done to stem the tide of manufacturing jobs moving out and the possibility of reversing it.[4] (authors' emphasis)

Recognizing the complex interaction of forces which had caused this decline Shore identified two major elements. First, there was an unexpectedly high level of voluntary migration of people and jobs from the conurbation centres caused by social and economic changes. This exodus of population, associated with rising levels of affluence and personal mobility, had been much larger than anticipated in the immediate post-war years. New and growing industries had located outside the older urban areas as road haulage replaced rail transport and inter-urban motorways were built. Second, planning policies of comprehensive redevelopment and dispersal were now reinforcing these market-led trends.

An essential element in devising new policies to rejuvenate the inner cities would be a reappraisal of the impact of the new towns programme, industrial location strategies and local planning policies. A policy review would also take account of the two 'no growth' factors: the marked downturn in recent forecasts of population growth; and the fact that 'widespread concern about the urban areas has arisen at a time of great strain on public resources...' with the result that extra resources for inner areas 'can only come from a redistribution of what is available at present. . .'.[5]

Planning for growth

Shore's speech heralded a reorientation of planning policies which had been pursued, with successive modifications, for a generation. The post-war consensus in favour of containment was undermined by unforeseen development pressures.

Post-war consensus

During and after World War II a consensus of opinion emerged about the nature of urban and regional problems and appropriate policies.[6] At the inter-regional level the problem was that of uneven economic development. This had emerged as a policy issue in the 1930s, as basic industries in the old industrial areas declined while new growth industries developed in the Midlands and South-East. In order to reduce inequalities in employment opportunities regional policies were strengthened. The Distribution of Industry Act, 1945 established the machinery for controlling industrial growth in more prosperous regions and diverting new manufacturing industry to the Development Areas. The main instrument of policy was the Industrial Development Certificate (IDC): in prosperous regions firms were refused IDCs for significant expansion.

At the city–region level the problem was defined in terms of the social and economic disadvantages of large urban concentrations. The inner areas were congested, polluted and dominated by slum housing. The sprawling low-density suburbs of both municipal and private inter-war housing estates lacked many community facilities, had resulted in long journeys to work and a massive land-take from agriculture. Prevailing ideas about appropriate solutions were epitomized in Abercrombie's 1944 Greater London Plan, which advocated containment of urban growth and planned decentralization of population and employment. Congested inner areas would be comprehensively redeveloped at lower densities, with the corollary that further peripheral growth would be strictly limited by a Green Belt, and overspill would be concentrated in a ring of new towns beyond. The Labour Government of 1945 created the statutory basis for implementation: the Town and Country Planning Act, 1947 established public control over land use; the New Towns Act, 1946 created special agencies to promote and manage the development of new towns to which some industrial growth could be steered through IDC control.

Thus the major themes of post-war strategic planning were containment of the growth of cities and prosperous regions, and redistribution of population within and between regions. The first generation new towns were designated in the late 1940s. Local planning authorities began the preparation of statutory development plans (often within the framework of advisory regional plans), embodying in varying degrees the dual concepts of comprehensive redevelopment and planned overspill. It was assumed that overall population and employment levels would remain basically stable, and that the main pressures for urban development, once initial housing shortages had been overcome, would be overspill generated by comprehensive redevelopment.

In the 1950s the development of dispersal policies, indeed of planning generally, lost impetus as the Conservative Government restored the market in the development value of land. Only New Town Development Corporations could purchase land at existing use value, but no further new towns were designated. Instead the Town Development Act, 1952 provided for conurbation overspill by the expansion of existing neighbouring towns. This involved complex negotiations between exporting and receiving authorities and initially yielded very limited provision. Many cities developed much of their remaining land but further peripheral expansion was restricted by the formal extension of Green Belt policy to provincial conurbations. This, combined with the limited progress of the new and expanded towns programme, began to pose major problems of land availability as comprehensive redevelopment programmes gathered momentum.

Exploding cities

It became apparent that the demographic and economic context of post-war planning had changed. Demographic demand for housing increased and it was clear that housing needs and planning policies were out of gear.[7] Housing shortages continued, especially in those cities which were attracting immigrants from elsewhere in the UK and abroad. It was no longer simply a question of planned dispersal of overspill from redevelopment: public overspill was also needed to reduce housing waiting lists and private overspill was increasing.

New manufacturing industry tended to locate in the most profitable locations on the periphery of the conurbations and in the towns within and beyond the Green Belt. At the same time, as service sector or 'tertiary' employment increased in both private and public sectors, office employment growth concentrated in city centres. The demand for office space fuelled redevelopment, in which the local authorities concerned were the willing but unequal partners of large property companies. Both more affluent office workers (trading off long journeys to work against the advantages of a suburban, village or small-town residential environment) and skilled workers moved outwards. Increased commuting by private car and the resultant peak hour congestion generated pressures for the renewal of primary urban road networks.

The extent to which these development pressures could be channelled into an efficient settlement pattern became the dominant strategic issue at the intra-regional level, as fears about loss of agricultural land and the limited progress of planned overspill raised the spectre of uncontrolled metropolitan expansion. During the 1960s a further generation of new towns were designated, but some cities argued that this was too little too late. Central government pressure to accelerate clearance and continuing housing pressure meant that public overspill had, in the short term, to be accommodated by peripheral expansion, often only after protracted conflict with adjoining county authorities defending dispersal policies. Much private overspill was accommodated in areas beyond the Green Belt.

At the inter-regional level economic growth again focussed attention on regional inequalities. There was a prolonged academic debate about the relative merits of 'taking work to the workers', or 'workers to the work'. But it was politically impossible to write off the social capital already invested in older industrial areas and planned emigration was considered impractical. Regional policy was strengthened as the 'stick' of the IDC was complemented by increased subsidies for firms; grants for capital investment, employment premiums subsidizing wages, rent-free periods for new factories, etc. On a scale never before achieved, new manufacturing industry was steered into the Assisted Areas. Peripheral green-field sites were developed by the English Industrial Estates Corporation, a policy which was often in direct competition with efforts to achieve dispersal of employment to new towns. The development of the national motorway network reinforced the locational attraction of the outer metropolitan areas.

Thus at the intra- and inter-regional levels post-war planning strategies were strengthened. Overspill from the cities consumed a considerable proportion of resources allocated by local and central government. In contrast, as discussed in Chapter 2, the provision of social infrastructure lagged well behind housebuilding in inner area redevelopment schemes. Until the mid-1960s this was confidently assumed to be a temporary problem and 'in 1965 at any rate nobody was as yet seriously suggesting that a better world would be created by leaving everyone living and working in a nineteenth century environment'.[8] Nor did the problems of twilight areas figure significantly in planning debates, except in so far as there was concern about the time that might elapse before they could be redeveloped. There was little understanding of the effects of decentralization on the economic and social structure of inner areas, and it was only from the late 1960s that:

> the inner city began to receive increasing attention in rather roundabout ways through house improvement policies and measures, based particularly in London and the West Midlands, to improve the position of coloured immigrants – although the problem could never be couched in those terms. Most important of all . . . was the development of thinking on positive discrimination in deprived areas.[9]

Shore's speech was dubbed not only 'memorable' but also as marking 'the end of the beginning' in the reorientation of urban policy.[10] Chapters 3 and 4 have dealt with the housing renewal dimension of government policy changes while Chapter 5 has outlined parallel developments in social policy. This chapter now examines the other 'roundabout ways' in which inner city problems became the central urban policy issue of the mid-1970s.

Spatial planning, urban management and social justice

Criticism of the consequences of post-war policies prompted the re-emergence of poverty and inequality as issues in urban planning. Local government reorganization provided a further impetus to management reforms. A burgeoning of community action stimulated increasing attention to both distribution (who benefits?) and accountability (who decides?) questions. The political and economic context of these emerging pressures changed drastically with the onset of 'no growth'. Deepening economic recession, together with a downturn in population growth forecasts, reduced urban development pressures and economic policy imposed cuts in social spending. A mounting volume of evidence testified to deteriorating conditions in inner areas. This tangled skein of influences and events shaped the policy making environment into which Shore's speech precipitated the results of the urban experiments. Their conclusions became pivotal in the inner areas debate.

Urban planning and equity

The rediscovery of poverty in the 1960s had little impact on urban planning. A system of structure plans and more detailed local plans was introduced in 1968, and there were rapid developments in the mathematical simulation of urban development, particularly in the field of land-use transportation planning. However, there was little explicit discussion of the social objectives and consequences of planning policies. If such issues were raised at all it was assumed that planning 'in the public interest' was a neutral, technical process, which benefited all groups rather than a political process which benefits some at the expense of others. This dominant view was gradually undermined. In 1977 a Royal Town Planning Institute (RTPI) Working Party commented:

> . . . many people in urban management, including planners, have become concerned that the positive results of their activities have benefited some areas and groups in the population more than others. The well-ordered development and high environmental standards of much peripheral, new and expanded town development are in stark contrast to the concentration of personal poverty, poor housing and physical chaos of such areas as inner Liverpool or parts of inner London.[11]

The statement reflected a changing climate of ideas stimulated by academic research. It was demonstrated that inequality had not been reduced under the Wilson administrations and the 'poverty lobby' was re-established as a feature of British politics.[12] Critical analysis of the performance of the welfare state was extended to include an assessment of the social consequences of urban planning.

The theoretical framework for much of this work was 'urban managerialism' which focussed on the relationship between social structure and spatial structure and the processes of resource allocation in the urban system. In a mixed economy market processes dominate the distribution of resources, but significant resources are allocated through non-market mechanisms: they are bureaucratically allocated by 'urban managers', including local government officers operating rules and procedures such as those governing access to council housing. Academics pointed out that planners are part of this system of allocation, as they influence the spatial distribution of, and therefore access to, goods and services: planning should contribute to the reduction of inequality by discriminating in favour of disadvantaged groups and areas.[13]

Judged from this perspective, planning was found wanting. An obvious example was that urban motorway proposals enabled middle-income car-owning commuters to move more easily between the outer suburbs and the city centre, but also imposed costs on low-income inner area residents – displacement, environmental intrusion and, indirectly, the erosion of public transport. At a more general level, strategic policies were judged to have reinforced rather than reduced inequality, by benefiting least the poor living in older inner areas.[14] Initially the planning establishment dismissed such criticism as the somewhat ethereal preoccupations of 'ivory-tower' academics or the worthy, but misconceived, concerns of younger professionals whose reforming enthusiasm would eventually be tempered by the harsh realities of experience. Nonetheless, the issue of social justice began to figure on a variety of strategic planning agendas – at the Greater London Development Plan Inquiry, the Examinations in Public of the first wave of structure plans, and during the preparation of a new round of regional strategies. Attitudes began to change as debates within the profession questioned the extent to which planning policies were contributing to inner area problems.

Corporate planning and area management

Dissatisfaction with physical planning was only one of the pressures for more effective urban government. In 1972 the Bains Report provided a renewed impetus for the development of corporate planning, and the upheaval of local government reorganization created the opportunity for implementing its recommendations.[15] Most of the new authorities established revised management structures, including a policy and resources committee, serviced by a chief executive and a chief officers' management team, with responsibility for integrating major policies. Corporate planning processes varied, but by the mid-1970s typically included the preparation of programme area position statements revising existing policies and commitments, e.g. in social services; issue analysis – the investigation of a policy area, e.g. provision for the elderly; the work of a Performance Review Committee, an internal watch-dog body; and an annual planning–budgeting cycle.[16]

The SNAP report had argued that 'since public action is always conceived in a fragmented fashion, resulting programmes have not been relevant to the real circumstances of the inner city'.[17] Moves towards corporate planning were an improvement, but several factors limited their potential. There was a mechanistic concern for management structures and processes with less emphasis on the identification of changes in policies. Internal reorganization of authorities' activities into broad programme areas (e.g. leisure and recreation) reduced the number of departments, but a service orientation continued to dominate. The new fragmentation of urban government reinforced the need for co-ordination between agencies, but this received relatively little attention. Innovations were mainly at the centre, tending to reinforce the power of senior councillors and chief officers. Above all, the tradition of administrative uniformity in the provision of services continued to militate against positive discrimination: corporate planning was more concerned with efficiency than equity.[18]

However, there was also growing interest in the concept of area management, which involves an integrated approach to the problems of particular localities.[19] Scaling down remote post-reorganization bureaucracies would increase their accountability and their capacity to adjust to varying needs. The concept means more than simple geographical decentralization of specific services, such as housing management. It has several key elements: area teams of officers with delegated responsibility for the co-ordination of local services; area committees comprising ward councillors and (possibly) representatives of residents' organizations, monitoring the impact of policies and providing an input to central decisions; area information systems analysing needs in relation to existing resource allocations; and, at its most sophisticated, area programming and budgeting systems and delegated spending powers. By the mid-1970s only a few authorities had introduced some form of area management, either taking the initiative themselves or participating in the DoE's area management trials. There were several reasons for this: argument in area committees could distract attention from basic decision making at the centre; area committees controlled by opposition parties was a prospect not relished by senior councillors; and servicing area committees would increase administrative costs. Nonetheless, there was a groundswell of opinion that area management could tune local authority activity to the diverse needs of neighbourhoods.

It was clear that innovations in urban management would not by themselves focus local authorities' action on problems of urban deprivation, but might increase their capacity to deal with these problems once so focussed.[20] From the local authorities' point of view, central government should provide that focus, but was not doing so, as it had no clear strategy to which they could relate their actions. The urban experiments were seen as spasmodic, unrelated, peripheral to the main issues, and a reflection of central government departmentalism. An INLOGOV report argued that authorities should be requested to prepare urban deprivation plans based on an analysis of problems and the impact of current policies; identifying key issues for action; and proposing policy changes committing all relevant agencies and departments to positive discrimination in favour of the deprived. These multi-agency plans should be funded by additional block grants from central government – 'the only means by which the attention of some authorities could be focussed'[21] – combined with the maximum possible internal redistribution of existing resources.

These proposals, like those of SNAP, emphasized adaptation of existing machinery, supporting the prevalent local government view that alternative channels could neither ignore the considerable activities of elected authorities nor replicate their local knowledge. However, many commentators were not convinced that better management could substantially alleviate deprivation, arguing that local authorities were unwilling to substantially shift their policies in favour of inner areas, as local politics would closely circumscribe the limits of redistribution from more affluent suburbs. Special agencies along the lines of new town development corporations were needed. Lack of democratic control would be more than offset by the benefits of swift action, deploying additional powers and central funding.[22] Such arguments tended to ignore the extent to which local authorities could improve their performance if they had the same special powers and finance.

The challenge of community action

Pressures for change did not only come 'from the top down'. During the early 1970s the rapid growth of locality-based groups in working-class areas generated political pressures 'from the bottom up'. The forgotten poor began to organize and challenge professional and political orthodoxies, by formulating their definitions of problems and priorities, demanding a more just allocation of resources and more influence over decisions vitally affecting their lives. The term community action embraced a diversity of ideologies, aims and types of organization which sustained a wide range of activities.[23] Its development was rooted in the failure of the welfare state to significantly reduce inequality. Deteriorating conditions in inner areas were the everyday experience of residents, alienating them from local government. While resigned acceptance in the face of apparent bureaucratic indifference to their problems was a common reaction, some residents began to organize groups outside the formal political process.

These local groups were often joined (and not infrequently formed) by a motley collection of middle-class activists who marched under the banner of community action. Some were committed socialists, disillusioned by the Wilson Government's retreat from basic principles, and seeking egalitarian social change through participatory policies.[24] Others were Liberals who grasped 'community politics' as the way to revive party fortunes among dissatisfied Labour voters. Their ranks were swelled by 'dissident professionals' who held the view that their professions were not adequately serving the interests of low-income groups. Working mainly on a voluntary basis, a minority of architects, planners, public health inspectors, lawyers and social workers sought to share their knowledge and skills with action groups. When added to the growing numbers of full-time community workers, they constituted a significant resource for some residents' groups, and exerted a liberalizing influence on the professions from whence they came.[25]

There were some common strands in community action. Most groups were non-party political, recognizing that explicit allegiance would render them vulnerable to the pendulum swings of local political control. Action groups tended to operate in a pragmatic and reactive way, organizing around immediate local issues. Housing conditions were the focus of much effort and earlier chapters have examined the role of groups in area renewal.[26] The typical inadequacy of provision in relation to needs prompted campaigns for facilities such as pre-school play groups, nursery schools, and community centres. Some issues were relatively short-lived, while others developed on a bureaucratically determined and seemingly geological time-scale.

The issues on which activity centred influenced the groups' organization: while many sustained their involvement through peaks and troughs of activity, others were ephemeral and collapsed in the face of local authority intransigence, internal conflicts, or loss of key personnel. Often groups were able to draw on independent neighbourhood centres with full-time housing and welfare rights workers, increasingly funded by Urban Aid. Initially, action groups were parochial but, as experience taught many that they were fighting the same battles, city-wide federations of residents' organizations emerged. Tactics varied. Many groups started on the basis of negotiations, while others, either sceptical of 'normal channels' from the outset, or disillusioned by a negative response, adopted a conflict approach emphasizing 'direct action' such as demonstrations.

By the mid-1970s the inner areas of most cities had dozens of active residents' organizations and the reactions of local authority officers and councillors varied from sympathetic support to downright hostility. Many action groups had become more sophisticated and independent: they were less reliant on middle-class activists, had learned much about the workings of local government, and were campaigning for more effective policies. In short, community action had become an established feature of local politics.

The end of growth

In the mid-1970s population projections were scaled down, a reflection of the declining birth rate and the cessation of net immigration. The rate of economic growth declined from 3 per cent p.a. in the early 1960s to 1 per cent by the early 1970s, and by 1975 'we could sum up Britain's economic position by saying that there will be no growth in real terms for some considerable time to come and there is a strong probability at least that real standards of living will fall'.[27] Unemployment rose to an unprecedented post-war level and the recession precipitated an abrupt end to an era of growth in local government services which had spanned three quarters of a century. In the aftermath of the financial crisis of 1976, expenditure plans were cut and a projected decline rendered a long-held assumption of continuous growth invalid.

The debate on urban planning intensified as the validity of post-war policies was sharply questioned. It was argued that massive decentralization of people and jobs was contributing to the rapid erosion of the economic base of the cities, especially the inner areas. The overall effect of decentralization had been initially debated at the GLDP Inquiry, and subsequently two related issues became prominent: the 'fiscal crisis' of the cities and 'social polarization'. Decentralization was producing a falling rate base, while the costs and demands for services to which the rates contributed remained the same, or rose. Rising costs and demands were partly attributed to the demands of commuters but also to polarization, i.e. selective migration increasing the proportion of residents dependent on state benefit or low incomes.[28] Falk and Martinos pointed to 'a growing crisis in the capacity of cities to sustain their basic services and to meet the demands of the most disadvantaged groups'.[29]

Against the background of description and analysis emerging from the urban experiments, several influential studies pointed to the relationship between decentralization and worsening conditions in inner urban areas. For example, Lomas highlighted two significant trends: first, the long-term decline of manufacturing employment in London had accelerated since the mid-1960s, and second, decline had been particularly marked in inner London.[30] He argued for the adoption of policies for economic renewal. Eversley, one of the strongest critics of urban policies, contended that the needs of inner areas should be given first priority, and that additional resources for these areas in a no growth situation meant redistribution from elsewhere. His statement that 'the new town programme will, at the very least, have to be put in cold storage' provoked considerable controversy.[31] It was strongly contested by those (particularly the Town and Country Planning Association) who argued that dispersal should continue, albeit modified to enable more of the inner city poor to move out, for by reducing pressures on land, such policies assisted inner area renewal.[32]

This changing climate of ideas was reflected in policy shifts. For example, the Strategic Plan for the North West recommended a reduction in dispersal and a concentration on the conurbation areas, with additional central government resources to deal with inner area problems.[33] In similar vein the GLC cut back its commitment to expanded towns and launched its own urban deprivation programme.[34] Concern about unemployment stimulated reappraisals of existing policies and the development of new ones. Prominent among the former were several well-publicized analyses by local authorities of the effects of comprehensive redevelopment on job loss; this set the scene for the development of policies to preserve existing jobs by minimizing disruption and to promote new employment through measures such as co-operatives.[35] Initiatives which were to assume considerable significance were those concerned with developing and applying the concept of Industrial Improvement Areas. Pioneering schemes in Rochdale and Tyne and Wear to foster employment by improving the infrastructure of old industrial areas (access, car parking, etc.), refurbishing old industrial property, and providing new accommodation, attracted considerable attention.[36]

In the wider field of urban management it was clear that corporate planning was at a crossroads: 'no growth' could either reinforce departmentalism as service chiefs sought to defend their budgets, or it could concentrate minds on the corporate determination of priorities to make the best available use of resources. Clearly the latter was necessary for improved action against urban deprivation, and in Newcastle the council adopted a priority areas approach involving the allocation of staff and modest budgets to deprived areas to be utilized in accordance with locally determined priorities.[37] Similarly, the 'end of growth' confronted community action groups with a dilemma: confining their activities to attacking local policies and officialdom was clearly limited when national policy was eroding local authorities' capacity to respond.

The inner areas debate

It was in this changing climate of ideas and emerging local initiatives that Shore made his speech in September 1976, which catalysed the developing debate and prompted the most widespread discussion of urban policy since the 1940s.[38] A succession of ministerial speeches at a proliferation of conferences maintained the momentum[39] and the urban crisis engaged the attention of the media – featuring in colour supplements,[40] television programmes and innumerable newspaper articles. The urban experiments came in from the cold. The CDP published two major and controversial reports.[41] The DoE published a quickly prepared summary of the IAS final reports and invited comments.[42] Local authorities and their organizations, professional institutions, academics, pressure groups and trades councils were among those who submitted their views.[43] In April 1977 Shore outlined the Government's proposals to Parliament. Three months later the IAS final reports[44] and the White Paper *Policy for the Inner Cities* were published.

The debate covered the symptoms and causes of decline, the aims of future policy and the means of implementation, but focussed on economic issues.

Hall encapsulated the thrust of the discussion:

it is essential not to treat symptoms but to isolate causes. That, surely, is the essential difference between the 1977 analysis of the urban crisis and the previous versions. There is general agreement that the central problem is economic: the rapid decline of the economic base of the inner city. Other evident problems need treatment too – housing, transport, administration. But they need analysing above all in terms of their effect on employment.[45]

Symptoms of decline

The facts were starkly chronicled: inner areas of the major conurbations contained one fourteenth of the country's population (nearly four million people), but an eighth of its unskilled workers, a fifth of households living in housing stress, and a third of New Commonwealth immigrants.[46] In these areas the overall unemployment rate was twice the national average (in Liverpool's inner area it had climbed to 17 per cent and in some neighbourhoods was over 30 per cent); the rate of job loss was twice the national average (in ten years Canning Town in London had lost 24,000 jobs, a net loss of 24 per cent); up to ten times the national proportion of families lived below the poverty line; there were more than double the national proportion of single parent families; and car ownership levels were less than half the national rate.[47]

The IAS reports confirmed that only a minority of inner area residents suffered any 'personal deprivations' and that there were significant concentrations of deprivation in the outer council estates, such as Kirby on Merseyside. But they were also unanimous in emphasizing the significance of what the Birmingham team termed 'collective deprivation' – 'that is, deprivation attributable to the shared environment and suffered by virtue of where people live'.[48] It is the sense of decline and neglect experienced by a majority of residents irrespective of their individual job and housing situation. In part it stems from the unattractive appearance of many neighbourhoods – poor quality housing, badly maintained council estates, litter, rubble strewn sites and boarded up buildings. Social problems such as racial tension, the anti-social behaviour of a minority of 'problem families', together with fear of vandalism and petty crime, contribute to the feeling that the area is going downhill. This is reinforced by the labelling of neighbourhoods, particularly in the local press, as 'problem areas' – a factor in the extra difficulties experienced by some residents in obtaining credit, jobs and mortgages. Poor services in relation to needs also undermine confidence in the future of these neighbourhoods and the agencies of government – further eroding 'community spirit'. The gist of the argument was that deprivation in inner city areas is greater than the sum of its parts. Concentrations of households suffering personal deprivation in areas characterized by more indirect, but pervasive, collective deprivation adds up to urban deprivation – a distinct and potentially explosive phenomenon, particularly in multi-racial areas.[49] This dimension of poverty was the basis of the IAS advocacy of an inner area policy initiative by government.

Causes of decline

The dominant view of causes of urban deprivation which emerged was in sharp contrast to that of the late 1960s: it emphasized structural factors. For example, the Liverpool consultants stated that 'poverty stems from the persistence of divisions of status and income in society at large'.[50] They posed a key question:

> to what extent does the decline of a particular inner city reflect social and economic changes, to be reversed only at very high cost, or is it at least in part the consequence of government action which could be more easily changed?[51]

For, as Hall pointed out, 'if the former then there must be doubt whether government, by thrusting policy levers into reverse can fundamentally change the situation'.[52] The debate centred on the relative importance of the processes causing the decentralization of population and employment and their impact on the inner cities. The prevailing view which emerged was that decline was the product of market forces, exacerbated by the consequences of government action.

The evidence substantiated the argument that concentrations of the poor in inner areas were, in part, the result of selective population decentralization.[53] The process was described as 'polarization' in provincial cities as the majority of those moving out are younger, middle- and higher-income families, leaving behind a rising proportion of unskilled and semi-skilled workers and elderly people. The London variation was 'bi-polarization', as the same trend is accompanied by gentrification of some of its older housing. Why are the poor unable to move out? They cannot afford to buy new private housing while access to desirable suburban council housing is constrained by allocation policies (a particular problem in London where the outer boroughs are reluctant to provide tenancies for families from the inner boroughs[54]), and the new towns selected mainly the skilled workers necessary to man their modern industries. This is the 'housing trap' highlighted by the Lambeth consultants.[55] The long-standing process of the market consigning the poor to the cheapest older housing had only been partly modified by state intervention.

The concentration of unemployment in inner areas was a major issue in the debate. This focussed attention on the operation of the labour market, about which there were (and still are) conflicting views.[56]

One view holds that the city is a single labour market and that workers losing jobs in one area would commute to jobs in other parts of the city. Hence very high rates of unemployment in inner areas are not primarily a function of declining job opportunities, but are due to a combination of the processes of residential segregation referred to above and high national levels of unemployment.[57] The labour force resident in inner areas contains disproportionate numbers of the unskilled who are most vulnerable to cyclical downturns in the demand for labour. When unemployment rises generally, the rate for the unskilled rises faster, not only because of the declining numbers of unskilled jobs but also because if skilled workers lose their jobs many can compete more effectively for any available unskilled work. The CDP pointed out that in order to survive industry has to maintain profitability in the face of fluctuating demands for its products. Firms therefore lay off labour to cut costs when demand is slack and re-hire when demand picks up. This 'expendable labour' at times of cyclical downturn in the economy is mainly the unskilled and semi-skilled.[58] Within this view it is clear that the concentration of unemployment can only be solved by lowering national unemployment rates and by policies aimed at vulnerable groups not areas, such as manpower training programmes or housing reforms to increase labour mobility.

A contrasting view, and one which dominated the debate, is that high unemployment in inner areas is due to the contraction of local employment opportunities, particularly as the result of the decline of manufacturing industry. In this view the urban area is a set of spatial labour markets and workers losing jobs in one area cannot easily obtain employment elsewhere. It is argued that inner area residents who lose local jobs cannot travel longer distances to alternative jobs and are unable or unwilling to move house.[59]

Decentralization of employment opportunities is a complex process. The decline of inner area employment is the net result of the birth of new enterprises and expansion of existing firms and job losses arising from closures of existing plants or shrinkage in their labour forces (see Figure 12).

First, there follows a description of the components of decline. For many years few jobs have been created in inner areas: births have been dwarfed by the scale of closures, and a minority of expanding firms have not offset the effects of others contracting. For example, the IAS survey of Liverpool 7 showed that during 1964–74 twenty-one new enterprises yielded less than 200 jobs, while thirty-five closures accounted for the loss of 1000; expanding firms generated 1800 jobs while other firms caused a shrinkage of 5000.[60] In general, the evidence indicated that the rate of new openings was much lower in inner areas, and that the average size of new plants, in terms of employees, was smaller.

Far less obvious are the different types of closures and their relative significance. Closures resulting from the death of firms produce an absolute loss of jobs – lost not only to inner areas, but to the economy as a whole. Other closures result from transfers, either to a new location or to an existing location within a multi-plant firm. These job losses may be gains for other areas, but relocation is often associated with an overall cut-back in labour.

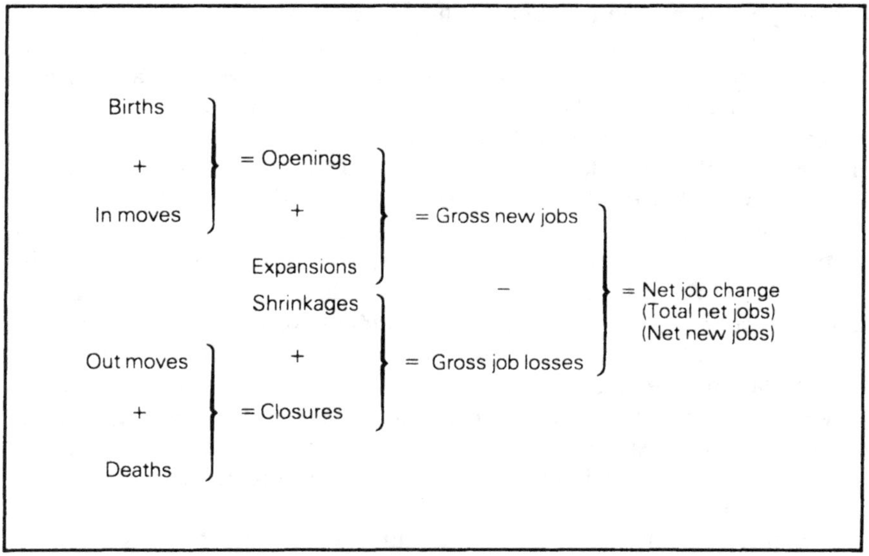

Figure 12 *Employment: the components of change*

Source: Adapted from D. Storey, *Job Generation and Small Firms Policy in Britain* (CES Policy Series 11, 1980)

In sharp contrast to the popular view that decline is due to firms moving out, research established the death of plants as the major component. Birmingham IAS concluded that the greatest cause of the extremely rapid loss of manufacturing jobs was not movement of firms but their death, and in inner London only a third of job losses was attributable to movement.[61]

Another popular view not supported by evidence is that job loss is mainly due to the closure of small firms. Although three quarters of closures in inner London were among firms with less than 100 employees, this accounted for only a third of employment loss from closures, and the Birmingham IAS found that much the largest part of closure losses were due to the death of large establishments. While the rate of closures in inner cities is similar to that of outer areas, the employment effects were more severe in the former because of relatively large closures.

Thus, while the balance sheet of the components of employment change in inner area manufacturing industry varies in detail, the general picture is one of low levels of new investment, and massive job losses stemming primarily from the death of shrinkage of larger plants, supplemented by relocation losses.

Why is industrial decentralization taking place on such a large scale? The explanations are complex and vary in the significance attributed to three groups of factors:

1 the changing locational preferences of industry – decline is a function of the relative disadvantages of the built environment of inner areas;
2 structural changes in the national economy – decline is a spatial consequence of the development of the national economy; and
3 government intervention – decline is the unintended consequence of planning policies.

The decreasing relative attractiveness of inner area locations is commonly held to be the major influence. An increasing scale of production and innovations in technology generate demands for large cheap sites with room for expansion. These factors, together with the importance of easy access to the national motorway network, make the outer areas of the conurbations, with their good communications, modern infrastructure, and relatively low private development costs, the most efficient locations for modern industry.[62] Conversely, many inner areas have poor road access, obsolete plant and land for expansion or new industry is both difficult to assemble and expensive to develop: 'the contrast that the modern industrial estate on the edge of town offers to the anarchy of the inner city could hardly be greater'.[63]

The locational requirements of modern industry explain the much higher rate of births, and larger average size, of firms in outer areas. Moreover, locational factors help to explain thc nature of the limited recent development in inner areas – the 'new industries of decline'.[64] Smaller firms are attracted by the availability of cheap premises and cheap labour – often non-unionized and immigrant. As well as not offsetting job losses such firms provide work which is often insecure, low paid and in poor conditions. Elsewhere, there is a tendency for the limited number of new industrial estates, with good access to major roads, to be dominated by warehousing and distribution. These new uses take up large areas of land, employ few workers and provide mainly low-paid, unskilled jobs. The heavy goods traffic they generate imposes noise and environmental pollution on local residents. For the CDP 'the new industries are no solution to decline – they are part of the problem'.[65] Locational disadvantages are also important reasons for closures due to firms moving. For example, surveys which examined the 'push' factors causing firms to move out of London showed that three quarters of moves were primarily motivated by the need to expand output: in most cases it was not possible to expand *in situ* because sites were fully occupied and existing buildings inadequate.

The pattern of births and closures due to relocation are clearly related to locational preferences stemming from technological changes, but this level of analysis leaves unanswered the question of why and how these changes have occurred. Moreover, the major components of manufacturing job loss – shrinkage in existing firms and closures due to deaths – are not so obviously explicable in locational terms.[66] The Liverpool IAS came to the view that many of the factors causing decline 'have little to do with the locational preferences of firms. They owe their causes to events far removed from those of the inner city'.[67] Similarly, academic researchers concluded that the decline in manufacturing can only be properly understood in terms of 'the link between locational change and developments at the level of the national and international economy'.[68]

Structural explanations of job losses in inner areas were thrust into the debate by the CDP report *The Costs of Industrial Change*. This argued that the collapse of local economies is a result of the acceleration of a process that has been going on for over forty years: at root, the problem is the declining profitability and competitive position of British industry. Low levels of industrial investment in the relatively profitable 1950s resulted in only marginal increases in productivity. Output per worker remained low as old plant was not replaced and the organization of production remained largely unchanged. In the 1960s profitability fell in the face of increasing competition from foreign firms which, after re-investment and reorganization, were achieving higher productivity. Many firms were unable to attract the re-investment necessary to increase their competitiveness and eventually went bankrupt. Inner areas, with large proportions of old plant, were particularly vulnerable to such closures and paid the price of companies failing. But inner areas also pay the price of some firms successfully adapting to changing conditions. Such companies reduce their aggregate labour costs by using new technology. Unless they also rapidly expanded output, increased productivity resulted in fewer jobs. In inner areas firms are part of older industries, in which demand is static or falling. Hence 'in older industrial areas increases in productivity almost always mean lost jobs'.[69]

However, an unfavourable industrial structure, in the sense of inner areas having a disproportionate share of industries in decline nationally, does not provide a full explanation. Some inner areas, such as London, have a structure biased towards industries in which employment is expanding. An important dimension is change in the ownership and organization of firms with the growth of multi-plant and multi-national firms.[70] Measures to increase productivity are often accompanied by a restructuring of production. Within multi-plant firms this can mean that goods formerly manufactured in several factories can be more cheaply produced at one location. Hence, rationalization results in a concentration of production and plant closures. Again inner areas lose out. Where there is a choice firms will not invest in their old, cramped sites but concentrate production in an existing or completely new factory in a more favourable location. In terms of both closures of some plants and shrinkage of employment at others, inner areas pay the price of companies successfully increasing profitability.

Measures to increase productivity and reorganize production have been accompanied by massive changes in the ownership and control of industry. In order to raise the huge amounts of finance necessary for investment firms have combined by mergers and takeovers. This increasing concentration of control has been a major feature of manufacturing industry for the past twenty years. In 1950 the top 100 companies accounted for 20 per cent of national output, by

1970 this had reached 50 per cent and by the mid-1980s it will be approaching 70 per cent.[71] The growth of national or multi-national companies has led to rationalizations and, again, the resultant closures and redundancies have a disproportionate impact on inner areas.

On this basis CDP argued that declining inner areas are not simply the legacy of a bygone era, nor are the processes which cause decline abnormal events within a broadly satisfactory system. Declining areas are an integral, normal and necessary part of the development of the economy as it is presently organized:

> The explanation of persisting poverty, unemployment and all the other features of 'deprivation' in our five areas is to be found in the nature of capitalist economic development itself: its need constantly to restructure, to find new outlets and new locations, and to keep down its labour costs throughout a variety of changing market and competitive circumstances. The development, stability and prosperity of expanding industries and areas implies and depends on the progressive under-development of other areas.[72]

The conclusion they reached was that the problem and inequalities generated and sustained by uneven development will persist:

> . . . until policies are implemented which seriously challenge the rights of industry and capital to move freely about the country (not to mention the world) without regard for the welfare of workers and existing communities.[73]

The CDP research moved from identifying the quantitative and qualitative decline in local employment opportunities in older areas to charting processes of restructuring. A concurrent academic analysis started from identifying the pressures in the economy which stimulated restructuring in twenty-five firms, employing a quarter of a million people in the electrical, electronic and aerospace equipment sectors – archetypal modern growth industries – then traced the effects of restructuring on the inner areas of the four cities with firms included in the survey.[74] The methodology was different but the results and conclusions are strikingly similar. Two thirds of the jobs lost were from the inner city, and of these 89 per cent were lost to the economy as a whole – only 11 per cent arrived elsewhere. This research stressed that closures and redundancies did not indicate failure, but the only possibility for success, a necessary process in the development of the national economy. It concluded that:

> . . . if there is a contradiction at the heart of this process of decline, our research would indicate that it is not between inner cities and the policy aided development areas, but between the cities and the demands of profitability and international competitiveness.[75]

The relationship between inner cities and regional policy was one dimension of the debate about the extent to which government policies were responsible for inner area decline. The 'planner-blame hypothesis' was widely canvassed by the media and some politicians, including the then Prime Minister, Callaghan, who accused planners of wrecking the inner cities and destroying worthwhile jobs.[76] The death of firms is the major component of job loss and many argued that comprehensive redevelopment was an important factor, as 'non-conforming' firms displaced were either not offered suitable alternative sites or were faced with prohibitively high rents for modern premises.[77] While the evidence suggested that between a quarter and a half of displaced firms had disappeared for good, the significance of this tended to be overstressed for several reasons. First, displaced firms were mainly small – big firms were 'planned around' because of enormous acquisition costs. Second, many of the small firms that disappeared would have died anyway as they were operating at very low levels of profitability – most of those equipped to grow survived redevelopment and moved into new premises. Finally, while redevelopment caused the death of many small firms, employment losses were mainly the result of large firms closing – the losses caused by redevelopment could therefore only have been a very small proportion of the total. Thus a balanced view of this issue suggested that a more sensitive approach to existing small firms was necessary, but that its potential for reducing the overall rate of job loss was very limited, particularly as this policy lever had already been thrown into reverse by the shift from redevelopment to improvement.[78]

Another element in the 'planner-blame hypothesis' was that job loss was in large measure due to dispersal policies taking industry out to new and expanded towns and regional policies diverting indigenous growth from inner areas of the prosperous cities to peripheral locations in Assisted Areas. While such policies did encourage the decentralization of employment it is clear that unplanned movement was dominant.[79] However, the major conclusion which emerged from IAS and CDP and from other research was that since the mid-1960s job losses due to movement have been only a quarter to a third of the total, and that the direct influence of planning policies has been a relatively minor and diminishing factor. For example, Gripiaos' study of south-east inner London showed that of the quarter of firms which closed because of relocation only 2 per cent moved to new towns and 3 per cent to the Assisted Areas, and Massey and Meegan's work indicated that the number of jobs lost to inner cities and gained elsewhere amounted to only 11 per cent of the total, of which two thirds went to the Assisted Areas.[80] The argument was not that inner areas do not lose employment as a result of strategic planning policies, but that the numerical significance of these losses tends to be exaggerated. Hence ending dispersal policy and further relaxing IDC control would have little impact on the loss of jobs although there was a case for regional policy being modified so that more of the subsidized firms located in the inner suburbs of the Development Areas.

Finally, government economic policies since the mid-1960s have actively encouraged company mergers and rationalization in the private sector through the work of agencies such as the Industrial Reorganization Corporation, and similar measures have been taken to increase productivity in the nationalized industries.[81] There is little doubt that these policies reinforced the processes which are the major cause of job losses in inner areas but, paradoxically, they attracted far less attention than the presumed effect of redevelopment, dispersal and regional policies.

A spectrum of prescriptions

The IAS concluded that the severity of the symptoms and the basic economic causes of urban deprivation warranted a new national policy which would channel additional resources to inner areas. However, they stressed that poverty is a national problem requiring nation-wide policies: while improved area-based policies could go some way towards relieving the inner city dimension of poverty, this should be complementary to, not in place of, changes such as a new income maintenance scheme providing higher pensions and child benefits.[82]

The aims of inner area policy would be to halt, if not reverse the processes of relative decline. In general terms the IAS argued for a more comprehensive approach to urban renewal which would include economic measures aimed at preserving and creating jobs in inner areas, and seek to achieve maximum benefit from limited public resources by improved urban management, greater community involvement and the encouragement of private investment. This prescription echoed many of the themes of policy debate since the late 1960s, but the significant difference was the emphasis on economic intervention.

However, there was a spectrum of views about appropriate economic measures:[83]

1 At one end CDP argued that effective action would necessitate public control of industrial investment, including measures such as nationalization of major profitable firms, extensive public shareholdings in private companies, planning agreements and direct public investment (via nationalized industries and the NEB) in areas of high unemployment – all of which required an end to public spending cuts.

2 At the opposite end the view was that the wealth of the nation depended on a thriving private sector, free to make its own location decisions and continue rationalization. The first priority was to restore profitability by reducing taxation and allowing unemployment to rise – the eventual improvement in the economy would create new jobs and training schemes would improve inner area residents' access to them. This strategy necessitated further spending cuts.

3 In the 'middle ground', chosen by the IAS, the argument was that in a mixed economy it was possible to change government policies and shift the balance back in favour of the inner areas. A range of incentives to both

large and small firms could be funded by increasing the proportion of available public expenditure devoted to industrial rather than, say, housing investment.

Conflicting views also characterized the debate about *methods of implementation*. The possibility of a national inner area policy at a time of resource constraints prompted arguments that effort should be concentrated in the big cities and counter-arguments that the needs of smaller cities and old industrial towns were also serious enough to warrant central government assistance. Similarly local government opinion was in favour of any new initiative being operated through local authorities rather than new agencies, but was split as to whether the prime responsibility should lie with metropolitan districts or county councils.

Policy for the inner cities

Competing explanations and prescriptions were distilled in a Cabinet review of urban policy. This resulted in the 1977 White Paper *Policy for the Inner Cities*, which gave an explicit priority to inner urban areas encompassing economic, social and environmental programmes, and embodied a long-term commitment to their regeneration. The following section describes the main features of the revised policy and outlines relevant powers and procedures.

The new approach

The main components of the White Paper[84] can be summarized under the following headings:

1 analysis of inner area problems;
2 aims of a long-term policy; and
3 methods of implementation.

The *analysis of inner area problems* focussed on unacceptable levels of economic decline, physical decay and adverse social conditions. While recognizing that deprivation exists in all older urban areas, it stressed that these problems are at their most serious in the major cities. Economic decline 'often lies at the heart of the problem', as inner areas suffer from high levels of unemployment and a mismatch between the skills of the workforce and the kinds of jobs available. Three factors were identified: the migration of skilled workers; heavy job losses – now attributed mainly to the closure of firms (sometimes brought about by redevelopment) and the shrinkage of employment in large firms, with movement out of firms a minor contributory factor; and insufficient investment in new manufacturing industry to counter-balance these losses. Physical decay – poor-quality housing set in a drab environment characterized by vacant and underused land and buildings – was attributed mainly to clearance and redevelopment 'getting badly out of step', leaving much vacant land in public ownership. Social disadvantage was discussed in terms of higher concentrations of poor people (reflecting both high unemployment and low earnings) and substantial numbers of people requiring help and support, but particular attention was given to 'collective deprivation'.

Several reasons were advanced for not leaving inner city areas to decay: continued neglect would cause mounting social bitterness and alienation; social infrastructure and land would be wasted; and while 'some of the changes which have taken place are due to social and economic forces which could be reversed only with great difficulty or at unacceptable cost', some decentralization had been assisted by public policies, the thrust of which could be changed to stem the decline.

With the provisos that policies need to be geared to varied conditions and that 'some of the solutions will be outside the inner areas', the White Paper specified four *aims of a long-term policy*:

1 'strengthening the economies of the inner areas and the prospects of their residents' by preserving and facilitating the growth of existing firms, attracting new ones, and improving travel to work arrangements, training and education;
2 'improving the physical fabric of the inner areas and making their environment more attractive', by improvements in housing, public services and land management, this helping to restore confidence in their future;
3 'alleviating social problems', by improvement in social services such as care for the elderly and the children of working mothers; and
4 'securing a new balance between the inner areas and the rest of the city region in terms of population and jobs' by reducing decentralization.

Methods of implementation centred on the development of comprehensive, area-based action: a comprehensive rather than a piecemeal approach justified by the interlocking nature of problems and an area approach because of the intensity of problems, particularly 'collective deprivation'. There were four key elements: resources, priorities, co-ordination and participation.

1 The bulk of public resources was to come from an extension of positive discrimination across the full range of government policies. Central government was to give 'an inner area dimension and priority' to its main policies and programmes, and would further discriminate in favour of authorities with severe problems. Similarly, local authorities were to redirect their policies. Supplementary resources were made available by an increase in Urban Programme funds. It was anticipated that this redeployment of public resources would stimulate private investment by creating opportunities for, and underpinning the confidence of, industry and financial institutions.
2 Two types of priorities were established. First, geographical priorities: although the aim was to tackle inner area problems generally, efforts in the first few years would be concentrated in those major cities with the worst problems. Second, policy priorities: the main emphasis was on

economic measures, by modifications in central government policies (such as those for industrial location) and the development of local authority action using both existing and additional powers.

3 The possibility of establishing a new town style special agency to secure co-ordination was rejected in favour of 'partnership arrangements' with certain cities. This joint machinery was intended to bring together a range of central government departments and agencies with both tiers of local government and the private sector in the development of comprehensive inner area programmes.

4 The new approach laid considerable emphasis on the participation of local communities and voluntary bodies.

Powers, procedures and professionals

The implementation of the new policy rested substantially on the modified use of existing powers: the only legislative proposals in the White Paper were for extending local authority powers to assist industry, which resulted in the Inner Urban Areas Act, 1978. However, the partnership approach required the development of new political arrangements and administrative procedures. Modifications in the use of existing powers, together with new powers and procedures are described in terms of measures to:

1 secure positive discrimination in resource allocation;
2 establish geographical priorities;
3 strengthen inner area economies;
4 declare Improvement Areas; and
5 develop Inner Area Programmes.

1 *Positive discrimination in resource allocation.* The extent to which public resources would be redeployed was unknown at the outset: an analysis of the processes of allocation shows why. These can be outlined in terms of central government main programmes, central government funding of local authority programmes, the Urban Programme, and local authority programmes.

(a) Central government programmes. While the momentum of the new towns programme was to be substantially maintained, the population targets of the third generation new towns were reduced, and a token £20m p.a. of the programme's resources diverted to the Urban Programme. Additionally, new towns were encouraged to take more retired, unskilled and unemployed workers. Outside this limited area, while the DoE has an overall responsibility, it has executive control over only a few relevant central government programmes and can only exhort other departments to support the policy. Thus, the Department of Health and Social Security (DHSS) and Area Health Authorities were asked to take account of inner area problems in allocating hospital resources and making decisions on local health services, and nationalized industries requested to release surplus land in inner areas or tidy up land held for future needs. Changes in the programmes of other departments and agencies are described below under economic measures.

(b) Central government funding of local authority programmes. The power of central government to affect local authority spending is considerable.[85] It can influence both total expenditure and its distribution between local authorities, but local authorities substantially determine its geographical distribution within their areas. Local authority spending is divided into two categories, subject to separate procedures. Capital expenditure creates fixed assets (e.g. building a school) and is usually financed by borrowing, with repayments over a period of years. Revenue spending comprises recurring expenditure which does not produce a permanent asset (e.g. salaries) together with annual payments on loans for capital expenditure. Capital expenditure is controlled by loan sanction procedure. For *key sector schemes* – mainly large projects in the main services of education, housing, social services and transportation, together with land acquisition and reclamation – approval for borrowing is required from the relevant government departments on a scheme by scheme basis. For *locally determined schemes* – small projects in some major services and schemes for other services (e.g. open space or land for industrial development) – a total annual borrowing allocation is given to local authorities who can then determine which schemes to finance. Loan sanction procedure is, by definition, a negative control and the extent to which it can influence the geographical distribution of expenditure between, and within local authorities, is limited. However, in making bids for the block allocations involved in HIPs and TPPs, authorities were requested to give priority to inner areas, and told that the extent to which they did would be taken into account in their allocations.[86] Revenue expenditure is financed from rates, government grants and charges for services. The latter (mainly council house rents) account for almost 30 per cent of total income. The remaining 70 per cent comprises a fluctuating combination of rates and government grants: of this, the proportion accounted for by government grants increased from 50 per cent in the mid-1960s to a peak of 67 per cent in 1975–6. The Rate Support Grant (RSG) accounts for four fifths of total government grants (£7000m in 1978–9) and is allocated by the DoE (in conjunction with the Treasury) in respect of rate fund expenditure as a whole, rather than being directed to particular services or areas within local authorities. The RSG has three elements; a domestic element which provides relief to all domestic ratepayers; a resources element which compensates authorities with low levels of rateable resources; and a needs element which compensates for variations in the level of needs. The latter is the largest grant element and is calculated by a formula incorporating 'objective' measures of need, e.g. in 1977–8 authorities received £508 per person over pensionable age. This formula is reassessed annually and it is by the inclusion of indicators of urban deprivation that authorities with inner area problems are allocated a greater share of the grant.

(c) Urban Programme. This constituted the only allocation of central government resources specifically directed to inner areas. With the launching of the inner cities policy, responsibility was transferred to the DoE and the total amount available increased from £30m p.a. to £125m p.a. (from 1979–80) with the level of subsidy remaining at 75 per cent.[87] Allocation procedures were significantly changed. Three quarters of the resources were concentrated in block allocations to those authorities required to produce IAPs, though within these allocations individual projects still have to be approved by the DoE. Other authorities continue to submit individual projects.

(d) Local authority programmes. Local authorities were requested to review their main policies and programmes – housing, planning, environment, education, social services and transport – in order to achieve 'wherever practicable . . . some switch of resources to the inner areas from other parts of the city'. Given limited government influence on local spending and the scale of the Urban Programme, this process was seen as the central task in the preparation of IAPs. However, it required significant innovations in budgeting procedures conventionally geared to resource allocation between services not areas.

2 *Geographical priorities* involved an initial concentration of effort in those authorities where problems were judged most severe. The Inner Urban Areas Act established a three-tier hierarchy of 'designated authorities', with variations in the availability of new powers, Urban Programme funding, and central government involvement.[88] Figure 13 summarizes the arrangements. As defined in the Act the term 'designated district authority' means both the district council and the county council for the areas designated.

(a) Partnership authorities. The 1978 Act empowered the Secretary of State and other ministers, when satisfied that special social need exists in any inner urban area which warrants concerted effort, to enter into, 'arrangements for determining action' with local authorities and others. This is the statutory basis of the inner city partnerships, 'the centre-piece of the Government's new policy for inner cities'.[89] There was no statutory definition of inner urban areas. Partnership authorities have some exclusive additional powers under the Act, and were allocated a large proportion of Urban Programme funds. The Government is directly involved at ministerial level in the preparation of Inner City Partnership Programmes (ICPPs).

(b) Programme authorities. These have only limited powers under the 1978 Act and receive much less support from the Urban Programme. Although they are required to prepare IAPs, there is no direct central

Designated district authorities	*Inner Urban Areas Act powers*	*Urban Programme resources*	*CG involvement*
Partnership authorities 14 districts grouped in 7 partnerships: Birmingham; Liverpool; Manchester and Salford; Newcastle* and Gateshead†; Lambeth; Hackney and Islington*; the London Docklands – Greenwich, Lewisham, Newham, Southwark and Tower Hamlets	General powers to (a) make 90% loans for acquisition of land or the carrying out of works on land; (b) make loans or grants towards cost of establishing co-operatives or common ownership enterprises; (c) declare Improvement Areas (d) adopt a local plan in advance of the approval or alteration of the structure plan and in 'special areas' (e) make loans, interest free for up to two years for site preparation, services and access roads (f) make grants to assist with rent (g) make grants towards interest on any loan made to a small firm for land acquisition or carrying out of works	Three year block allocations for inner area programmes varying from £5m p.a. for Lambeth to £15m p.a. for Docklands Total annual allocation from 1979–80 onwards of £66m p.a.	Inner City Partnerships established to prepare ICPPs Partnership Committee chaired by SoS or DoE minister ICPP prepared by Inner City Teams, comprising officers of district and county, DoE and other government departments and agencies
Programme authorities 15 districts Bolton, Bradford†, Hammersmith, Hull, Leeds, Leicester, Middlesbrough, North Tyneside, Nottingham, Oldham, Sheffield, South Tyneside, Sunderland, Wirral, Wolverhampton	(a), (b), (c), (d) above	Three year block allocations for Inner Area Programmes varying from £1m to £2m p.a. Total annual allocation from 1979–80 onwards of £25m p.a.	IAPs required by DoE No direct central government involvement but ministers share responsibility for Programme Authorities Inner City Teams from districts prepare IAPs in consultation with county, DoE and Area Health Authority
Other designated districts 14 in England: Barnsley, Blackburn, Brent, Doncaster, Ealing, Haringey*, Hartlepool, Rochdale, Rotherham, St. Helens, Sandwell, Sefton, Wandsworth and Wigan 5 in Wales: Blaenau Gwent, Cardiff, Newport, Rhondda and Swansea	(a), (b), (c), (d) above	Allocations on individual project basis Total allocation of £6m for England and £4m for Wales, but non-designated authorities with areas of special social need can also bid for this allocation	Preparation of IAPs at discretion of districts No new machinery for co-ordination between central and local government

* Authority involved in Area Management Trials; the other AMTs were in Dudley, Kirklees and Stockport.
† Denotes authority preparing Comprehensive Community Programme.

Figure 13 *Inner city policy: geographical priorities, 1978*

government involvement in this work, only strengthened consultation procedures.

(c) Other designated districts. These have the same 1978 Act powers as programme authorities but no block funding. The preparation of IAPs is discretionary and central government involvement is through normal channels.

This classification of authorities was determined partly on the basis of a statistical analysis using various 'inner city indicators'.[90] The DoE was not specific about the other evidence used, but intensive lobbying was undoubtedly relevant.

3 *Strengthening inner area economies.* This was the central feature of the new policy. Implementation relies on a combination of modifications to central government programmes and the development of more positive intervention by local authorities. The intention was to add an intra-urban dimension to industrial and employment policies to help inner areas and stimulate private investment.

(a) Central government policies and programmes. The Department of Industry (DI) undertook to continue some advance factory building in inner areas and to further relax IDC controls; while the assisted areas remained the first priority for mobile industry, inner areas of London and Birmingham were given a higher priority than new and expanding towns, and similar minor modifications were made to office development policy. The Department of Employment (DE) undertook to adapt employment subsidies and training schemes within the developing framework of IAPs.

(b) Local authority policies and programmes. The White Paper suggested various ways in which local authorities could use their existing powers and procedures more effectively to assist industry, and more detailed advice was given in Circular 71/77.[91] This stressed the need for improved liaison with industry by centring industrial work on a named official or co-ordinating unit. Particular emphasis was given to planning and transport powers: processing applications for industrial development and the preparation of local plans with a large industrial content; the disposal of publicly owned land; mixed developments; relaxation of policies on non-conforming industrial uses; and transport proposals to improve access for industry and commerce.

New powers and procedures were amplified in Circular 68/78 and are summarized in Figure 13. Within the constraints imposed by geographical priorities, they are available to both district and county authorities, who jointly determine whether both or one of them will exercise the powers.

Expenditure could be met from three sources:

(a) Revenue – Section 137 of the Local Government Act, 1972 enables local authorities to incur expenditure up to the product of a 2p rate for purposes not authorized by other legislation (several local authorities had already used this to promote industrial development) and these provisions

remained in force as if the 1978 Act had not been enacted;
(b) Locally Determined Sector – authorities were encouraged to give priority to industrial and employment related capital projects;
(c) Urban Programme – the scope of this was widened to include economic and environmental projects, and the Government expected about a third of funds allocated to partnership and programme authorities would be spent under the provisions of the 1978 Act.

Grants and loans were to enable firms to develop and expand in inner area locations when they might otherwise have gone outside or not undertaken development. While the use of the new powers should result in permanent improvement to the environment, 'the main aim . . . must be to secure permanent employment opportunities either by the creation or preservation of jobs'.[92] It is up to local authorities to determine criteria for assistance, but Circular 68/78 offered various suggestions which included: the economic viability of assisted projects; loans for acquisition or work on land for projects unable to secure long-term finance from other sources; preference in making interest-free loans in 'special areas' within partnership authorities for site works which will provide industrial or commercial premises; priority in providing assistance with rent and interest relief grants in 'special areas' for firms displaced and new firms starting up; and careful consideration of assistance to service enterprises which compete in essentially local markets.

4 *The declaration of Improvement Areas* (IAs) is intended:

> . . . to secure a stable level of permanent employment in an older industrial or commercial area where economic activity might otherwise steadily decline owing to adverse environmental factors, inadequate buildings and a pattern of land use that is unsuited to modern industrial or commercial needs.[93]

It was stressed that IA designation should involve a commitment to concentrated effort by the local authority using the whole range of its powers, and implied the diversion of significant manpower and financial resources in order to work effectively with firms in the area. IAs were not to be regarded merely as areas where some extra powers are available, but as a focus for comprehensive action.

(a) Choice of area. No statutory limits were placed on the condition, character, size or duration of an IA, other than it must be predominantly industrial and/or commercial, or if developed in accordance with the development plan would be predominantly such an area. A norm of 50 ha was suggested as realistic in view of the demands on management effort and resources. A life span of up to ten years was recommended: an initial period of intensive work of three to five years followed by a similar period for residual works. IA powers were considered to be most useful where substantial physical improvement was necessary but only likely if begun by the local authority. In contrast, predominantly commercial areas which could be improved by normal private investment, together with areas with extensive dereliction and few viable firms, were considered unsuitable. Advice also stressed the need to select areas where there was a reasonable chance of success and to secure effective, speedy and visible improvements. Local authorities were advised to consider:

the extent to which the use of their powers would improve the area, e.g. opportunities for land assembly and improvement of access;

whether employment opportunities could be stabilized, e.g. by assistance to a declining industry which dominates the area;

the attitudes of local firms to remaining in the area and improving their properties; and

the relationship of a proposed area to adjacent residential areas, involving the co-ordination of IA work with HAA and GIA programmes.

(b) The establishment of an IA. The declaration of an IA is subject to ministerial approval. After consultation with the other designated district, an authority can resolve that an area should be declared, after which it must publish a notice of its intention, and send a copy of its resolution and map of the area to the Secretary of State. In addition, further information on the context of the proposal (e.g. relationship to other IAs or the overall inner area programme), the intended policy towards the area (e.g. on loans and grants for environmental work, management, estimated expenditure and time-scale) and a brief statistical statement (e.g. concerning employment, vacant land and buildings in the area) are requested. The Secretary of State can 'negative the declaration' as a whole or in part. Beyond this it is up to the local authority to determine procedures.

(c) Environmental improvement. In a declared IA local authorities can make loans or grants for the following types of work: construction of fencing or walls; landscaping; clearance or levelling of land; cleansing of watercourses and reclamation of land covered by water; cleaning, painting, repair or demolition of structures or buildings; and construction of parking spaces, access roads, turning heads or loading bays. The amount and form of loans and grants is discretionary.

(d) Improvement grants for converting or improving buildings. Works eligible for grant aid are the conversion, improvement, or extension of industrial or commercial buildings, and the conversion of other buildings to industrial or commercial buildings. Normal maintenance work is excluded. The amount of a grant is limited to 50 per cent of the cost of carrying out the works, or £1000 for each job that is likely to be created or preserved. In determining the amount authorities were advised to assess the return to the firm or developer on this investment and to consider imposing conditions, e.g. on occupancy. Circular 68/78 provided illustrations of cases for aid, e.g. an incoming firm wanting to use an empty building could be awarded a grant based on the total number of jobs likely to be accommodated.

5 *The development of Inner Area Programmes* has three main components: an

analysis of local conditions; a spending programme for the deployment of Urban Programme resources; and adjustments to main programmes and policies designed to shift resources to inner areas. They are three-year rolling programmes revised annually.

The White Paper acknowledged difficulties in the way of securing co-ordination of government activity and the involvement of residents and the business community. The development of an area approach, when central and local government departments are organized on a functional basis 'requires special efforts of co-ordination and joint working which cut across established practices': the task of the partnerships was to develop effective joint machinery.

The administrative arrangements established for partnerships are complex. The Partnership Committee is chaired by a DoE minister and comprises elected local members and appointed members of other government bodies. It is serviced by an officer steering group, chaired either by the Regional Director of the DoE (provincial partnerships) or a local authority chief executive (London partnerships). The Co-ordinating Team comprises officers of central and local government departments and agencies, some specifically appointed for this work, others are part-time secondments. Further arrangements typically involve the establishment of working groups responsible to the Co-ordinating Team, organized around key topics such as employment, housing and physical environment. Arrangements for programme authorities reflect the much lower level of central government involvement, and usually comprise an inner city team of officers responsible to the main policy making committee of the district council.[94]

Inner Area Programmes

The 1977 White Paper stressed the need for 'early and demonstrable results'. All partnership and programme authorities prepared their first IAPs during 1978 and rolled them forward by the end of 1979, although implementation is still in its early stages. In significant respects a threshold has been crossed in the development of urban renewal policy, but there are serious doubts about its capacity for generating the 'powerful and countervailing action' which Shore had justifiably proclaimed necessary. The most common prognostication is that unless the policy is significantly strengthened it will, at best, result in only marginal improvements. This section provides an assessment of the potential and limitations of the 1977 initiative by examining the aims, resources and organization for the implementation of IAPs, and four key issues – employment, land, participation and race.

A threshold crossed or the illusion of a policy?

The 1977 White Paper was a synthesis of a decade of developments in housing, planning and social policy. Urban deprivation was officially acknowledged to be widespread rather than confined to a few small pockets, and to be caused by the changing demands of the economy rather than the personal inadequacies of the poor – a shift from 'victim blame' to 'system blame'. *Ad hoc* initiatives were replaced by changes in major policies within a broadly based, phased and long-term national strategy. Urban deprivation is being tackled through positive discrimination in main programmes, and supplementary Urban Programme funds. Most importantly, the emphasis on economic renewal reflects recognition of the limitations of attempting to resolve housing, environmental and social problems in isolation from underlying economic trends. Finally, for the first time, central government made the preparation of comprehensive and integrated urban renewal programmes a precondition for the allocation of resources.

These changes are significant but only a modest step in the right direction: the principles of the new policy limit its potential, and implementation is constrained by the same political and economic context which defined its basic parameters. The 1977 White Paper was a selective response to the IAS reports. It accepted the case for a specifically inner areas policy, but ignored the argument that for such a policy to be more than marginal it should be part of a wider programme of more substantial redistributive measures to help the deprived wherever they live. Rather than introducing major reforms to redistribute resources from the rich to the poor, the inner cities policy simply extended area-selective positive discrimination which, in the context of overall cuts in public expenditure, meant redistribution among less affluent areas.

While there are those who remain unconvinced by the case for area-based policies,[95] there is widespread support for the basic aim of reducing urban deprivation. Debate about means continued. The 'middle ground' policy of 1977 was criticized by both those arguing the necessity for more direct state intervention, and those demanding further reduction of government restrictions on private enterprise.[96] Another line of argument is that urban policy should not seek to stem decentralization, but should take advantage of the opportunities it offers for planned dispersal linked more closely to inner area renewal.[97] Others argue that concentrations of the retired, the unemployable and the unemployed are inevitable, and dismiss conventional policies as expensive impositions serving mainly the interests of welfare state professionals. They assert that it would be cheaper to provide free heating, lighting and house maintenance and to encourage an informal, self-help household economy based on sharing and organizing activities such as bulk buying of food, home brewing, and passing on children's clothes.[98] Leaving aside the practicalities and consequences of sacking large numbers of public employees to provide the funds for free services, the criticism that this concept of the inner city 'good life' is a naive irrelevance has yet to be satisfactorily refuted.

The limitations of the inner cities policy, within its own terms of reference, emerged as IAPs developed. They stem largely from inadequate resources. In the debate on the Inner Urban Areas Bill, Walker stated that:

> . . . welcome though it is, the Bill makes only a small contribution and is chicken-feed compared with what is needed. . . . The idea of designated districts and partnerships is right in principle, but the restraints on public expenditure and the uncertainties in local government will make this a slow process. . . . We should not decide on a limited number of designated districts as an experiment. We should decide on a whole range of districts where there is desperate need for action. . . . We should say that we agree that the situation needs a programme of public expenditure so that in five to seven years those areas move from deprivation to at least the average position for the country. That would be a big commitment for public expenditure.[99]

His argument was that, eventually, in *net* terms this would not mean massively increased public expenditure because it would reduce expenditure on unemployment benefits and the cost of dealing with a crime rate which would continue to rise.

The new policy was launched with a £100m 'one-off' allocation for capital projects in inner areas (known as 'the Healey construction package'). This allocation was for 1977–8 and 1978–9 and was succeeded by the enhanced Urban Programme of £125m p.a. This is 'chicken-feed', constituting less than 1 per cent of local authority expenditure. Moreover it does not mean £125m for new projects each year. As IAPs are developed and implemented they become 'silted up' with recurrent revenue expenditure stemming from commitment in the first and second rounds, pre-empting money and reducing the proportion of the allocation available for new schemes.[100] Prior to the 1979 election the Labour Government had indicated that the annual allocation was to be increased to take account of this. The need to do this was becoming increasingly urgent as cuts in revenue budgets (see below) were making it impossible to transfer Urban Programme revenue schemes into main programmes.

Shore's response to the 'chicken-feed' criticism was that specific urban programme grants were only the smallest part of the total available and instanced the RSG as a major source of finance.[101] But the resource provisions were widely criticized in the debate. It was pointed out that cuts in the housing programme were exacerbating conditions in inner areas and that the partnerships were a smokescreen – they partly offset cuts but did not provide additional funds:[102]

> The question of whether this is additional money or a redirection of existing money is important. There is a danger that the Henley description of 'the illusion of a policy' will result.[103]

The allocation of additional resources had been ruled out by the Treasury and, for reasons discussed in the previous section, the Government were unable to give any indication of the volume of resources to be redirected to inner areas from elsewhere. The difficulties of 'bending' main programmes in an era of retrenchment can be exemplified as follows:[104]

1 Central government main programmes. The DHSS was 'rationalizing' allocations by shifting funds from relatively well-resourced Area Health Authorities to those that are less fortunate, but in the absence of 'bending' within AHAs this reduced resources for inner London and inner Birmingham.

2 Central government funding of local authority programmes bore the brunt of expenditure cuts. For example the Liverpool IAP pointed out that capital expenditure by the City Council fell from £56.2m in 1974–5 to £38.7m in 1978–9:[105] even in a partnership area the Urban Programme allocation was less than half the cuts in capital expenditure. The DES gives priority to the provision of new schools in expanding residential areas, thus in the absence of additional resources there was no scope for accelerating the improvement or replacement of inner area schools. The inadequacies of redirected HIP allocations in the context of overall cuts were discussed in the previous chapter. The Locally Determined Sector was cut (the 1979–80 allocation was less than 60 per cent of the 1978–9 figure), yet this is a source of finance for, among other things, industrial development.

The RSG was cut from 65.5 per cent of local government revenue expenditure in 1976–7 to 61 per cent in 1978–9, but in an attempt to support inner cities policy was increasingly diverted from the shire counties to the metropolitan authorities. However, the complexities of allocation techniques meant that, although the counties fared least well, inner London boroughs and cities such as Liverpool and Newcastle received considerably less assistance than more affluent outer London boroughs and metropolitan districts. This anomaly dwarfed the effects of Urban Programme allocations. But the prospects of a smaller slice of a shrinking cake prompted considerable opposition from the shire counties and redistribution approached the limits of what was politically possible.[106]

3 Local authority main programmes. The bending of local authority main programmes is a major task for the partnerships, but there was little progress in the first round of IAPs as effort was concentrated on spending Urban Programme funds in this first year. Minds have been focussed on this issue, but positive discrimination within contracting budgets remains both technically demanding and politically sensitive.[107]

Resource constraints underlay the complex hierarchy of geographical priorities. The concentration of effort in the partnerships remained controversial as the paucity of resources rendered promotion from the 'second division' of programme authorities to the 'first division' of partnerships a distant prospect. The problems of 'robbing Peter to pay Paul' were reflected in variations between IAPs. Some, such as the Wirral, concentrated resources in quite small localities, while others drew their boundaries more widely to include inter-war council estates – the inner area of Newcastle/Gateshead contains 200,000 people, some 40 per cent of total population.

In terms of policy priorities IAPs are tending to concentrate on economic development, physical environment, leisure and recreation, as opposed to education and housing which dominate main programme expenditure. However, there were considerable variations in the extent to which the Government's emphasis on economic renewal was given effect locally – a variation not related to differences in economic conditions – prompting comments such as:

> . . . the primary impression emerging from these programmes is that they represent less a coherent strategy for the regeneration of England's decaying inner city areas, and rather more a list of projects that have long been on departmental and committee shopping lists.[108]

The significance of potential yields from improved management had undoubtedly been exaggerated:[109] they could not offset the effects of expenditure cuts. Moreover, the fact that IAPs are the 'investment partnership' of housing improvement writ large means that a multitude of agencies and groups are involved and yields could be only slowly realized. From the outset concern has been voiced about the bureaucratic complexity of partnerships, and a lack of co-ordination between central government departments exacerbating difficulties at local level.[110] Similarly there has been only limited progress in involving the private sector, which emphasizes the importance of public sector investment to create more attractive conditions for private investment which benefits inner area residents.[111] Nonetheless, IAPs have brought together a wide range of organizations in collaborative working and they provide a potentially more productive setting for the development of area management.

Job-led recovery programmes

Given the emphasis on economic renewal an important test of inner city policy will be its effectiveness in raising incomes by reducing the proportion of inner area residents who are unemployed or have low earnings. If successful it could increase effective demand for better housing standards, reduce numbers dependent on state benefits and services and improve the resource base of local authorities. An apparently simple formula, but can IAPs stem the tide of job loss, create additional well paid jobs and improve access to job opportunities elsewhere?

A fundamental point is that the development of IAPs is taking place in the context of persisting mass unemployment. There are two major underlying trends: first, continued restructuring (particularly the application of microprocessing) will result in reduced labour demand in manufacturing, which is unlikely to be offset in the service sector; second, the labour supply will expand by an extra 2½ millions by the mid-1980s.[112]

The overriding goal of *national economic policy* is an increased growth rate. Faced with a world recession, the Labour Government embarked on deflationary policies, the industrial strategy, manpower planning and a whole battery of selective employment measures.[113] Social expenditure was cut in order to divert resources into the 'productive' sector, with consequent reductions in public sector employment. The industrial strategy gave priority to the stimulation of manufacturing investment. However, increased productivity and increased employment can only be achieved if output grows faster than productivity. Unemployment can only be checked, let alone reduced, if there is an expansion in the economy, but there is little sign of an end to the recession which would allow this to happen. Continued industrial restructuring will undoubtedly cause further closures and redundancies, particularly in large-scale enterprises. Acknowledgement of this was a major factor in the resurgence of interest in small firms. In essence the argument is that it is possible to create a climate in which a huge increase in the birth and growth rate of small firms can 'mop up' labour shed by larger firms. By the time IAPs got under way the future of small firms had been elevated to the status of a key component in national economic recovery: small-scale capitalism is seen not only as beautiful, but essential.

Falk has elaborated this view.[114] He argues that small firms (under 200 employees) account for 20 per cent of industrial output and employment and that their decline may have been reversed. Even with an upturn in the economy there will be no large increase in employment for manual workers in large enterprises. In contrast, employment in small firms could expand for a variety of reasons: they are more flexible in meeting new and specialized needs, more likely to innovate and give a higher return on assets; as they are more labour intensive any given level of investment could lead to double the employment compared with large firms; finally they are more likely to respond to positive public intervention.

However, such optimism is misplaced. The increasing dominance of large national and multi-national firms ensures that small firms (particularly in the manufacturing sector) are marginal and vulnerable, often dependent on large firms for whom they carry out peripheral operations such as component production. When a large firm closes down it often takes small firms with it. This role, which may be tantamount to 'servicing the dinosaurs of British industry',[115] together with the brake on change which results from dynastic and gerontocratic management structures, renders anachronistic and romantic the view of small firms as the seedbed from which new large companies will grow. Moreover, the growing interest in 'the small trader – the really small firm, which puts craftsmanship, quality and social responsibility above the demands of rapid turnover'[116] may produce worthwhile innovations, but in the absence of wider changes any impact on unemployment will be peripheral. Finally, the high labour turnover, low level of training, low wages and insecurity of many small firms contrasts with the stereotype image of better management–worker relations and higher quality of work uninterrupted by strikes.[117] However, the Labour Government was committed to bolstering the small firms sector. A Cabinet review paved the way and in 1977 the small firms employment subsidy was introduced for firms with fewer than 50 workers; the 1978 budget made substantial tax concessions to small firms at a cost of £200m; and the Department of Employment Small Firms Counselling Service was extended.[118]

For reasons discussed earlier in this chapter developments in the national economy will have a disproportionate effect on inner area unemployment levels, and the extent to which this can be offset will depend on spatial policies. Regional policy is the major instrument for influencing the location of industrial investment, disbursing some £650m p.a. Even in the relatively favourable climate of the 1960s, such aid could only prevent the widening of, rather than eliminate, regional inequalities. This is unlikely to be achieved in the future as job loss in the assisted areas increased while the volume of mobile industry is now much lower than in the 1960s. These problems underlie the DI's marked lack of enthusiasm for 'bending' its policies in favour of inner urban areas, and token changes reflected an overriding preference for the most efficient locations, which in practice means 'green-field sites'.

Thus the economic content of IAPs heavily depends on *local authority policy*, but economic renewal meant the development of a main programme virtually from scratch. In the mid-1970s, most local authorities had very limited experience of intervening in their local economies and economic policy was seen as a central government responsibility. Circular 71/77 then stressed their role in the implementation of the industrial strategy.[119] The view emerged that realistic local employment planning must be mainly concerned with 'mopping up', i.e. minimizing the local impact of industrial restructuring, which, given the limited amount of mobile industry, means developing the existing economic base.[120] Many authorities are evolving local economic development plans with an explicit inner area dimension including: establishing potential and priorities for job conservation and creation; mobilizing resources; developing an organizational framework; and allocating resources to measures best suited to local needs.[121]

The range of possible measures to promote economic renewal is considerable but can be briefly summarized as follows:[122]

1 Land and premises. This traditional area of local government involvement includes the allocation of land in development plans; the granting of planning permission for industrial development; the assembly, reclamation, preparation and release of land for industrial development; and the provision of new buildings for manufacturing, warehouse and office use, possibly in partnership with the private sector. There is a growing interest in the refurbishment and conversion of old industrial buildings. New

powers for IIAs facilitate the implementation of this type of work on an area basis.

2 Local authorities and firms. This includes: advice and information, e.g. concerning the availability of government assistance, and establishing fora for the exchange of ideas and views; assisting existing firms by the provision of grants and loans, sometimes as risk capital linked to municipal shareholding; intervention in the event of a proposed closure; promoting the development of co-operatives; identifying new products and services, e.g. by financing new enterprise workshops; and giving more sympathetic treatment to industry in the exercise of planning powers.

3 Local authorities and the labour force. While training schemes are predominantly the function of the Manpower Services Commission, local authorities can assist by helping identify needs and linking the MSC's work to that of local educational institutions.[123] Other policies include improving bus services to industrial areas and providing housing for 'key workers'.

A combination of measures can be determined by an analysis of the potential and priorities for job conservation and creation. This involves the considerable task of developing a working understanding of local labour market conditions, the needs of local firms, and existing patterns of investment and disinvestment, including the impact of national trends and policies. Some authorities, particularly through the partnership machinery, have established consultative groups to draw on the knowledge and experience of industrialists and trade unions. A range of important questions have emerged as local economic renewal policies have started to take shape.

Which type of firm should be the focus of attention? There is a widely held view that small firms are particularly important for two reasons. First, they tend to be concentrated in inner areas and as a result of job losses in large firms they have assumed increased relative significance. Second, while inner areas are unattractive to large firms, they still offer small firms locational advantages which could be exploited: both existing and new firms can utilize cheap premises in refurbished buildings and often need to be close to city centres for linkages with suppliers and customers. However, the extent to which the inner city still acts as an incubator for new small firms is arguable. Although limited surveys of small inner area firms have indicated varying proportions of enterprises which are declining, stable or growing, it is likely that only a small proportion are growth oriented compared with medium-sized firms, which some argue should take priority. There is clearly no 'right' size, but small firms are heavily emphasized in national policy and given a high priority in IAPs, despite the fact that one closure of a firm employing 500 workers could offset the gains from the establishment of 50 new small firms.[124] The importance of ownership patterns is increasingly recognized: recent research suggests that inner areas with a high proportion of locally owned firms will benefit most from policies to improve the local working environment.[125]

Should the emphasis be on new build or the improvement of the existing older stock of industrial buildings? An important issue here is the need to establish basic information about the condition of existing buildings and processes of change – the present situation is analogous to housing renewal in the early 1960s. Much is claimed but little is known of the demand for workshops in converted premises. Most IAPs include building new small units but how far this will simply mean vacated railway arches rather than additional employment remains unknown.[126] This issue also raises the question of working conditions: some argue that in conversions certain standards could be relaxed, while others take the view that public money should not be used to preserve substandard premises – echoing a long-standing debate in housing renewal.

How far should economic renewal strategies concentrate on a small-area approach? All IAPs include proposals for Improvement Areas which are seen as a means of drawing together various initiatives, and concentrating a proportion of public resources to make a visible impact and provide a catalyst for private investment. The parallels between the GIAs of the early 1970s and the IAs of the early 1980s will be striking. Government specified selection criteria leave much room for local discretion and a variety of objectives could be pursued. In particular, there will be varying weight given to environmental objectives and those of preserving or creating jobs. An evaluation of the pioneering work in Rochdale suggests that both can be achieved but the latter is placed in perspective by the fact that while 100 or so jobs may be added to the Crawford Street area as a result of improvement, total employment fell by over 600 in the four years under review.[127]

Finally, what is the most appropriate relationship between the public and private sectors? Conventional policies such as subsidizing private development costs by the provision of serviced industrial land and reversing planning policies are prominent in IAPs. However, some argue that IAPs should concentrate on innovations such as co-operatives and a more directly interventionist approach involving financial involvement which is publicly accountable, such as municipal shareholding.[128] Others advocate an approach reliant on reducing government controls on the private sector to stimulate investment. Again there are parallels with the long-standing debate in housing renewal.

Until answers are found for these kinds of questions, economic renewal 'strategies' will remain a series of pragmatic initiatives. Moreover, resources and organization pose serious difficulties. Expenditure under the Inner Areas Act was expected to be £20m p.a. nationally, compared with the £650m p.a. on regional aid. There is no main programme funding as such and resources have to be pulled together from a variety of sources: in cities such as Liverpool and Newcastle a combination of Urban Programme funds, rate fund contributions (up to the product of a 2p rate) and the remnants of the Locally Determined Sector yield some £5m p.a. With the exception of inner city hypermarkets and the establishment of small firms by large companies there is little sign of the return of private investment. Furthermore, a variety of departments (planning, estates, treasurers, solicitors, etc.) and agencies are involved and it will take time to weld effective organizations. The co-ordinating machinery for IAPs is assisting this but, as with housing renewal, much depends on the commitment and drive of key personnel.

As IAPs entered their third year of operation there was clearly little prospect of a job-led recovery programme. Rigorous analysis of the scale and components of inner area industrial decline has extended to include provincial cities, emphasizing the magnitude of the task, but the policy levers which have been put into neutral or reverse are those which can have limited impact on job losses.[129] Neither measures to take work to workers living in inner areas, nor to take workers to the work outside by retraining and increasing their mobility, can have an appreciable impact on high levels of unemployment, given the overwhelming effect of residential segregation which continues to concentrate the growing numbers of the unemployed in deprived areas.[130]

The following comment illustrates the scepticism surrounding the much vaunted attack on causes of decline:

> Unless the government is prepared to direct both private sector and its own major employment creating investment into the inner city, to set up stronger local economic development agencies and to commit itself to spending a lot more on infrastructure, the current inner city programme can at best only smooth an inevitable path of decline.[131]

Economic renewal is a new field, arguably a minefield. Although it focusses attention on the causes of urban deprivation, it has become apparent that, within the parameters of the 1977 policy, arresting (let alone reversing) economic decline is an unrealistic ambition. The rhetoric of the inner areas debate is being superseded by the more modest aim of alleviating the worst consequences of industrial change.

Urban wastelands

The development of IAPs promoted improvements in policies and programmes to deal with environmental conditions. In particular the problem of vacant and underused land and buildings has received considerable attention.

It has long been argued that decentralization would reduce demand in inner areas and cause a fall in land values, creating opportunities for renewal at lower densities, with the provision of open space and other community facilities at modest costs.[132] Yet large-scale decentralization since the 1950s has been accompanied by continued high values and the emergence of urban wastelands. This paradox raises important questions: why is there so much underused land; why do land values remain relatively high when there has been an exodus of investment; do high values impede urban renewal? The key issues are patterns of ownership and the interaction of public policy with the land market.

Although information is sparse, research indicates that between 5 and 15 per cent of inner city land is vacant, half of which is in local authority ownership (mainly in small sites), a quarter is owned by nationalized industries and statutory undertakers (often large sites), and the remainder is privately owned.[133] Much of this land is held at theoretically high valuations. The 1977 White Paper implied that land costs were not significantly inhibiting development, but 'it is common sense to critics of the property market that if derelict dockland is worth £30,000 per acre when there is almost no demand for it then something must be wrong',[134] and an RTPI Working Party argued that high land values are a serious impediment to urban renewal.[135]

This is a complex issue and there are conflicting views, but one explanation is the way land law artificially inflates prices in inner areas. When land is acquired by compulsory purchase the price is set by the district valuer who, bound by statutory rules governing compensation, estimates what the land is worth in its existing or permitted use, i.e. an estimate of what a willing buyer would pay a willing seller. Existing use includes 'eighth schedule rights' under which derelict land retains a presumptive right to its previous use and scale of building, no matter how long it has been disused; permitted use includes that established by a development plan zoning or valid planning permission. These planning assumptions frequently create values much higher than current use value. This formula is easily applied in areas where there is a flow of voluntary transactions. But in inner areas private development has been minimal; there have been very few recent transactions by willing sellers, so the establishment of values has largely been a result of the public sector acting as buyer or seller. If significant quantities of land were simultaneously put up for auction the price obtained would probably be very low. For reasons discussed below, this has not happened and it is likely that district valuers are valuing land in relation to 'a largely fictitious demand'.[136] Thus compulsory acquisition tends to set a floor below which other transactions do not drop, as owners will not sell for less than the local authority would have to pay in compensation. Once a series of valuations sets prices higher than current use value the process becomes self-sustaining because these transactions are recorded and used in subsequent valuations.[137]

Vacant land in *local authority* ownership is largely a legacy of delays in comprehensive redevelopment and highway schemes as clearance ran ahead of rebuilding in the early 1970s. The 'end of growth' exacerbated these problems. Further reductions in resources, particularly for public open space and highway schemes, left many areas in limbo. Liverpool illustrates the extremes of the problem: in 1976 the City Treasurer estimated that the council owned 452 ha of vacant land which would cost £139m to develop, but only 62 ha were in firm capital programmes at a cost of £28m.[138] Much of the land holdings of local authorities have been acquired at relatively high costs, and where land has been acquired relatively cheaply, site preparation costs are high.

All the case studies examined by the RTPI Working Party involving acquisition by local authorities and subsequent disposal to the private sector recorded a substantial loss: even if sites were acquired for virtually nothing, clearance and infrastructure costs exceeded the amount recouped. Rather than incur significant losses authorities hold land, waiting for resources to become available for them to undertake development, although this ignores the costs incurred in keeping land vacant while paying interest on capital borrowed for purchase. Hence vacant land has accumulated in local authority ownership.

Nationalized industries and statutory undertakers have substantial holdings of vacant land in inner areas. But redundant railway sidings, dockyards and gasworks are littered with the substantial detritus of a century's development, making redevelopment extremely costly. Some of this land is held in reserve for possible reuse, although when gas boards argue that they are retaining sites for when North Sea gas is exhausted, 'temporary redundancy' means long term underuse. The development of surplus land is inhibited by institutional constraints, e.g. British Rail is required to obtain the highest possible price for land which it sells. While this may help to keep down rail fares it can encourage the retention of unused sites in the hope of being able later to sell at a higher price, perhaps as the result of securing new planning permissions. Hence large tracts of neglected land and buildings in public ownership continue to disfigure inner areas.

In certain areas, usually on the fringe of the central business district, *private owners* are available to drive up land prices by exerting speculative pressure. This happens in some parts of inner London (and to a lesser extent in provincial cities) where there is the hope of a planning permission for a higher value use, or where eighth-schedule rights can be claimed.[139] It can work against the interests of local residents in two ways. First, there is an incentive for existing manufacturing firms to leave in order to realize capital from an otherwise viable plant for investment elsewhere, adding to local job losses. Second, it can make acquisition prohibitively expensive for local authorities wanting to develop sites for housing and other community facilities. Hence hope values and existing use rights can cause private land to remain vacant.[140]

The problems posed by poor environmental conditions have emerged as major areas of work for two main reasons, which generate conflicting priorities. Ministerial speeches reiterated the call in the White Paper for more positive land management and stressed the importance of improving the physical environment in order to stimulate private investment in economic regeneration.[141] This implies a concentration of resources in industrial and commercial areas where large-scale investment is necessary, e.g. in site preparation. Second, it became clear in the formulation of IAPs that residents wanted improvements in their immediate environment, suggesting a high priority for more modest initiatives in residential areas, e.g. tidying up of small sites, improved refuse collection, provision of amenity and play spaces.

There is no doubt that many local authorities have changed their attitudes to land management, not least in that underused land is no longer regarded as an inevitable but temporary concomitant of urban renewal. A considerable range of initiatives are being developed and a wide variety of approaches to implementation are being adopted. Although early work tended to be characterized by an opportunist appproach, authorities have started to evolve more coherent policies. Many took the long-overdue first step of setting up a register of vacant sites, classified by physical characteristics, ownership, causes of vacancy and existing development proposals. This paved the way for a systematic review which could achieve two results. First, temporary uses, such as landscaped open spaces, could be devised for sites where permanent reuse by existing owners will be reasonably delayed. Second, information on sites identified as surplus to requirements could be used in the preparation of local plans. These plans can update zoning proposals, (e.g. by allocating additional land for industry and linking this to measures to improve access and site conditions), and minimize blight (e.g. by removing unrealistic highway reservations). They can provide a framework for the co-ordinated deployment of urban programme and main programme resources in ways which encourage private investment and/or meet the needs of residents, according to the priorities adopted.[142]

As with other areas of IAP work, initial practical experience has raised questions which need to be answered in order to develop more effective programmes of environmental improvement.[143] To what extent should the emphasis be on developing an integrated approach? How are the mounting revenue implications of capital schemes to be dealt with, e.g. the maintenance of landscaped sites? What is the most appropriate balance between short-term and long-term work? Should effort be concentrated in a few areas, or more widely dispersed?

These issues are relevant to the immediate future, but in the longer term a substantial impact on environmental conditions in inner areas will require the input of more public resources, necessitating measures such as writing off local authorities' historic acquisition costs and securing a more equitable balance between public and private gains from the development of land.

Unequal partners

The White Paper stressed that the active participation of the people who live, work and invest in inner areas is essential to the success of the policy:

> Involving local people is both a necessary means to the regeneration of the inner areas and an end in its own right. Public authorities need to draw on the ideas of local residents, to discover their priorities and enable them to play a practical part in

> reviving their areas. Self-help is important and so is community effort. Some things will be better done, or done more satisfyingly if they are undertaken by voluntary groups and bodies.[144]

It was a 'necessary means' because it was hoped that it would enable limited public resources to be used to maximum effect by turning policies to local needs and stimulating private investment. It was 'an end in its own right' by increasing consumer involvement in the provision of services.

The Government envisaged two levels of participation: first, a process of *consultation*, giving opportunities for views and ideas on problems and priorities to be voiced and for comment on proposals; second involvement in *implementation* through voluntary sector projects funded by the increased Urban Programme. Consultation in the early IAPs was limited.[145] It primarily involved two types of voluntary organization. The emphasis was on those agencies organized around specific issues at a district level, e.g. services for the elderly. Much of their work is in inner areas, and they are often long-established charities, many with significant resources. The majority of authorities consulted these agencies, often after pressure, but this apparently had little effect on proposals. Neighbourhood organizations are usually more recently established, less well resourced and, perhaps, not so polite. Only half the authorities made any attempt to consult local residents, mainly through these groups, some of whom organized their own meetings to discuss IAPs.

In terms of implementation the overall allocation of Urban Programme funds for voluntary sector projects from 1979 onwards was much larger than in previous years. However, the bulk of this went to voluntary agencies: in some authorities neighbourhood organizations were not even given an opportunity to submit proposals. In most authorities such participation as was achieved was through 'umbrella' organizations which attempted to disseminate information and co-ordinate the input from this sector. Local Councils of Social Service, backed by technical advice from the NCSS, tended to take a leading role.

This very modest progress stemmed in part from the tight schedule for the first IAP submissions. The demands of establishing internal co-ordinating machinery left little time for the development of new participation procedures and authorities had to rely on adaptations of those already established. This created the impression that participation was viewed as an appendage rather than an integral part of the process. Subsequently there have been efforts to develop more effective procedures, including: a formal time-table of events (release of consultation papers, submission of project bids, etc.) integrated in the annual cycle of programme preparation; better information; increased opportunities for consultation; clarification of Urban Programme allocation procedures; and improved liaison between officer steering groups and 'umbrella' organizations by the appointment of staff to work with officers of voluntary organizations.

These types of arrangements will probably enable voluntary agencies to increase their involvement, but are of less value to residents' organizations who are primarily concerned about the combined impact, or lack of impact, of proposals affecting their area. Beyond developing methods of describing problems, and itemizing Urban Programme (and in some cases main programme) investment on an area basis, proposals currently envisaged are patchy and limited. A few authorities are proceeding with ward-level meetings or area committees, but Newcastle's initiative in allocating limited block budgets to local committees remains exceptional. Despite lobbying by organizations, it is clear that the influence which residents and ward councillors will have on IAPs will remain severely limited.[146]

Increasing the effectiveness of participation means changing existing power relationships. The management structure for IAPs concentrates power in the hands of a small minority of leading councillors and senior officers. Not only do Partnership Committees meet in private, in sharp contrast to normal committee practice, but inner area ward councillors are effectively excluded from the decision-making process (unless they happen to be senior party members), despite the White Paper statement that 'local councillors are vital in maintaining the link between the community and the authorities'.[147] Unless this structure is modified by a significant devolution of power, participation will be little more than tokenism.

Race

Questions of involvement and power are most sharply posed when the substantial black minority in inner areas is considered. The 1977 White Paper was at pains to point out that 'Inner area problems and racial problems are by no means co-terminous. . .'[148] and commented that some conurbations, e.g. Tyneside, had not seen substantial coloured immigration. It acknowledged, but understated, the significance of ethnic minorities' settlement in the inner areas of the major cities. The Poverty Programme had its origins partly in the political response to racist sentiment. By the mid-1970s coloured immigration had sharply declined in quantity and changed in nature, having been restricted to the families of previous immigrants. But Britain's black population of 1.8m was almost exclusively urban and heavily concentrated in the inner areas of London, the Midlands, North West and West Yorkshire: 'the geography of urban despair tends to coincide with the geography of immigrant settlement and concentration within the conurbations'.[149] Racist political parties have re-emerged while the bitterness and frustration of black youth (often not immigrant) is increasingly evident. Unemployment among blacks is growing more rapidly than among the rest of the population (an increase of 350 per cent between 1974 and 1977 compared with a 120 per cent increase in total unemployment).[150]

In this context official discussion of policies for regenerating the inner city is inadequate. The White Paper's reliance on more general anti-discrimination measures and a further passing reference to investment by immigrant communities in housing and shops[151] hardly constitutes serious attention to this issue. Confronting this racial dimension undoubtedly raises complex issues, but a first step would be to encourage further identification of the more indirect pattern of racial disadvantage which often results from policies which at face value have a 'colour-blind' orientation, in addition to those resulting from more conscious discrimination.[152] While some official action could then be tailored to particular local needs, e.g. by amending planning policies on Muslim prayer houses, more substantial changes are likely to flow from community initiatives. The black population is effectively excluded from formal politics. Although blacks may derive some benefit from inner city policies, their relative position will only be improved by a transfer of power and influence and by specific funding of projects aimed at countering particular disadvantages.

Conclusions

Within two years the policies embodied in the 1977 White Paper and subsequent legislation were beginning to have an impact in many older urban areas. These changes were the result of the Government's synthesis of a decade of debate and policy development which had established inequality within cities as a priority for intervention, just as in the 1930s the acknowledgement of regional inequality had prompted the beginnings of regional policy:

> . . . cities serve and sustain the whole region around them in social, cultural and economic terms. If cities fail so to a large extent does our society. That is the urgency of tackling the problem. . . .[153]

The basic causes of urban deprivation are now more widely understood than was the case when poverty was rediscovered in the 1960s, although there are those who would still 'blame the victim'. There is wide agreement that the causes are economic and that action should be taken to alleviate urban deprivation, but there are conflicting views on appropriate solutions, which reflect different political and professional perspectives.

In the absence of major changes in the economic organization of society the market will continue to distribute resources unevenly, and the issue is that of the scale and effectiveness of redistributive measures. Such reforms are relatively painless if the economy is growing. But when it is stagnating or contracting, redistribution is politically far more difficult: it means a reduction in the standards of living of the 'haves' in order to improve the lot of the 'have nots'. For this and other reasons the wider economic and social programmes necessary for a significant reduction of inequality and, therefore, poverty have not been forthcoming. Instead the Labour Government cut social expenditure in an attempt to restore national economic prosperity.

This was the context in which the inner cities policy was introduced. In principle, it was a continuation of the trend towards area-selective positive discrimination. Notwithstanding the exaggerated claims surrounding its introduction, it clearly provided an improved framework for the co-ordination of action across a wide range of issues. However, in practice, area-based policies have been undermined by the deterioration in conditions stemming from the diminishing effectiveness of wider policies to reduce inequality. At best, inner cities policy can reduce the rate of decline in the priority areas, but at the expense of more rapid decline in other areas where conditions are only marginally better. A genuine attack on the causes of inner area problems must combine specific inner area programmes with wider economic and social programmes. Only then can causes rather than symptoms be dealt with, and the rhetoric of the inner area debate be translated into the reality of more effective action.

7 Birmingham: second city first

This chapter examines the impact of the major phases of national policy on the physical and social fabric of England's second largest city. The economy of Birmingham has, until very recently, been relatively prosperous. Sustained economic growth in the inter-war and post-war years meant that the context for urban renewal was strong demographic pressure on housing. In Birmingham there are particularly clear relationships between the historical development of the built environment and urban renewal policies, because the city 'has grown principally by the addition of successive peripheral zones around the original nucleus'.[1]

By 1875 housing conditions in the inner ring had been defined as a 'civic problem'. Seventy years of debate about the relative merits of reconditioning and clearance produced very limited action. But from the 1940s it was the target area of comprehensive redevelopment, and Birmingham's massive programme came to epitomize this approach to renewal. The middle ring was developed in the late nineteenth and early twentieth centuries. It became the 'twilight zone' of the 1960s, as a combination of housing market pressure and the effects of comprehensive redevelopment in the adjacent inner ring caused rapid deterioration. The huge improvement-based Urban Renewal Programme, launched in the early 1970s, was directed to this area which is now the focus of the city's version of gradual renewal. The outer ring was substantially developed in the inter-war years by a combination of public and private sector building, and more recently huge high-density estates were added to rehouse families displaced by inner ring redevelopment. By the end of the 1970s there was growing concern about the deterioration of much inter-war property, and ageing council housing is competing with the Victorian middle ring for limited renewal resources.

The substantially redeveloped inner ring and the partially improved middle ring form the core of the Birmingham Inner City Partnership Area. For the first time in its history the city is now attempting to implement renewal policies in the context of a declining local economy. Housing pressure is not as obvious, but resource constraints are undermining housing improvement policies, and economic renewal is a remote prospect.

Slums and the civic gospel

In 1913 the council set up an inquiry to examine the housing conditions of the poor. It found that 200,000 people were living in 43,000 back-to-backs, described as 'cavernous conditions', unfit for human habitation.[2] This was the product of a century of rapid growth, and the limited impact of forty years of sanitary reform.

Inner ring growth

During the nineteenth century the local economy developed rapidly on the basis of an increasing variety of metal trades. Until the late 1860s production was predominantly organized in small workshops owned by master craftsmen, employing skilled artisans. Economic prosperity had a magnetic effect. The city's population increased from 71,000 in 1801 to 184,000 in 1840 and, as immigration accelerated, exceeded 400,000 by 1875.[3] This phase of economic development necessitated the housing of large numbers of people on high-value land, within walking distance of their work, at rents they could afford. The resultant built environment was dominated by some 50,000 back-to-backs, in courtyard arrangements, lacking sinks and drains, with communal water supplies and toilets sited in the yards. There was no public open space. Small workshops were intermixed with, and often not structurally separate from, the housing (see Figure 14).[4]

There was little intervention during this phase of growth. But a worsening of housing conditions in the 1860s coincided with the transformation of the city's complacent government, under the compelling leadership of Chamberlain.[5] A tradition of innovative municipal intervention was established: 'civic pride was the driving force of a whole civic philosophy, known at the time and since as "the civic gospel" '.[6] This development had a two-fold impact on housing, for '. . . at the same time as it laid down building regulations for the future, the corporation made itself responsible for the wreckage from the past'.[7] The former significantly influenced the growth of the middle ring, while the latter initiated a seventy-year debate about slum clearance in the inner ring.

Middle ring growth

From the late 1860s the factory system of production dominated the local economy, and the development of medium and light engineering ensured continued prosperity. Skill was subordinated to capital, and the proportion of unskilled, low-paid jobs increased. There was an outward shift in industrial investment as new factories were built on cheap green-field sites, in corridors along the major canals and railways. The population continued to increase, and by 1911 had reached 840,000. This suburbanization of industry was accompanied by speculative residential development, adjacent to the new

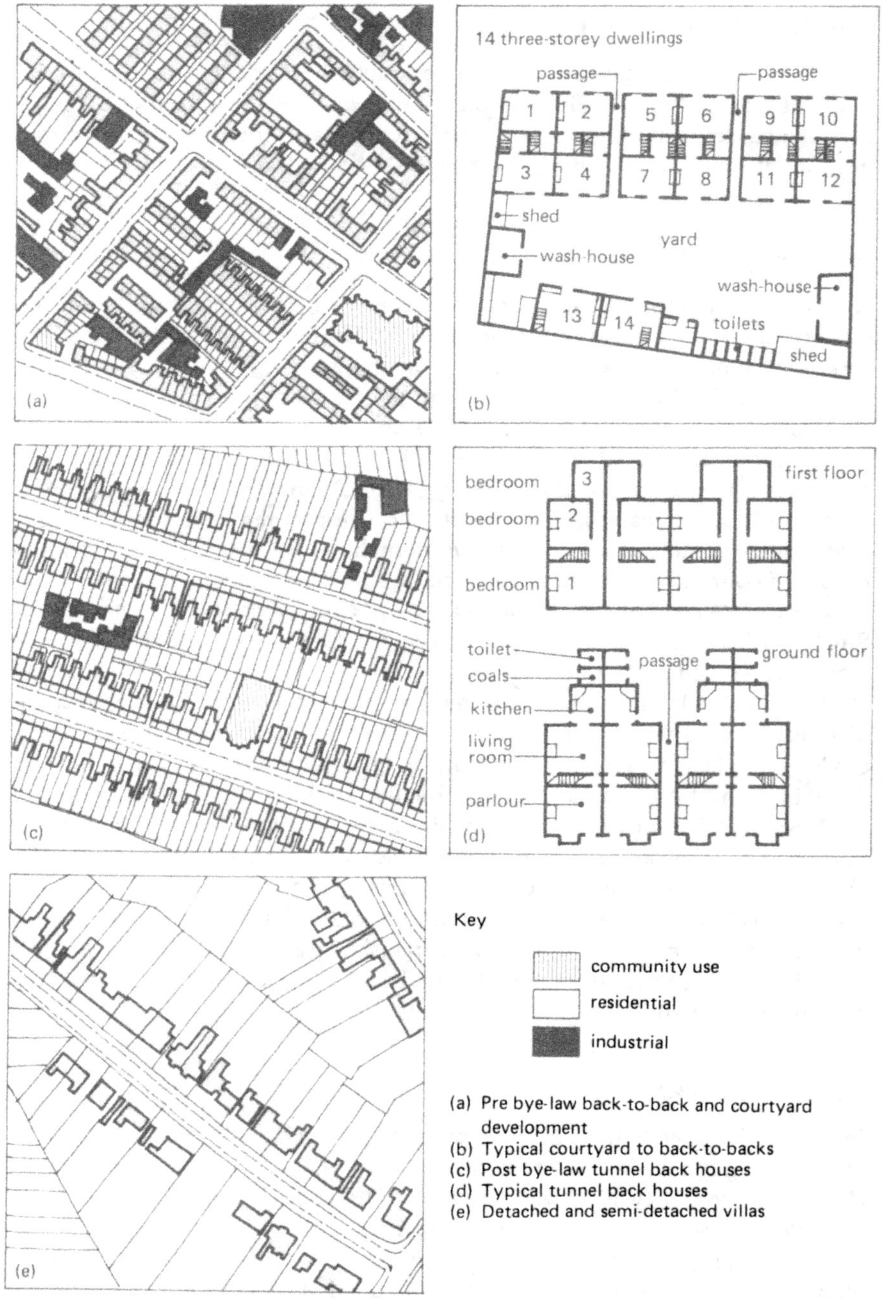

(a) Pre bye-law back-to-back and courtyard development
(b) Typical courtyard to back-to-backs
(c) Post bye-law tunnel back houses
(d) Typical tunnel back houses
(e) Detached and semi-detached villas

Figure 14 *Birmingham: pre-1914 housing*

The street plans are reproduced from Ordnance Survey maps.

factories and encircling the older districts. However, the construction of back-to-backs was banned by the Chamberlain administration's bye-laws.

The built environment produced was markedly different from that of the inner ring. The predominant house type was the tunnel-back, some 50,000 of which were built mainly in long uniform terraces. They were larger than the back-to-backs and had piped water, sinks, and gardens. The majority were individually equipped with an outside w.c., but very few had bathrooms. Some parks were provided and industry was less intermixed with housing. Improved standards resulted in higher rents and, as public transport developed, the skilled working-class moved into these new suburbs. Similarly, the middle-classes left the inner districts for new estates of large, expensive villas with spacious gardens. These estates were eventually engulfed by tunnel-back development.

The slum problem identified

Suburban development and selective migration left the deteriorating back-to-backs as a reservoir of cheap accommodation. In the inner ring the population declined, but there was a growing concentration of the lowest paid and immigrants. At the turn of the century the exodus slowed as housebuilding rates declined. Yet the city's population continued to expand and pressure on the inner districts increased.[8] The result was renewed overcrowding and accelerated dilapidation. By the time of the 1913 inquiry these processes had:

> . . . set the seal on the slow transformation of Birmingham's back-to-backs from modern efficient housing into hard-core slum. All those who could afford to live elsewhere, or whose employment would allow them to move, had now left. Those who remained were condemned to perpetual residence in housing conditions which the middle classes now came increasingly to regard as detrimental to health, morals and education.[9]

These conditions also reflected the failure of forty years of municipal intervention. Chamberlain was at the height of his power in Birmingham at the time of the Cross Act of 1875, which he regarded as a watershed as '. . . for the first time the claims of large communities had been recognized as superior to . . . the sacred rights of property'.[10] Within months of the new legislation the council had approved his ambitious and controversial renewal project, the Birmingham Improvement Scheme. This was one of the first, and by far the largest, of the schemes carried out under the Cross Act. The objective was the clearance of ninety-three acres of one of the most congested central districts and its redevelopment for commercial and residential purposes.[11]

Chamberlain argued that slum clearance would necessitate cheap high-density replacement housing in the form of flats '. . . if the poor are to be housed in close proximity to their work, and at a reasonable rent'.[12] But the market showed no interest in such provision, as suburban development was a more profitable and less risky investment. By 1885 the Improvement Committee was advocating municipal flat provision.

Chamberlain had allowed his imagination to run away with him. There was considerable opposition to his strategy: landlords objected to the acquisition of their property; the Conservatives considered municipal housing unnecessary (in view of vacant private houses) and expensive (in the absence of central government subsidy); the Trades Council pressed for municipal provision of suburban low-rent terraced housing, rather than flats in the poor environment of the inner ring; the slum dwellers were known to dislike the idea of flats, and proposals to overcome this by high design standards foundered as the consequent rents would be beyond the means of the poor.

The debate ebbed and flowed for twenty-five years and the city failed to develop a positive housing policy from the Improvement Scheme initiative. By the turn of the century, only two municipal housing projects had been built. In sharp contrast, profitable commercial and civic rebuilding had transformed the city centre.

In 1901 responsibility for housing policy was given to the newly formed Housing Committee chaired by Nettlefold. The result was the adoption of the private enterprise 'suburban solution', with three key elements:

1 a holding operation involving reconditioning the back-to-backs, by enforcing minimum repairs and selectively demolishing end houses to open up the courts;
2 a gradual thinning out of the inner ring by 'filtering' to new private suburbs built within the framework of municipal town planning schemes; and
3 the eventual private redevelopment of the partially evacuated inner districts, again within a planned framework.[13]

This strategy was a total failure. Reconditioning (which reduced the supply of cheap housing) combined with the rejection of municipal housing (when private building was declining and the city's population expanding) contributed to a worsening housing situation.[14] The 1913 inquiry recognized some of the problems, but '. . . it was unwilling to propose what it saw as the only feasible solution – the clearance of large areas of central Birmingham, and the construction of at least 50,000 municipal dwellings there to replace the back-to-backs'.[15] The objections to this were those which the Chamberlainites had encountered from 1875, and the result was a recommendation to continue Nettlefold's suburban solution.

The genesis of comprehensive redevelopment

During the inter-war years there was little improvement in the 'cavernous conditions' of the inner ring. A separate water supply was installed in most back-to-backs, and between 1930 and 1938 some 8000 of the worst houses were demolished. It was not until the end of the Second World War that a policy of large-scale comprehensive redevelopment was established.

Council housing, reconditioning and piecemeal clearance

The local economy was cushioned from the worst effects of national economic recession by the growth of another generation of industries, including electrical engineering and motor vehicle manufacture. There was a further outward shift in industrial investment as new mass production enterprises located on cheap land beyond the middle ring. The population continued to increase until it had exceeded one million by 1931, and decentralization accelerated. With further selective migration the population of the inner and middle rings fell by a quarter, while that of the outer ring doubled.[16]

State intervention significantly influenced residential development and modified Nettlefold's suburban solution. With the advent of central government subsidies, municipal housebuilding, which before the war had been rejected as 'too socialistic',[17] was now seen as the only practical solution to the chronic post-war housing shortage. Birmingham embarked on the country's largest council building programme, and 50,000 houses were built by 1939. Both public and private semi-detached estates were built within the framework of town planning schemes; densities were low; sites were allocated for community facilities; and industry was segregated.[18]

During the 1920s national housing policy and the city's housing shortage ruled out clearance. The first renewal scheme in 1928 was for the reconditioning of a small area of back-to-backs, and the controversy surrounding it illuminated the conflicting views and interests of politicians, officers, landlords and tenants.[19] Clearance was opposed by influential property owners and the Conservatives, who considered reconditioning sufficient. Existing tenants did not want demolition unless low-rent rehousing could be provided. The failure of a small experimental block of municipal flats at Garrison Lane had underlined the council's incapacity to make such provision. They had been let at a loss to avoid prohibitively high rents. The Labour opposition and the MoH, both pressing for slum clearance, shared the tenants objections to low housing standards, the absence of community facilities, and the location of new housing in an oppressive and deteriorating environment. The flats were compared unfavourably with suburban council estates.

After 1930 a combination of factors prompted the gradual abandonment of the 'suburban solution'. The national slum clearance campaign and changes in housing subsidies undermined the local reconditioning lobby. Although the inner ring was 'thinning out', it was increasingly accepted that many slum dwellers could not afford higher rents and travel costs resulting from moving to a suburban council estate.[20] Attitudes to suburban development began to change, as its volume and low density had caused an unprecedented expansion of the city's built-up area.[21]

However, Birmingham's slum clearance programme during the 1930s was the smallest of any large city.[22] In 1930 the Conservative controlled council adopted a five-year programme for the demolition of 4700 back-to-backs and the construction of 7000 replacements.[23] This low level of activity remained council policy until 1938, and was attributed by Sutcliffe to continued all-party opposition to flat-building.[24] While this was clearly important, Schifferes' argument that '. . . the important property holdings of some Conservatives, with the uncertainty of compensation, was undoubtedly the main factor'[25] is more persuasive.

Clearance was carried out on a piecemeal 'worst first' basis, and because of continuing opposition to flats, small groups of replacement maisonettes were built. With low-density replacement, only a minority of residents could be rehoused locally. Most of the remainder were moved to council-owned slum property, often by preference (because the rents were low) but also because the council was reluctant to allocate suburban estate tenancies to clearance families.[26] This weakened Labour opposition to large-scale, high-density flat building, as did the fact that the enclaves of new maisonettes suffered the same environmental disadvantages as the Garrison Lane scheme.

The restriction of subsidies to clearance rehousing in 1933 focussed attention on the flats' issue, and in 1934 a scheme was proposed for the clearance of five acres of back-to-backs and their replacement by high-density flats. Labour Party and local residents' meetings showed divided working-class opinion, but by now middle-class opinion had shifted from the suburban ideal and the council was under pressure from a pro-flat Minister of Health. After a two year debate the scheme was approved and the St. Martin's flats were completed in 1939. This decision was the watershed in the flats debate, but the evolution of renewal policy was significantly influenced by the appointment in 1935 of Manzoni as city engineer.

The concept of comprehensive redevelopment

Manzoni altered the terms of the policy debate. He argued that a piecemeal approach was inadequate, given the physical and social characteristics of the inner ring. A wider perspective was needed, involving comprehensive redevelopment on the largest possible scale. For Manzoni:

> . . . the object of redevelopment, if it is to be successful, is to bring back an obsolete district to a high standard and this can only be achieved if the whole layout is changed with the provision of new roads, open spaces, and good shops, proper zoning, and all the amenities of a new and up-to-date development; to rebuild a few groups of houses in an already dingy setting will never do this – the whole area must be new and it must look completely different.[27]

Only comprehensive redevelopment with high-density housing, including flats, would enable a substantial majority of residents to be rehoused locally and the provision of a full range of community facilities. It would also avoid the environmental disadvantages of piecemeal schemes, for the developed areas would extend 'from the core to the proximity of good property'.[28] He applied this concept in a draft layout for 267 acres of Duddeston and Nechells, designated in 1937 as the first large-scale redevelopment area under the provisions of the Housing Act, 1936.

This advocacy of comprehensive redevelopment was one element in a reappraisal of policy in the late 1930s, which by 1938 had resulted in the Conservative council finally adopting a substantial five-year programme for the clearance of 17,500 slums. However, there was more to the rehousing question than the issues raised in the flats debate. Large-scale clearance necessitated a massive increase in council housing production, and changes in allocation policies. The 1938 proposals were for the construction of 25,000 dwellings at double the rate then being achieved, of which 20,000 were to be allocated to clearance tenants and only 5000 to meet the needs indicated by a 10,000 strong waiting list.[29]

The viability of the strategy rested on a means test. When applied to prospective tenants this would eliminate some 5000 from the waiting list, and extended to existing tenants would persuade the 'richer' ones (who would be charged full economic rents) to move into the private sector. At the same time a rent rebate scheme for poor families would enable clearance tenants to take up the resulting vacancies. The indignity of the means test provoked demonstrations and a massive rent strike, and the council had to withdraw its proposals.[30]

Wartime plans and municipalization

Thus at the outbreak of war the council was committed to large-scale clearance. Yet, despite the acceptance of flats, it had failed to solve the rehousing problem and had not seriously confronted the issue of large-scale acquisition.

In 1941 the council initiated an intensive period of planning for post-war reconstruction. Under Manzoni's guidance, four more large redevelopment areas were designated. Draft layouts were prepared incorporating the design principles of segregated land-uses, restructured road systems, neighbourhood units, and public open space. Manzoni cultivated local support and in 1943 his advocacy of comprehensive redevelopment extended to the national arena, when he was appointed to serve on a panel considering the powers needed for the acquisition of blitzed areas for redevelopment. Knowing that a restriction of emergency powers to blitzed areas would be of little assistance to Birmingham, he successfully argued that blighted slum areas presented similar problems and that sweeping powers of acquisition were necessary in both cases. The Town and Country Planning Act, 1944 provided these powers and became known as 'the blitz and blight act'.

The council lost no time. A CPO for the five redevelopment areas was submitted in February 1946. Notification of individual owners was not required. There were only 300 objections and, after an inquiry lasting only a week, the Order was confirmed in June 1947. At a stroke almost 1000 acres of the inner ring, some 32,000 houses accommodating over 100,000 people, and hundreds of industrial and commercial premises, were taken into municipal ownership (Phase I in Figure 15). As Manzoni put it: 'Birmingham was launched upon an uncharted sea, and like Columbus, it believed that there was a landfall to the west, but couldn't be certain'.[31]

Inner ring development

The optimism of the 1940s was succeeded by two decades of unexpectedly slow progress, the result of inadequate resources for the implementation of this massive programme. Then in the late 1960s there was a spectacular acceleration in the rate of demolition and rebuilding. By 1970 most of the inner ring had been cleared and much of it redeveloped.

Containment and slow progress

During the early post-war years comprehensive redevelopment proposals were incorporated in a planning strategy designed to contain the city's growth. The Ministry of Town and Country Planning endorsed an advisory plan prepared by Abercrombie and Jackson.[32] This assumed that the major strategic issue was the accommodation of overspill from inner area redevelopment rather than overall population growth. The main proposals were for limited suburban development and the definition of a Green Belt, with overspill to be accommodated in selected areas within and beyond it. No new towns were proposed. It was assumed that expansion of nearby towns such as Bromsgrove, Cannock and Tamworth would cater for the decentralization of population and employment. In a slightly modified form, these assumptions were embodied in the city's Development Plan in 1952, but the scale and timing of overspill provision was left indeterminate.[33]

In the nine years to 1954 only 3000 slums were demolished in the redevelopment areas, less than half the 1930s clearance rate (Figure 16). National policy discouraged clearance. Locally a combination of the suspension of house-building during the war and immigration (sustained after the war) produced a massive housing shortage. Despite restrictions on eligibility, the waiting list rocketed to 78,000 in 1951. Local political opinion changed and general needs were given top priority. Building rates were initially abysmally low, but from 1949 a marked improvement resulted in a fall in the waiting list. However, this expanded programme rapidly exhausted available large green-field sites. Densities of suburban development were increased by flat building and sites started to become available in the redevelopment areas. But the cleared sites were limited in number and too small for rapid development. After 1953 the building programme declined sharply.[34]

Initially, the council undertook only minimum repairs to the houses acquired in the redevelopment areas. But, as it became clear that many of

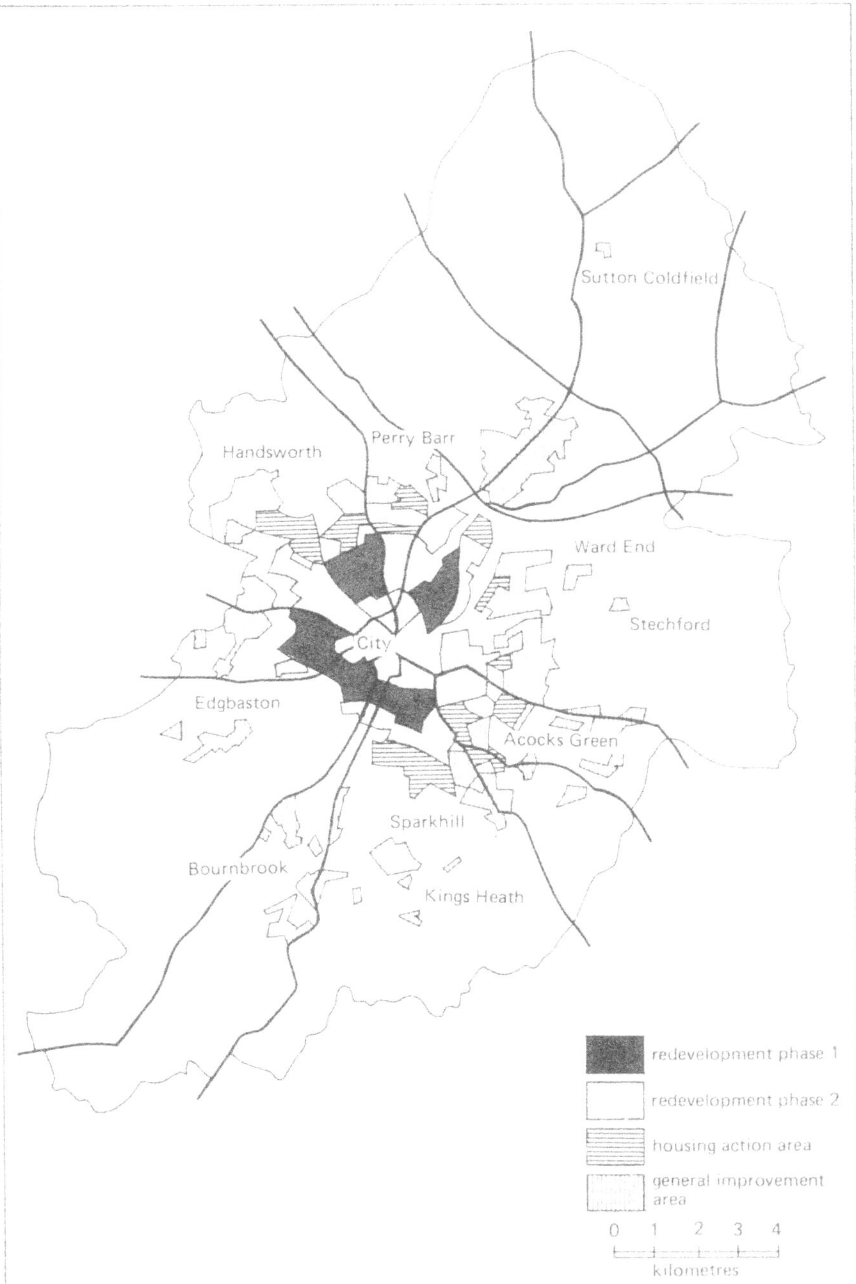

Figure 15 ***Birmingham: renewal areas***

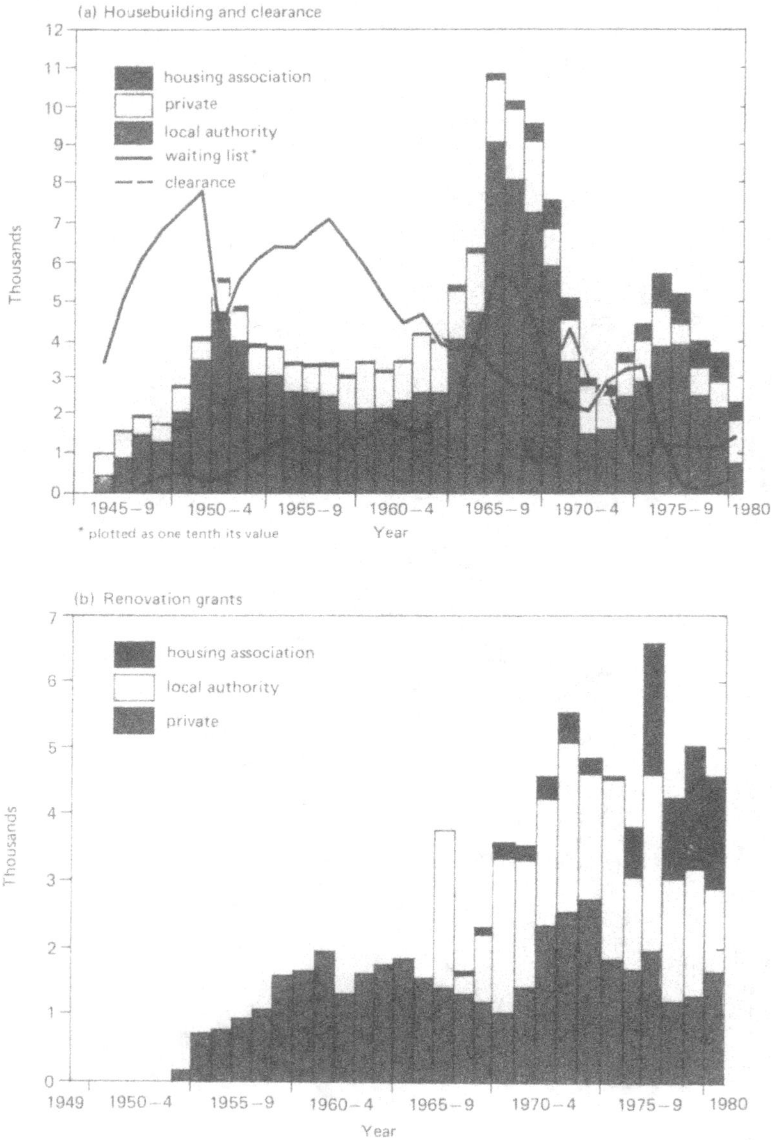

Figure 16 *Birmingham: renewal progress 1945 to 1980*

Notes: Data for Housing Association and Local Authority Grants is not available for the years before 1967
1954–66 figures are grants approved; 1967–70 figures are grants paid; 1971–8 figures are grants approved; 1979–80 figures are grants paid

Sources: City of Birmingham, *Annual Abstract of Statistics* and DoE, *Local Housing Statistics*

them would remain for much longer than had originally been envisaged, it started to carry out more extensive renovations. In 1953, accepting the inevitability of its role as a slum landlord, the council adopted a policy of renovating houses to provide 'reasonably tolerable living standards'.[35]

The launching of 'Operation Rescue' in 1954 marked the resumption of a national slum clearance campaign. Birmingham's involuntary renovation procedures were incorporated in national policy, and subsidies were made available for this process, which became known as *deferred demolition*. As in 1945, the council lost no time in utilizing the new powers, and in 1955, despite opposition from property owners and the Conservatives, a further fifteen smaller areas were designated as Phase II of the redevelopment programme (see Figure 15). Some 25,000 properties (later increased to 30,000) were to be purchased in advance of clearance, but demolition was not programmed to start until Phase I was completed. These houses were to be renovated at a unit cost of £200 – more than the standard grant for private owners introduced later in 1959. By 1964 virtually all the houses in Phase II had been represented as unfit, some 17,000 had been acquired, and over 10,000 reconditioned.

Compared with the relatively rapid progress of acquisition and reconditioning of Phase II properties, the rate of Phase I clearance was much less impressive. In the period 1955–64 an average of 1500 houses p.a. were demolished, only 50 per cent better than the 1930s rate. This left a third of the properties acquired in 1946 standing. The key factor was the very low level of council housing production (an average of 2500 p.a.) in relation to a massive and continuing housing shortage.

In 1956, the Conservative Government restricted subsidies for new building to slum clearance rehousing. This, combined with the council's long-standing commitment to clear the slums and the fact that building sites in the Phase I area were essential to the maintenance of even a modest building programme, resulted in changes in housing allocation policy. By 1957 60 per cent of allocations were made to clearance area families.

In this context the piecemeal acquisition of houses in the Phase II areas was strategically necessary for the implementation of Phase I redevelopment. Acquisition partially offset demolition and Birmingham was able to maintain a large pool of old substandard housing in its ownership. The additional availability of relets in acquired property helped to maintain a modest rate of clearance. But the council was still trying to both clear the slums and cope with a continuing housing shortage: with a low building rate it was unable to do either satisfactorily. Slum clearance progress was slow and the waiting list rose to 70,000 again in 1958.

Many factors were involved in the poor level of housing production, but two were particularly important. First, there was the contradictory nature of national policies. Housing policy emphasized the need to clear the slums but planning policy resulted in a serious shortage of land available for council building. This stemmed from the Government's refusal to designate a new town to meet overspill needs, the inadequacy of town development schemes, and the increasingly rigid enforcement of Green Belt policy. Faced with mounting difficulties, the council shifted from its post-war policy of acquiescence in containment. In 1959 it attempted to secure peripheral building land in neighbouring Warwickshire. The attempt failed at the Wythall Inquiry, partly as a result of the Government's reluctance to alter the strategic planning framework, an attitude reinforced by the intervention of the Midlands New Town Society advocating policies of long-distance dispersal.[36]

However, the city's case was seriously weakened by the second factor – its housebuilding organization. In the late 1950s there were long delays in the development of the one remaining large suburban council housing site at Castle Bromwich. These were due to political arguments about the use of system building and to interdepartmental wrangling.[37] Thus by 1964, the year after a White Paper had talked of the end of the slums and the need to start planning for action in the twilight areas, Birmingham's housing situation was desperate – there was a backlog of slum clearance and a huge waiting list.

Breakthrough

During the early 1960s the Government accepted that overspill provisions for Birmingham were inadequate and designated Dawley (later Telford) and Redditch new towns. Of more immediate relevance was the new Labour Government's decision to give Birmingham permission to develop a 6500 acre peripheral Green Belt site at Chelmsley Wood. Furthermore, subsidies for council housebuilding were substantially increased. These changes prompted the Labour controlled city council to put aside its long-standing objections to system building (stemming from a concern about reduced standards) and to reconstitute its housebuilding organization.

The effect of these changes was dramatic. Council housebuilding rates soared and in 1967 a staggering total of 9034 dwellings were completed, easily surpassing the previous best annual total of 6715 which had stood since 1930. Between 1965 and 1970 39,000 houses were built by the council and the waiting list was sharply reduced. 23,000 houses were demolished, which virtually completed Phase I clearance, and accounted for 60 per cent of the clearance in Phase II. In the same period a further 18,000 houses were renovated as the rate of acquisition of Phase II properties increased. The city's official history summed up the situation as follows:

> . . . the city's housing machine attracted nationwide attention. Birmingham was now renewing itself faster than any other city in Europe. . . . By 1970 almost all of the original central redevelopment areas had been cleared and redeveloped on a scale unparalleled in Britain. And demolition was proceeding so fast in the newly acquired areas that all the city's unfit houses were expected to disappear by 1975.[38]

But the slums did not all disappear by 1975. To explain this, it is necessary to turn to the problems of the twilight areas and the reappraisal of policy in 1972.

The twilight areas

The Bournville Village Trust report of 1941 described the middle ring as:

> . . . a blighted residential quarter destined, unless brought into a general plan, to descend in the end to the condition of slumdom.[39]

At the end of the war it was an area of stable second- and third-generation communities. The families of semi-skilled and skilled workers occupied mainly privately rented tunnel-back housing, which was structurally sound, but beginning to show its age as a result of minimal repair and maintenance. The more substantial villas were still predominantly in single-family, middle-class owner-occupation. By the early 1970s the interaction of market forces and the council's housing and planning policies had reproduced conditions in the middle ring approximating to those which had emerged in the inner ring at the turn of the century.

Housing pressure and exploitation

While the council was preoccupied with inner ring slum clearance, the middle ring underwent substantial social change, and housing and environmental conditions deteriorated through a lack of adequate private and public investment. The middle ring replaced the inner ring as the source of the cheapest private housing in the city and selective migration led to an increasing concentration of low-income groups, most of whom had no choice but to live there. The people who moved in were predominantly low-income households, often large young families. This was facilitated by, and later reinforced, the movement out of higher-income groups and of children leaving home and forming new households. Older residents and others who could not afford or did not want to move remained.

The processes which produced these patterns of change were complex, but an underlying factor was the continuing post-war housing shortage and the council's policy for managing this shortage while implementing its clearance programme. Aggregate housing needs in the post-war period were much greater than initially anticipated for two main reasons. First, the rate of natural increase of population and household formation accelerated unexpectedly. Second, the city's prosperous industries and expanding public services drew in immigrant labour from elsewhere in the UK and overseas, particularly the New Commonwealth countries. While overspill (both voluntary and planned) contributed to a marginal decline in the city's population, the housing situation remained one of continuous pressure.[40]

Movement of population out of and into the middle ring was the outcome of inequalities between the housing opportunities of different groups. Higher-income groups moved to owner-occupied houses in the outer suburbs and beyond. In contrast, the housing opportunities of lower-income groups depended on access to council housing or cheap private accommodation.[41]

The availability of *council housing* for residents living outside the redevelopment areas was severely limited by a combination of the inadequate house-building programme and the high priority given to slum clearance rehousing. Many of these families remained in the waiting list 'queue' for years. Furthermore, restrictions on eligibility excluded single people under forty, and residential qualifications known as the 'five-year rule' made it very difficult for newcomers to the city to obtain a tenancy.[42] In addition, single people under forty displaced by clearance were not normally eligible for council rehousing, and others displaced preferred to rehouse themselves. Thus there was a continuing demand for cheap private accommodation from new households, immigrants and people displaced by slum clearance – groups for whom council housing was either unavailable or unacceptable.

But the municipalization of the inner ring properties drastically reduced the availability of cheap private accommodation, and concentrated continuing demand for it in the middle ring. There the availability of *privately rented* accommodation was being progressively reduced by sales for owner-occupation, while access was limited by low turnover and the 'handing down' of tenancies.

The progressive transfer of small terraced housing to *owner-occupation* significantly altered ownership patterns in the middle ring, but many were sold to sitting tenants and were not available to newcomers. The increasing reluctance of building societies to lend on this property, particularly at the lower end of the quality scale, was partially offset by the council's mortgage scheme, introduced in 1960. By the early 1970s the purchase of some 10 per cent of middle ring properties had been financed in this way.[43] The new owner-occupiers included a significant proportion of the city's coloured immigrants and by 1969 40 per cent of them owned their homes.[44] Although by the late 1960s over a third of council mortgages were allocated to coloured immigrants,[45] many of these (along with other low-income groups) had to fund purchase through 'fringe finance' or informal personal arrangements. Moreover, for most immigrants owner-occupation was a second-stage process.

Many low-income households in housing need were unable to obtain access to council housing, to the traditional private rented sector, or to owner-occupation. This contributed to the accelerated development of *multi-occupation* from the 1950s onwards, which predominantly took the form of the subdivision of large villas coming on to the market as their middle-class owners moved out. Initially, the process was piecemeal but 'once multi-occupation began in an area it snow-balled. . . . What had been the smart streets of the twilight areas now became the centres of multi-occupation'.[46]

Many of these villas were bought by immigrant owner-occupier landlords, who lacked capital to purchase outright, could not obtain building society mortgages and had to rely on short-term, high-interest loans. This involved heavy repayment costs, and the property was sublet at high rents to service the loans. In the context of the city's housing problems these lodging house entrepreneurs can be regarded as a pariah group of landlords, doing the necessary job of housing themselves and others, while taking the blame for doing it. This is the interpretation offered by Rex and Moore.[47] Although no doubt accurate in many cases, it ignored both the persistence of high rents long after the repayment of loans, and an increasing proportion of absentee landlords. Many landlords bought property as a short-term investment and 'milked it', letting cramped substandard units at high rents and carrying out little or no maintenance, let alone improvement.

By the end of the 1950s there was growing concern about multi-occupation in the middle ring, and a report to the council drew attention to the '. . . large and substantial older houses, mainly in the Handsworth, Aston, Sparkbrook, and Balsall Heath areas, where living conditions have become much worse than in those houses known as slums as a result of overcrowding, inadequate amenities and neglect'.[48] A survey in 1962 estimated that 38,000 people were living in multi-occupation. The local press was full of lurid accounts of the problem and the council found itself the butt of much criticism as areas of acute housing stress were identified in certain parts of the middle ring. The problem of multi-occupation became inextricably bound up with the question of the housing of coloured immigrants in the city and race relations in general.

The policing of multi-occupation

The council had some powers to tackle the problem positively, but lacked the necessary resources. The overcrowding provisions of the Housing Acts could only be effectively used if displaced households were eligible for council rehousing. But the scarcity of council tenancies was a crucial factor in the development of the problem, and political pressures generated by both a long-drawn-out clearance programme and a high waiting list precluded an adjustment of allocation priorities in favour of families living in multi-occupation.

Faced with this dilemma, the council adopted a combination of 'policing policies'.[49] The first was vigorous action by public health inspectors against the worst cases of overcrowding. This involved the use of housing legislation to enforce the provision of adequate facilities, restrict the numbers of people occupying houses and secure minimum standards of maintenance. While this did not solve the problem, it helped curb the worst excesses of exploitation. A parallel policy was that of containing the geographical spread of multi-occupation, initially utilizing planning legislation. Later, the council used special powers, obtained under the Birmingham Corporation Act, 1965, which required compulsory registration of houses in multiple occupation. Permission could be refused if the council considered the house, the area, or the landlord, unsuitable. Available evidence suggests that in broad terms the spread of multi-occupation was checked.[50] But the scale of the problem undoubtedly increased: by 1970 some 13,000 houses were in multi-occupation. Thus the policy intensified the problem in certain areas. Both these policing policies were negative and controversial: they had the effect of 'writing off' certain neighbourhoods, and arguably also restricted areas of immigrant settlement.[51]

Housing improvement – keeping the options open

Although the problem of multi-occupation dominated discussion and policy, four fifths of the houses in the middle ring were still in single-family occupation at the end of the 1960s. While there was no formal public strategy, improvement was based on an informal 'lifing' of property.[52] This divided the middle ring into two broad zones. Some 11,500 houses in the worst condition and adjacent to existing redevelopment areas were included in *pink areas* with a life of less than fifteen years. They were envisaged as the third phase of redevelopment from the mid-1970s onwards. In general, improvement grants were not given in these areas and the official prognosis of decline acquired the certainty of a self-fulfilling prophecy. Many of the multi-occupied properties were in these areas.

The remaining 56,000 properties were included in *green areas* with a life of over fifteen years, where standard grants were approved on request. But there was a marked reluctance to award discretionary grants in many areas, because improvement was seen as a short-term holding operation. Between 1954 and 1969 some 21,000 private improvement grants were approved, mainly in the 'green areas', of which some 90 per cent were standard grants. Birmingham was one of the few authorities to implement the 1964 area improvement powers. Twenty-nine Improvement Areas were declared, mainly in the outer suburbs of engulfed villages, where there was a high proportion of owner-occupiers and the houses were in good basic condition – only 1770 out of a total of 4800 lacked any basic amenities.[53] In the late 1960s Birmingham's demonstrated willingness to use compulsory powers to secure the repair and improvement of privately rented accommodation was an important factor in the proportion of grants approved for private landlords exceeding that for owner-occupiers – counter to the national trend.

Policy in transition

The initial response to the 1969 Act was the addition of a GIA component to existing policies. In the redevelopment areas problems of implementation became increasingly controversial. Organized opposition to the extension of clearance began to emerge in some of the areas earmarked for the third phase of redevelopment, as a slump in council housebuilding exacerbated difficulties in existing redevelopment areas.

Early GIAs – buffer policy and no man's land

Nine GIAs were declared in 1970–1, containing 5600 dwellings. But there was no comprehensive review of older housing and no overall assessment of the balance between redevelopment and improvement.[54] GIA selection was the responsibility of an interdepartmental working party accountable to the Health Committee. The first two GIAs were declared in Summerfield, as part of a scheme comprising redevelopment and improvement in discrete areas. At this point improvement was seen as complementary to clearance in marginal areas.[55]

This perspective changed when the Health Committee laid down guidelines for GIA selection:

> The Working Party was instructed primarily to concentrate on areas which . . . after improvement . . . would be likely to stand for at least thirty years and so form parts of the city's stock of permanent houses. As a principle it was laid down that old, worn-out and overcrowded houses which ought to be pulled down should not be included in General Improvement Areas. The Working Party was asked to devote their main effort to consideration of areas containing the better type of house built between the turn of the century and the First World War. One of the important matters for consideration in choosing General Improvement Areas was the desirability that they should act as a buffer between the present stock of good suburban houses and those properties which had deteriorated too far to the point where slum clearance and total redevelopment would be necessary.[56]

A further seven GIAs were declared on the outer periphery of the middle ring, in which only a third of the dwellings lacked basic amenities and less than 2 per cent were multi-occupied. No GIAs were declared on council housing estates.

Thus intervention leapfrogged from the outer edges of the redevelopment areas over the worst of the twilight areas which were left in a policy 'no man's land'.[57] There was no formal decision about the long-term future of either the large areas of small terraced houses in poor condition on the fringes on the redevelopment areas, typified by Summerfield, or the housing stress areas affected by multi-occupation such as Handsworth and Sparkbrook.[58] By implication their prospect was one of continuing neglect and eventual redevelopment. In essence the buffer policy was a modification of the informal 'lifing' policy of the 1960s. In much of 'no man's land' grant applications were still refused and no special grants were made for HMOs.

The buffer policy was, in part, an interpretation of advice given in Circular 65/69, but two local factors were of particular importance. First, redevelopment had only just passed its post-war peak when national policy changed in

1969 and it was still the dominant concern. Phase II was not scheduled for completion until 1975 and a formal decision on the scale of further redevelopment was considered premature. Second, the Health Committee was the dominant influence in the development of improvement policy. The city's PHIs maintained their pessimistic view of housing improvement in the twilight areas, an attitude reinforced by the Government's renewed emphasis on voluntary grant take-up.[59]

Total private sector grant approvals increased only gradually but by early 1972 had reached 2000 p.a. (Figure 16) with a marked increase in the proportion of discretionary grants. While Birmingham was immediately off the mark with GIAs they had minimal impact. By mid-1972 no environmental works had been implemented outside Summerfield. Although the council accepted the principle of public participation, the practice was rudimentary. Draft proposals were drawn up by the Architect's Department prior to declaration. After declaration residents were invited to a public meeting to discuss the scheme. The meetings were well attended and usually resulted in the formation of a residents' association. But schemes were dominated by often unpopular proposals for rear access roads and garage provision and the council failed to establish an ongoing dialogue with residents' groups. Residents pressing for action met with little response and rapidly became disillusioned.[60] At the time limited progress was attributed to staff shortages and the absence of a special GIA agency.

Improvement versus the slow death of the slums

In the early 1970s the problems of the redevelopment process became acute, particularly in the Phase II areas.[61] Here residents had by now endured fifteen years of planning blight and appalling living conditions.[62] Private investment had virtually ceased. Very few landlords had undertaken repair and maintenance work. Owner-occupiers were in a minority: while some had attempted to maintain their property, others sold to the council and either bought elsewhere or accepted a council tenancy.

In sharp contrast to Phase I, the acquisition of Phase II properties was undertaken on a piecemeal basis by the Estates Department. Some were purchased by negotiation well in advance of clearance, others represented as unfit by the Public Health Department and acquired through a series of small Housing Act CPOs. Finally, acquisition was completed by a Planning Act CPO covering the remaining houses and non-residential uses.[63] During this gradual process many acquired properties were reconditioned and relet by the Housing Department. But in accordance with long-established management practice this 'Part III accommodation' was allocated to families who were judged unsuitable for anything better, by virtue of their rent paying capacity or their housekeeping standards: this group of tenants were labelled 'problem families'.[64]

The city's official policy was that, as far as possible, residents would be rehoused locally if they wished. But tenancies in a particular area were allocated on a city-wide basis, and even when rebuilding was taking place locally, local residents were not given special preference.[65] For many the result was dispersal despite preferences: for some this meant Part III accommodation in another redevelopment area at a less advanced stage: for others the result was a long-distance move to an inter-war or peripheral estate.

The Housing Department was also responsible for demolition. Since acquisition was piecemeal and rehousing protracted, demolition was initially patchy. Rebuilding was the joint responsibility of the Housing, Public Works' (Planning), and Architect's Departments. But, because of the importance attached to the restructuring of areas and economies of scale, rebuilding awaited the availability of large sites. By the early 1970s it had only just started in many Phase II areas.

At this time residents in many of these areas were suffering 'the slow death of a slum', the product of inadequate resources and ineffective co-ordination. There were delays at all stages in the process. Living conditions were appalling: many houses were damp, in bad repair (some literally crumbling), dangerous and insanitary – the result of neglect by private landlords and, in the later stages, the council; in the final stages houses were often boarded up and left empty; cleared sites were dumping grounds for rubble, breeding grounds for vermin and training grounds for vandals. These problems were exacerbated by poor communication: many residents had had no formal contact with the council. There was confusion about acquisition, contradictory or vague information about the timing of demolition, and uncertainty about rehousing.

Local reaction to these situations was mixed. In the fifteen years since designation these areas had changed from being relatively stable and uniform communities, to neighbourhoods characterized by diversity. Of the remaining long-standing residents, many were embittered by the decline of their area, (which they variously attributed to the council, the 'coloureds', or the 'problem families') and wanted to leave as quickly as possible. Others wanted to remain in the area after redevelopment, and in the meantime press the council to minimize the impact of the process. Of the newcomers, many owner-occupiers (particularly Asians) intended to purchase similar property elsewhere if possible, while council tenants all wanted a better standard of housing, some preferring to remain in the area, others not.

In some redevelopment areas residents formed community organizations in an attempt to influence the processes which dominated their lives. However, at this late stage effective collective action was virtually impossible. While local pressure often resolved individual problems, it could not change policies and procedures. The situation in the St. James Redevelopment Area was particularly acute and attracted both local and national publicity.[66] In several areas there was pressure for local rehousing, but this coincided with renewed housing pressure and the council was unwilling to alter its allocation policies.

In 'no man's land', particularly in neighbourhoods adjacent to the Phase II redevelopment areas, there was limited but growing opposition to the possible extension of comprehensive redevelopment. This was in part a reaction to the process and product (particularly multi-storey flats) of redevelopment.[67] However, there was not only little prospect of reforming the process, but also opposition to the principle of redevelopment. The majority of houses were in better condition than those in the redevelopment areas, appeared worth 'saving', and owner-occupation had now reached significant levels: redevelopment would mean dispossessing thousands of owner-occupiers. Neighbourhood organizations included several advice centres supporting a few formally organized community groups. Prompted by the declaration of GIAs in the 'buffer zone', and sometimes supported by local councillors, they were campaigning for the council to extend its GIA programme: for example, the Sparkbrook Association was pressing for improvement on the basis of the Sparkbrook Community Plan.[68] Several neighbourhood agencies began co-operating with housing associations, which had been steadily increasing their involvement in the conversion and improvement of middle ring housing since the late 1960s and were themselves lobbying the council to adopt improvement policies there.[69] The only part of 'no man's land' for which formal proposals were being formulated was 'Sparkbrook West Two', where the Residents' Council successfully campaigned for the inclusion of proposed GIAs in the Action Area plan.[70]

A housing crisis

In early 1972 optimism about the end of the slums evaporated as the housing programme ran into serious difficulties (see Figure 16). Council housebuilding collapsed and completions in 1972 were the lowest since 1949. Chelmsley Wood was completed and the city again faced an acute shortage of large building sites. More importantly, the council was unable to secure tenders for housebuilding within government yardstick limits: these remained fixed despite soaring building costs, and more profitable office development work was available in the city centre. Concurrently the house price explosion increased the rate of applications for council housing and reduced the outflow of council tenants into owner-occupation: this, together with council house sales, meant that relets declined and the waiting list increased for the first time in a decade.

The rate of clearance did not fall as rapidly as housebuilding (because of the time-lag between the representation and demolition of unfit houses) and by 1971 the council was demolishing more houses than it was building, with a resultant increase in vacant sites and adverse publicity. The only hopeful sign was the steady increase in private improvement grant approvals. There was growing concern about the costs of redevelopment and that the city's emasculated rehousing capacity would further delay completion of existing redevelopment areas and prejudice any future extension of the programme.[71]

Gradual renewal

In 1972 the Labour Party regained control of the council and within seven months the city's renewal strategy had been recast. The middle ring became the focus of intervention as an improvement dominated Urban Renewal Policy was launched. Although modified since, the decisions taken in 1972 remain the basis of contemporary policy – the city's version of gradual renewal. As the policy was refined there were significant management innovations. But progress on the ground was limited. Clearance and redevelopment continued to decline, an upsurge in housing improvement was short-lived and little environmental work was implemented. By 1976 the policy was clearly failing to meet its objectives.

The Urban Renewal Programme, 1972

Immediately after the elections the council established a Standing Conference on Urban Renewal. This non-executive body of councillors and officers was given a brief to develop an urban renewal strategy, co-ordination of implementation and public participation. Circular 50/72 had requested the submission, by October, of an overall renewal strategy and information about constraints on implementation. This provided the Conference with the opportunity and impetus for a policy initiative.

Urban renewal had not been a major issue in the elections, but the Labour Party had made clear its intention to reform and restrict redevelopment and expand the improvement programme.[72] Shuttleworth, the chairman of the Standing Conference, had first-hand knowledge of the problems of redevelopment and was critical of the Conservatives' 'buffer policy'. Although Circular 50/72 had requested a systematic assessment of the needs and wishes of residents, the Conference had neither the time nor the resources to do this. However, the bitterness and disillusionment in redevelopment areas was well known and some neighbourhood organizations in 'no man's land' made formal submissions to the Conference. These inchoate views were taken to mean that middle ring residents were opposed to further comprehensive redevelopment and in favour of improvement.

In October the Conference produced the city's response to Circular 50/72, an outline strategy to meet the Government's objective of eliminating all substandard houses by 1980. These proposals were approved as the Birmingham Urban Renewal Policy by the city council in January 1973.[73] The intention was to accelerate *both* slum clearance *and* improvement in a phased programme with three components.

1 *Redevelopment areas.* Phase II was to be completed by 1977. In the mean-

time problems of implementation were to be alleviated by better environmental maintenance (clearance of rubbish, provision of skips, grassing of vacant sites), an increase in the number of local Family Advice Centres to improve communication, and more local rehousing.

2 *General Improvement Areas.* Sixty-eight GIAs were to be declared by 1978, embracing some 60,000 structurally sound houses, to be implemented through voluntary improvement to high standards by private owners.

3 *Renewal areas.* Twenty-six renewal areas, comprising 15,000 dwellings located between the redevelopment areas and the proposed GIAs, were scheduled for a combination of improvement and redevelopment (along the lines of the Summerfield and Sparkbrook West II schemes). It was estimated that 60 per cent of these houses were unfit or would be by 1980, and would be acquired for demolition. Blocks of houses would be retained where owners were willing to improve to high standards – some might eventually be declared GIAs. Immediate work would include the identification of retention properties and temporary environmental improvements. After 1976, when redevelopment area clearance was completed, partial clearance and, where possible, local rehousing on infill redevelopment sites would take place, together with extensive environmental improvement and the provision of community facilities.

An explanatory booklet was distributed to community groups and the policy was launched at a public meeting in the council chamber in January 1973. There was a generally favourable reaction to the apparent resolution of the future of the middle ring, the emphasis on improvement 'to avoid breaking up local communities'[74] and the commitment to participation. Some doubts were expressed about staff resources and the likelihood that the voluntary emphasis would do little to help private tenants.[75] However, the constraints on implementation identified by the Conference and conveyed to the Minister were not widely understood: the acceleration of clearance depended on both significantly increased cost yardstick limits to restore the building programme, and more rapid processing of CPOs. Moreover, there was little understanding of the inner city housing market: owners' lack of confidence was seen as the main constraint on private improvement and it was assumed that 'blanket' GIA proposals would remove uncertainty and restore the flow of investment. The huge GIA programme was seen as:

> . . . reasonable and feasible appreciating that the city council is responsible only for the implementation of the environmental works – the physical improvement of the dwellings occurs if and when the owners decide that the time is appropriate – subject to a policy review should the rate of improvement be considered unsatisfactory.[76]

and it was estimated that annual costs to the rates would rise to about £½m by 1979, approximately the product of a penny rate in 1972–3. No costings were prepared for the redevelopment and renewal areas programmes. An urban renewal officer was appointed to service the Conference and chair a team of officers from relevant departments which were also requested to provide additional staff. No other management changes were introduced: the Public Works and Housing Departments were responsible for redevelopment and renewal areas and the Health Department remained responsible for GIAs.

The technical basis of the policy was a limited exercise to crudely differentiate older housing areas by physical condition. In essence it was a modification of policies which had originated in the 1960s: the previously informally blighted 'pink areas' became the renewal areas rather than the third phase of comprehensive redevelopment, while the 'green areas' became proposed GIAs. The policy was launched more as an act of faith than a carefully programmed intervention in the twilight areas. Its scale and timing derived from the objectives set by Circular 50/72 and successful implementation was largely dependent on national policy. Additionally, the Conference was looking to the newly established Saltley Community Development Project and Small Heath Inner Area Study to further the development of its outline strategy.

Policy development 1973–6

Although changing national policy was the main influence, by 1974 local circumstances had already shifted the programme's centre of gravity to the renewal areas, initially earmarked for a 'holding operation' until 1976. At the first public meeting the council had agreed that the definition of clearance properties in renewal areas should have priority and this was first done on the basis of external inspections by PHIs. However, the council made it clear that where a majority of owners in the blocks proposed for clearance were willing to carry out full improvements, the classification would be changed to retention. The massive press publicity given to the council's proposals, together with the subsequent individual notification of classification sent to the occupants of the 15,000 houses, precipitated a flood of requests for a full survey from owners of demolition property seeking reclassification.[77]

The council then embarked on a programme of detailed inspections on a block by block basis. A crash programme of public meetings was mounted to further explain and gain support for the policy. Owners were provided with schedules of work required to bring their houses up to the full standard and asked if they were prepared to go ahead. Where there was a majority positive response, blocks of houses were classified for retention and the council adopted a policy of acquisition (by agreement or compulsory purchase) of outstanding properties. Where only a minority of owners were willing to improve blocks were classified for clearance. This time-consuming process of negotiation, prolonged by staff shortages, was still in progress when the Housing Act, 1974 came into operation.

At this point the Urban Renewal Policy was reviewed as part of the corporate management procedures established after local government reorganization. A Performance Review Committee report revealed conflicting officer views on achievement to date, but concluded that the programme 'was not adequately defined', made a 'major plea for a tightening up of the whole programme formulation process, with a detailed, tangible programme appearing at the other end', and identified the urgent decisions necessary to achieve this.[78] The report drew attention to the high input of *resources* of manpower and finance necessary to convert the existing commitment to a firm programme. It highlighted the urgent need for planning briefs, essential for the co-ordination of inputs such as schools, open space and traffic management schemes in detailed phased, environmental work programmes. The Standing Conference had been disbanded on reorganization. Its responsibilities were transferred to a new Urban Renewal Sub-Committee of the Environmental Services (formerly Health) Committee, whose role in the *management* of urban renewal was extended to include more influence over clearance, to achieve more effective integration of the three components of the programme. At officer level the management structure was extended and consolidated.[79]

The report identified three key issues which required decisions. First, the *area improvement programme* had to be modified to take account of changes in national policy. But the die had been cast in 1972. With minor exceptions the renewal areas were designated proposed HAAs, together with a few areas originally intended as GIAs. In 1975 the council approved the declaration of four HAAs, as part of a programme of eighteen embracing some 12,400 houses. The policy of improving retention properties to the full standard was reaffirmed, the corollary of which was the decision that most HAAs would be declared GIAs after three to seven years.

A priority list of HAAs was defined partly in accordance with DoE guidance (using census indicators, supplemented by a house condition index) but also took account of experience in the renewal areas, including a joint project with the IAS on a pilot HAA in Little Green and similar detailed work by the Saltley CDP. Although this selection process identified housing stress areas, the 'objectivity' of a statistical ranking was tempered by the legacy of past decisions and resultant commitments.[80] Two types of HAA were selected: 'high demand areas' such as Sparkbrook East (HAA No. 1), declared a decade after Rex and Moore's study, and characterized by 'villa' housing with multiple occupation, furnished tenancies, large families and immigrants: 'low-demand areas', such as Little Green (HAA No. 2) and Havelock, Saltley (HAA No. 3), characterized by small terraced houses lacking basic amenities, mainly in single-family occupation, with a high proportion of unfurnished tenancies and/or low-income owner-occupiers.

Two years' work in the renewal areas had generated political and administrative commitment, produced a slight amelioration of environmental conditions, but yielded only a trickle of grant-aided house improvement.

However, residents' expectations had been raised and their organizations were pressing for early HAA declarations, on the reasonable grounds that conditions in all proposed HAAs warranted the immediate availability of 75 per cent grants. In these circumstances Birmingham opted for a rapid programme of declarations.

The review had recommended a detailed assessment of resource implications and priorities for council departments and outside agencies, particularly the new West Midlands Metropolitan County Council and the new Severn–Trent Regional Water Authority. Given the scale of environmental deprivation in many areas and a commitment to full standard housing improvement, the council took the view that substantial environmental works were essential, to the level of £600 per house – £900 when the whole cost of buying out non-conforming uses was included. By scaling up from a single-area assessment, the resource implications for a revised ten-year programme were estimated at £300m. This was a far cry from the 1972 discussion of resources and embodied a rejection of '. . . the concept of trees, shrubs and no-entry signs' and the Government's 'irrelevant and misleading' figure of £200 per house.[81] In the light of this more detailed work a revised programme was established in 1976 including twenty-one HAAs and high priority given to some fifty GIAs out of a total of ninety-two.

The second key issue was *compulsory action and social ownership*, now more important as the limits of voluntary improvement became clear and the 1974 Act emphasized a more interventionist approach. There had been little progress in acquisition of properties in blocks identified for improvement (with the exception of some voids[82]): identifying them had been a time-consuming process, extended by a reassessment of owners' intentions in the light of grant increases, and a lack of clear commitment.[83] In 1975, the policy was redefined. Various compulsory repair and improvement powers were to be used as a means of inducing owners to improve; where this proved ineffective, the properties would be compulsorily purchased for improvement – unless owners offered them to the council or a housing association. This strategy was devised principally for HAAs, but was to be applied selectively in some GIAs.[84]

Houses in multiple occupation posed special problems. It was not until 1976 that a prolonged review was completed, and the new policy emphasized control rather than elimination of HMOs. It was considered that for the forseeable future single-person and transient households could only be catered for in privately owned HMOs and that planning approval should be granted for suitable premises. For existing HMOs, owners are offered a range of options involving the use of various renovation grants, and where this fails compulsory improvement or acquisition powers are used.[85]

The third key issue was the completion of the *redevelopment areas*. Rather than accelerating, the programme had slowed considerably: 6000 houses awaited demolition and there were large tracts of undeveloped land. There had been considerable delays in the confirmation of CPOs and, despite strenuous efforts, the council's housebuilding programme had recovered only slowly. The council had taken several initiatives to check the growth of the waiting list: estates were purchased 'off the peg' from private builders; the provision of 100 per cent mortgages to council tenants, waiting list families and first-time buyers was massively increased; and equity sharing schemes were pioneered with the Housing Corporation. By 1975 the housing situation was improving, but there was little prospect of completing the redevelopment areas by 1977. In this context and in view of government policy, the council decided to apply the same retention criteria in redevelopment areas as had been applied in the renewal areas. The result was that 1250 properties were scheduled for retention twenty years after their designation for clearance. Residents were given the option of remaining in improved property or being rehoused elsewhere.

Implementation

By 1976 the council had declared eleven HAAs comprising 8400 dwellings and twenty-four GIAs containing 17,200 dwellings but the rate of private improvement grant approvals had slumped (Table 6 and Figure 16) and they were by no means concentrated in declared areas. In HAAs only seventy-five grant-aided improvements had been completed, with a further 187 in progress – a limited return for three years effort since their designation as renewal areas. In GIAs 10 per cent of dwellings had grant-aided work completed or in progress, but only 500 improvements were in post-1972 GIAs. Public sector improvement had also been very limited and environmental work had been started in only six of the (mainly pre-1972) GIAs.

Why was progress on the ground so limited? This question can be answered by examining the complexities of the 'investment partnership' and its vulnerability at a time of economic recession.[86] There were significant developments in the day-to-day management of implementation, particularly its partial decentralization. The area affected by the policy was divided into eight sectors, each served by a multi-disciplinary team operating from a local office. Teams typically comprise a team leader and clerical support staff, seconded environmental health officers, architects and technical assistants, and are serviced by peripatetic housing, planning, social work and engineering staff. They are responsible for a rolling programme of declarations, the preparation of environmental schemes, the administration of grants (jointly with divisional environmental health staff), and liaise with the Housing Department and housing associations. They are backed up by the Urban Renewal Educational and Publicity Unit producing information in readable 'Know the Facts' sheets, together with leaflets explaining environmental schemes and local newsletters. These developments were not without problems. For example: with an average 9000 dwellings in up to fifteen

Table 6 *Birmingham: special area declarations*

Year	*Improvement Areas*		*General Improvement Areas*		*Housing Action Areas*	
	number	*houses*	*number*	*houses*	*number*	*houses*
1965	7	1200				
1966	11	1341				
1967	5	1050				
1968	4	794				
1969	2	401				
1970			6	3940		
1971			2	1574		
1972			—	—		
1973			6	5216		
1974			—	—	5	2643
1975			5	5173	12	6929
1976			15	3234	9	3821
1977			7	2180	1	449
1978			—	—	—	—
1979			—	—	—	—
Totals	29	4786	41	22317	27	13842

Notes: All figures are Birmingham CB before 1974; Birmingham MD after 1974.

Sources: Annual Report of the Medical Officer of Health, and City of Birmingham Environmental Health Department.

declared or proposed HAAs and GIAs in each 'patch' the teams are somewhat thin on the ground; their executive powers are limited – implementation of major works remains the responsibility of various council departments and outside agencies; relationships with residents are closer but not always harmonious.[87]

Although these innovations were positive, they coincided with a downward trend in *private sector improvement.* Implementation was substantially dependent on voluntary improvement, particularly by owner-occupiers, but the extent to which a policy commitment to improvement would restore confidence was overestimated. By 1976 a developing understanding of market conditions established the significance of a series of interlocking constraints.

Low incomes, static grants and rising costs. Apart from the fact that many owners were satisfied with their houses,[88] most were unable to afford the costs of achieving the high standards required by the council. As the average cost of improvement rose from £2500 in 1973 to £6000 in 1976 many were further deterred by the lack of a corresponding rise in the eligible expense limit – in 1976 an owner's share of a £6000 improvement in an HAA was £800 (25 per cent of £3200) plus £2800 (the non-grant-aided balance).

Mortgage finance. Local research established the extent of building societies' reluctance to invest in the middle ring for the general reasons discussed in Chapter 3. The Urban Renewal Policy was seen as creating rather than reducing uncertainty. Of particular concern were the adverse effects on resale prospects of the 'valuation gap' (in many areas, particularly HAAs, the market value of an improved house was less than unimproved value plus the onwer's costs of improvement) and the five-year occupancy condition.[89] Conventional mortgages were a minority form of finance for house purchase in older areas (Table 7).[90] A massive increase in council mortgages in 1974–5 meant increased lending on new properties while the numbers of loans for pre-1919 properties remained constant. In 1975 the council decided to give priority to mortgages for older housing, but its aim of 'a near monopoly of housing finance in areas of older housing'[91] was immediately rendered unattainable by a halving of its mortgage allocation for 1975–6 (resulting in a nine-month suspension of lending) and a reduction to £6.5m in 1976–7. Hopes of increased building society lending were quickly dashed when under the 'support scheme' less than a quarter of the council's 220 nominations for loans on pre-1919 properties had been accepted by the end of 1976.

Leasehold. An idiosyncratic but important feature of the local housing market is the fact that in many inner areas a high proportion of owner-

Table 7 *Birmingham: sources of mortgages in older areas 1972 to 1974*

	Saltley per cent	*Sparkhill* per cent	*Soho* per cent
Bought outright/informal loan	21.8	14.9	23.0
Formal loan from			
Building society/insurance company	7.5	37.3	9.7
Local authority	7.6	11.7	20.4
Total conventional mortgages	15.1	19.0	30.1
Clearing banks	49.5	24.5	34.5
Fringe bank or finance company	11.4	8.5	8.9
Others	2.5	3.3	3.6

Notes: Nationally, 85 per cent of all funds for house purchase in 1972–4 were provided by building societies and insurance companies, and 9 per cent by local authorities, a total of 94 per cent from conventional sources.

Source: Adapted from V. Karn, *Priorities For Local Authority Mortgage Lending: A Case Study of Birmingham*, Research Memorandum No. 52, Centre for Urban and Regional Studies University of Birmingham (1976), p. 18.

occupiers are leaseholders. While they have a legal right to purchase the freehold, this is time-consuming and expensive (£500 plus). Without the security of freehold, owners and building societies are reluctant to invest, and many owners are ineligible for grants and loans.[92]

£175 rateable value limit. This excluded 10 per cent of houses in HAAs and 15 per cent in GIAs, and in Sparkbrook East HAA 25 per cent were excluded. Ample evidence of the bluntness of this instrument of redirecting resources was submitted to, but for two years ignored by, central government.

Owner-occupiers not excluded by these constraints were often deterred by the fact that many others in their neighbourhood were, and this 'externality effect' was exacerbated by minimal improvement by private landlords. In 1975 only 19 per cent of grant approvals were for rented property, as most landlords preferred to sell when they could obtain vacant possession.[93] Although *public sector acquisition and improvement* was recognized from the outset as a vital component of the strategy, implementation was slow. No CPOs for improvement had been submitted by 1976. Government restrictions on acquisitions and improvement presented further difficulties. While the rate of improvements to properties acquired by agreement had more than doubled since 1974 to over 700 p.a. this was at the expense of inter-war modernizations. Housing associations substantially increased their programmes. Their work was gradually concentrated in HAAs and a system of 'lead' associations was introduced. But in many areas there were adverse reactions to delays between acquisition and improvement.[94]

The considerable efforts made to stimulate grant applications were impeded by the fact that prompt implementation of *environmental improvement*, regarded as critical for stimulating confidence, proved unattainable.[95] Local government reorganization resulted in a two-year moratorium on GIA declarations and the new county council embarked on a review of the road hierarchy and associated road widening lines, making it impossible to finalize traffic management proposals which were often critical for schemes in existing GIAs. Moreover, the location of many off-street works, e.g. play areas, parking and garaging, depended on the resolution of on-street proposals. The new Regional Water Authority took a long time to formulate its programme for the relining or relaying of water mains, on which the replacement of unsatisfactory branch supplies to private houses depended; in addition, surface work to roads and footpaths is impractical before this work is completed.

As a dialogue with the county was established, declarations were resumed and the council developed a more sophisticated system for the preparation and execution of environmental works. Following the recommendations of the Performance Review Committee the council started to prepare informal local plans for all HAAs and for GIAs where appropriate. In some cases, they encompass a combination of HAAs, GIAs and redevelopment areas. Significant work is undertaken before declaration to reduce the delays between public participation and implementation. After declaration and initial public meetings a residents' planning committee is formed to prepare proposals with the local project team.

Area plans are broad in scope and the GIA type scheme is but one element. In addition to proposals for housing clearance, retention and new build, these plans establish a framework for the preparation of detailed environmental schemes. The work is divided into three phases: Phase I comprises off-street works including walls, fences, gates, improved rear access (footpaths) and minor landscaping; Phase II works are mainly on-street, including traffic management and related landscaping, together with resurfacing work, but also include facilities such as play areas; Phase III consists of costly works outside the scope of GIA subsidy (e.g. parks, shopping facilities, the removal of intrusive industries) to be implemented in the longer term.

Despite these innovations there was little progress beyond the drawing board. Generally, the city's system of capital programming was inadequately tied to the pace of declarations and sudden government cuts wrought havoc with existing frail arrangements;[96] similarly, constraints on revenue spending impeded adequate staffing. More specifically, the preparation of schemes followed a lengthy sequence of activities. For area plans the complexity of committee referrals was a key factor accounting for thirty of the one hundred weeks involved, and in GIAs extensive public participation accounted for thirty-one of the fifty-three weeks between declaration and the earliest start date for off-street works. In HAAs early implementation was confined to Phase I works on private land (the city 'topped up' the £50 curtilage grant) as Phase II had to wait several years for redesignation as GIAs. Thus, as with housing improvement, environmental work was not going where it was most needed. Attempts to persuade the DoE to allow earlier implementation of GIA type work were fruitless.

Moreover, opportunities for slippage were legion. Traffic management schemes remained particularly vulnerable, as proposals to prevent commuter traffic entering residential areas frequently involved increased pressure on already overloaded nearby major road junctions. In the county's view such junctions should be improved first, but it was unable to allocate the funds: in 1976 there was deadlock in Small Heath where problems with one major road junction were holding up schemes in several GIAs declared in 1973. The time-lag between declaration and the start of capital works emphasized the importance of increasing current expenditure on maintenance and environmental services. The city responded, for example, by providing supplementary rubbish skips, and the Inner Area Study mounted an experimental 'area caretaker' scheme,[97] but such measures were of only limited value given, say, the continued presence of intrusive industry.

The council's commitment to *public participation*, reinforced by the neighbourhood based activities of CDP, the Inner Area Study and various voluntary organizations, resulted in the programme becoming the main focus of an unprecedented development of community action. In four years from 1972 the number of residents' groups increased from less than a dozen to over forty. Their characteristics varied considerably: they were unevenly distributed; many tended to be dominated by white owner-occupiers, reflecting the problems of building representative organizations in multi-racial areas characterized by diverse tenure groups; most were informally organized around a small core group, though a minority were based on formal street representation; there were differences in continuity, cohesion and range of activities – some groups were ephemeral, while others flourished and developed their activities beyond urban renewal issues. Although there were inevitable conflicts, area plans generally reflected residents' views. The project teams' commitment to maximizing residents' involvement posed problems. As the Inner Area Study observed:

> the more they worked with residents and developed a better understanding of their problems and perspective, the greater their tendency to become advocates on residents' behalf. At times this gave rise to considerable differences of opinion between local officers and more senior, centrally based officers, some of whom were anxious to ensure that their teams' involvement with residents did not extend to an actual or apparent association with open criticism of the council, and doubtless many councillors shared their concern.[98]

A parallel development to this neighbourhood involvement was the emergence of Community Forum, a federation of residents' organizations active in areas affected by the renewal programme. Soon after the launching of the programme the chairman of the Standing Conference suggested the formation of a liaison group, comprising officers and councillors from the Conference and half a dozen representatives of residents' organizations, to act as an additional channel of communication and provide the opportunity for airing 'across the board' issues. A liaison group was established accountable to a wider body – Community Forum.

Three phases in Forum's approach to participation have been identified.[99] A 'dialogue approach' when the emphasis was on co-operating with the council, e.g. to improve publicity through the joint preparation of leaflets. A 'more militant approach' adopted as the programme's slow progress and problems centring on officers' claims that they could not present written reports to non-elected bodies such as the liaison group led to increasing frustration and the suspension of meetings. Finally, a 'wider political approach' as sustained pressure resulted in the liaison group being replaced by regular informal meetings of the full Urban Renewal Sub-Committee and Forum's executive committee, and growing awareness of the effects of expenditure cuts prompted discussions with UCATT and the Birmingham Trades Council which eventually led to the short-lived Birmingham Campaign Against the Cuts.

Direct access to the Sub-Committee improved communications and enabled Forum to put forward its views on key policy issues. For example, Forum pressed for rapid declarations of HAAs to reduce the divisive effects of area-based policies and presented detailed evidence on the effects of the £175 r.v. restriction. However, involvement in policy was always more problematic than in local plans, and after more than two years effort it was considered that 'Community Forum cannot claim to have achieved anything more than a minimal influence on decision making and management procedures'.[100]

Inner City Partnership Programme

In 1976 the Conservatives regained control of the council and began to reorientate the housing programme. Efforts to secure environmental improvements started to yield results but housing improvement remained in the doldrums. A further reappraisal of the Urban Renewal Programme produced major initiatives to accelerate progress in HAAs. These emerged during the preparation of the first ICPP, and are being implemented as part of this more broadly based policy.

The enveloping and block schemes

The housing programme was reorientated to place greater emphasis on the role of the private sector. In the late 1970s council housebuilding fell from over 4000 p.a. to under 1000 p.a. and, together with housing association new build, was increasingly concentrated on infill sites in inner areas. The clearance rate declined to 300 p.a. Council housing sites were sold to developers in pairs – an inner city site coupled with one in the suburbs. Subsidizing inner city land costs resulted in the reintroduction of private new build in several inner area neighbourhoods.

Corporate planning fell from favour. The chief executive was made redundant and the embryonic corporate planning machinery was dismantled. Resultant changes in the management of the Urban Renewal Programme placed it more firmly in the ambit of the Environmental Health Department. The project teams were consolidated and declarations continued, but at a rapidly reducing rate. There are currently twenty-seven HAAs (14,000 dwellings) with a further eleven proposed (2000 dwellings), and forty-one GIAs (22,000 dwellings) with sixty-eight proposed (43,000 dwellings). The painstakingly created machinery for environmental improvement began to produce results, and expenditure increased from £0.2m in 1976–7 to £10m in 1979–80. By early 1981 Phase I works (now £1200 per house) will be completed in eighteen HAAs and thirty GIAs, Phase II works (£1000 per house) will have been implemented in one HAA and five GIAs, but no Phase III schemes (£600 per house) will have been carried out.[101]

The continuing problems of housing improvement stimulated significant innovations. The visible expression of constraints on private grant take-up and limited public sector activity was a 'pepper-pot' pattern of improved houses. By early 1978 only 600 grant-aided improvements had been completed in the HAAs. The prospect of failure to complete the first HAAs declared in 1975 within the five-year period, together with the Government's inner city initiative, prompted a review of the following options for HAAs:[102]

1 Large-scale and accelerated public sector acquisition and improvement? The intention had been to 'underwrite' private investment by a combination of municipalization and housing association activity to 'finish' an area, but with the low rate of private improvement the prospective scale of public ownership was enormous – about two thirds of the properties. This option was discounted for several reasons: it contradicted the promotion of owner-occupation; there were insufficient resources for both municipalization of pre-1919 houses and the urgently needed improvement of inter-war estates, and the experience of municipalization as part of comprehensive redevelopment had left officers with little enthusiasm for another large programme.
2 Reduce standards of improvement? This was rejected on the grounds that it would be tantamount to 'deferred demolition', as neither owners nor building societies would invest in the uncertain future of areas improved to lower standards.
3 Extend the time-scale? This would be counter-productive as it would undermine the confidence of owners and building societies.
4 Increase clearance? While it was acknowledged that the pendulum had swung too far to improvement, the peppering of fully improved houses and commitments given in extensive participation exercises constrained a reversal to substantial clearance.

The review concluded that further incentives for private improvement were needed. The council decided to spend £1.5m of its allocation from the Inner City Construction Package (money made available by government to launch) the inner cities policy) on 'Operation Facelift' in two HAAs. External works – including new roofs and chimneys, and the replacement of gutters, windows and doors on front elevations – were carried out free of charge to 600 houses at a cost of some £2500 per house, on the basis of large block contracts which were completed within a year. Encouraged by this rapid progress the council decided to allocate Urban Programme funds in the first ICPP to an extended scheme. Known as *enveloping*, this package entails complete external renovation free of charge to owners, with a 75 per cent central government subsidy.[103]

The case for enveloping is that it enables resources to be effectively concentrated in an area through a planned and controlled investment programme, rapidly implemented on a street by street basis. A signed indemnity form from each owner is all that is required for the scheme to be started – administratively far simpler than processing improvement grants. A single contract between the council and a large reputable builder minimizes the cost of supervision, while maximizing quality control and scale economies. Private owners are subsequently more likely to be able to afford to undertake the complementary internal works with grant aid, and building societies will be more inclined to invest as the structure of whole areas is secured. Finally, total public expenditure per house for full improvement is about two thirds that of municipalization.

However, the DoE did not approve this part of the ICPP submission for a 1979–80 start. This opposition stemmed from concern that the scheme undermined the principles of the grant system because there was no guaranteed owner's contribution, and such a substantial alteration in the terms of the 'investment partnership' of housing improvement would result in heavy public expenditure. Nonetheless, although the council does not compel private owners to undertake internal works, a majority have done so in the first two HAAs which are now completed. The Conservative Government has subsequently approved the scheme as an experiment. In the three years from 1980–1 2000 houses in HAAs will be enveloped at a unit cost of £3600 – the largest single project within the ICPP.

The concept of enveloping was extended with the development of *block schemes* which offer owners a comprehensive package of internal and external improvements and rest on a liberal interpretation of existing legislation. The internal works are funded from improvement grants fixed at the maximum eligible expense level. Most owners are considered hardship cases and their contribution is generally limited to 10 per cent. The external works include both enveloping and Phase I environmental works, funded from the limited government expenditure and HIP allocations for environmental works. These various funds are paid into a suspense account which finances large block contracts organized and supervized by the council. While administratively more demanding than enveloping and attracting less subsidy, this alteration in the terms of the 'investment partnership' results in full improvement at a total cost of £12,000 per house for an owner contribution of £500.[104] Following a pilot scheme in the Roshven HAA the 1980–1 HIP allocation provided for schemes in nine other HAAs incorporating approximately 1000 houses.

The development of techniques for systematic housing improvement was welcomed by residents' organizations who are pressing for an extended programme. In particular the new schemes are seen as a solution to the problem of 'cowboy builders'. Growing concern about the standards of work in grant-aided improvements prompted Community Forum to organize a mock public inquiry and the resultant publicity, including a television documentary, added weight to the case for this new approach. A reservation about enveloping is that it places a premium on neglect, particularly in the case of the private rented sector, and it has been suggested that the 100 per cent grants should be made a charge on landlord owned property.[105] More fundamentally the CDP, while supporting the principle of systematic improvement, pointed out that enveloping is an expensive way of maintaining the private market in inner areas and questioned the validity of continued support for owner-occupation at the expense of programmes of social housing.[106]

Economic decline and priorities

The decline of the hitherto prosperous local economy, heavily reliant on the car industry, became a major policy issue in the mid-1970s. A number of studies highlighted the impact of economic changes on the inner areas which lost 10,000 manufacturing jobs p.a. during the 1970s, mainly as result of rationalization and closures.[107] This further accentuated the trend for better-off skilled workers to move to the suburbs and the population of the Inner City Core Area (see Figure 16) declined by a third between 1961 and 1976 to 294,000, by which time 32 per cent of households had incomes of under £2000 p.a. (compared with 26 per cent in the West Midlands as a whole) and a third comprised New Commonwealth born people and their dependents. In some areas, such as Saltley, traditional industries were partly replaced by warehousing, causing a significant increase in heavy traffic in residential streets. The contraction of traditional industries contributed to the problem of vacant land which in 1978 totalled almost 6 per cent of the core area. Local shopping facilities declined markedly as a result of changes in the organization of retailing and the falling spending power of local communities. Inadequate local authority and health services added to the range of problems facing the ICPP Committee.

The initial Urban Programme allocation was £10m p.a. for three years from 1979–80. Not surprisingly, the first ICPP made no attempt to specify redirection in main programmes and stated that:

> ... in the medium term the scope for doing this may be limited, particularly on revenue expenditure programmes where debt charges on establishments, running expenses and staff costs are fixed, unless policy decisions are taken to close establishments and services. Capital expenditure offers more scope for redirection, although a balance will have to be maintained between inner city areas and other areas with increasing population.[108]

However, an increasing proportion of HIP expenditure has been allocated to the Urban Renewal Programme, and the ICPP Committee now publish area statements for each of ten parts of the core area, identifying Urban Programme and main capital programme expenditure, together with details of planning proposals.

In determining geographical priorities the extensive Partnership Area was justified by the need to apply measures to improve employment opportunities for residents of the smaller 'core' area over a wider area. Nevertheless, in order to avoid spreading resources too thinly for other aspects of the programme, four priority areas were selected within the core (Figure 17).

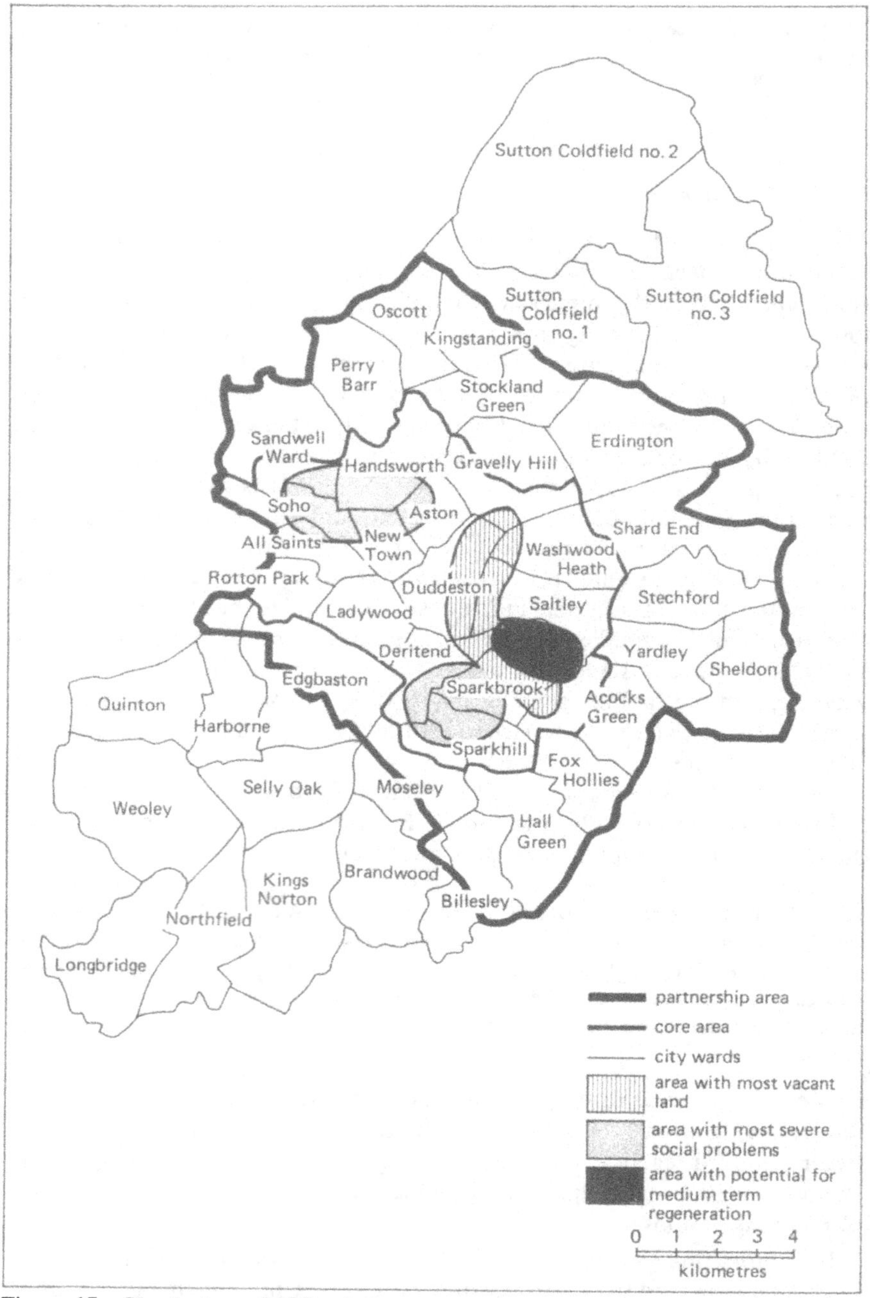

Figure 17 *Birmingham: ICPP priority areas*

Source: Birmingham ICP, *Inner City Partnership Programme Summary* (1978)

Policy priorities and the diversity of projects are indicated by the Urban Programme allocations shown in Figure 18 which demonstrates the emphasis on economic renewal. The ICPP acknowledges that the employment effects of wider economic changes and cuts in public expenditure will mean that:

> . . . future industrial developments may not lead to an overall increase in employment opportunities in the inner city especially of a kind suitable for residents. . . .[109]

but justifies its policies in terms of ameliorating the growing spatial concentration of unemployment.

The strategy currently emphasizes improving the physical infrastructure of industry by the reclamation of sites for development, the refurbishment of industrial buildings, the construction of advance factories (mainly small units) and an Industrial Improvement Area programme with three initial declarations. A study of the city's inner area building stock has indicated considerable scope for such intervention.[110] Nearly half the buildings surveyed completely covered their site, leaving no room for *in situ* expansion and necessitating all loading taking place in the street. Recent investment in premises has been limited and piecemeal. The researchers concluded that there is a demand for space, but that fragmented ownership patterns and density of development preclude significant private sector renewal. They recommended local authorities taking advantage of the rapid turnover of premises (obviating the need for compulsory relocation) and using short leases to assemble sites and secure gradual renewal to a more modern layout at modest public expense.

More direct measures to generate employment include the Birmingham Business and Employment Scheme, providing financial assistance and a range of advice aimed at small manufacturing firms, and New Enterprise Workshops, providing a 'sheltered' environment for small firms, in the form of subsidized premises and communal facilities and services. Whereas the ICPP seeks to increase the significance of such measures, many depend on as yet unrealized responses from the private sector.

Considerable efforts have been made to tackle the problem of vacant land. Following a systematic survey of sites during the first ICPP all public authorities have identified land surplus to requirements. A recent report documents the extent and characteristics of the problem, progress in the past two years and future proposals.[111] It optimistically concludes that with a more positive approach by public bodies the majority of vacant sites over 0.2 ha will be developed in the next three years, including the long overdue completion of the public open space programme in the redevelopment areas.

New methods of revitalizing older neighbourhood shopping streets are being developed, including an extension of enveloping. The renovation of shop fronts, provision of off-street parking and minor landscaping schemes are having a visible impact, stimulating modest private investment.

There has been a massive increase in the scale of Urban Programme funds allocated to voluntary organizations, significantly boosting their activity.

Schemes	Proposed start date(s)	Cost 1979–82 Capital	Cost 1979–82 Revenue
		£000	£000
Economy			
Inner Urban Areas Act projects. Various environmental work, aid to assist non-conforming uses, aid to industrial development, including firms in old premises, industrial improvement areas	April 1979	3520	900
Advance factories	April 1979	1400	—
Refurbished industrial premises	April 1979	1500	—
New enterprise workshops	April 1979–81	168	102
Reclamation of major sites	June 1980–81	695	30
Industrial promotion special campaign	April 1979	—	150
Support for new enterprises	April 1979	—	90
Economy sub-total		7283	1272
Physical environment			
Improvements to various older shopping centres	April 1979	950	—
Development of open space in redevelopment areas	April 1979–81	384	—
General environmental improvements	April 1979	260	—
Improvement to parks		240	—
Special projects	April 1979–80	259	—
Physical environment sub-total		2093	—
Housing			
Extensive external work to private properties in HAAs (enveloping)	April 1979	4562	—
Warden service schemes, primarily to serve the private sector	April 1979	225	57
Housing sub-total		4787	57
Movement			
Additional highway maintenance in priority areas	April 1979	— }	490
Contribution to off-site highway works	April 1979	— }	
Traffic Regulation Orders and parking measures	April 1979	—	85
Small highway schemes and traffic management measures, etc.		1697	—
Community bus service (1 year Experiment)	April 1979	—	150
Movement sub-total		1697	725
Learning and Leisure			
Education			
Extra home/school liaison teachers and non-teaching helps	April 1979	—	117
Withdrawal units in secondary schools	April 1979	—	117
Aston Manor sports hall	November 1979	290	—
Repair and maintenance of buildings	April 1979	—	120
Minor works to adapt buildings especially for community involvement	April 1979	150	—
Other projects	April 1979–81	156	657
Amenities and recreation			
Garrison Lane playing fields	April 1979	140	—
Play centres in parks	April 1979	—	273
Libraries, museums and art gallery		9	52
Learning and leisure sub-total		745	1336
Society			
Community self-help			
Community projects based on primary schools	April 1979	30	180
Youth and community workers attached to Urban Renewal Project teams	April 1979	—	81
'Community chest' provision	October 1979	—	50
Other self-help projects		—	215
Special groups			
Children and youths	April 1979–81	180	451
Elderly and handicapped	April 1979–81	20	21
Additional adult training centre	April 1980	500	70
Society sub-total		880	1133
Health and personal social services			
Primary health care facilities	April 1979	600	38
Six social workers specializing in mental health in inner areas	April 1979	—	102
Social worker input to primary care	April 1979	—	150
Other projects		478	651
Health and personal social services sub-total		1078	941

Figure 18 *Birmingham: Urban Programme allocations 1979 to 1982 (total capital £19.77m, revenue £6.8m at 1977–8 prices)*

Source: Birmingham ICP, *Inner City Partnership Programme Summary* (1978)

After prolonged negotiations Community Forum, whose formal access to the Urban Renewal Sub-Committee had been severed by the incoming Conservative council, was accorded the status of an 'umbrella organization'. Forum's full time officer works in close co-operation with the Birmingham Voluntary Service Council's Inner City Unit (funded by the ICPP) which produces newsletters and pamphlets, provides assistance to groups seeking Partnership funding, and generally promotes the role of the voluntary sector. Community Forum is campaigning for a higher proportion of resources to be allocated to neighbourhood-based action groups. It helped establish informal area committees but the council have refused to introduce formal area committees with budgets and powers to make decisions. Instead a 'community chest' scheme has been established which provides small grants (£100 maximum) to voluntary organizations, on the recommendation of advisory groups of area-based officers (particularly from Education and Social Service Departments), who also advise on major funding of voluntary organizations. There is clearly a need for a further development of the local area input to decision making, not least because ward councillors still have a very minor role.[112]

The development of the ICPP has stimulated an awareness of the processes of decline, focussed the attention of a variety of departments and agencies on inner area problems, and resulted in some progress towards a more comprehensive approach.[113] Significant innovations have underlined both the possibilities for the effective deployment of limited public resources and the difficulties of stimulating private investment which would benefit inner area residents. The first two years have seen a growing realization of the limitations of the ICPP in the face of the wider forces generating unemployment, poverty and environmental degradation.

Conclusions

The history of urban renewal in Birmingham is punctuated by 'grand strategies' generated by the 'civic gospel' tradition of municipal intervention. But, just as the Chamberlain Improvement Scheme failed in the absence of subsidized council housing, so the impetus of Manzoni's Comprehensive Redevelopment Programme was lost as national policies curbed the rate of implementation. More recently the progress of the Urban Renewal Programme has been constrained by overriding economic influences. Nonetheless the city's innovations have also contributed to the development of overall policy: the principles of comprehensive redevelopment established during the war years were subsequently adopted by many other authorities, and the renewal areas of 1972 can be regarded as prototype HAAs. It is ironic that having pioneered deferred demolition through force of circumstances in the 1940s, the city is now pressing for the use of enveloping as an alternative to its reintroduction. The second city has often been first, but the fact that in the

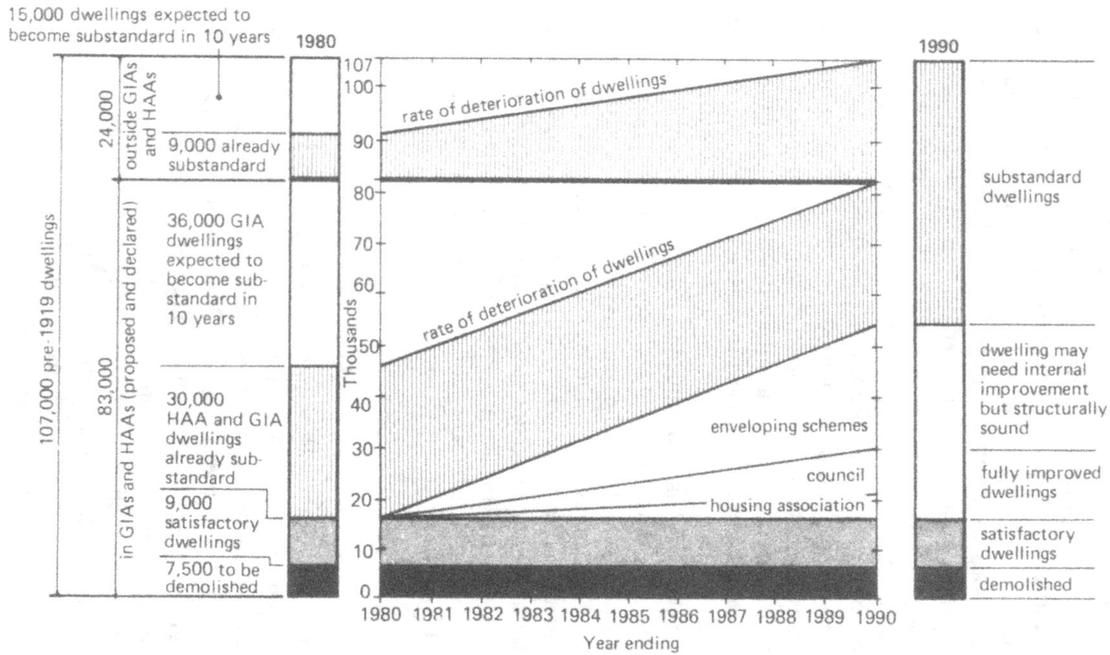

Figure 19 *Birmingham: Housing Investment Programme: Urban Renewal 1980 to 1990*

Note: This projection is based on capital expenditure being achieved at the level envisaged in the 1981–2 HIP submission.

Source: Adapted from City of Birmingham, *Housing Strategy and Investment Programme* 1980 to 1984

long run progress has not been markedly better than elsewhere testifies to the primacy of national policies and economic conditions.

The fortunes of the Urban Renewal Programme during the 1970s clearly illustrate the limitations of national policy. A combination of inadequate public finance and market processes resulted in failure to meet the target, set in response to government advice in 1972, of eliminating substandard housing by 1980. A contributory factor has been the council's reluctance to effectively employ compulsory powers in the private rented sector although this has, to some extent, been offset by housing association activity. The problems of low-income owner-occupiers came sharply into focus but the resource intensive response in the form of the enveloping and block schemes contradicts national policy.

The city's renewal programmes are now at a crossroads. Without significant changes the prospect is one of continued aggregate decline of older housing areas. A continued concentration of Urban Programme and HIP funds will produce a chequer-board pattern of improved areas and, if present rates of progress continue, the future of a substantial proportion of these marginal areas may be secured during the 1980s. But a pepper-pot pattern of improvement will continue to characterize the bulk of the Victorian middle ring, failing to arrest decay. Similarly, without accelerated investment the municipal inter-war suburbs and post-war estates will continue to deteriorate.

This is the message of the 1981–2 HIP submission in which the returning Labour council argue that the recent breakthrough in the Urban Renewal Programme can only be sustained on the basis of increased public expenditure. A bid of £97m included expenditure on pre-1919 housing of some £38m. However, an allocation of £47m means substantial reductions in all component programmes. At the point when a decade of effort has built up an effective local machine for urban renewal the impact of central government policies will preclude its potential being realized and will ensure massive problems for the 1990s.

Overall, changing conditions in Birmingham's 'rings' illustrate the unpalatable reality of urban renewal policies, limited by the demands of a market economy, failing to prevent problems shifting around. The concentration of effort on inner ring redevelopment precluded preventative action in the middle ring, which deteriorated badly. There is now the very real prospect that before the renewal of the middle ring is implemented the municipal suburbs will have reached crisis point. The causes of urban decay are now better understood: Birmingham is an unequal city because it is the product of an unequal society. At root, the problems which are the concern of the ICPP are those which faced Chamberlainite reformers a century ago.

8 Leeds leads

This chapter examines the development and contemporary problems of urban renewal in Leeds. As in Birmingham, state intervention has had a massive impact on both the built environment and social conditions in the city's older residential areas. But, as the following discussion demonstrates, there are important differences between the two cities.

The local context for urban growth and renewal is the city's changing economic base. After rapid industrial and population expansion in the last century, Leeds had a stable economy in the inter-war years. In the post-war period a decline in manufacturing employment was only partly offset by the growth of service employment. A stagnant local economy and a lack of immigration have meant that urban renewal has generally operated in a comparatively low-pressure housing market.

The legacy of rapid expansion was the dominance of a particular type of working-class housing: the back-to-back. In the 1930s a vigorous clearance drive provoked intense debate. The scale of obsolescence remaining in the 1950s and 1960s was massive and the city pursued tandem policies of clearance and improvement. The 'Leeds method' of improvement through Conversion Areas and Improvement Grant Areas was influential in the development of national policy. Paradoxically, the success of housing improvement eventually gave rise to new problems for the council's overall strategy. In the 1970s an initial attempt to extend comprehensive redevelopment was painfully abandoned. The local response to the national emphasis on gradual renewal has been a much reduced and refined clearance programme and a second area improvement programme. The premises of this current strategy are being challenged while its impact does not match the rate of decay.

Within the framework of the Government's inner city policy Leeds has been designated a Programme Authority. Despite some local innovations, a limited allocation of urban programme funds, in the context of much reduced main programmes, is unlikely to lead to a significant impact.

The legacy of nineteenth century growth

The inner city of Leeds was a creation of the industrial revolution. Expansion was accompanied by the construction of vast numbers of back-to-back houses and local complacency about sanitary reform. The city structure which resulted has been the setting for later policies of urban renewal.

Back-to-backs

Soon after the First World War Chamberlain, chairman of the Parliamentary Unhealthy Areas Committee, commented, 'the City of Leeds is perhaps confronted with the most difficult problem to be found in any of the provincial towns, owing to the enormous number of back-to-back houses . . . it is difficult to suggest any method of dealing with them satisfactorily short of complete clearance'.[1] The Unhealthy Areas Report of 1920 suggested that 30,000 houses needed to be demolished.

This was the first official recognition of the scale of the problem left in the wake of rapid nineteenth century population and industrial expansion. When Queen Victoria came to the throne in 1837 the city's population had already more than doubled in little more than a third of a century to over 130,000. By the time she died in 1901 it had trebled again to reach 429,000.[2] The industrial base of expansion was initially textile manufacture, particularly flax-spinning. Later ready-made clothing and engineering became dominant.

The characteristic form of housing built for the working-class in this period was the back-to-back, which constituted over two thirds of the city's housing stock in 1920. Although back-to-backs were also built in other cities, nowhere else were they built in such numbers (78,000) and over so many years (from 1787 until 1937). The house type began in the yards of inns in the city centre. It was soon adopted by speculative builders who reduced the costs of roads and drainage by building back-to-backs in closed courts. Very high densities were achieved by 'one-up, one-down' houses and by 1840 the Select Committee on the Health of Towns was commenting on the filth and disease in these courts.[3]

The most extensive form of working-class housing development in the early part of the last century was the Type I back-to-back, built in long unbroken rows, with blocks of shared w.c.s and ash-pits at the end of each row. The explanation for the continued use of back-to-backs in independent streets put forward by Beresford is that it was a result of the tyranny of building to a pattern of pre-existing long narrow fields:

> . . . the economical beauty of back-to-backs in a property developer's eye was not only their density, yielding maximum rents per square yard, but the neat way in which they fitted into the shape of the vacant spaces available in Leeds as building land.[4]

Very few large estates became available for building; instead new housing had to be crammed into these long narrow fields which came onto the market one at a time. Subservience to this field pattern is demonstrated by the way the ends of back-to-back streets are often blocked by a wall, by a change of level or by the sides of other houses in an unconnected street, and most strikingly by the construction of 'half-back' or 'blind-back' houses.

Local complacency

When the sanitary reform movement developed nationally there was still a prevalent local apathy about housing conditions in these pre-bye-law back-to-backs for:

> The back-to-back house, which distinguishes Leeds from other commercial centres, is more respectable than slums and is considered a desirable residence for work-people. It lacks ventilation it is true . . . but then it is warm in the winter, and if you have been working all day in a stuffy factory you don't notice the bad air at home.[5]

The city council confined itself to piecemeal clearance, between congested houses and courts. This process of 'opening up' was much favoured by Lupton, chairman of the city's Unhealthy Areas Committee.[6] Not only was it cheaper than wholesale clearance, it did not require the rehousing of families displaced.

One large-scale clearance scheme was attempted for 2790 houses in York Street and Quarry Hill from 1895 onwards. However, little progress had been made by 1912. Lupton blamed the Local Government Board for delays as they insisted on replacement housing being provided for those displaced, an unnecessary imposition, he felt, with so many vacant houses in the vicinity. In fact, the only two council housing schemes built before the First World War proved difficult to let because of their high rents.

A more significant result of this complacency was the continued construction of back-to-backs at a time when almost all other cities were prohibiting them. By the time building began in larger fields and estates around Leeds in the 1860s the back-to-back was firmly established as the accepted form of mass housing provision and action under the bye-laws was limited to improving standards. The Type II back-to-back was established by the Leeds Improvement Act of 1866 and built in terraces split into blocks of eight houses, with yards containing shared w.c.s and ash-pits between. Each house consisted of a living room, usually with a side scullery on the ground floor, two bedrooms above and a skylight attic on the second floor. Streets were 36ft wide and densities were commonly fifty to sixty houses and up to 200 people to the acre. Some 30,000 Type II back-to-backs were built between 1870 and 1900.

A further modification emerged around 1890, and Type III back-to-backs were built with a basement kitchen, a small front garden, and a w.c. (either private or shared with the adjoining house) under a flight of steps leading to the front door. Densities were normally forty houses to the acre. By this time through terrace houses were being built, often intermixed with and to the same grid as the Type III back-to-back. Yet, even when the Housing and Town Planning Act, 1909 banned the further building of back-to-backs nationally, there was an escape route for local builders. The Act did not apply to development proposals previously approved by the council. This clause meant that there were some better Type III back-to-backs built in the 1920s and 1930s. The last street was not completed till 1937. In total approximately 14,000 Type III back-to-back were built.

City structure

The spatial structure of the inner city was established by 1920. Around the city centre, along the valley of the Aire and its tributaries and in some scattered townships, especially south of the river, there were concentrations of heavy industry and the canals, railways and main roads which sustained them. In the immediate vicinity were the congested Type I back-to-backs. A little further away were the industrial suburbs of Armley, Holbeck, Hunslet, Woodhouse, Harehills and Richmond Hill, where Type II back-to-backs had been built in the second half of the nineteenth century. Adjacent to these were the Type III back-to-backs and small through terraces. On the higher ground particularly in the north, were villas and spacious three-storey terrace houses with large gardens and often set in tree-lined avenues. Figure 20 illustrates these house types. The pattern was basically concentric but complicated by the old industrial townships which were later incorporated into the city.

Back-to-back housing was almost exclusively owned by private landlords.[7] The better types were let at higher rents and enjoyed a higher social status, though rents in general were noted as being comparatively low in Leeds. Until housebuilding began to fall off after 1870, the availability of an adequate supply of cheap, small houses made sharing by families relatively rare. The Leeds Permanent Building Society had started to provide facilities for owner-occupation of newly built back-to-backs, making them available to the regularly employed 'respectable' sections of the working class.[8] The growing middle-classes were the owner-occupiers of more substantial villa developments.

Red Ruin

In the 1930s Leeds became noted for a vigorous slum clearance drive. Red Ruin was not without its critics and the debate engendered was intense.

Majority report

New housebuilding declined considerably in the years immediately preceding the First World War and this, combined with the cessation of building during the war and an influx of munition workers, generated a housing shortage. The first priority was action to meet this shortage in the form of suburban council housing development. The city's Development Committee approved a programme for 6000 council houses before the Addison Act changed national policy. Land was acquired and council estates built at Middleton, Wyther,

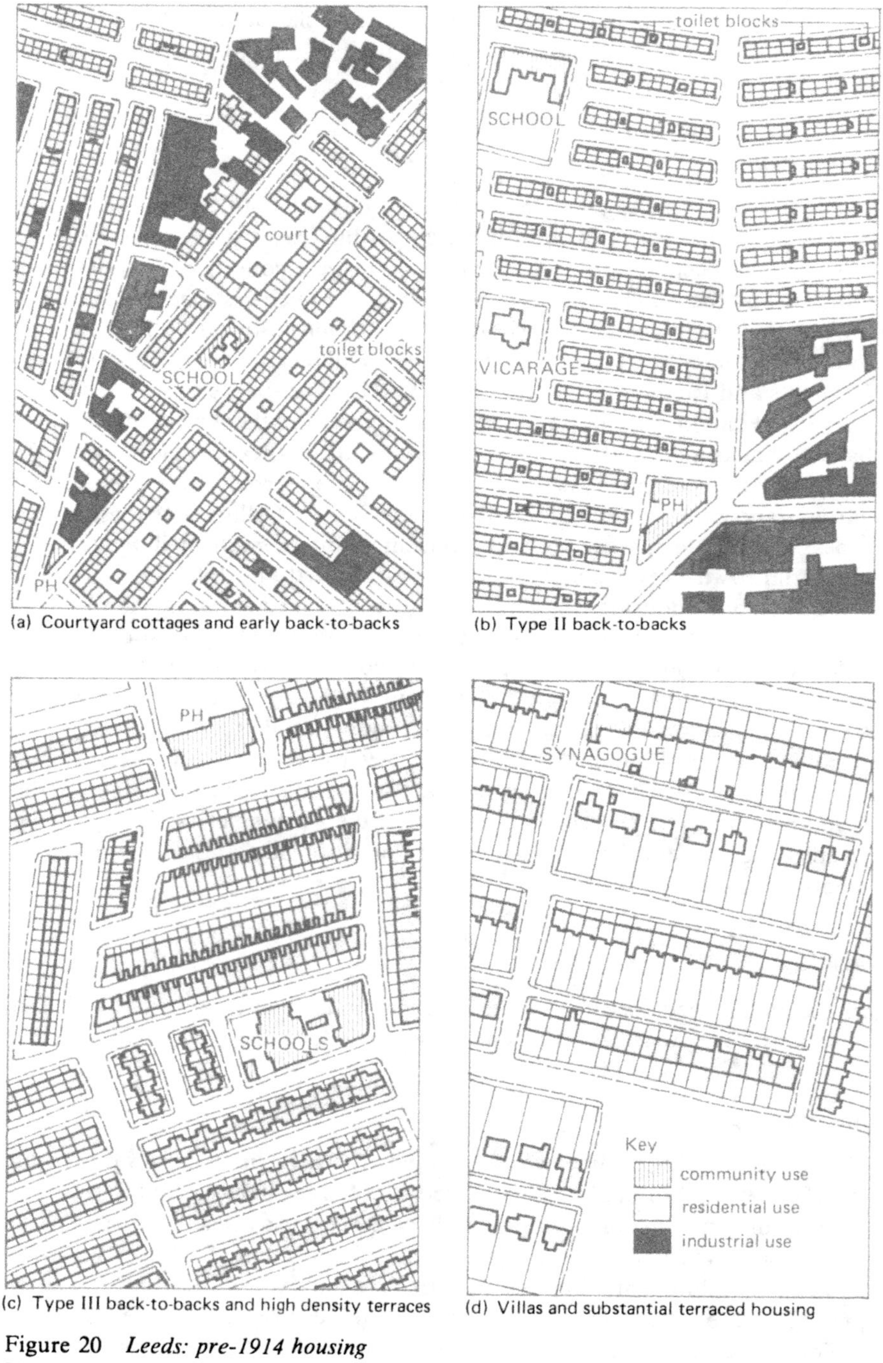

(a) Courtyard cottages and early back-to-backs

(b) Type II back-to-backs

(c) Type III back-to-backs and high density terraces

(d) Villas and substantial terraced housing

Figure 20 ***Leeds: pre-1914 housing***

The street plans are reproduced from Ordnance Survey maps.

Crossgates, Hawksworth and Meanwood. Under the Addison Act council housebuilding forged ahead but the impetus was not maintained in the late 1920s.

Until 1930 virtually no slum clearance was undertaken and the only major clearance project, West Street, was delayed through cost and procedural problems. The call for a national slum clearance campaign after the Housing Act, 1930 was initially met with a 'woefully inadequate'[9] set of proposals from the council, and throughout the 1920s the annual reports of the city's Medical Officer of Health indicated growing impatience with the council's lack of action to deal with slum housing. When a subcommittee of the Improvements Committee was eventually set up in 1931 to investigate the housing situation his report revealed that of the 128,000 houses in Leeds, 75,000 were back-to-backs of which 33,000 were built prior to 1872. He continued:

> The problem in Leeds centres around the 33,000 back-to-back houses of the old type. They constitute the slums . . . can they be improved and made habitable? . . . A small proportion may be amenable to a process of reconditioning but only at a cost which would make the experiment a doubtful proposition and at the best would be a palliative and not a cure. . . . There remains only one alternative . . . complete demolition.[10]

In 1932, despite this advice, the majority report of the subcommittee recommended minimal action.[11] Piecemeal clearance of 400 houses would be combined with the building of low-quality council houses – 1000 at once and more later.

However, two events in 1933 substantially altered the climate of policy making. At a national level there was the major shift of policy towards building solely for the needs of slum clearance. At a local level the publication of a minority report of this subcommittee set the scene for dramatic intervention.[12]

Minority report

The minority report was an impressive document. It proposed that clearance should proceed at a rate of 3000 houses p.a. over five years with a further 30,000 by 1948. Total replacement of the demolished houses was necessary, with more care being given to the needs of small households. Rent differentiation should be applied to all council houses so that slum dwellers could afford the rents of decent houses. With provisos, the principle of flats was agreed, for 'if large numbers of people cannot go out, then they must go up'.[13] These and many other recommendations, together with the establishment of a housing committee with its own director and department, provided inspiration for the intensive action which followed.[14]

The report was soon adopted as Labour Party policy and its clearance proposals taken on board by the Improvements Committee, under mounting public and ministerial pressure. Housing was a major issue in the local elections later in 1933 when Labour was returned and Jenkinson (one of the authors of the minority report) became the first chairman of the new Housing Committee. Immediately the clearance programme was boosted to 30,000 houses in six years – more than a tenth of the national total.

In the event this programme was by no means fully implemented. Nonetheless, achievement was impressive and the controversy surrounding it intense. In the period of Labour control from 1933 to 1935 over 8000 houses were represented for clearance and contracts were let for nearly 7000 new houses and flats. From being a city noted for its slum housing, Leeds acquired a reputation as a dynamic housing authority. To a great extent this was due to the dominant role of Jenkinson – 'by his industry and ability he was able to change the great City of Leeds, in the space of a few years, from being an outstanding example of the evil consequences of the industrial revolution to the Mecca of all housing reformers'.[15]

The clearance programme was announced in 1933 and copies of the map widely sold. It quickly became known as the 'Red Ruin Map' because of the way patches of red signified prospective clearance areas. Clearance action concentrated on the Type I back-to-backs (see Figure 21). At the same time proposals were announced for the construction of 3000 houses in a large new garden suburb at Gipton, for new tenements to assist with local rehousing, and for a massive block of flats 'on the continental plan' at Quarry Hill.[16] These broad plans were rapidly refined. Five per cent of new houses were to be 'sunshine houses' for TB patients; council shops were to be provided on the new estates; a municipal hostel for single persons would replace the demolished lodging houses; a hire purchase scheme would enable tenants to furnish their new homes by weekly instalments paid with the rent; and a free disinfestation service would be provided for tenants being rehoused from their slum dwellings.

Controversy and rents

What was being attempted was a 'social transformation which must cut across many interests before becoming an accomplished fact'.[17] It could hardly be expected that such plans would be implemented with opposition. A lively propaganda war developed between supporters and opponents of the plans with pamphlets, social surveys, spirited exchanges at public inquiries and electioneering all playing their part in the controversy.[18] The opposition on the city council were against the cost of the scheme and its implied 'policy of communal socialism',[19] whereby the eventual result would be 40,000 council houses – 'an attempt to sap the independence of the individual and to turn a body of people into supplicants at the expense of the public purse'.[20] They were also opposed to the building of council estates in the more affluent suburbs.[21]

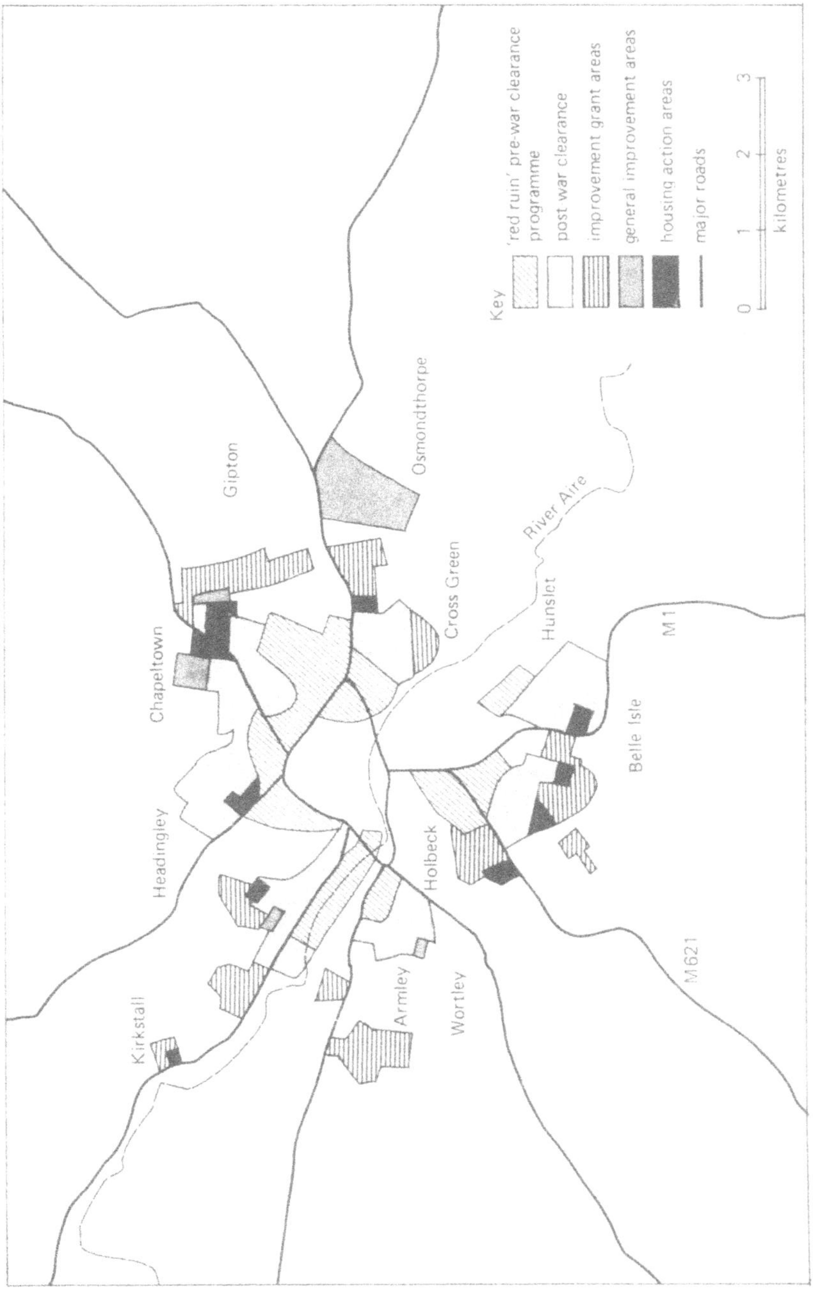

Figure 21 ***Leeds: renewal areas***

At this time almost all the back-to-backs affected by slum clearance were still in private rental and the local Property Owners and Ratepayers Association was also prominent in this opposition. They were incensed when Sir Hilton Young, Minister of Health, commented on the need for action to deal with the 'hovels of Leeds'.[22] Lack of compensation for landlords increased their anger and Leeds was cited at their national conferences as the most prominent exponent of political robbery.[23] Proposals were made for the building of replacement houses by landlords at economic rents, to be aided by larger compensation and state loans.[24]

At a more philosophical level objections centred on the way that:

> The whole tendency of our present day municipal policy with respect to housing, is to treat the mass of people in the manner of a herd, destined to be moved hither and thither according to the dictates of a despotic authority which professes to know better than the individuals concerned, not only what they desire, but what they ought to need.[25]

As residents of slum areas found themselves moved to council estates on the edge of the city, the hardships caused by increased rents and travel-to-work costs, resistance to change and to new disciplines imposed by life on a council estate provoked reactions against the plans. The churches took up the argument against slum clearance or, alternatively, in favour of local rehousing schemes.

The most hotly disputed aspect of Jenkinson's programme was the differential rents scheme, introduced in 1934 to pool the financing of houses built under various Housing Acts and to abolish rent anomalies. Ironically, the scheme had been introduced not only as an attempt at rationalization, but also to enable the rehousing policy to work by using pooled subsidies to provide rent relief for needy families moved to the new estates by clearance action. While subsidy of the poorest families (some families rehoused paid no rent at all) reduced the sharp differentiation of council estates into superior/general needs and inferior/clearance needs, it also meant rent rises for most houses.[26] To the Conservatives it was turning the Housing Committee into a public assistance board: to most tenants rent differentiation was simply another name for the introduction of rent rises and the loathed means test. Rent strikes followed on the older council estates.

It was differential rents more than any other aspect of housing policy which contributed to Labour losing control at the 1935 election. However, many aspects of their programme continued. The Red Ruin Map's proposals remained a council policy. Although representations fell sharply because of the need 'to slow down the programme at the destructive end and speed it up at the constructive end',[27] by 1938 they were rising again. At the outbreak of war nearly half of the infamous 30,000 Red Ruin houses had been represented for clearance and of the 11,000 families displaced by clearance, 85 per cent had been housed by the council, mainly in new properties. The building contracts placed by Labour resulted in just over 5000 new council houses during 1937 and 1938, and, despite delays in the building of Quarry Hill and Gipton, the 20,000th council house was completed by 1939.

Debate about the need to replace slum housing with high-density flat developments intensified during the late 1930s.[28] It was associated with continuing complaints about lack of local rehousing at clearance inquiries.[29] Only the 'model estate' at Quarry Hill[30] was actually built but the issue was to reappear after the war.

Tandem policies

Notwithstanding the impact made by the inter-war clearance programme, the scale of older housing in Leeds was still considerable. The city adopted a tandem approach in the 1950s and 1960s, incorporating both comprehensive redevelopment and housing improvement to modest standards on an area basis. Eventually, the very success of improvement led to tensions within this strategy.

Comprehensive redevelopment

Immediately after the Second World War the council purchased over 1000 acres of land for its building programme and council housebuilding gradually increased. Initially, little action was taken to clear the houses still remaining from the Red Ruin Map. This lack of action conformed with central government policy: it also reflected the urgent housing shortage in Leeds. The housing waiting list reached a peak of over 30,000 in 1952 and only 10 per cent of allocations were earmarked for applicants from clearance areas.[31]

Leeds needed little encouragement to resume clearance in 1954. The Development Plan of 1949 had concluded that 90,000 dwellings were obsolescent, of which 56,000 were back-to-backs, and the clearance target adopted for the period to 1971 was 31,000. By 1956 the number of families rehoused from clearance areas exceeded the total number of families housed from other priority groups on the waiting list for the first time since the war.

By 1961 about 10,000 of these houses had been cleared, but a survey carried out for the Development Plan review found that 96,000 dwellings 'already or becoming obsolete or unsuitably located, would require removal during the remainder of the century'.[32] The annual rate of houses actually cleared had doubled from the 1954–8 rate to over 2000 p.a. and, encouraged by this success, the council adopted a representation rate of 2300 dwellings p.a. The general housing situation was regarded as one of non-pressure with the number of dwellings roughly equalling the number of households.

Nevertheless, the most contentious aspect of the Development Plan Review was the clearance rate and its relationship with council building. Partly because of disagreement about the respective roles of clearance and improvement, the review was not submitted until 1967. In the meantime, the eventual review plan policy on clearance had been incorporated in the Housing Redevelopment Areas Map 1961–81. This policy envisaged the clearance of some 41,000 dwellings by 1981 and the rate adopted to meet this target was 2300 p.a. until 1971 and then 1800 p.a. The council house-building rate would be slightly less, and the arguments used to justify this were a rising number of relets, and an increasing trend for households displaced by clearance to find private accommodation rather than be rehoused by the council.

The representation rate achieved between 1961 and 1971 kept pace with this programme, though the rate of actual demolition fluctuated, largely determined by variations in the council building rate (see Figure 22). The net result of the post-war clearance drive was the representation of 40,000 dwellings by 1971 and the demolition of 30,000. The last remaining slums identified in the Red Ruin Map were cleared by 1965.

In this post-war period clearance became part of the wider approach of comprehensive redevelopment. The review of the Development Plan laid great stress on the need for clearance to proceed on an area basis, a policy which 'enables satisfactory layouts and groupings of buildings to be achieved in redevelopment with an effective separation of pedestrians and vehicles'.[33] The tightly packed back-to-back houses with their obsolete road patterns, lack of open space and inadequate social facilities would be discarded and be replaced by new housing estates, incorporating all other modern facilities. This 'restructuring of the inner city along the lines of modern town planning theory and practice'[34] became associated with the implementation of the 'Leeds approach' to transportation planning in the late 1960s.[35] High density development would be concentrated in the inner city and also massed around transport termini and shopping centres on suburban estates.

Two features of this policy were particularly significant for the physical environment. First, there was the use of multi-storey flats. The inter-war debate on the use of flats was resurrected in 1954 and contracts let for the first multi-storey flats.[36] By the 1960s they comprised roughly one third of council building. Multi-storey flats were usually in mixed developments (Figure 23) and, perhaps because of a more careful allocation policy, appear to have been socially more successful than in some other cities.[37] Second, there was the extent of cleared land remaining undeveloped for considerable period of time – creating the impression of a scorched-earth policy. A survey in 1971 found over 500 acres of cleared land unused, over two thirds of it allocated for other purposes than housing.[38] Lack of resources causing delays in implementing such supposedly linked programmes as public open space was primarily responsible.

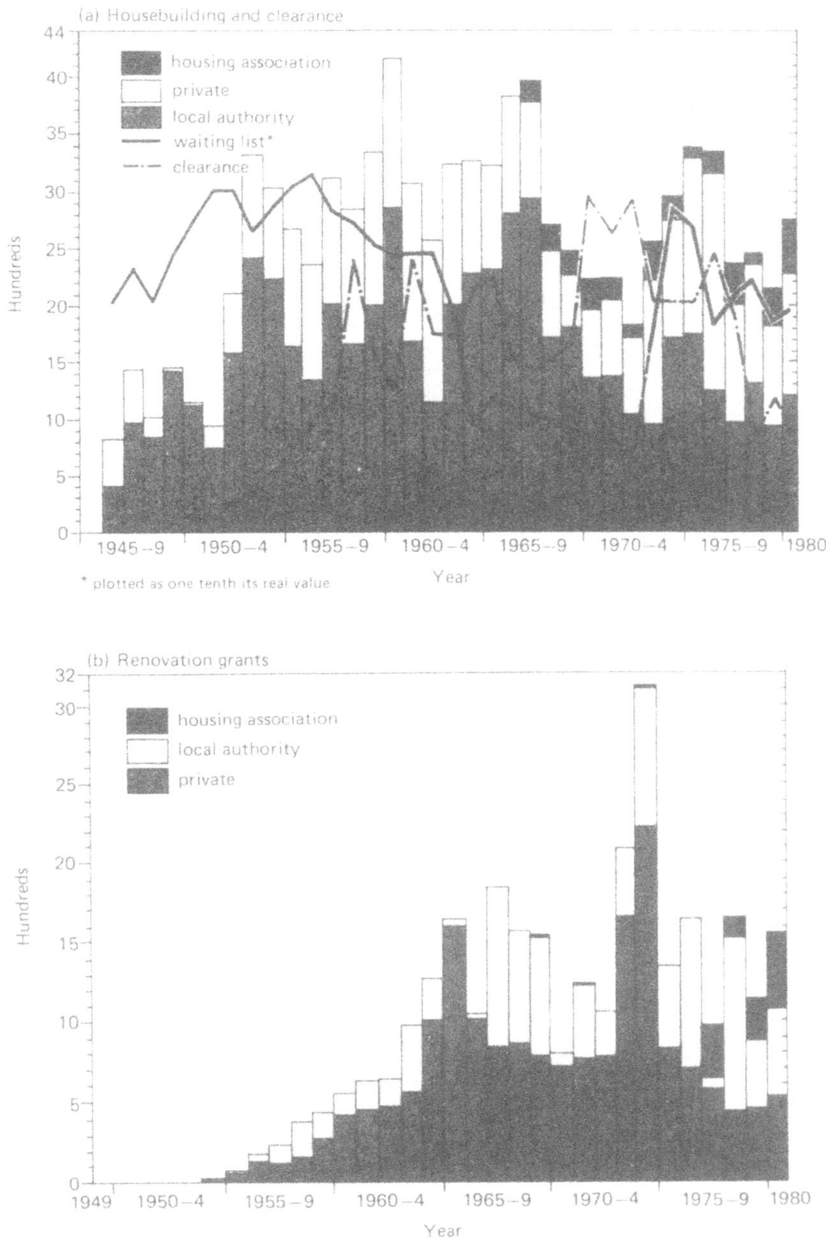

Figure 22 *Leeds: renewal progress 1945 to 1980*

Sources: 1946–65, Annual Report of the Housing Committee to the City of Leeds Council; 1966 onwards, MOHLG and DoE *Local Housing Statistics*; waiting list figures are from various reports to the Housing Committee, but the complete series is not available

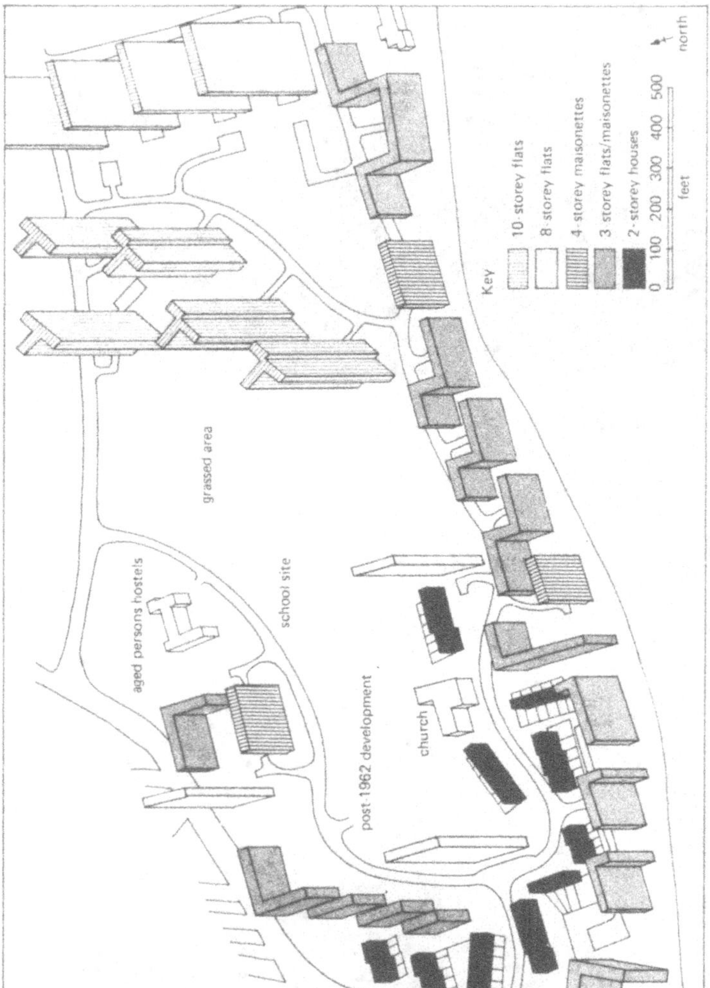

Figure 23 *Leeds: comprehensive redevelopment at Ebor Gardens*

Source: Adapted from MOHLG, *Families Living at High Density: A Study of Estates in Leeds, Liverpool and London*, Design Bulletin 21 (HMSO 1970)

Improvement – the 'Leeds method'

Renewal policy in Leeds during the 1950s and 1960s is best known for the way in which this clearance programme was complemented by housing improvement. In both the size of the programme and the style of implementation used, Leeds was unique in this period. The emphasis was on area improvement, firstly through the operation of Conversion Areas and secondly through Improvement Grant Areas.[39]

The emergent problem of large villas, previously occupied by the middle-class but later abandoned and increasingly multi-occupied, was noted by the MoH in 1938.[40] In the early 1950s the city council embarked on a scheme to compulsorily acquire multi-occupied houses and convert them into self-contained flats and maisonettes. Grants and loans would also be available to private owners to carry out conversions and extensive environmental improvements were planned.[41]

Action first began, and was later concentrated, in the Chapeltown area of the city. In 1954 a CPO was served on forty-three large houses. Although there was an attempt to encourage voluntary improvement when a further part of Chapeltown was tackled three years later, almost all improvement and conversion work was undertaken by the council itself. Acquisition followed the use of CPO powers or, more frequently, the threat of such powers. 1000 houses were included in the four major *Conversion Areas*. Acquisition and conversion was spread out over many years, delayed by the housing management and decanting problems inherited with such houses.[42]

Chapeltown became the heart of the main coloured immigrant area of Leeds during the early years of Conversion Area policy. Before that it had been an area into which Jewish families moved from their original area of settlement close to the city centre, and a reception area for East European and Irish immigrants immediately after the Second World War. The policy was originally conceived 'not as a response to a "colour problem", but purely in terms of preservation of good housing stock threatening to slide into lodging house decay, the natural consequences of changes in family size and housing need as these affected late Victorian middle-class family houses'.[43] Nevertheless, it became inseparable from the issue of housing for coloured immigrants. Increasingly the route to a council tenancy for the West Indians coming to the city was via living in a multi-occupied house soon to be purchased by the council in Chapeltown.

The other vehicle for Leeds' improvement policy was the *Improvement Grant Area* (IGA). Declarations began in 1955 and IGAs soon dominated the programme. By 1970 105 IGAs had been declared, containing over 22,000 dwellings (see Table 8).

The first of these IGAs was the Hill Street/Lincoln Road project which consisted of 200 Type II back-to-backs, 90 per cent lacking basic amenities. The response of landlords to the offer of grants was cautious, with the result

Table 8 *Leeds: special area declarations*

Year	*Improvement Grant Areas*		*General Improvement Areas*		*Housing Action Areas*	
	number	*houses*	*number*	*houses*	*number*	*houses*
1955	1	197				
1956	—	—				
1957	2	334				
1958	3	210				
1959	9	1077				
1960	—	—				
1961	—	—				
1962	3	308				
1963	11	1516				
1964	11	1839				
1965	12	3741				
1966	17	4683				
1967	10	2550				
1968	11	3692				
1969	12	2513				
1970	3	196	2	511		
1971			2	65		
1972			2	433		
1973			3	362		
1974			2	805		
1975			—	—	1	212
1976			1	90	3	818
1977			2	682	3	878
1978			2	564	3	606
1979			2	423	1	79
Totals	105	22656	18	3935	11	2593

Notes: All figures are Leeds CB before 1975 and Leeds MD after, except GIAs. Only two GIAs (inter-war local authority estates) were declared before local government reorganization in Leeds CB – the remainder were in the 'outer districts' incorporated in the new area.

Source: Leeds City Council, Department of Housing.

that almost all were purchased by the council. Financial cut-backs led to a temporary halt in the programme in 1956. When it resumed a year later, the momentum built up and the programme was accelerated from 1962 onwards.

The justification of the IGA approach was the need to secure comprehensive improvement of a whole area by the provision of basic amenities in each house. If older houses could be tackled on an area basis 'as opposed to the existence of a number of scattered improved houses which must result from a purely voluntary method', efforts to secure improvement could be concentrated. It had the advantage 'that all the houses can be expected to enjoy a lengthened life and avoids the difficulty which results when some houses are allowed to decay in among those which have been improved'.[44]

The programme used no special legislation, relying on that generally available for grants from 1949 onwards and powers to purchase houses compulsorily in the 1957 Act. The interesting aspect of implementation was the combination of encouraging voluntary improvement and the use of compulsory purchase powers – the 'iron fist in the velvet glove' philosophy. 'Strategically the operation hinged on a large number of units being pushed into a pipe-line of some administrative complexity'[45] and departmental liaison was crucial.

By 1970 some 8000 houses had been improved out of 13,000 without amenities in IGAs. Progress in persuading private owners to improve their homes and in the purchase and improvement of houses by the city council was most rapid in the mid-1960s under the direction of Cohen, Labour chairman of housing.[46] The rate of improvement declined after a change in local political control in 1968, when one essential component of the 'Leeds method' – the threat of compulsory purchase – was suspended.

Improvements to back-to-backs (both Type II and III) usually involved the installation of a bathroom in the small bedroom and the provision of a dormer window in the skylight attic (Figure 24). Accompanying repairs were often minimal, particularly before the 1969 Act made them grant-aided.

Tensions within the strategy

The rationale for tandem policies of clearance and improvement was derived from the characteristics of the nineteenth century built environment and the scale of obsolescence identified in 1949. The clearance programme was aimed at the Type I back-to-backs remaining from the Red Ruin Map and the worst Type II back-to-backs. This implied an extended life for large areas of better back-to-backs and the small through houses which were the focus of the IGA programme. Improvement was thus complementary to clearance, as the installation of basic amenities was, it was often stressed, a 'palliative', reflecting the scale of obsolescence in Leeds. IGAs were conceived as a short-term expedient, which did not eliminate the longer-term need for comprehensive redevelopment. The compatibility of the policies was further strengthened by the argument that basic housing improvement was geared to the limited (fifteen- to twenty-year) life of IGAs.

Leeds' renewal strategy meant that it was one of the very few authorities to implement the tandem approach enunciated by central government from the 1950s. Moreover, in municipalizing stress areas of multi-occupation it was leading the way to later developments in national policy. The pioneering aspect of Leeds tandem approach to older housing is illustrated by its

Figure 24 *Leeds: typical improvement of a back-to-back*

Source: Leeds City Council, *Improvement* (booklet about Burley Lodge Road (1965))

influence on the Denington Committee's recommendations in 1967 (Cohen was a member of the committee).[47]

The impact of the clearance programme on the private rented sector was considerable. The vast majority of houses demolished were in private rental and their occupants were rehoused in new suburban council estates or comprehensive redevelopment schemes around the city centre.[48] Studies by Wilkinson and Sigsworth revealed little opposition to the principle of clearance from residents of slum areas at this time and less preference for local rehousing than might be expected.[49] They did, however, comment on the uncertainty and anxiety which resulted from a lack of information about the process.[50]

The improvement programme both reflected and reinforced the decline of private rental in other older housing areas. Owner-occupation increased rapidly in IGAs and provided an impetus for voluntary improvement. Although some landlords also improved their houses (particularly large philanthropic trusts), others sold to the council. Over 7000 acquired properties were managed by the council by 1973 and most of these were in IGAs and Conversion Areas. There was little difficulty in letting these for their attraction lay in comparatively low rents, even after improvement, and a location in established communities with easy access to the city centre and local social facilities. As the then director of housing commented:

> I cannot stress too much the attractions of these small type dwellings for those people who have grown up in a gregarious atmosphere; there is a degree of chumminess and awareness of community which is certainly not immediately reproduced in the large estates developed on the perimeter of our large cities.[51]

He identified three groups for whom an improved back-to-back house was popular – the elderly, those with low incomes, and those with other priorities for spending than housing. The complementary nature of clearance and improvement is also illustrated by the fact that relets in improved back-to-backs were often allocated for clearance rehousing.

Not surprisingly, the very success of the improvement programme raised the possibility of it having a longer-term role. This challenge to the view of improvement as a palliative was led by Cohen and in 1966 the council duly decided to adopt a reduced rate of clearance.[52] The issue was far from settled, however, for there was considerable opposition to any weakening of resolve about comprehensive redevelopment.

The vexed question of a longer-term strategic role for housing and environmental improvement is illustrated by the early history of proposals for Burley Lodge Road – an area which was later to become the unstable barometer of subsequent changes in Leeds renewal policy. The area consists of two different types of housing: Type II back-to-backs removed from the clearance programme and declared an IGA in 1965; and small through terrace houses also declared an IGA in the same year. The whole area of 664 houses was proposed for environmental improvement in 1966 and a scheme developed in co-operation with the Ministry as one of the demonstration projects before the Housing Act, 1969. Phase I of the environmental improvements was implemented in 1969 and concentrated on street closures to restrict through traffic, limited tree planting and hard landscaping at a total cost of £6 per dwelling.

It is not intended to discuss the merits of the scheme or the style of consultation with residents adopted.[53] Its importance in changing perspectives of the role of improvement is that it was presented as an alternative to clearance. Significantly, Cohen was quoted as saying that the scheme 'will enable people to go on living there in a more modern environment and keep their old associations with the district. We are giving the area new life, and we anticipate that it will last this century well out'.[54] Such an objective was contradictory to the original concept of improvement as a palliative: it ensured that Burley Lodge Road would subsequently be at the centre of debate about Leeds' renewal policies.

Strategy D

The debate engendered by the introduction of a revised strategy for urban renewal in 1971 illustrates the clash between the comprehensive redevelopment philosophy of the 1960s and changing views on improvement. Though introduced as a natural progression from previous tandem policies, Strategy D caused intense argument in the city: it attempted to extend redevelopment at a time when nationally the pendulum was swinging the other way.

Review of older housing stock

By 1971 remaining areas defined for clearance in the next ten years included 13,600 dwellings, as against the 18,000 which would be required to match the review plan's predictions. A review of the programme was considered desirable to make up 'deficiencies in the requirements of the existing clearance programme during the next decade' and to roll it forward to 1991.[55]

The methods adopted to survey housing obsolescence as a guide to redevelopment potential and priorities were ambitious, involving studies of both housing conditions and the surrounding environment.[56] The information thus gathered on the pre-1919 stock was then combined in a penalty points framework of obsolescence factors.

In order to formulate alternative strategies a series of constraints and opportunities were identified. Factors which would encourage a high clearance rate included:

1 demographic considerations – a dip in demand for housing from new households was forecast in the late 1970s;

2 rising public expectations of housing quality associated with continuing increases in real incomes;
3 no overall shortage of land for the new housing needed for replacement; and
4 the need to enhance the image of Leeds by removing the drab environment of the older areas (the relationship between such action and the attraction of modern industry to the region had been recently stressed by the Economic Planning Council).

On the other hand, factors which were identified as leading to a more modest level of activity included the need to:

5 avoid undue physical disruption of existing communities;
6 ensure a continuing pool of cheap older housing, particularly privately rented;
7 avoid overstraining the administrative machinery for rehousing;
8 retain old housing of character; and
9 honour the past commitments of renewal policy, i.e. to recognize the extended life of fifteen to twenty years given to IGAs.

Strategy D then emerged from a consideration of several alternatives. It would continue the then current representation rate of 2300 p.a. till 1977, and then a lower rate of 1700 p.a. in 1977–87, leaving the scale of action in 1987–91 for determination later. The strategy was agreed by the Conservative council in 1972. Ravetz comments:

> The arguments for Strategy D were quite happily accepted by the majority of council members; no doubt largely because the report presented them in such a way to make this appear the only reasonable strategy to adopt. But over and above this, the strategy was presented and accepted as a means of regenerating and restructuring the old-fashioned and decaying parts of the city, improving life for their residents, and upgrading the image of Leeds, to bring it more into parity with the fortunate south.[57]

The assumptions of Strategy D were essentially those of the 1960s: comprehensive redevelopment was seen as necessary and this inevitably meant large-scale clearance. A lack of housing pressure at this time provided an opportunity for such action before new household formation increased in the late 1970s. While acknowledging the fact that only 7000 dwellings were statutorily unfit and not yet represented, the report confidently expected that either increased standards would be incorporated into housing legislation or the clearance powers of the Planning Acts would be used. Leeds could thus move from an era of slum clearance into an era of clearance determined by higher standards and expectations.

Aftermath

Strategy D added 17,000 houses to the clearance programme. Areas previously identified in the HRA Map would be represented up to 1977 and thereafter newly identified areas (including some 8000 houses in IGAs) would be affected. The outcry when the actual streets designated became known was considerable, orchestrated in part by the new found 'community politics' of the Liberal Party, who had won some inner city wards in the previous two years. When the Labour Party took office in 1972, it found itself inundated by pressure from community groups established to fight Strategy D. Areas were rephased back in the programme; in the next year the 1982–6 phase was scrapped altogether.

As before, the Burley Lodge Road area was at the centre of the controversy. In 1972 the northern half was included in the 1977–81 phase of clearance. Uproar followed, and residents besieged the information centre set up to explain the decision.[58] A now well-established community association commissioned a study of future options for the area by planning consultants.[59] After stormy public meetings the decision was eventually revoked and the area again given extended life.

The Strategy D debacle left Leeds without a coherent strategy. The representation rate of houses for clearance had fallen to 850 by 1974. Furthermore, at a time when the rest of the country was taking up opportunities for GIA action, Leeds was slow to respond. Although the *Older Housing in Leeds* report of 1972 had identified several areas of terrace housing for possible GIA action, only two inter-war council estates were actually declared and schemes implemented. Improvement was now the major component of renewal activity. But a dramatic rise in grants depended little on local initiatives, rather it had been stimulated by the temporary provision of 75 per cent grants in assisted areas.

Gradual renewal

Local government reorganization and the Housing Act, 1974 resulted in a revised strategy, which reformed the clearance programme and established a second area improvement programme. Implementation was affected by both local decisions and government cuts, while the assumptions of the strategy are still contested.

Local government reorganization and a housing strategy

The reorganization of local government boundaries and functions in 1974 resulted in the establishment of a metropolitan district corresponding very closely to the local housing and labour market, the Leeds city–region. Surrounding towns and commuter settlements such as Morley, Pudsey, Garforth, Horsforth, Rothwell and Wetherby were all included in the new district which has a total population of about 735,000, compared with just over 500,000 in Leeds CB. The new authority now managed some 93,000 council houses.

In the period 1971–4 housing pressure had increased significantly. One reflection of this was the housing waiting list which by 1974 had reached 28,000. Council housebuilding had dropped dramatically and private building, which had been dominant in the commuter areas, was now in the doldrums. The new authority inherited a clearance programme consisting of the remains of Strategy D plus some small areas in Morley, Pudsey and Rothwell. Of the eleven GIAs inherited, nine were in the new areas. In most of these substantial housing improvement had already been completed during the 75 per cent grant period, but complex environmental problems remained. They had often been declared just before reorganization.

The new district's review of housing policies concentrated on housebuilding (public and private), improvement and clearance up to 1981.[60] It evaluated evidence on overall housing need and resource availability and set policy options within the context of changing national legislation and guidelines. This housing strategy and subsequent more detailed work are the basis of current renewal policies, though the context for their implementation has been altered by local political decisions and cuts in expenditure by central government.

The recommendations eventually agreed involved a redirection of emphasis from clearance to area improvement in the light of changes in the overall housing situation, reactions to Strategy D and central government policy. A six-year clearance programme was adopted, to be 'rolled forward' each year. It comprised 1250 dwellings for initiation each year.[61] Discretionary powers were then used to reduce the 'minimum life' of dwellings eligible for intermediate grants to six years and for improvement grants to ten years. 13,700 dwellings were included in investigation areas for area improvement and the intention was to declare four HAAs and four GIAs p.a. At the same time there would be phased increases in the council housebuilding programme which would then average 2000 p.a.

Clearance and local rehousing

As well as reviewing the content of the clearance programme, the housing strategy also recommended a review of the process. There were two innovations: improved publicity and a system of local rehousing opportunities backed up by pre-allocation schemes.

The study of clearance administration discussed in Chapter 2 had concluded that Leeds' decentralized housing management system and emphasis on professional training aided individualized attention for families rehoused.[62] However, it also found that residents in clearance areas did not understand earlier steps involved in the process. Measures were now taken to remedy this situation. A revised pattern of publicity was adopted, the most important change being the involvement of housing visitors at representation to explain the sequence and timing of events, rights of objection and rehousing opportunities. These visits were combined with the distribution of short explanatory booklets.[63]

A more significant refinement was the introduction of a system of local rehousing. The basis of the new approach was that 'the separate elements of the redevelopment process should be integrated more closely by jointly programming, for a longer term than hitherto possible, the six-year clearance programme and the related part of the building programme'.[64] Dates of representation and new building starts were related so that forecast rehousing needs could be matched with local new building schemes. Although local rehousing opportunities could not be provided in every area, an attempt was made to maximize these by splitting some larger areas into phases and by inserting some new schemes into the building programme. Figure 25 illustrates the type of programming adopted. The approach involved continuous monitoring to identify 'slippages' while the housing mix of linked new schemes was to be influenced by information collected during visits at representation.

The corollary of this policy in housing management terms was the introduction of pre-allocation. The first scheme was the Rocheford estate in Hunslet, where families from the immediately adjacent clearance area were rehoused. Hunslet as a whole exhibits the classic cycle of nineteenth century industrial expansion and housebuilding for the new working class,[65] followed by industrial decline and the dispersal of the community through clearance and redevelopment. Lack of local rehousing, destruction of facilities without speedy replacement and vacant land accompanied the clearance drive of the 1950s and 1960s.[66] This later approach of providing local rehousing opportunities was, in part a reaction to criticism of this process. On the Rocheford estate allocation of new houses took place a year before they were completed, thus reducing uncertainty among clearance area residents. 'Swops' were possible at the local temporary office and limited involvement in the design of the new estate was also encouraged. Overall the experiment was welcomed[67] and it was followed by further schemes.

Area improvement

There was less local innovation in the content or implementation of the second area improvement programme, which in many ways was a development of previous IGA and Conversion Area policies.[68]

By the end of 1979 eleven HAAs containing 2600 houses had been declared (see Table 8). They were aimed at two very different problems. First, areas of Type III back-to-backs and small through terrace houses lacking basic amenities occupied by unfurnished tenants and owner-occupiers. Second, areas where multi-occupied villas house furnished tenants sharing amenities. The pattern is complicated by local variations such as Asian owner-occupation or increasing numbers of single young people.[69] Seven further

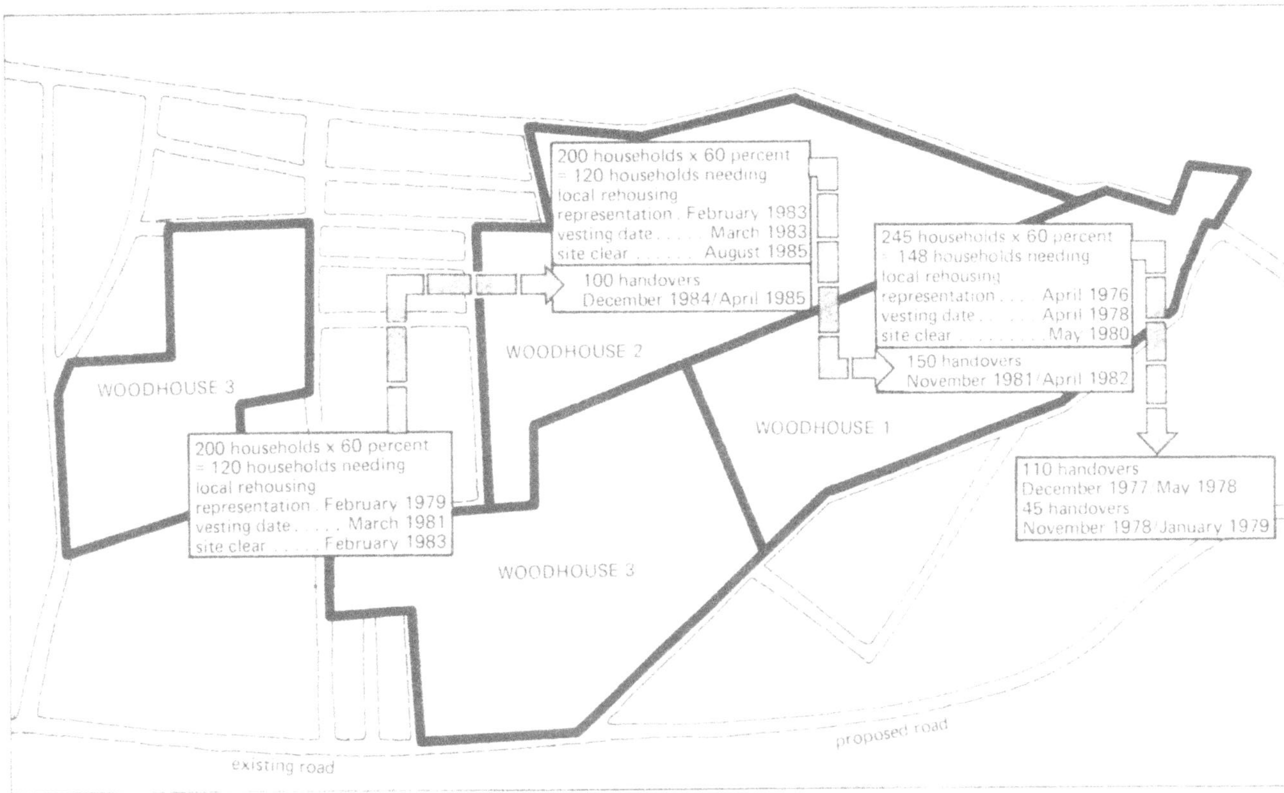

Figure 25 *Leeds: local rehousing*

Source: Adapted from Leeds City Council Clearance and Local Rehousing Programme (1975)

GIAs containing some 1800 houses had also been declared in areas with a lower proportion of private rental. These areas had more scope for environmental improvement which Leeds had never seriously attempted before.

Unlike many other authorities, the council established no special multidisciplinary teams or local offices to implement this programme. Instead, it was intended that the activities of the several departments involved would be directed by a co-ordinator in the housing department leading a small 'core team'.

A major new dimension was the involvement of housing associations. They had almost completely confined themselves to new building prior to 1975, as the council was itself active in supporting its improvement programme by purchasing and improving older houses.[70] However, the availability of extra resources from the Housing Corporation and a disinclination to pursue widespread municipalization by the ruling Conservative Party encouraged housing association involvement. By 1979 they were heavily involved in HAAs. For example, Leeds Federated Housing Association had purchased and improved half the houses in the first HAA, the Arthingtons, and a zoning arrangement was in operation for several associations to buy and improve houses at a rate of about 300 p.a.

Resources and management

Implementation of this renewal strategy in the period 1975–9 was undertaken in the context of changed local political control from Labour to Conservative and increasing central government cuts in relevant spending programmes. Although it is difficult to disentangle the relative significance of these two factors, their combined result was a slump in investment.[71]

Locally, the change of control was directly responsible for the promotion of council house sales.[72] It also stimulated a large programme of selling building land to private developers in a situation of overall land shortage.[73] Cuts in the council housebuilding programme followed a housing waiting list revision in 1976, which reduced the list from 27,000 to 18,000.[74] This, in turn, influenced a reduction in the representation programme to about 500 houses p.a. but vacant sites evidenced the problems of implementing local rehousing schemes from existing clearance areas. Some inner city sites were sold to private developers.

In this period the national resource situation examined in Chapter 4 seriously undermined the improvement programme. The impact of inflation and declining real incomes, combined with the end of a general availability of 75 per cent grants, caused a drastic fall in private improvement.[75] Restrictions on the acquisition of houses and Section 105 controls reduced the council's own improvement activity.[76] HIP allocations of £31m for 1978–9 and £33m for 1979–80 failed to reflect the extent of local needs.

Cuts in the council mortgage allocation probably had the most disastrous effect on confidence in older housing areas and best illustrate the problems caused by arbitrary quotas. To assist the new area improvement programme and to maintain previous investment in IGAs, Leeds restricted its mortgage scheme to older, cheaper houses on which building societies had hitherto refused to advance loans.[77] But in 1976 a succession of cuts by central government began. At a time when the council's mortgage allocation was disappearing in a few hours,[78] there was mounting evidence that building societies refused to lend in certain older housing areas (called 'blue zones' in Leeds)[79] and the support scheme was demonstrably not 'filling the gap' as claimed by central government. Building societies still refused to lend on most of the remaining back-to-backs, in areas with substantial Asian ownership, or where some houses are in multi-occupation.[80] Even after maximum use of *virement* within HIP allocations demand for council mortgages exceeded supply.

Other problems can be more clearly laid at the council's own door. The second area improvement programme had not been matched by any commitment to adequate staffing levels and responsibilities were still split between several departments, notably Housing and Environmental Health. Compulsory action was virtually non-existent with only a handful of properties compulsory purchased despite policy decisions to proceed with CPOs on unimproved privately rented properties within two years of declaration. Multiple occupation was increasing with little effective enforcement action by the council.

The programme had only a marginal impact on older housing problems by the end of 1979. First, within declared areas private improvement has been minimal – only 220 private grants had been completed in HAAs. Although housing associations had made a significant impact, their acquisitions were slowing down. In GIAs environmental work was still being completed in those areas declared before reorganization. Second, the programme itself was limited and the number of declarations fell well behind those agreed in the 1975 strategy.

An alternative way?

At the same time the policies themselves were under challenge. Their rationale, even with the substantial reduction in the rate of clearance over recent years, was basically the same as that adopted in the 1950s and 1960s. Clearance was seen as the most appropriate solution for the majority of the remaining Type II back-to-backs, while improvement should be concentrated on Type III back-to-backs, through terraces and areas of unsatisfactory multi-occupation. It was still essentially a tandem approach. The justification for policies operated on such an area basis is that development in the nineteenth century was generally on a comprehensive scale. Older housing is therefore usually differentiated in type, age and condition by area rather than individually or in small pockets.

In continuing with clearance of the worst Type II back-to-backs the local authority had been supported by the DoE inspectorate when the alternative of improvement had been raised at inquiries. One of their more forceful conclusions was:

No doubt it would be a great deal cheaper to improve these houses than to redevelop with new ones; but this is an over-simplification as there can be no comparison between new houses built to contemporary standards and developed at a proper density with space and air around them and with attention to external amenity, and the deplorable substandard overcrowded back-to-back houses that would remain even after improvement.[81]

The confusing provisions of Section 5 of the Housing Act, 1957 relating to back-to-backs also supported a continuing policy of replacement.[82]

However, the clearance component of this tandem approach was still attacked. Some areas which have substantial numbers of houses in which basic amenities were installed with the aid of grants were now in the clearance programme. The logic of the tandem approach meant that more should be introduced. Opposition came from owner-occupiers, but one problem which the compensation laws create is the site value rule for unfit houses owned by private landlords. Not surprisingly, in cases of more recent improvement landlords were concerned about the loss of this investment should their houses be later classified as unfit.[83]

A more substantial challenge was mounted in the late 1970s by a loose grouping of neighbourhood organizations, academics and the local Civic Trust. The group argued that Leeds' policies were not in tune with the ideas and practices suggested in post-1974 Act circulars. It criticized the distance involved in some local rehousing proposals; 'planning blight' during phased redevelopment; loss of housing stock suitable for smaller households, including students; and lack of public involvement in decisions about the principle of clearance.[84]

In the view of these critics, resources and organization were secondary issues, the principal change required was in the perception of the problem. The key definition which should be changed was that of the inherently unsatisfactory back-to-back, some 20,000 of which remain:

In any discussion on slum clearance the back-to-back has been the object of much criticism. Its very existence has been used as a reason for clearance, often in emotional and unreal terms. Its defence has been apologetic, with schemes put forward to convert it into conventional housing. It must be emphasized that back-to-backs were designed and built as a complete housing unit, with large living room and small kitchen, very well suited to the present day tendency of small adult families, a group the present system is just not providing for. Structurally they compare well with traditional houses and are easily maintained. They are used by older households; by young married couples as a first home; as a stepping stone, if buying, to a larger home as the income grows and by the many non-family households which are a real development of modern society. They are compact, low-cost, easily run accommodation for which the demand is great.[85]

The alternative solution advanced was the removal of blight through ending any firm clearance programme; developing a system of neighbourhood-based working and participation; and implementing cellular renewal.[86]

The future influence of these arguments is uncertain. At a 1977 clearance inquiry the council's case for the demolition of 350 (mainly Type II back-to-back) houses was contrasted with a local community group's arguments for an HAA and limited cellular renewal. The result was the confirmation of the CPO, but with some changes of classification from 'unfit' to 'fit'.[87] Paradoxically, a much less controversial CPO for part of the first IGA (judged to have reached the end of its extended life) was rejected.[88]

Pressure from critics then resulted in the investigation of the potential of an alternative approach in Woodhouse – an area of 700 older houses identified in the clearance programme for phased redevelopment (see Figure 25), Five options were evaluated:

1 demolish and rebuild – phased redevelopment with local rehousing;
2 improve as a GIA or HAA;
3 short-life retention with repairs;
4 demolish some houses to provide better external standards and convert back-to-backs to through terraces or flats;
5 gradual renewal – a complex and small-scale combination of 1–5.[89]

The study emphasized the implications that option 5 would have for the overall rate of replacement of the city's older housing stock and for its management of renewal: it raises '. . . the need for co-ordinated management of widespread change on a continuous basis which is quite unlike the area-programmed departmentally-based approach to renewal currently operated'.[90] The outcome in this area was the continuation of phased redevelopment – a decision influenced by ground stability problems and the fact that many residents' experience of years of blight meant that the non-definitive nature of gradual renewal held little appeal. Nevertheless, debate about the general issues raised continued;[91] continuing confusion at a national level about the future direction of urban renewal is sure to be reflected by dissent from the city council's current policies. A lack of innovation in the management of urban renewal (with the exception of clearance rehousing) makes the council vulnerable to criticisms of a failure to secure local involvement.

The inner city

The present position in Leeds clearly illustrates some of the problems and limitations of current inner city policy. Hitherto, causes of decline have not been the same focus of attention as in those cities which were the setting for 'urban experiments' and strategic planning studies in the early 1970s. Within the framework of national policy Leeds has been designated a Programme Authority, with resource implications which fail to recognize the seriousness of its problems.

Problems

City-wide statistics present Leeds in a comparatively favourable light, but this is because local government reorganization meant that several relatively prosperous areas were absorbed. The inner areas of Leeds present basically the same problems as are found in other large cities.

In some respects post-war strategic planning policies were less significant in explaining the progress of urban renewal in Leeds than in many other authorities. In the 1950s and 1960s there was the same emphasis on comprehensive redevelopment and transportation policies. However, limited population growth, combined with the availability of ample building land within the city's boundaries, meant that long-distance dispersal was not a factor affecting the progress of clearance. Overspill from clearance areas and other council housebuilding requirements were catered for by the development of suburban estates within the city, like Seacroft, rather than in new towns or town development schemes. This planned movement of population was accompanied by voluntary migration to private housing estates in the suburbs and surrounding towns, such as Garforth. Decentralization of the city's population was selective, leaving inner areas with disproportionate numbers of the elderly, the unskilled, and recent immigrants.

Although some decentralization of employment took place, a general decline in the city's economic base, and resultant job loss, have more significant implications for the inner city: 37,000 manufacturing jobs disappeared between 1951 and 1973.[92] The city was losing jobs at a faster rate than the national average. The clothing industry of East Leeds is in rapid decline and the engineering industry is far from healthy.[93] With the promotion of Leeds as a regional centre, nearly as many new jobs were created in the service sector in those years, but these were largely taken up by commuters. Moreover, the boom in office development and local government employment has ended. By 1978 unemployment rates in the inner city had reached 10 per cent and in the worst parts was over 15 per cent.[94]

Inner Leeds has been subjected to considerable planning blight, caused mainly by the development of the primary road network.[95] During the 1960s it was anticipated that Leeds would become the 'motorway city of the 1970s', a vision prompted by the emergence of its strategic position in the national motorway network. The M1 and M621 have penetrated almost to the heart of the city and the inner ring road has been partially constructed. However, many other major road proposals were still at the drawing board stage when the programme lost its impetus, primarily because of the harsh reality of resource constraints. Access to south Leeds was improved, only to encourage warehousing rather than new industry, and the unbuilt sections of the network have had a significant blighting effect in many older industrial and residential areas, such as Richmond Hill.

Planning and the Urban Programme

Two planning exercises are influencing the development of policy for Leeds' inner city – the West Yorkshire County Structure Plan and the city's local plans programme. The overall strategy set out in the structure plan is based on three principles: the efficient use of resources; priority to the improvement of the local economy; and assistance to deprived groups.[96] The preparation of this strategy focussed attention on the competing needs of the smaller urban settlements of West Yorkshire and its inner city areas. In particular, on the Pennine fringe of the county job and population losses are severe. Leeds is set within a region with widespread problems of urban decline, making the channelling of resources to its inner city problematic. Not surprisingly, the plan proposed that investment be focussed on both types of area.[97] An ambitious local plans programme was started by the city council while this structure plan was being prepared, but, with a realization of the lack of influence of the local plans process over key spending programmes, this was amended. The Chapeltown local plan provided a painful lesson of the limitations of land-use planning when faced with major problems of deprivation.[98] After production of the structure plan formal plans were concentrated on those outer areas identified for expansion.

In the meantime, informal plans were geared to the new framework of the Government's inner city policy. Despite representations, Leeds failed to secure Partnership status in 1977, and was designated a Programme Authority.[99] The city's first Inner Area Programme was prepared by a group of officers reporting to the Policy and Finance Committee. Leeds was allocated £2m in 1979–80 (effectively £1.5m).[100] As far as main programme resources were concerned, the working party attempted to establish the existing geographical distribution of expenditure as the basis for its possible redirection, and to strengthen future programme bids to central government. The problems of a priority area approach to urban deprivation are reflected in the fact that the council included within the boundaries of its 'inner city' substantial inter-war suburban council estates, on the very reasonable grounds that the problems of social deprivation and unemployment are at least as severe as in the older neighbourhoods (see Figure 26).

In this first phase public involvement was inevitably limited but somewhat controversial. The council adopted the approach of working with 'umbrella' organizations; the Leeds Council of Voluntary Service and the Community Relations Council. However, the first explanatory publication about the programme met with a hostile reception from local community workers.[101] By the second phase there was strengthened member input through a special subcommittee and more extensive consultation with voluntary organizations.

The city adopted an area-by-area approach to implementation, whereby resources at any one time are concentrated in a specific part of the inner city.

Figure 26 ***Leeds: inner city – priority areas***

Source: Adapted from Leeds City Council *Second Urban Programme Report* (1979).

The first priority area to be selected was Woodhouse/Lower Meanwood Valley/Sheepscar and 75 per cent of the urban programme resources concentrated there. It was added to by further areas in Richmond Hill and Holbeck in the second submission.[102] Industrial development and employment-generating schemes were emphasized but probably the most interesting aspect of implementation is the comprehensive treatment given to untidy land. This flowed from the identification of problems in local plan appraisals and in 1978 a comprehensive survey of all underused and vacant land in the inner city was carried out. Work to landscape and tidy up such land has been funded under Operation Clean-Up, the extended criteria for Derelict Land Reclamation Grant and Urban Programme Funding.

Overall, despite providing the impetus for action on issues such as vacant land and funding for some innovatory projects, the resources allocated to a Programme Authority are considerably less than those going to a Partnership. More important, urban programme funding cannot compensate for limited spending on main programmes. During the late 1970s reductions in capital budgets, e.g. HIPs, were applied in the context of local cuts in spending – by 1979 Leeds had the lowest rates devised of any large city and consequently the lowest expenditure per head.[103] The overall result was a decline in services.

Conclusions

This analysis demonstrates the reciprocal but unequal relationship between central and local government. Changing national perspectives and policies have been the most significant influence on the development of urban renewal in Leeds. Its main phases – the growth of council housing and the clearance drive of the 1930s; the commitment to comprehensive redevelopment in the 1950s and 1960s; and the move towards gradual renewal in the 1970s – derive essentially from the local application of national policies.

Yet in both the nature of the problem faced and the emphasis given to particular policies, local variations have been important. Three influences are central to an understanding of this variation: the particular built environment of back-to-backs created in the nineteenth century; a stable economy and lack of housing pressure which enabled a concentration on the renewal of existing housing; and local politics and personalities. In two key phases Leeds led in its application of national policy. First, its clearance drive in the 1930s was the most vigorous of any city. Second, it implemented tandem policies of clearance and improvement in the 1950s and 1960s when other cities were devoting all their attention to comprehensive redevelopment. The latter example influenced national policies and thus altered the context for subsequent intervention.

The city's response to its nineteenth century built environment has been that obsolescence is not a finite problem. Once the Type I back-to-backs were identified as only suitable for clearance, a continuing process of improvement and clearance was necessary for the remainder. Yet, the pursuit of a complementary improvement policy raised further issues. On the one hand, back-to-backs were regarded as inherently unsatisfactory and improvement could only be a temporary expedient. On the other hand, the very success of housing improvement reinforced the virtues of older housing areas. Two competing interpretations of older housing were developed. One emphasized the substandard nature of the houses and their environment and the need for eventual replacement. The other stressed the importance of cheap housing, and the need to retain settled communities of people living in their 'little palaces'. With hindsight the attempt of Strategy D to extend comprehensive redevelopment had no chance of success in the changed housing situation of the 1970s. The growth of low-income owner-occupation, a rising housing waiting list, and the promotion of improvement as an alternative nationally all ensured strong opposition.

The 1970s have seen a much reduced clearance programme and a second phase of area improvement. But, despite significant refinements to the clearance process, its assumptions are still under attack. Notwithstanding the new contribution of housing associations, this area improvement programme is not making any fundamental inroads into poor housing and environmental conditions. The Blue Zone Map has replaced the Red Ruin Map and continuous investment in older areas is not occurring at a rate necessary to arrest decay. Conversion areas were a predecent for HAAs but the wider social problems of Chapeltown as a 'municipalized stress area' remain. Of 64,000 remaining pre-1919 houses only some 6000 lack one or more basic amenities, but many of the others improved since the mid-1950s are now in need of substantial investment in reimprovement or clearance: they are often set in drab environments.

Despite a past record of considerable improvement to modest standards and widespread municipalization, a daunting challenge is presented by continuing decay. At the same time the momentum of intervention has been lost. Clearance and improvement have been viewed as separate programmes and there has been little attempt to establish an effective organization for area renewal. The incoming Labour council of 1980 found its HIP bid of £63m yielded an allocation of only £25m for 1981–2. In the medium term its review of housing strategy and, perhaps more important, of departmental organization may generate changes. Initiatives in economic renewal and in supporting voluntary groups have been launched and a supplementary rate levied. However, the problems of economic decline are beginning to assume a greater significance and expose the inadequacies of both the Government's inner city policy and a local emphasis on low expenditure and reduced services in the 1970s. 'Leeds leads from behind'[104] is a sad description of urban renewal in the city as it entered the 1980s.

9 Unequal cities in an unequal society

Variations in the quality of the built environment are a manifestation of long-established and persistent inequality which stems from the economic organization of society. Market forces tend to concentrate those on irregular or low incomes in poor-quality, mainly older, areas and urban renewal policies have been developed in an attempt to alleviate the resultant conditions. An analysis of the national and local dimensions of urban renewal has demonstrated the complexity of both the problems faced and the factors influencing intervention. This final chapter draws together key themes, assesses trends and discusses prospects for the 1980s.

A historical overview identifies the key characteristics of a century of state-sponsored urban renewal, providing a basis for defining contemporary problems and the challenges to be met if more effective policies are to be devised. Against this the policy response of the Conservative Government is described and its likely impact assessed. The prospects for the early 1980s are bleak and it will be important to sustain the arguments for urban renewal policies which contribute more to the reduction of inequality. The book concludes by outlining some practical reforms while recognizing the very real constraints that stand in the way of significant achievement.

Historical perspective

A historical perspective shows how ideas are translated into policy under specific economic and political conditions, sometimes with consequences unintended by their originators, with yesterday's solutions becoming part of today's problems. The main phases of urban renewal have each seen the onset of disillusion and a debate about the consequences of established orthodoxies; then new legislation, implementation and reappraisal. Yet contemporary discussion about private versus public solutions, redevelopment versus improvement, the relative roles of central and local government, the validity of area-based policies and the involvement of residents, echoes the arguments of previous generations.

Fluctuating state intervention

The general historical trend has been towards greater state involvement, but national policy has fluctuated as an increased level of intervention has been succeeded by a period of withdrawal, followed by a resurgence of activity in the face of accentuated problems.

The expansionary phase of industrial capitalism transformed Britain into an urban nation, but did not provide adequate housing for the new working-class. The conditions created set the scene for sanitary reform measures and, after it became apparent that the private sector found it unprofitable to build mass housing, led to the introduction of council housebuilding.

Throughout the first three decades of this century the prevailing view was that it was sufficient to encourage landlords to recondition their property to minimum standards.[1] During the 1920s and the early 1930s, the economic crisis and resultant public expenditure cuts limited clearance to the demolition of the very worst property. It was argued that this strategy would gradually improve conditions as displaced slum dwellers filtered into the privately rented property vacated by emigrants to the expanding suburbs. It inevitably failed and the complacency of policy makers was eroded by the organized political pressure of the working-class and social reformers who chronicled the resultant human misery. The easing of economic conditions from 1933 onwards permitted more substantial intervention.

In 1930 Arthur Greenwood introduced an Act which was to stimulate the first real drive against the slums. One commentator at the time wrote: 'The solution to the problem of the slum is in sight. The Housing Act of 1930 has brought it perceptibly nearer. Under it bad houses are regarded in the same light as bad food, something to be discovered and destroyed'.[2] In 1969 Anthony Greenwood, his son, introduced another Act which heralded an equally significant change. It was argued that both clearance and improvement would be accelerated, but a later official summary of urban renewal rationalized what eventually transpired, when it claimed that the 1969 Act 'marked a deliberate shift of emphasis from redevelopment towards improvement, especially on an area basis'.[3]

Between the two Acts, with the enforced interruption of war, there was continuity of direction. Goals which had once seemed hopelessly idealistic became accepted as obvious, necessary and feasible: 'What the private sector had constructed in the industrial revolution of the 19th century the state had now to rebuild in the 20th'.[4] Slum clearance was succeeded by comprehensive redevelopment and successive ministers saw this as a finite task. But each time the end was sighted a further survey of unfit houses revealed the reality of continuing obsolescence and the mirage-like quality of ministerial visions.

Although comprehensive redevelopment meant massive intervention, the state did not invade profitable areas of house production. The money for council housebuilding was borrowed from private capital and the houses were mainly built by private firms. Private housebuilding continued, but now for owner-occupation. Despite controversy about compulsion, clearance was increasingly seen as the euthanasia of worn-out houses in the already dying private rented sector. Until the move by the Labour Party to the middle ground in the 1960s, the ebb and flow of political debate was between those who saw council housing meeting general needs and those who saw it as a residual activity, competing philosophies which were part of a wider debate about the welfare state.

The shift to improvement was a means of minimizing public investment in twilight area renewal as post-war prosperity came to an end, and also a reflection of both the state-encouraged growth of owner-occupation in older housing areas and disenchantment with the impact of comprehensive redevelopment. When improvement was 'the name of the game' in the early 1970s the state's role was seen as the stimulation of voluntary private improvement: it would be party to an investment partnership with owners. In terms of numbers of properties improved the policy was remarkably successful. However, the problems of housing stress areas prompted more direct intervention. There was a reawakening of interest in social ownership and in diverting effort towards areas of most need. But the prospects of a public sector led programme were short lived as expenditure cuts emasculated local renewal strategies. The subsequent reduction of activity re-emphasized the crucial role of the state in financing urban renewal. Experience in Birmingham where, within seven years, the Urban Renewal Programme moved from being envisaged as implementing minor environmental works and processing grant applications to assuming responsibility for the whole fabric of residential areas, illustrates the necessity for extensive intervention to achieve the progress promised.

In the nineteenth century one school of thought held that sanitary reform measures could create a healthy workforce which would then be able to afford better housing provided by the private market. This could not and did not happen, and it was eventually recognized that the creation of a large public sector was necessary to improve working-class housing conditions. However, urban renewal policies have recently returned to this theme of raising effective demand, albeit in a modified form. The central problem of the inner city is now held to be its rapidly declining economic base. Successful implementation of gradual renewal and the amelioration of social deprivation is seen as dependent on resolving the employment problems of the inner city poor. Hence the emergence of comprehensive urban renewal, with an emphasis on local economic measures. But, in essence, the inner cities policy of 1977 was an across the board extension of the investment partnership of housing improvement, and the lesson of history is that such a partnership is destined to fail in the face of much stronger forces ensuring economic decline.

Why is it that a century of intervention to improve the living conditions of a large proportion of the population has fallen short of creating socially just cities? To answer this question demands some consideration of the origins of social policies and an understanding of the role of the state in our society.

Conventionally, analyses of social policies present their development as a natural progression. Problems are brought to light by research and practical experience and new solutions devised in a rational manner by men of goodwill. This view promotes the role of the state as neutral, pursuing the common interest, occasionally prodded by reformers but essentially responding to identified needs. Any inadequacy in response is explained in terms of bureaucratic inefficiency and insensitivity, or occasionally by the immediate pressing demands of the national economy, which when met will allow the resumption of effort on welfare activities.

Marxist analyses would reject such a view, emphasizing instead the complex relationship between the role of the state and the interests of capital. While there are considerable theoretical disagreements about the precise relationship, and in particular about the role of the bureaucracy, they would point to the contradictory roles of the welfare state whose civilizing effect on the economic system simultaneously represents advances by the organized working-class, and a functional response by capitalism to ensure both the reproduction of a healthy and competent labour force and the legitimation of existing grossly unequal class relationships.[5] The political economy of the welfare state is complex but should be viewed within the dynamics of the capitalist state. This approach has been developed as a new urban theory by sociologists such as Castells, who have focussed on patterns of 'collective consumption' of goods and services like housing and schools which provide the back-up to centralized production and are directly or indirectly subsidized by the state.[6]

Within this perspective 'urban problems' are not seen as stemming from inadequacies in the processes of resource allocation by urban managers, but as rooted in the processes of production which determine the scale of the resources available and mechanisms for redistribution. The role of the state is not neutral but it is contradictory. Government policies aid the processes of restructuring production in the face of changing economic conditions in the capitalist world, while at the same time intervening to ameliorate the consequences of these changes without threatening the established economic order.

Such a perspective, in general terms, sheds light on the structural limitations of state-sponsored urban renewal. Inequalities in housing remain because intervention on the scale necessary to substantially reduce them is not possible without fundamental social and economic changes to end the domination of the market processes which generate and sustain inequality. Hence the role of the state has resulted in a 'partitioning' of housing renewal into public redevelopment and predominantly private rehabilitation.[7] The latter has re-emerged as individual home ownership has increased and the economic crisis has reduced the scale of public resources available. Government policy has increasingly relied on stimulating effective demand for rehabilitation and has withdrawn from municipalization. Similarly, urban decay can be seen as a function of changes in the way industrial production is organized in an advanced capitalist society, changes which are assisted by government policies. Attempts to stem inner area economic decline are confined within the limits set by the need to maintain profitability, and as such can only have a marginal impact.

Local initiative

An important dimension of the role of the state is the question of central direction or local autonomy. The chief concern of many local powerholders in the last century was to hold down the rates, press for thrift in the town hall and oppose grandiose schemes for reform. But, as local government was given responsibility for implementing housing renewal, vigorous programmes frequently became a matter for civic pride and progress has been the aggregate of local authorities' programmes.

How much local initiative is possible? For Muchnick the formulation of policy, the pattern of implementation and the possibilities for reform in Liverpool of the 1960s were essentially local matters. 'Admittedly, central advisory opinions, financial incentives and regulatory prohibitions are strong influences; however, they are not the ultimate determinants of the municipal approach'.[8] In contrast, and more convincingly, a more recent study of Birmingham by Lambert and his colleagues identified 'the role of local government as interpreter and agent of central power, not as creative initiator of autonomous policies and practices'.[9]

Local authorities are the recipients of central dictates which closely determine their policies: they are circumscribed by legislation and increasing dependence on central finance. The case studies of Birmingham and Leeds demonstrate overarching central government control. This is exemplified by the comparable collapse of council housebuilding and clearance programmes in both cities in the 1970s and the effect of cuts on improvement programmes. In the management of capital expenditure (through HIPs, TPPs, IAPs, etc.) the procedure of local bids theoretically allows more discretion, but always within centrally prescribed limits.

Nevertheless, the case studies also highlight variations in the local articulation of policies during the main phases of urban renewal. The slum clearance programme in Leeds during the 1930s and the wholesale municipalization of large tracts of Birmingham's slums in the late 1940s are cases in point. Birmingham's current enveloping and block schemes illustrate the continuing scope for local initiative. The inherited built environment and subsequent development of the local economy, together with the impact of local politics and administration, have been influential in variations between the two cities at different points in time. Moreover, initiatives developed in a particular local context have often paved the way for changes in national policy. This was the case with deferred demolition in Birmingham in the 1950s, area improvement in Leeds in the 1960s and economic renewal initiatives in Rochdale in the 1970s. But such initiatives are only embodied in national policy when they are consistent with centrally determined directions of change.

Finally, this limited autonomy is important because local authorities have significant discretion regarding the mechanics of the renewal process. There are many nuances of style and emphasis in those aspects of implementation which are less closely related to economic factors than the overall direction and progress of local strategies. While the parameters of action are determined centrally, the emphasis given to comprehensive area-based action, the standards adopted for housing improvement and the management of redevelopment are examples of important issues subject to local discretion. Moreover, the competence and commitment of both local politicians and officers can make a significant difference to results on the ground. The sensitivity of housing allocation practice, the quality of assistance to owners negotiating the labyrinth of improvement grants, and the care with which environmental works are devised and implemented are not the key determinants of success or failure, but they are susceptible to local decision making and do matter to residents.

Area-based policies

A prominent feature of urban renewal is action in defined geographical areas. Last century the description of 'black-spots' was often the starting point of social reformers. The earliest legislation was concerned with both individual unfit houses and groupings of them but 1930s clearance and post-war comprehensive redevelopment reinforced the area dimension. An initial focus on the improvement of individual houses has been complemented by housing and environmental improvement on an area basis. Most recently, development of comprehensive inner area policies has involved a more sophisticated classification of 'black-spots', with priority areas defined by computer analyses of urban deprivation – the mechanized equivalent of the campaigning work of Booth and Rowntree. The policy response to recognition of the causes of decay has extended the area approach into economic renewal.

This emphasis on priority areas has long been the subject of criticism. A major stimulus for urban renewal has been concern about the dangers of concentrated problems to the established social order. The case for sanitary reforms was recognized in the context of both epidemic disease spreading from slums and the 'stirrings of the mob'. More recently, an underlying concern in the development of inner city programmes is the threat to social stability posed by concentrated unemployment and, in some areas, its racial dimension. However, a response which carries the implication that the causes of problems lie within such areas can be diversionary. Uneven economic development and inequality of incomes are not seriously challenged by policies dealing with some of their symptoms in discrete areas. A never-ending catalogue of abbreviations – CDA, GIA, HAA, CDP, IAS, IAP – has replaced the earlier label of slums. This has achieved little save the proliferation of bureaucracies with vested interests in devising such programmes, but 'it is evidently functional to preserve the ideology of area-based troubles as a cheap and convenient way of avoiding unpleasant alternatives'.[10]

Such arguments have much force but run the risk of throwing the baby out with the bathwater. It is in those policies aimed at the physical fabric that the validity of geographical areas as a focus for intervention is most apparent. The original development of older housing areas concentrates the need for clearance in pockets of varying sizes, while the underlying justification of area improvement is that to encourage individual and institutional investment it is essential for whole areas to be systematically improved and confidence raised. The framework provided by realistic, programmed and resourced local planning is necessary if the infrastructure is to be renewed in a co-ordinated fashion and community facilities provided. Outside any areas defined there will always be, for instance, houses in multiple occupation or in poor repair which demand intervention but it can be forcefully argued that one of the problems of area-based renewal, particularly since improvement has been the major tool, has been that it has been too selective. More special areas should have been declared and action programmes of varying intensity progressed.

In other areas of social policy the justification for area-based intervention is more difficult: some policies are best served by universal provision and others more effectively aimed at specific deprived groups rather than areas, although others still necessarily have a geographical dimension when they involve locating a building such as a health centre. Overall, the criticism of area-based policies is more properly aimed at all policies geared solely to symptoms rather than causes. Area-based programmes are a necessary but not sufficient condition for effective urban renewal but such intervention is limited if it is not part of a wider package of reforms.

Community involvement

The extension of the area approach has been accompanied by the growing involvement of residents' organizations. Slogans such as 'planning with people, rather than for them' are nowadays frequently voiced from the platform at public meetings before they are expressed from the floor.

The case studies reveal a longer history of tension between city-wide policies and narrower interests than is often acknowledged. Much local debate has contrasted town hall concern about overall housing conditions with the more immediate preferences of residents in the localities affected. Opposition to the 1930s clearance drive produced an earlier version of the arguments and tactics more extensively used against comprehensive redevelopment in the early

1970s, notwithstanding the fact that leadership was previously more likely to be provided by aggrieved landlords and the local vicar than threatened owner-occupiers and the temporarily resident sociology graduate.

During the past decade community work has been established as a welfare state service, a development which received considerable stimulus from the urban experiments. Its emerging theory and practice have provided a fertile field for critical analysis and ideological debate about the state's response to urban problems. The rapid growth of community work can now be seen as the outcome of a changing relationship between two contradictory sets of forces: the development of a variety of self-help groups pressing for more resources for disadvantaged areas and increased residents' control; and the needs of the state to reduce resources for social programmes while being seen to respond to the emerging urban crisis.[11]

These analytical developments have led to a more sophisticated understanding of the role of residents' organizations in urban renewal. It was commonplace a few years ago to assume a causal relationship between residents' opposition and the abandonment of redevelopment proposals. It is now clear that the shift to improvement was primarily determined by national economic circumstances, and that residents' opposition served to legitimate decisions taken in response to more fundamental pressures. This awareness has, in part, been prompted by the subsequent misfortunes of the improvement programmes activists campaigned to establish.

In the wake of public expenditure cuts many grass roots organizations moved from attacking the welfare state to defending it and, as the economic causes of decline became apparent and community action became more involved in employment issues, increased efforts were made to forge links with the trade union movement.[12] The range and style of action has changed but the contradictions remain, nowhere more apparent than in IAPs. Nonetheless, continuing community involvement in urban renewal may help lay the ground for a more democratic and socially just process, by promoting a wider understanding of the mechanics of decision making, the dominant interests now being served and the constraints on reform.

Contemporary crisis

The officially received view of the problems to be tackled by urban renewal changed from impatience with delays in reaching the end of the slums in the 1960s to concern about the 'urban crisis' in the 1970s. By conventional housing standards much has been achieved but much remains to be done, and judged by relative standards achievement has been limited. Massive urban inequalities persist. The 'inner city problem' is a spatial manifestation of deeply rooted changes in the economy, yet the area approach is not accompanied by national policies which strike at the external causes of decline.

Housing needs and standards

The prospects of a crude housing surplus emerged in the late 1960s. In the past decade official statements have implied that with the end of post-war shortages and the clearance of the worst slums, major national problems have been succeeded by more manageable local difficulties. This is mystification. The case studies demonstrate local variations, but the sum of local needs remains a major national problem. An attempt to assess the scale of current problems and future needs must take account of the extent to which housing conditions have improved when judged against official standards, the validity of such conventional standards, the investment which has been necessary to achieve improved conditions and the adequacy of prevailing investment levels in relation to outstanding and future needs.

A century of urban renewal has transformed the housing conditions of the mass of the population. There is no longer an acute danger to public health from insanitary housing. The shoddily built, often overcrowded slums which characterized great swathes of the cities in the 1930s have mostly been cleared. In 1951 9.7m households (69 per cent) in England and Wales lived in overcrowded conditions or sharing a house, in unfit houses or houses lacking basic amenities. By 1976 the comparable figures for this backlog were 2.7m (15 per cent) of which 2m were in England.

However, a recent analysis using official statistics illustrates the extent to which these conventional indicators underestimate current need.[13] When allowance is made for factors such as a 'vacancy reserve' (necessary to permit moves) and second homes, a crude surplus of 540,000 dwellings becomes a crude shortage of 330,000. But as dwellings are often in the wrong place or at prices beyond the reach of needy families, the real issue is the sum of local shortages. The HIP returns showed 540,000 households lacking a home in 1978 (and a similar figure was forecast for 1983 – double the standard DoE projection). Similarly, conventional indicators ignore the emerging problem of disrepair: between 1971 and 1976 the number of fit houses with amenities, but requiring over £1170 of repairs at 1976 prices, increased from 393,000 to 992,000 in England alone, a rate of 120,000 p.a. which in part offset the significant reduction of unfit houses and those lacking amenities. Thus a more realistic assessment of the backlog in England is 3.6m (see Table 9).

The process of obsolescence is complex and forecasting is hazardous.[14] A house is not necessarily obsolete at, say seventy or a hundred years old – witness exquisitely maintained and expensive Tudor cottages and Chelsea mews. Physical obsolescence through both external weathering and internal wear, and functional obsolescence caused by changing requirements, can both be offset by investment. As investment prospects vary with ownership, the key issues affecting major tenures signpost challenges for the 1980s.

The private rented sector has borne the brunt of slum clearance, and improvement policies have been linked with a transfer of ownership from this

Table 9 *Housing needs and past performance (England only)*

(a)	*The 'backlog' of housing needs 1977 ('000s of households)*		
	Households in shortage		1.602
	Unsatisfactory dwellings		
	Households in unfit dwellings	0.570	
	Households in dwellings that are fit but lack basic amenities	0.700	
	Households in dwellings in serious disrepair but that are fit and have all amenities	1.110	
		2.380	2.380
			3.550
(b)	*Annual increases in housing requirements ('000s p.a.)*		
	Increase in households		140–165
	Dwellings becoming unfit		50–70
	Dwellings falling into disrepair		75–120
	Miscellaneous demolitions, etc.		15–25
	Total annual increase in housing requirements		280–380
(c)	*Past performance ('000s p.a.)*		
	1971–5 inclusive: average new build (all sectors)	271	
	average improvement (all sectors)	228	
	total per annum	499	499
	1976–9 inclusive: average new build (all sectors)	231	
	average improvement (all sectors)	122	
	total per annum	353	353

Source: B Crofton 'Hard Core Mythology' *Roof,* vol. 4, no. 2 (1979), pp. 51–4 – (c) updated to include 1979 figures.

sector into owner-occupation or social ownership. Conditions are still at their worst in privately rented housing. It accommodates some of the poorest families and is geographically concentrated, mainly in the inner cities and especially London. It is unlikely that any new measures would now engender either the ability or willingness on the part of most landlords to maintain or improve their property, since the relationship between costs and rents ensures that they can never both secure economic returns and assist low-income families (see Figure 27). The issues for the 1980s are the speed of transfer to different ownership, the nature of that ownership, and the implications of different alternatives for the extent of state intervention and the resources required.

In recent years both main political parties have vied with each other in promoting home ownership but the extension of owner-occupation to those

Example

Property in Berens Road, London, NW10. Four-storey terraced house for conversion to 4 × 2 persons (1 bedroom) units. Purchased vacant.

Housing Association	£	**Private Landlord**	£	
Capital cost		*Capital cost*		
Purchase price and legal fees	17,500	Purchase price and legal fees	17,500	
Conversion cost and fees	46,763	Conversion cost and fees	46,760	
Housing Association administration	955			
Estimated capitalized interest*	8,650	Estimated capitalized interest*	7,500*	
	£73,868		£71,760	
Less Housing Association grant	£70,471		*Pre-Housing Act, 1980*	*After Housing Act, 1980*
		Less maximum possible improvement grant	11,600	17,400
NET CAPITAL COST	£3,397		£60,160	£54,360
Annual cost		*Annual cost*		
Annual repayments	615	Annual repayments	10,890	9,841
Management and maintenance	1,297†	Management and maintenance	1,297†	1,297†
ANNUAL COST TO BE SERVICED FROM RENTS	£1,912	ANNUAL COST TO BE SERVICED FROM RENTS	£12,187	£11,138
i.e. 4 × 2 person flats at £9 and £9.50 per week each (1979 Fair Rent)		i.e. 4 × 2 person flats at £58.60 or £53.50 per week each		

* The finance is assumed to be borrowed at 18 per cent over 30 years, the current Housing Corporation terms for fair rent projects.
† Based on Department of the Environment permitted levels for Housing Associations.
* Assumes private landlord has less scheme scrutiny than a Housing Association, is therefore faster and so has less capitalized interest.

Figure 27 *Housing associations and private landlords: costs and rents*

Source: Adapted from a table presented by G. Randall at the 1980 Shelter conference

with low incomes has not been matched by any relevant subsidy system. On the contrary, low-income owner-occupiers in older properties often pay higher interest rates and face large bills for repairs while subsidies in the form of tax relief are related to income and size of mortgage. The precarious benefits of marginal owner-occupation in older areas and the long-term consequences of this 'solution' to the twilight areas of the 1960s is now emerging as a key policy issue. As the level of owner-occupation rises and the age of both properties and their owners increases, the continued absence of significant changes in the subsidy system will result in issues of social equity being joined by problems of mounting physical decay.[15]

In the public sector, issues of relative standards and obsolescence are crystallized in the 'difficult-to-let' phenomenon – new jargon referring to those estates which are most unpopular with existing tenants and where applicants are only prepared to accept tenancies if they have little choice. The type of housing found to be so unacceptable varies considerably, but almost all towns and cities have one or more areas labelled in this way. Inadequate design standards, unsuitable location, lack of facilities, poor management and maintenance, and the poverty and behaviour of some residents combine to stigmatize them. Local authorities estimated that some 230,000 dwellings were difficult-to-let in their 1980–1 HIP returns. To avoid expensive demolition (a last resort already implemented in a few cases) central and local government are currently sponsoring some improvement and management initiatives. Such estates, whether 1930s low-rise or 1960s high-rise, are the harbinger of public sector renewal problems for the 1980s, created by inadequate 'solutions' to the slums.[16]

Finally, problems are emerging in that part of the stock which has already been improved. An absence of external works, increasing obsolescence of amenities installed up to twenty years ago and inadequate continuing investment mean that the question of reimprovement or demolition of houses improved to basic standards, already raised in Leeds, may well become prominent. There is also growing concern about the quality of work in the 'full improvements' of the 1970s. In both the private and public sectors inadequate cost limits for improvement subsidies have played their part. Particularly when areas have been reprieved from clearance and then rehabilitation schemes pared to the bone, the results will be seen in expensive and disruptive programmes for items such as reroofing in the future. The problem is often compounded by shoddy workmanship and the use of poor-quality materials. This raises the long-standing issue of the capacity of the private building industry to sustain improvement programmes.

The annual average increase in housing requirements is 280–380,000 p.a. (see Table 9 for the components). The improvement in conditions in the early 1970s was the result of a much bigger combined housing programme than that of the late 1970s. As we enter the 1980s it is clear that the prevailing levels of investment are such that little or no progress is being made to reduce the quantitative housing shortage or to improve the quality of the existing stock. According to one estimate, the combined impact of clearance and renovation is a net improvement of a meagre 15,000 dwellings p.a.: if major disrepair is included in the definition of substandard housing, at present activity rates it will take nearly 200 years to eliminate the backlog.[17]

Thus even by the absolute standards of a sound structure and basic amenities, housing problems are far from residual. Moreover, these definitions are elements of a subsistence definition of poverty and ignore the issue of relative standards. For example, after thirty years effort to install bathrooms in older houses occupied by the poor, houses occupied by many of the more affluent have in the meantime been equipped with central heating, double glazing and double garages. The argument that minimum standards should be raised to reduce inequalities receives scant attention these days.

Accelerated investment to increase the size and improve the quality of the stock is essential. But it will also be important to maximize its impact where it is most needed. The improvement of housing conditions generally, and in the inner areas in particular, depends on effective policies to deal with current and emerging physical problems, coupled with changes in the public sector designed to widen access to its stock and to improve housing management.

Urban deprivation

In their efforts to re-establish poverty on the political agenda the analysts of the 1960s focussed on income. By this measure recent years have seen the tide of poverty rising. The supplementary benefit level remains the official poverty line, despite evidence that many families with incomes only slightly above this level experience hardship. By the late 1970s some 6.2m people were dependent on incomes at or below s.b. level and a total of 14m on incomes less than 40 per cent above it (25 per cent of the population compared with the 14 per cent revealed by *The Poor and the Poorest*).[18]

Poverty is changing its face. A decade ago the majority of people below the poverty line were pensioners. Demographic changes are increasing the proportion of the population who are pensioners, the majority of whom have earned insufficient income during their working lives to adequately save for retirement, so the aged poor are still growing in absolute terms. But the majority of the poor are now the low-paid and increasingly the unemployed.

While inequality in incomes is a basic consideration, accumulated findings about inequalities in housing, education, health and so on have led to a widening of the definition of poverty by reference to the concept of relative deprivation.

> Individuals, families and groups in the population can be said to be in poverty when they lack the resources to obtain the types of diet, participate in the activities and have the living conditions and amenities which are customary, or at least widely encouraged

and approved, in the societies to whom they belong. Their resources are so seriously below those commanded by the average individual or family that they are, in effect, excluded from ordinary living patterns, customs and activities.[19]

These resources include not only private income and capital assets, but also the whole range of benefits and services derived from the welfare state.

Since the 'rediscovery of poverty' the overall structure of inequality has changed little. A long-term trend towards the more equal distribution of wealth has continued, but the rate has remained almost imperceptibly gradual: contrary to popular myth, the rich are in no imminent danger of extinction. More so than in the 1960s it is acknowledged that poverty is not significantly the fault of its victims. The underlying causes are the mechanisms which systematically deprive some people of adequate resources while consistently providing others with a disproportionate share and continually reproduce the overall structure of inequality. But policies which aim to alleviate symptoms by modifying the position of individuals within an unequal structure tend to be the focus of attention, rather than those which aim to more directly alter that structure.

The geography of deprivation became a major growth industry in the 1970s, as academics were joined by central and local government in efforts to apply the concept of urban deprivation to policy development.[20] The resultant maps describing the contours of deprivation testify to the complexity of its spatial distribution while the degree of concentration remains in dispute because of methodological weaknesses in the analyses. In particular, there is a tendency to describe deprivation by indicators which can easily be measured, thus exaggerating some of its dimensions and ignoring others. Many available statistics more accurately record responses to deprivation, e.g. social work referrals. These limitations are compounded when scores on various indicators are aggregated, often without resolving weighting problems, to give a priority ranking of deprived areas. Thus 'the facts' of urban deprivation are no simple matter.

Overall, there is broad agreement that the degree of concentration of problems varies with different dimensions of deprivation and that the majority of the deprived live outside those areas with the most intense concentrations of deprivation. To the extent that 'problem areas' do exist, urban renewal policies are failing to prevent their reproduction in different locations. The case study of Birmingham illustrated the validity of a model of growth, maturity and decline in large tracts of the city – a life-cycle of working-class neighbourhoods determined by the changing demands of the economy. The locus of the most intense deprivation shifted from the inner ring to the middle ring and now conditions in some outer council estates are threatening to reach crisis point.

The processes of uneven economic development have varied over time with changing economic conditions and state intervention but they continue to create deprived areas. Radical analysts argue that this is because the real basis of urban deprivation has not been acknowledged: uneven economic development is an essential feature of a capitalist economy, not an unfortunate side-effect. The need to maintain competitiveness results in the restructuring of the space economy, and currently inner areas 'are areas where capital has moved on leaving labour and infrastructure in its wake'.[21] Hence intervention which falls short of social control of the volume and location of capital investment can only ameliorate the symptoms of industrial change rather than resolve the causes of urban deprivation.

Policy challenge

The limited impact of current policies constitutes a considerable challenge. The improvement of housing conditions will require increased levels of public investment for programmes of both new building and improvement. In some areas a major council housebuilding programme is needed to meet housing shortages. In others clearance also needs to be expanded to deal with conditions in slums which have been identified for many years and where housing improvement could make no real impact.

More generally the problem is one of the older housing stock sliding increasingly rapidly into decay. In inner London, but also in many other cities and towns, the private rented sector still gives the greatest cause for concern. But at the same time the decay of many owner-occupied properties is a growing problem. The social survey carried out as part of the 1976 English House Condition Survey has clearly demonstrated that home ownership does not, by itself, maintain the housing stock, and that improvement grants under the current terms of the investment partnership will not prevent the rapid growth of another generation of slums.[22] It indicated that only a third of those who live in substandard houses are dissatisfied with their accommodation, and that the more serious the state of disrepair the more likely are the owners to underestimate the severity of defects and the costs of remedying them. Continuing investment in the maintenance of their dwellings by owner-occupiers was very limited in the period covered by the survey, was not concentrated on properties requiring the most urgent action to prevent further deterioration, and was not used on those remedial works most needed. Not only are owners' perceptions of needs for investment and actual expenditure low, but their capacity for investment is limited: even with grant aid, over 40 per cent of owner-occupiers of dwellings needing improvement would have to find a sum equivalent to their annual income to bring their houses up to the full standard.

There is no room for complacency when traditional comprehensive redevelopment has been discredited but the innovations of the past decade have yet to deliver the goods. Attempts to secure area improvement dominate practice, but there are conflicting views about appropriate standards and a combination of resource constraints and management problems are severely limiting achievement. Cellular renewal has been widely canvassed but has yet to achieve the status of a credible alternative. The basic premises of current policy are clearly false and changes are urgently needed which ensure that the rate of effective investment in older housing areas will significantly exceed the rate of decay. The means for deploying these resources should minimize the conflict between housing stock objectives and social objectives. This would entail significant changes in housing finance and legislation to ensure that subsidies go to those in greatest need and to allow the choice of forms of area renewal to be based on a more balanced appraisal of residents' needs and wider strategic considerations, rather than on expediency induced by variable constraints on implementation.

For such changes to have maximum impact they should be part of integrated urban renewal programmes. Comprehensive renewal is in an embryonic stage and the challenge to policy makers is twofold. First, there is a need to identify and implement those modest practical changes which will prevent it from being stillborn. An important issue here is that the possible employment yields from area-based economic measures are so small that opportunity costs of the current emphasis on economic regeneration should be carefully assessed. Are the returns on such attempts to 'attack causes' greater than those on policies to treat symptoms? The development of better methods of 'economic firefighting' is worthwhile. But if national policies and economic conditions continue to preclude significant improvement in the employment prospects of inner area residents, it may make more sense to concentrate on policies which provide tangible social and environmental benefits, even if their economic benefits are limited. An unselective commitment to economic measures runs the risk of sacrificing modest achievements on the altar of unattainable ambition.

Second, there is a need to ensure effective longer-term developments without which IAPs will never be more than 'Peter Pan programmes'. The progress of urban renewal in the 1980s will be determined by the outcome of conflict between two opposing views. One holds that stronger interventionist policies are necessary, involving the allocation of additional public sector resources to IAPs which will themselves be set within a framework of more effective economic and social policies. Within this view urban renewal can become an instrument of social change in the direction of a more egalitarian society. A contrary view is that less direct state intervention is more likely to resolve problems by encouraging private investment in inner areas. It is also essential, because without further reductions in public expenditure it will not be possible to create the conditions for economic growth, which is a prerequisite for inner city regeneration. The next section examines the implications of this latter view.

Urban renewal into the 1980s

For the past twenty-five years urban renewal policies have been the product of the 'middle ground' of politics. However, the Conservative Government is committed to radical change. The early 1980s will see an attempt to break decisively from the post-war development of the welfare state, with measures designed to bring about a more selective and residual approach. Changes in both resource allocation and the statutory and administrative framework for urban renewal are now in motion with the intention of reducing state intervention and enhancing the role of the private sector. The broad aims of the 1977 inner cities policy have been adopted but the changing means of achieving them will produce less effective action.

Abandoning the middle ground

The Conservative Government does not subscribe to the view that the state should be heavily engaged in the promotion of redistributive taxation and social welfare policies to reduce inequality. Such measures are considered both undesirable, as they impede the growth of the economy, and unnecessary because society has become more equal and there is little evidence to show that ordinary people want this process to go further.[23] The welfare state is therefore to be reduced in scale, with its eventual role seen as providing mainly means-tested services and benefits for a minority of the most deprived.

The Government's strategy for economic recovery rests on bringing down the rate of inflation and interest rates by curtailing the growth of the money supply and government borrowing; restoring incentives; and public spending 'which is compatible both with the objectives for taxation and borrowing and with a realistic assessment of the prospects for economic growth'.[24] This has resulted in plans not simply to halt the growth of public expenditure, but to reduce it. The planned level for 1983–4 is 4 per cent lower than that of 1979–80.

The effect of this change of direction on the level of public resources for urban renewal emerges with the distribution of funds between and within main programmes is examined (see Figure 28). A greater priority is given to defence and law and order. The substantially increased social security budget, despite real cuts in some benefits, is a reflection of rising unemployment. A reduction in total public expenditure will be achieved by major cuts in other areas, mainly in services provided by local government. Education spending will be reduced by 12 per cent as will that on roads and transport (with major reductions in local transport) and other environmental services. The brunt is borne by the industry, energy, trade and employment, and housing programmes. A 40 per cent reduction in the former includes a one third scaling down of regional aid by 1982, with the reduced resources concentrated in Merseyside, the North East and Glasgow. Spending on housing will be halved

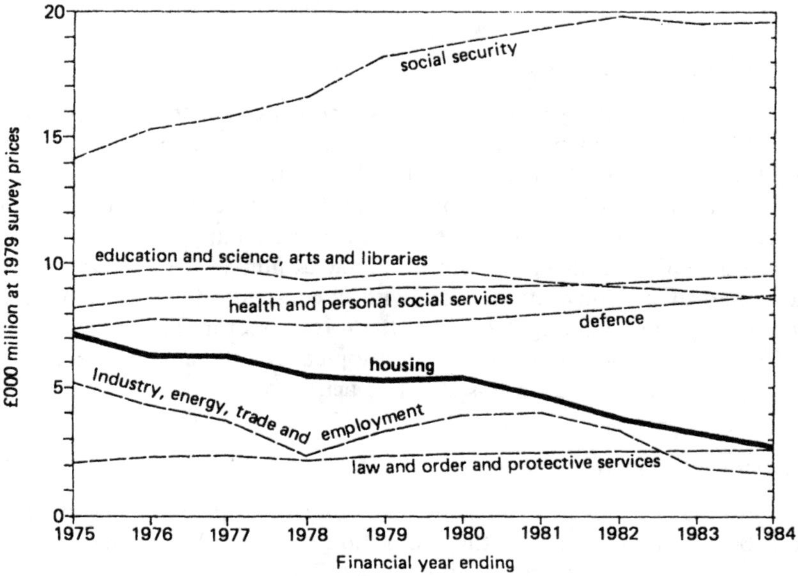

Figure 28 *Public expenditure 1974 to 1984*

Source: The Government's expenditure plans for 1980–1 to 1983–4, cmnd. 7841 (HMSO)

by 1983–4. Thus the majority of the main programmes on which urban renewal depends are being substantially reduced.

Private enterprise to save cities

These public expenditure cuts are accompanied by changes in policies, powers and procedures, intended to control local authority spending and to encourage hitherto reluctant private capital to reinvest in inner areas. The Government's objective is:

> . . . to make the inner cities places where people want to live and work and where the private investor and institutions are prepared to put their money.[25]

The relevant legislative changes are mainly embodied in the Local Government, Planning and Land Act, 1980, where the provisions which will have most significance for urban renewal are those concerning local authority expenditure, Urban Development Corporations, Enterprise Zones and land development.

Reductions in *local authority expenditure* will be implemented by a significantly changed system of control. Measures are being introduced to ensure central government control over the volume of local authority spending, while freeing local authorities from some detailed controls. In 1981–2 the present RSG system will be replaced by the block grant contribution to revenue (current) spending. The Government will calculate what each authority needs to spend to achieve a nationally determined level of service – its 'grant-related expenditure'. Then it will calculate the rate each authority would have to levy to pay for services at that level – its 'grant-related poundage'. The block grant will be the difference between these centrally assessed spending needs and the yield of centrally determined rate levels. Authorities will be able to spend above the standard level, but excess spending will have to be borne by increased rates and the Government will be able to penalize 'overspending' authorities by reducing their block grant.

Similarly the Act provides for the introduction of a new system for control of local authority capital expenditure by empowering the SoS to set a total figure for each authority split into five single block allocations – housing, education, transport, personal social services and other services. There will be provision for *virement* between blocks and 'tolerance' in spending up to 10 per cent more than an allocation in any one year. Capital receipts from disposals (sale of assets) and repayments (of grants and mortgages, etc.) may augment these allocations. Scheme by scheme project control will be reduced by the introduction of a system whereby local authorities will make detailed costings of proposals publicly available and publish the actual cost on completion. Central government would then only intervene if a scheme is too expensive or gives poor 'value for money'.

In some cities the role of local authorities will be reduced by the creation of new agencies for urban renewal, with special powers and resources modelled on the new towns. *Urban Development Corporations* (UDCs) are being established in the first instance for the London and Merseyside docklands. Elsewhere IAPs will continue under existing arrangements, with some streamlining of procedures. This initiative reflects the Government's view that in certain areas there is a need for a body which can adopt 'a single-minded determination not possible for the local authorities with their much broader responsibilities'.[26] The Act enables the SoS to designate an area of land as an 'urban development area' and establish a UDC, run by appointed members, to secure its regeneration. UDCs will be expected to achieve this by bringing land and buildings into effective use, encouraging the development of existing and new industry and commerce, creating an attractive environment, and ensuring that housing and social facilities are available.

The SoS is enabled to confer extensive powers on UDCs. As part of the designation order land from local authorities and some other public bodies may be transferred to them and they will be able to acquire additional land at market value (inside and outside the designated area) by negotiation or compulsion, and sell land for development. The SoS is empowered to establish

UDCs as local planning authorities, and make a special development order granting automatic planning permission for development in accordance with agreed proposals. Building land sold or let by a UDC can be assisted by loans, and they will have the same powers as a designated district authority to make loans and grants under the provisions of the Inner Urban Areas Act, 1978. UDCs are also given powers to secure the provision of infrastructure, such as roads.

The exact range of powers for UDCs will be specified in their designation orders, as will their precise areas, but it is envisaged that some 5000 acres of London and 1000 acres of Merseyside docklands will be involved. The financial memorandum to the Bill indicated that the total direct cost in grants and loans in the early years is expected to be some £100m p.a. Much of this will come from diverting existing main programmes, although there will be some new expenditure. The general intention is to secure the efficient deployment of public funds in ways which will render the docklands attractive to private development.

The stimulation of private investment is the aim of *Enterprise Zones* (EZs), an initiative announced in the 1980 budget speech as part of a package which also encompassed measures to assist small businesses generally. The Government sees EZs as an experiment to pioneer a new approach to economic renewal by testing:

> . . . how far industrial and commercial activity can be encouraged by the removal of certain fiscal burdens and by the removal or streamlined administration of certain statutory or administrative controls.[27]

Financial incentives are 100 per cent capital allowances over four years (for corporation and income tax purposes) for commercial or industrial buildings; exemption from development land tax; and the abolition of general rates on industrial and commercial property, with the revenue foregone reimbursed by central government. The relaxation of controls comprise: reduced planning controls; exemption from the requirements of industrial training boards; accelerated handling of applications for warehousing free of customs duty; abolition of remaining IDC requirements; and reduced central government requests for statistical information.

The statutory procedures for establishing an EZ can be summarized as follows:

1 the SoS has the power to invite district councils, London borough councils new town and urban development corporations, to prepare a draft plan – this invitation must specify the area for the scheme, and may contain directions as to its form, content and required consultations;
2 an invited authority may prepare a draft plan, making provision for publicity and representations;
3 after any modifications the authority may adopt the plan by resolution, which must then be sent to the SoS, placed on deposit, advertised and made available for sale;

4 the SoS may then designate the area an EZ – the designation order must be advertised and specify its effective date, the period for which the scheme will be operational, its boundary and the 'designated Enterprise Zone authority'.

Prior to designation the SoS and the invited authority will agree administrative arrangements to ensure the rapid determination of planning and building regulations. The plan will show which classes of development are permitted in each part of the EZ, set out any conditions governing development, e.g. those needed for health or safety or the control of pollution, and specify any 'reserved matters', e.g. access. After designation permission will not be required for development that conforms to the plan's zoning and conditions, except for reserved matters.

No selection criteria have been formally defined, but initially local authorities were invited to make submissions for some 500 acres in areas of physical and economic decay, where conventional policies have not succeeded in regenerating self-sustaining economic activity. From the many submissions received the Government initially announced nine EZs: in Liverpool (Speke in the outer suburbs), Manchester/Salford (Trafford Park), Newcastle-upon-Tyne/Gateshead, London (Isle of Dogs in Tower Hamlets), Corby and Dudley in the Midlands, the Lower Swansea Valley in Wales, and one each for Scotland and Northern Ireland. These nine EZs will be designated in 1981, at an estimated cost of some £10m p.a. in foregone taxes and compensation to local authorities for lost rate revenue.

Measures concerned with *land development* are to be more widely applied to encourage private investment capital. The Act makes provision for the SoS to designate areas where land owned by public authorities which is vacant or underused will be recorded in a register. The SoS has the power to require the necessary information for these land registers, which will be made available for inspection. Some twenty-one local authorities have been designated. Given that up to three quarters of vacant and underused land in inner areas is in public ownership, this innovation is potentially important for urban renewal. It is the corollary of the repeal of the Community Land Act and, coupled with measures to relax detailed planning controls on development, streamline statutory development plans and the processing of planning appeals, constitutes the Government's attempt to ensure an adequate supply of building land and the removal of 'unnecessary constraints' on private development.

The new Government's *housing policy* also aims to reduce the role of the public sector and create conditions in which private enterprise can make a greater contribution. The relevant legislative changes are embodied in the Housing Act, 1980 which adds two key measures to those contained in Labour's Bill – the 'right to buy' for council tenants and 'shorthold tenure' in the private rented sector.

The right to buy is available to every secure tenant of three years standing of a council or non-charitable housing association. It is backed up by statutory discounts of up to 50 per cent of the valuation, guaranteed council mortgages and a range of other measures including the option to purchase later at a frozen price. The only exemptions from the right are purpose-built accommodation for the disabled and sheltered housing for the elderly. A massive publicity campaign has been mounted to stimulate take-up.

The Act seeks to encourage expansion of the private rented sector by introducing shorthold tenure whereby landlords can let new tenancies on the basis of one to five years, and assured tenancies where privately rented homes, newly built by an approved body, can be let at economic rents. It also contains a number of other provisions designed to revive this sector, including rent registration every two years with a reduction of phasing stages and the abolition of controlled tenancies.

Subsidies for council housing are to be amended by the introduction of the deficit financing system anticipated in Labour's Bill, but with the expectation that the Government's discretion to specify appropriate rent rises in the calculations will push rents up much faster than the overall level of inflation. The tenants' charter provisions of the previous Bill are also included, though are watered down in some respects. Public sector tenants are given formal security of tenure and can only be evicted on specific grounds. They are also given the rights to sublet, do improvements and have a written tenancy agreement.

Comprehensive guidance on the renovation grant provisions of the 1980 Act is contained in Circular 21/80, which also deals with the many matters left to the discretion of the SoS in the legislation.[28] The two major aims of these changes are to reduce administrative restrictions and increase flexibility. Its detailed provisions are outlined in Figure 29.

Among the restrictions which have been eased or removed are: grants can be made for dwellings to be occupied by members of an applicant's family; the 'twelve-month rule' preventing sitting tenants who purchase their homes in HAAs or GIAs from getting grants in the first year is abolished; and r.v. limits no longer apply in HAAs. In addition the sale of a house by one owner-occupier to another no longer constitutes a breach of grant conditions. Public and private sector tenants can now apply for most types of grant and a system of provisional approvals is introduced to assist prospective purchasers where a mortgage offer is often conditional on grant approval.

The aim of increased flexibility is to channel resources toward the worst properties and those households in greatest need. A reduced repair standard for the improvement grant has been combined with increases in the proportion of the grant which may relate to repairs (where these are 'substantial and structural') from 50 to 70 per cent. Similarly the standard for intermediate grants is reduced to the single requirement that, after improvement, the dwelling should be fit for human habitation. Most important of all, the scope of the repairs grant is widened to deal with substantial and structural repairs of older houses wherever they are situated, subject to a r.v. limit.

Special grants are also extended to include an element for repairs and, more significantly, means of escape from fire. Eligible expense limits for all types of grant are increased and the new rates of grant distinguish between priority and non-priority cases. Priority cases cover dwellings which are either in an HAA, are unfit, lack any standard amenities, or are in need of substantial and structural repair: the grant percentage for these cases is 75 per cent (up to 90 per cent in hardship cases). Non-priority cases cover all other circumstances and the grant percentage payable is 50 per cent (except in GIAs where it is 65 per cent).

Changes in area improvement powers include: the abolition of Priority Neighbourhoods; removing the need for central government consent for GIA declarations and sale of land held under GIA powers. The most important change is that environmental works in HAAs are put on the same basis as those in GIAs with cost limits for subsidy increased to £400 per house in both. There is a simplified administrative procedure for subsidy claims towards these works.

The Act introduces powers for improvement for sale (IFS) and shared ownership schemes to be implemented by local authorities and housing associations. For IFS, the maximum difference between qualifying costs (acquisition and improvement) and market value which can be subsidized is initially £5000. Local authorities are also encouraged to sell unimproved houses for improvement by adopting 'homesteading schemes' on the lines pioneered by the GLC. The Act provides for local authorities to guarantee building society mortgages.

Increasing urban inequality

The 1980s should prove the effectiveness or otherwise of this shift in emphasis of urban renewal. The latest round of specifically inner city initiatives add to, rather than supersede, the 1977 policy, but the wider context of area-based policies has changed significantly for the worse. The consequences of an apparently unshakeable belief that 'public expenditure is at the heart of Britain's present economic difficulties'[29] is that for the first time since its inception the welfare state is to go firmly into reverse:

> . . . those on housing waiting lists, the homeless, the families in unsatisfactory accommodation, the unemployed, the less fortunate who are most dependent on the social services must take comfort in the fact that their sacrifices are helping to put the country on the right lines. Those of us who are comfortably housed, in work, will steel ourselves, as realists, to the necessary sacrifices of others.[30]

International economic recession, combined with the Government's economic policies, are driving up unemployment – now well over 2m and still rising. The planned increase in social security expenditure will not meet the

Renovation grants	*Improvement*	*Intermediate*	*Special*	*Repair*
1 Purpose of grant	Available at the discretion of LA for improvement or conversion of dwellings to modern standards *or*, in cases of hardship, partial improvement.	Available as of right (subject to conditions below) for provision of some or all of the standard amenities, and for associated repairs if the applicant wishes.	Available at the discretion of LA for provisions of more standard amenities in HMOs, and for means of escape from fire, and associated repairs. But see (11) below.	Available at discretion of LA for substantial and structural repairs only. But see (11) below.
2 Maximum eligible expense	*Priority cases:* £8500 (£9800 per dwelling for conversions of houses of three-storeys or more). In Greater London (GL) £11,500 (£13,300). *Non-priority cases:* £5500 (£6400). In GL £7500 (£8700). The maximum percentage of the eligible expense allowed for repairs (where house is in need of substantial and structural repairs) is 70%; otherwise 50%.	£4400 (£1900 for specified sums for each of seven specified amenities and £2500 for repairs). In GL £6000 (£2500 and £3500). For reduced standards of repair £250 (£350 in GL) times number of amenities up to a maximum of £1000 (£1400 in GL).	As intermediate grants for specified amenities (but more than one of each may be allowed) and for repair. For means of escape from fire £6750 (£9000 in GL).	£4000 (£5500 in GL).
3 Maximum grant rate	*Priority cases:* 75%, but in cases of hardship up to 90%; *Non-priority cases:* 50%, but in cases of hardship up to 65%.			All are *priority cases*.
4 Central government contribution	*Priority cases:* 90% of grant paid. *Non-priority cases:* 75% of grant paid.			
5 Minimum life	Thirty years. LA discretion to reduce to ten years.	Not specified, but for short life properties reduced repair standards encouraged.	LA discretion.	LA discretion.
6 Standard	Ten-point standard with LA discretion to reduce; repair standard 'reasonable', with LA discretion to reduce.	Reasonable repair and fit – can be reduced at LA discretion.	LA discretion. But see (11) below.	'Reasonable'. But see (11) below.
7 Rent increase allowed to private landlord	Where landlords carry out work they can apply for new 'fair rent' with increases phased over two years. Where tenants fund improvement, landlords cannot increase rent on basis of tenants' expenditure.			
8 Occupancy conditions	(i) If grant paid to *private landlord*, dwelling has to be let for five years, or otherwise grant to be repaid at LA discretion. (ii) If grant paid to *tenant*, no repayment can be imposed on him, but private landlord may have been required to meet letting conditions in (i) above.			

	(iii) If grant paid to *owner-occupier*, dwelling has to remain occupied by existing owner of close relative for five years, *or* can be sold to another owner-occupier, *or* can be let after first year – otherwise repayment at LA discretion.			
9 Land tenure	Owner of freehold, or five years unexpired lease, regulated (private) tenant, secure (public) tenant.			
10 Age of house	Pre-1961 (except for works for disabled persons).		Not applicable.	Pre-1919.
11 Compulsory improvement/repair	Not applicable.	Improvement notice at LA discretion where tenant requests and house lacks one or more amenities. Reduced standard can apply.	Where notice under S.15 of Housing Act, 1961 or Sch. 24 of Housing Act, 1980 served, grant becomes mandatory.	Where repair notice served under S.9 of Housing Act, 1957 grant becomes mandatory.
12 Rateable value limits for owner-occupied houses.	For improvements £225 (£400 in GL). For conversion £350 (£600 in GL). Not applicable in HAAs or for works for disabled persons.	Not applicable.		£225 (£400 in GL).

Priority cases	*Ten-point standard*	*Standard amenities*
(i) dwellings or HMOs in HAAs; (ii) dwellings or HMOs which are unfit for human habitation; (iii) dwellings which lack one or more standard amenities and HMOs which lack sufficient standard amenities for the occupants; (iv) dwellings in need of 'substantial and structural repairs'; (v) HMOs which lack adequate means of escape from fire, where the works remedy the condition in question.	(i) be substantially free from damp; (ii) have adequate natural lighting and ventilation in each habitable room; (iii) have adequate and safe provision throughout for artificial lighting and have sufficient electrical socket outlets for the safe and proper functioning of domestic appliances; (iv) be provided with adequate drainage facilities; (v) be in stable structural condition; (vi) have satisfactory internal arrangement; (vii) have satisfactory facilities for preparing and cooking food; (viii) be provided with adequate facilities for heating; (ix) have proper provision for the storage of fuel (where necessary) and for the storage of refuse; (x) conform with the specification for the thermal insulation of roof spaces laid down in the Building Regulations in force at the time of grant approval.	(i) fixed bath or shower; (ii) hot and cold water supply at fixed bath or shower; (iii) wash-hand basin; (iv) hot and cold water supply at wash-hand basin; (v) sink; (vi) hot and cold water supply at sink; (vii) water closet.

Figure 29 *Private renovation grant system, 1980*

Criteria	*Local authorities*	*Housing associations*
For rent 1 Cost limits	None fixed, but under project control procedure all schemes with expenditure per dwelling above £4000 (£6000 in GL) or within a total contract costing more than £100,000 must be submitted to the DoE at sketch design stage and before tender acceptance where costs rise more than 15% above estimates at sketch design. DoE will consider a cost/value ratio and any special considerations in deciding whether to approve.	Cost limits act as a sieve for approval not a ceiling. They are expressed in a matrix form, taking into account size and area. For *Acquisition and Works*, together with fees, the limits in August 1980 were: *A* / *B* / *C* / *D* / *E* 1p dwelling: 18,640 / 14,360 / 10,600 / 9,740 / 8,380 2p dwelling: 20,340 / 18,810 / 14,520 / 14,020 / 10,260 3p dwelling: 24,780 / 20,000 / 15,730 / 14,880 / 11,460 4p dwelling: 27,860 / 24,960 / 17,100 / 16,920 / 11,970 5/6p dwelling: 31,280 / 28,850 / 18,460 / 16,920 / 11,970 Where vacant properties are acquired there is an increase of 50% of the actual cost of acquisition. Examples of areas are: A – Inner London, B – Outer London, C – Birmingham, D – Leeds.
2 Standards	None fixed. Ten-point standard and 'thirty-year rule' for age of dwelling abandoned.	Ten-point standard and standard amenities, amplified in Housing Corporation's Technical Brief.
3 Subsidy	75% of loan charges on admissible costs – but only payable when 'national' Housing Revenue Account in deficit.	Capital Grant (HAG) to reduce loan charges to a level which can be met by rental income (less DoE defined management and maintenance costs).
For sale 1 Eligible dwellings and Standards	In need of substantial repair or improvement. Standards for LA and HA to determine, but influenced by building societies. Can be acquired for IFS or transferred from rented stock.	
2 Subsidy	75% of net cost (acquisition, works, fees, and interest minus market value) up to £4000 and 25% of next £1000, that is, a maximum of £3250.	100% of net cost (as LA but also including administrative allowances of HA) up to £5000.
Area improvement	*General Improvement Areas*	*Housing Action Areas*
1 Declaration procedure	LA declares and then notifies SOS for information only.	LA declares and submits specified information to SOS who can, within twenty-eight days, choose to cancel declaration or exclude part of area.
2 Compulsory improvement	Discretionary improvement notice powers available to LA for a rented dwelling lacking one or more amenities or for an owner-occupied dwelling where satisfactory improvement works could not otherwise be carried out to an adjoining dwelling.	
3 Compulsory acquisition	Discretionary 'last resort' power for any dwelling in the interests of the area as a whole.	Discretionary power for any dwelling to lead to improvement, better management and use of accommodation, or increase well-being of residents in area.
4 Grant availability and rate	All grants available. For non-priority cases 65%.	All grants available. All are priority cases.
5 Environmental subsidy	50% of number of dwellings at declaration times £400.	50% of number of dwellings, HMOs and hostels times £400.
6 Eligible environmental works	(i) street works and traffic management, excluding normal highway maintenance; (ii) landscaping – including open space, play areas, parking areas; (iii) exteriors and curtilage of buildings – improving external appearance but excluding routine maintenance; (iv) community buildings – conversion of existing buildings for facilities to benefit community as a whole; (v) miscellaneous – not covered by other subsidies and not more than half the total costs. Works not covered include those producing revenue to LA or significant profits to owner of commercial and industrial premises.	

Note: Powers to declare further Priority Neighbourhoods were repealed in the 1980 Act.

Figure 30 *Public sector renovation and area improvement, 1980*

needs generated by rising unemployment and demographic changes. Unemployment and many other national insurance benefits are being reduced in real terms, making more people dependent on means-tested supplementary benefits. These economic and social policies, coupled with income tax changes which favour the more affluent, will result in increasing inequality.

Within these parameters there is still a consensus on the need for discrimination in favour of inner areas. IAPs, tantamount to area means-tested benefits, have a place in a declining welfare state: it can be claimed that necessarily reduced public expenditure is being concentrated in areas of greatest need. Some academic commentators argue that it would be more rational to accept that the inner city will remain an unsuitable location for many economic activities. Training and housing mobility should be given more emphasis to enable workers with upgraded skills to move to where there is work as part of a balanced strategic programme. This debate will remain academic, as there is no prospect of the resources for such intervention. For example, the capacity of the new towns to contribute is being eroded by measures to force the sale of their assets rather than allowing recycled proceeds of publicly sponsored urban development to be used to provide further housing and jobs. Moreover, proponents of dispersal have not allayed concerns about the concomitant waste of resources.

In these broad terms IAPs will continue to develop along the lines established in the late 1970s, but the net effect of changes in national policies can only be to undermine their already limited impact as the level of resources being applied to them are reduced. Not only does the Government not see the solution to inner area problems in terms of an injection of public funds, but its expenditure policies will severely constrain those local authorities which do hold this view. Neither a significant expansion of the Urban Programme, nor the diversion of additional main programme resources are realistic prospects for the early 1980s. Relevant central government programmes, such as investment grants to industry, are being drastically run down. The 1981–2 RSG settlement, under the new block grant procedures, reduced the central government contribution to 59 per cent and assumed a 3 per cent reduction in local government expenditure, with a tight cash limit on pay. Within the settlement, authorities with inner area problems, particularly the London boroughs, lose out as resources have been redistributed back to the rural shires. Reductions in services are inevitable, as is the further erosion of limited local autonomy.[31] The shrinkage of the cake will be such that no matter how dextrous local authorities are in using their new freedoms to divide it up, it will not be possible to protect inner areas from centrally imposed cuts.

The success of recent innovations ultimately depends on a positive response from private investors, both institutions and individuals. There is clearly some limited scope for reduced public resources to be used more effectively as a lever on private investment. But increased incentives and reduced restrictions in a few small pockets, better working relationships with the private sector and more community enterprise will not offset withdrawal of public funds. Market forces, not government intervention, are primarily responsible for inner area problems. The Government's belief that, freed from 'unnecessary controls', these forces can be relied on to spearhead regeneration in ways which will benefit those in need flies in the face of historical experience and contemporary evidence. As the former Conservative SoS, Walker, stated for the benefit of his colleagues during the debate on the Inner Areas Bill in 1978:

> . . . there is no way in which this problem can be solved by easy application of free market forces. Mr Milton Friedman has only to take a short cab ride from his university in Chicago to see what free market forces have done to some districts of that city. Such forces will not operate in some districts. . . . We either neglect these districts or we put in considerable resources.[32]

More recently, the Property Advisory Group came to similar conclusions, emphasizing that:

> Financial institutions will become involved only in property development schemes which are profitable in relation to final costs, and offer growth of income and asset values comparable with those available from alternative investment opportunities. . . . It is therefore unrealistic to hope that any large part of the growing income of the financial institutions can be channelled towards property investment in locations of low demand and high risks as an act of social responsibility towards declining areas. Some relaxations of institutional criteria are possible, but these are more likely to result in investment in schemes where there is confidence that an environment conducive to economic growth is being created.[33]

Its report identified the crucial role of public investment in environmental improvement, providing infrastructure and generally pump-priming to provide a catalyst for private investment. The result of the Government acting on the 'planner blame' hypothesis and the assumption of private sector led investment with minimal supporting public expenditure will be the continued general decline of inner areas.

These fundamental points can be elaborated in a brief discussion of the more specific changes now in train. It illustrates that increased private investment in inner areas does not automatically guarantee better prospects for existing residents; that with the erosion of public investment private initiatives will also be reduced rather than expanded in some fields; and that some of the new proposals are hastily conceived and little thought out even within their own frame of reference.

The introduction of UDCs, a new breed of 'quangos', is a mixed blessing. The contradictions of development corporations in inner areas – the availability of greater resources and powers than those of the local authorities whose accountability they are exempt – are at their least severe in relatively thinly populated dockland areas. A well resourced single agency in sympathy with, and geared to, the needs of developers may well be better equipped to rapidly implement infrastructural work and lever private investment.[34]

Against this, residents and elected representatives of docklands and nearby run-down areas will be substantially disenfranchised in terms of their influence over, for example, the needs met by the types of housing provided and the extent to which jobs for local people are created by the developments embarked upon. The UDCs will be under considerable pressure from the Government to deploy public funds in ways which generate the most rapid rate of private investment. The docklands UDCs are a means of giving specialized, innovative treatment to what are by definition, atypical inner areas. The success of this dimension of the 'private enterprise solution' will be measured by the Government in terms of the quantity of private investment they generate by the use of public funds.

Justifications for a departure from normal local democratic control of urban renewal has been debated since the 1960s: the 1980s will present opportunities to evaluate its results. The basis of the evaluation will be important. The two UDCs will be first in the pecking order for government resources – they are to receive more special funds than all the partnerships put together. The acceptability of the trade-off between efficiency and accountability should be judged by the contribution of these organizations to improving the lot of disadvantaged inner area residents. Given the context in which they are being established, it is difficult to conceive of UDCs substantially benefitting other than investors, developers and the relatively affluent.

The prospect for economic renewal, defined in terms of improving employment opportunities for inner area residents, were frail enough under the previous administration. They are now fast receding in the face of the continuing recession, a national 'employment strategy' reliant on stimulating job generation by tax incentives and the reduction of bureaucratic impediments to the formation and growth of small firms, and the application of this overall approach to area-based economic renewal initiatives.

The Government's faith in the capacity of small firms to revive the economy stems from a political ideology untrammelled by any ambivalence about the virtues of small-scale capitalism and is buttressed by popular interpretations of a study of the role of small firms in the US economy.[35] The most frequently quoted results of this research are that two thirds of all new jobs are generated by small young firms (less than 20 employees) which should be the main target for government support. This is interpreted by some as justification for increasing reliance on small firms: they are as important a source of new jobs here as in the USA, or they would become so if taxation levels and attitudes to enterprise there could be replicated here.

Careful examination of Birch's study shows that this is a misleading, if convenient, misconstruction of reality. The two thirds proportion is of *net* new jobs (i.e. gross new jobs minus gross job losses) not all new jobs – failure to appreciate this results in a substantial exaggeration of the importance of small firms. Moreover, the study included both manufacturing and service firms, with the latter overwhelmingly dominant – the performance of small manufacturing firms is very similar in both countries and increased jobs in small services firms in the USA have been a consequence, not a cause, of economic growth.

Concurrent research on recent trends in manufacturing in Britain show that while small and new firms have provided some net growth this is very limited in numerical terms. Although new firms are important in the long term, increasing the rate of firm formation is an inadequate response to current employment problems compared with arresting the decline of existing firms. Moreover, the only long-run study in this country shows that the birth rate of firms has not fallen during the past thirty years, during which taxation and red tape are held to have progressively stifled enterprise. The conclusions from this research are that an emphasis on new and small firms to achieve economic and employment growth is misplaced in the manufacturing sector. They are not sufficiently important to improve the economy, without which service sector firms will not be able to increase. New and small firms are important, but measures to assist them should be part of a range of programmes which also assist existing and larger firms, and should concentrate more on mechanisms other than tax relief and reduced controls which have little effect.

These criticisms also apply to area-based policies. The contraction of regional aid means that many inner areas will soon lose their assisted area status, a change which will be only marginally offset by the introduction of Enterprise Zones. Whereas IA special powers are designed to promote grant-aided investment mainly by existing firms, EZs rely on reduced controls and 'no-strings' funding to stimulate new development. The absence of any meaningful selection criteria can only be interpreted as a desire to hedge bets. If the chosen sites have development potential they will probably attract investment in the next few years, regardless of EZ status. If they are unattractive areas the inducements are sufficient to stimulate some development. In the unlikely event of this not happening it could be argued that further reductions of controls are necessary, such as those for health and safety.

While there will be some increase in employment in EZs in run-down areas, this is likely to be limited, of low quality and achieved at considerable social costs. It will be difficult to attract institutional investors. Pension funds will not benefit from capital allowances as they do not pay tax. They and insurance companies (who would benefit from allowances) will be discouraged by the uncertainty implicit in their experimental status. Moreover, local authorities will argue strongly for retaining control on retail development, fearing the impact of hypermarkets on existing shopping centres. The financial incentives will be insufficient to give large firms a competitive advantage from locating in EZs. Small firms will probably be attracted, but a mushrooming of Steptoe-like scrap metal yards and similar enterprises is an image which may well not be very far from reality. An increased demand for space in these 500 acre zones could inflate prices and rents and, in part, offset subsidies to industrialists, leaving private landowners and developers as the major beneficiaries. Any substantial reduction in planning controls will inevitably mean lower development standards. EZs could well precipitate further decline in employment levels and environmental standards in adjacent areas by sucking in existing economic activity, rather than stimulating new investment, and by increasing pressure on local infrastructure such as roads.

Even on the most optimistic forecasts, EZs will do little to improve employment prospects in the inner areas in which they are located. But they are serving to divert attention from the erosion of national and regional policies to curb mounting unemployment. In this sense the EZ initiative is a throwback to the urban experiments. Despite their weaknesses they are an offer that many authorities could not refuse. In the current political climate EZs have a wider significance as mechanisms for promoting the ideology of private enterprise. Their mixed parentage included Howe, a monetarist chancellor, and Hall, a Fabian academic; in some cases their midwifes will be Labour councils whose reluctance has been overcome by the prospect of any mechanism to create some local employment.[26]

Prospects for housing renewal are now rapidly declining. Job-led recovery programmes are no longer even a pious hope for inner areas, where increasing unemployment and declining disposable incomes will further reduce the capacity of residents to participate in an investment partnership. Concurrently the policies being pursued by expenditure cuts, the legislative changes in the 1980 Housing Act and related use of administrative discretion, will ensure both further overall decline in the older housing stock and failure to help those in greatest need.

The full impact of cuts in the housing programme remain largely a matter of guesswork, not least because the Government either does not know, or refuses to disclose, how far the pattern of housing expenditure will be changed as total spending declines from £5370m in 1979–80 to £2790m in 1983–4, and how far public and private investment will meet housing need. When the House of Commons Select Committee on the Environment requested clarification, the general message of Heseltine's bland reply was that the 1980 Public Expenditure White Paper's figures were based on 'what the country could afford'.[37] He could not support the statement made in the Paper that they also had regard to the 'present size and condition of the housing stock, trends in household formation and the capacity of the private sector to meet housing needs' with any evidence at all, and refused to relate their consequences to the 1977 Housing Policy Review's forecast of housing need.

The new controls on capital expenditure and new subsidy system will in future years enable the Government to determine the breakdown between capital and current expenditure, but, whatever way this unprecedented power is used, reduced totals render the breakdown of the housing programme inevitable. The Select Committee estimated that allowing for capital receipts from projected council house sales, rent increases of 16 per cent above the rate of inflation (to reduce the subsidy bill) and no shift of investment from new build to improvement, council housebuilding will fall to 30,000 by 1984. This, combined with the continuation of private new build at its present low level (an expectation shared by the building industry) means that the volume of housebuilding, now at its lowest peacetime level since 1924, is set to decline further. By 1984 this would produce a shortfall of 500,000 dwellings. The AMA further examined this gloomy picture and pointed out that the deterioration of the housing stock is now out of control by current policies and levels of expenditure. Furthermore, it will soon be beyond the capacity of the rapidly contracting building industry to tackle older housing and new building at the same time, should an upturn eventually materialize.[38] Shelter have drawn attention to the accelerated growth in council waiting lists which they predict will reach two million by 1984.[39]

Already the obsession with cash limits has slashed reduced programmes. The Housing Corporation's cash limit for 1980–1 was in danger of being exceeded halfway through the year, and this resulted in a stop to any further tender approvals for new contracts by housing associations or loan approvals for the acquisition of properties or sites: houses stood empty and vandalized and sites unbuilt on.[40] A similar moratorium was introduced for local authority HIP expenditure one month later and all council new build and improvement schemes, mortgages and renovation grants (other than statutory intermediate grants) halted. The HIP allocation for 1981–2 was reduced by 30 per cent on the previous year (or 15 per cent if capital receipts on housing and land sales are achieved). Some local authorities will be able to do little more than continue existing contracted commitments, while others will face harsh decisions on competing priorities. The Housing Corporation's expenditure level will remain constant, but the effect of past commitments on spending means that only 18,000 new or improved dwellings will be introduced into the development pipeline compared with 43,000 in 1979–80 and tender approvals will continue to be rationed. In this context the contribution made by initiatives such as improvement for sale and shared ownership schemes is only marginal.

The regressive effects of other housing policies are broadly predictable. Many council tenants who cannot afford to buy their homes will have their rents increased substantially, while tax relief to owner-occupiers remains unchanged. Some families in need, with owner-occupation beyond their means, will not be able to gain access to the public sector and will be forced into private rental. While the introduction of short-hold tenure and the abolition of controlled tenancies may marginally increase the volume of lettings, it will substantially increase the housing costs and insecurity of many private tenants.

Those in greatest need will also suffer most from the inevitable decline of investment in the older housing stock. As with the overall housing programme, the detailed outlook is difficult to forecast because the SoS has taken the powers to modify the renovation grant system at will, and local authorities have the discretion of a single capital allocation. Generally, however, it is clear that the potential benefits of some of the more sensible modifications will not be realized because of the withdrawal of public resources.

While grant take-up by owner-occupiers could be increased by relaxed grant conditions, the introduction of new eligible expense limits and the wider availability of repairs grants, low-income owner-occupiers will remain unable to afford grants for substantial improvements, even if they are available from councils' severely reduced HIP budgets. Few tenants are likely to exercise their new right to improve their landlord's property, and there is little prospect of the increased incentives for landlords producing accelerated investment. Those local authorities that want to underwrite private improvement by compulsory action and municipalization find themselves thwarted by the Government's administrative controls. Similarly the modest increase in subsidy for environmental works in GIAs and HAAs will be offset by the reduction in HIP allocations. The uncertainty that this generates will further discourage building societies from investing in the most needy areas and the capacity of local authorities to provide mortgages will remain low. As in other components of urban renewal programmes, a reduction of public funds will curtail the flow of private investment, reduce standards and ensure decay.

Not only will the effectiveness of housing improvement in older areas be reduced, but at the same time the problems of an eventual return to clearance will be compounded by policies which will reduce the attractiveness of council rehousing. As the most desirable housing is sold it will leave behind the least attractive stock and the poorest tenants.

> The danger to council housing of policies which concentrate on owner-occupation is not . . . that it will be killed off but rather that it will be maimed and disfigured.[41]

A stigmatized public sector with little choice will strengthen opposition to the rehousing necessary for an expanded clearance programme. When coupled with inadequate investment in the remaining stock it will ensure increasing renewal problems on what will have become 'impossible-to-sell' estates.

Except in a few favoured areas, the more positive land management and substantial environmental improvement necessary to stimulate private investment in industry and housing will not be forthcoming. The repeal of the Community Land Act and the prospective large-scale transfer of publicly owned land at relatively low prices will weaken the positive influence that public bodies can have on the development process. While the disposal of some large sites owned by statutory undertakers may facilitate desirable development, the sale of publicly owned land does not guarantee development, let alone development which will benefit local residents. Similarly, while the receipts from sales can be used to boost local authorities' capital spending, such receipts cannot possibly offset massive reductions in these programmes, now running at less than half the peak level of £6000m in 1974–5 and set to decline even more rapidly.

The withdrawal of public resources contradicts greater public involvement in regenerating inner areas. This concern was manifest in the Government's enthusiastic support for the European Campaign for Urban Renaissance, at the launching of which King, Minister for Local Government said:

> In the United Kingdom we are encouraging the ordinary citizen to play a role in improving his own environment. In essence we are endeavouring to create a climate within which people have as much control as possible over the environment.[42]

It is difficult to envisage 'constructive' citizen participation as the impact of public expenditure cuts and escalating unemployment takes its toll on the morale of community groups and exposes the limitations of area-specific policies. Moreover, increasing central control of local government renders the key decisions ever more remote from local influence, and residents affected by UDCs and EZs have little prospect of influencing decisions geared primarily to the needs of investors.

The main features of urban renewal under the Conservative Government have now emerged. Further developments may result from a resurgence of interest in overseas experience, stimulated particularly by the Trinational Inner Cities Project. This government sponsored comparative study of practice concluded that cities in West Germany and the USA have more varied and flexible relationships between government, the private sector and local communities, than is usual in the UK, and that these relationships can be very fruitful in assisting inner city regeneration.[43] In the field of economic development two key interrelated concepts were identified. First, 'leverage', i.e. using limited government finance to stimulate private investment. Second, 'merit financing', i.e. directing any assistance towards those inner areas with the best prospects of success. Organizational structures such as joint venture companies, involving local political leaders, local financial institutions and local employers were recommended for providing infrastructure, arranging finance for development and manpower training. Similarly, useful lessons were identified from American experience of community enterprise – the involvement of community groups (particularly of ethnic minorities) in the creation of economic enterprise for their own areas.

However, it is in the revitalization of residential neighbourhoods that efforts to transfer American experience may have an impact in the near future. The work of the Neighbourhood Housing Services Programmes has attracted considerable attention.[44] While in many ways similar to GIAs, these schemes are larger in scale (approximately 5000 dwellings) and wider in scope (involving the improvement of all neighbourhood facilities). A central agency, the Neighbourhood Reinvestment Corporation, helps to establish NHS schemes by feasibility studies of potential areas, staff training, and maintaining a revolving loan fund for improvers who are not good credit risks. Each local NHS scheme is a non-profit-making corporation whose board includes representatives of the local authority, private lending institutions and residents (who are in a majority). Staff salaries are paid for in part by tax deductible contributions from private organizations, who also provide seconded staff for the neighbourhood-based teams which undertake similar work to that of their counterparts here, but with much more emphasis on 'financial packaging'. The NHS schemes are 'targeted' on the better quality older housing areas where there are prospects of a 'turn around'. Interest in them may well reinforce the development of building society investment on an area basis being pioneered by the Abbey National Building Society, currently involved in approximately 100 declared GIAs and HAAs, providing loans to bridge the gap between the total cost of works and the renovation grant.

While further policy developments along these lines may marginally increase private investment in some inner areas, 'there is no magic policy currently being pursued in the United States which could achieve dramatic effects if transferred to Britain'.[45] A reliance on private solutions to replace rather than augment the public sector will reduce the aggregate quantity of investment in urban renewal and in distributional terms will preclude resources being allocated to those in greatest need: the result will be increasing urban inequality.

The renewal of intervention

It is clear that expanded and redirected state intervention is needed if urban renewal is to make more impact. Analyses of social policy traditionally end in one of two ways. For some, incremental changes are both desirable and practicable: marginal shifts of policy need to be identified, debated and tested.[46] A list of recommendations is drawn up and confidence expressed or implied about the ability of policy makers to meet the challenges outlined. For others, it is futile to propose remedies for artificially fragmented problems by minor adjustments to policies: such problems are so entrenched in the structure of our society that no policy package at all will work within the present system.[47] This final section briefly outlines an agenda of practical measures, while acknowledging they must be accompanied by more fundamental economic and social change.

Practical reforms

The immediate prospects for urban renewal could well engender an attitude of resigned 'muddling through' – doing less of the same. A more positive response would be a sustained commitment to working out initiatives and, where possible, applying them on a pilot basis. Rather than the simple pragmatism of making virtue of necessity, this work should be conceived of as both making better use of limited resources by identifying more relevant powers and procedures *and* maintaining pressure for increased resources.

At a national level the aim should be to identify those changes in renewal codes which would enable more effective intervention by local authorities to be geared to the particular circumstances of their areas. At a local level the aim should still be to further develop an integrated approach which ensures that limited resources go to those whose needs are greatest. The present national situation will place a heavy premium on imaginative ideas and effective implementation to secure any improvements. Management innovations will therefore be important. More committed interprofessional effort would enable local authorities to firstly utilize increased 'freedoms' to refine procedures for allocating resources between main programmes and geographical areas in accordance with more locally determined priorities. Every possible attempt should be made to maximize the bias towards innovative schemes in the use of Urban Programme resources rather than simply funding conventional schemes delayed by cuts in main programmes. Such an agenda for reforms can be elaborated in terms of some key components of inner city policy which, despite its limitations, provides the most coherent framework to date for urban renewal.

The powers and procedures for *housing renewal* have accumulated over many decades and there has never been a comprehensive review of the wide spectrum of legislation involved. The result is a Byzantine complexity of administrative procedures before one brick is placed on another in a redevelopment scheme or a bathroom installed in an old house. While the patchwork of existing powers is used with varying success by local authorities, there is an urgent need for a new Housing (Urban Renewal) Act which would establish a simplified system for individual house improvement and a unified area renewal code. This would include the following measures.[48]

1 A single private improvement grant for all work necessary to bring a dwelling up to the ten-point standard, with an emphasis on securing the structure and external fabric. Local authorities should be given complete discretion as to eligible works, and the distinctions between different types of work, e.g. the repair/improvement split, would be removed. The appropriate percentage of grant would similarly be at local authority discretion, between a minimum of, say, 30 per cent and a maximum of 100 per cent, taking account of the total cost of the work and the applicant's income. Mandatory grants should be restricted to cases where statutory notices, e.g. for repairs, have been served.
2 Raising minimum standards of fitness by incorporating standard amenities (extended to include adequate electricity and mains water

supplies), and retaining 'unfitness for human habitation' as the level at which clearance, closure action or improvement would be legally required. However, the ten-point standard could be used as the basis for rationalized compulsory improvement and repair notice procedures.

3 Simplifying project control procedures for public sector improvement and new build schemes in a way which places accountability with local authorities and housing associations.

4 Ending distinctions between powers and procedures for clearance areas, GIAs and HAAs so that Housing Renewal Areas (HRAs) could be declared by local authorities within which total demolition, total rehabilitation or mixtures of the two would take place. This would enable local authorities to adopt a 'horses for courses' approach to area renewal, varying the mix of techniques and the balance of public and private sector funding, according to local housing market conditions and political preferences. For example, in those areas where the private market has almost collapsed so far as investment in the stock is concerned, substantial public investment is needed in selective demolition and high-standard improvement of both houses and infrastructure. In such areas a planned and controlled public investment programme is needed, implemented on a street basis, using methods ranging from enveloping (to be subsidized) which, in essence, reconstitutes the private market, to social ownership programmes which replace the private market. At the other end of the spectrum, in areas comprising the best of the nineteenth century stock and where the market is still relatively buoyant, it may be possible to achieve revitalization on the basis of limited public funds and a concerted effort to harness additional private institutional investment. In these areas there is some prospect of successfully building on recent initiatives attempting to enhance the role of the private sector. Between the extremes are a range of varying conditions, and priorities between them will be a matter for local political decision.

5 Within HRAs there would be widened powers of compulsory acquisition for clearance so that it could be justified on environmental grounds, to enable the provision of community facilities, as well as in situations where houses are incapable of being improved to the ten-point standard (or some other lower standard determined by the local authority) at reasonable expense. These powers would incorporate a revised compensation code based on market values in all situations.

6 The implementation of an HRA would be accompanied by statutory participation procedures and any compulsory purchase proposals would be subject to a local public inquiry procedure.

For any given level of resources the effective use of such reformed powers and procedures would enhance both area renewal sensitive to the needs of particular older private housing areas and improvements outside priority areas. Similarly, innovations in management practices in the public sector, together with imaginative schemes of environmental improvement on problem estates could also increase the effectiveness of limited resources. Implementation should further extend the progress already made in establishing locally-based area teams and collaboration between agencies.

The very recent development of *economic renewal* and limited experience of implementation makes the identification of specific reforms in this area more difficult. However, a 'jobs at any price' approach would not constitute the most effective use of public resources. As experience develops, local measures should be increasingly selective, giving priority to the preservation or creation of better quality jobs, in terms of working conditions, wage levels, security of employment and environmental impact. This could include:

1 support for small firms being directed towards co-operatives and other community-based initiatives, rather than 'sweat shops';
2 linking any subsidies to private industry with the development of accountability in the use of public funds, such as municipal shareholding, and of the use of pension fund investment;
3 the development of IA programmes in which environmental works are clearly justifiable in terms of environmental benefits rather than solely their uncertain and limited employment effect;
4 giving significant priority to the relocation of 'non-conforming uses' which are identified as conflicting with investment in housing renewal;
5 the rigorous monitoring of all measures of economic renewal, to maximize the impact of programmes and define their limitations, in order to strengthen the case for direct intervention.

Both housing and economic renewal programmes include *environmental improvement* measures to stimulate private investment, and attention has become more sharply focussed on the need to tackle the problems of under-used and vacant land and buildings. Environmental improvement is often too readily dismissed as 'cosmetic', and this component of IAPs should be strengthened. Relevant measures would include:

1 the development of Environmental Policies and Programmes, analogous to HIPs and TPPs, which would establish overall needs, determine priorities between different types of work, and secure a sensible balance between capital works and environmental maintenance;
2 implementation within an extended framework of local plans more clearly related to expenditure proposals;
3 the extension of direct labour organizations, taking advantage of a programmed flow of publicly financed projects to maximize quality control – a development which could be dovetailed with government sponsored training programmes to create stable jobs;
4 strengthening the powers of local authorities to acquire and develop land for socially beneficial uses and ensure that any disposals are for development which will benefit inner area residents.

With all its contradictions the mechanisms for *public participation* programmes should be strengthened with particular emphasis placed on the enhanced involvement of neighbourhood-based organizations. A steady increase in the proportion of Urban Programme funds allocated to such groups for a variety of initiatives, ranging from job creation to welfare services, would assist the development of effective organizations and could enable them to secure more influence in debates about main programmes. This should be accompanied by other measures to devolve some degree of decision making through the extension of area planning, management and budgeting.

The need to devise such reforms and, to hone them in critical debate about their wider applicability, has implications for *educational programmes*. While developments within initial professional education are necessary, it is essential that post-qualification 'education for urban renewal' crosses conventional professional demarcation lines. Advanced courses in urban renewal studies should bring together practitioners and researchers from different departments and agencies in discussions centred on worked examples of innovative practice. Similarly, while residents are exhorted to participate in IAPs, 'education for participation' remains a slogan. There is a need to extend and improve access to informal adult education programmes.

Overall direction of urban renewal programmes should firmly rest with local authorities. In the 1970s housing renewal strategy implementation saw the effective combination of authorities with housing associations or co-operatives and valuable links made with building societies. In economic renewal a variety of agencies, including local enterprise trusts, are being spawned to undertake tasks such as the conversion of old industrial buildings. Within the framework of the accountability, both political and financial, necessary for public sector supported organizations, the aim should be to further explore such organizational options and not to lose flexibility and responsiveness by creating monolithic bureaucracies.

Such modifications of powers and procedures and local developments would maximize the impact of limited resources. But arresting the growth of another generation of slums (this time in both private and public sectors) and the significant amelioration of other problems besetting inner areas will depend on significant changes in national policies and resource allocation.

Continuing constraints

The history of urban renewal reveals the ebb and flow of activity with shifts in political ideology and economic conditions. The obvious paradox of urban renewal in the 1970s has been an increasingly sophisticated analysis of the symptoms and causes of urban decay paralleled by a declining commitment to investment in programmes to deal with either. At present a monetarist response to economic recession precludes any significant development of urban renewal policies reliant on state intervention. Developing and sustaining the arguments for practical reforms would mean that, with a return to the 'middle ground' or some progression beyond it, the lessons learnt from local innovations and debate on new powers and procedures could be more widely applied in the implementation of a substantial agenda of reforms.

To achieve significant results such reforms would have to be accompanied by increased public expenditure. It is currently argued by the Government that public spending harms economic growth and cannot be afforded. A cogent counter-argument can be made that increased expenditure, particularly on capital investment, can stimulate economic expansion and be financed partly from tax paid by workers in employment rather than tax income being spent on workers on the dole.[49] Priorities between the various sectors could be redefined to ensure that more relevant social needs are met, e.g. by reducing defence expenditure. Similarly, there is more scope for redirection of expenditure within each sector than has been officially acknowledged. For example, the present system of housing finance ensures that far too little is spent on repairing, improving and replacing the older housing stock. Proposals have been canvassed for switching funds from subsidies for owner-occupiers and tenants to investment. They would recognize the problems of low-income owner-occupation and amend the system of tax relief, while at the same time introduce cross-subsidization between local housing authorities with different problems. Financial reforms would be coupled with other changes in the management and allocation of housing designed to equalize the financial and social advantages of renting and owning.[50]

Even with such resource changes a reforming programme in the late 1980s will be hard put to offset the effects of the changes in motion now: we may reach the end of this century with conditions not significantly better than that at the end of the 1970s. The 'practicality' of the reforms listed earlier partly rests on the fact that none of them threatens the present version of a mixed economy. It can be argued that, with a resurgence of reform, a 'barrier', last confronted in the 1940s, will once again be reached and that:

> Bridging the gap between plans and powers will eventually mean not simply improving arrangements in the public sector, but must mean a more or less fundamental leap from a market-based and market-led economy to a public-sector-led economy.[51]

Developing a radical inner city policy as the geographical component of an alternative economic strategy, which also includes extending public ownership in industry (combined with experiments in self-management by the workers concerned), will require fundamental economic and democratic changes.

Earlier discussion has noted that a major development in academic critiques of renewal in the 1970s was the revival of a Marxist political economy perspective and its specific application to urban problems. In the main such writing is long on explanation and brief on the routes to radical change. Nonetheless, if achievement in urban renewal during the 1980s is as limited as appears likely, the diagnosis offered by this perspective may well become more widely accepted. An understanding of underlying constraints, on the part of both those who are employed to resolve inner area problems and those who suffer the consequences of policy failure, would contribute to the creation of conditions in which current definitions of 'practical reforms' could be substantially changed.

Urban renewal has been an important element of government policy for over a century, yet the limitations on achievement have been such that the question has recently been posed 'will the inner city problem ever go away?'.[52] Unequal cities reflect an unequal society. Until society becomes more equal urban renewal may ameliorate and modify the form of 'the inner city problem' but it will not go away.

Appendix 1 Evolution of private renovation grant system 1949 to 1977

Key to grant characteristics

1 maximum eligible expense
2 grant rate
3 central government contribution to LA
4 minimum life of dwelling
5 standard of improvement
6 rent increase allowed
7 occupancy conditions
8 land tenure
9 age of dwelling
10 compulsory improvement
11 rateable value limit for owner-occupied dwelling

Legal provisions	Types of grant	
	Discretionary (Improvement) Grant	*Standard (Intermediate) Grant*
Housing Act, 1949	1 £600 (total cost £100 minimum, £600 maximum) 2 50% 3 75% 4 thirty years 5 sixteen-point standard 6 6% of landlords share of cost 7 if rented, had to remain so for twenty years, otherwise grant repayable *pro rata*, with interest 8 owner of freehold or thirty years, plus lease	
S.I. 1819, 1952	As in 1949, except: 1 £800 (total cost £150 minimum, £800 maximum)	
Housing (Repairs And Rents) Act, 1954	As in 1952, except: 1 £800 (£100 minimum) 4 fifteen years 5 twelve-point standard 6 8% of landlords share of costs	
House Purchase and Housing Act, 1959	As in 1954, except: 1 £800 (for conversions £400 per flat to maximum of £1,200 per house) 4 thirty years, LA discretion to reduce to fifteen 7 restriction reduced to ten years 8 owner of freehold or fifteen years, plus lease 9 pre-1945	1 £310 2 50% 3 75% 4 fifteen years 5 fit and five-point (all standard amenities) 6 8% of landlords share of costs 7 if rented had to remain so for ten years 8 owner of freehold or fifteen years, plus lease 9 pre-1945
Housing Act, 1964	As in 1959, except: 1 £1000 (£500 per dwelling for conversions) 5 twelve-point standard, LA discretion to reduce 6 12½% of landlords share of costs 7 restriction reduced to three years 8 owner of freehold or five years, plus lease	As in 1959, except: 1 £350 4 fifteen years, LA discretion to reduce 5 fit and five-point or three-point (some standard amenities) 6 12½% of landlords share of costs 7 restriction reduced to three years 8 owner of freehold or five years, plus lease 10 LA discretion, at tenants request, to five- or three-point standard, where fifteen years life

Housing Act, 1969	As in 1964, except: 1 £2000 (£2400 per dwelling for conversions) 4 thirty years, LA discretion to reduce to ten 6 usually resulted in 'qualification certificate' for change from controlled to regulated tenancy (fair rent) with five-year phasing of rent increase	As in 1964, except: 1 £400 (£900 when extension needed) 5 seven-point standard, LA discretion to reduce 6 as discretionary grant, but where reduced standard as in 1964 7 as discretionary grant 9 pre-1961	*Special Grant* 1 specific sums for standard amenities 2 50% 3 75% 4 LA discretion 5 LA discretion 6 not applicable 7 none 8 as discretionary grant 9 none	
Housing Act, 1971	As in 1969, except: 1 LA discretion to increase to £3000 (£3600) in Assisted Areas 2 75% in Assisted Areas for work completed by June 1973 (extended to June 1974) 3 90% of grant paid in Assisted Areas for work completed as in 2	As in 1969, except: 2 as discretionary grant 3 as discretionary grant	As in 1969, except: 2 as discretionary grant 3 as discretionary grant	
Housing Act, 1974	As in 1971, except: 1 £3200 (£3700 per dwelling for conversions) 2 50% 3 75% 5 ten-point standard, LA discretion to reduce 6 three year phasing of rent increase 7 if rented, had to remain so for five years; if owner-occupied had to remain so by same owner or be let by him for five years – otherwise repayment at LA discretion 9 pre-1961 11 £175 (£300 in GL) or £350 (£600 in GL) for conversion	As in 1971, except: 1 £1500 (£700 for specified amenities, plus £800 for repairs) 2 50% 3 75% 5 standard amenities, good repair and fit, with LA discretion to reduce 6 as improvement grant 7 as improvement grant 10 LA discretion at tenants request to achieve full or reduced standard	As in 1971, except: 1 sums increased in line with intermediate grant	*Repair Grant* 1 £800 2 only available in GIAs (60%) and HAAs (75% and up to 90% in cases of hardship) 3 90% 4 LA discretion 5 Good repair, LA discretion to reduce 6 as improvement grant 7 as improvement grant 8 as improvement grant 9 as improvement grant
S.I. 1211/1213, 1977	As in 1974, except: 1 £5000 (£5800 per dwelling for conversions) 11 £225 (£400 in GL); for conversion as in 1974	As in 1974, except: 1 £2700 (£1200 for specified amenities, plus £1500 for repairs)	As in 1974, except: 1 sums increased in line with intermediate grant	As in 1974, except: 1 £1500

Appendix 2 Evolution of area powers 1964 to 1974

Legal provisions	**Areas for special action**			
	Improvement Areas (IAs)			
Housing Act, 1964	1 at LA discretion for rented dwelling lacking standard amenities but with a life of fifteen years 2 no specific powers, but general powers under Housing Act, 1957 (Part V) 3 as elsewhere 4 as elsewhere 5 as elsewhere 6 none			
Housing Act, 1969	Powers to declare Improvement Areas repealed, but compulsory improvement powers of 1964 Act still available in declared IAs	*General Improvement Areas (GIAs)* 1 at LA discretion for rented dwelling lacking standard amenities, at tenants request 2 'last resort' power for any dwelling in interests of area as a whole 3 as elsewhere, except Standard Grant at LA discretion 4 as elsewhere 5 as elsewhere 6 (a) maximum eligible expense: £100 per dwelling (b) CG contribution: 50%		
Housing Act, 1971		As in 1969, except: 6(b) 75% in Assisted Areas for work completed by June 1973		
S.I. 440, 1972		As in 1971, except: 6(a) £200 per dwelling		
Housing Act, 1974	All 1964 Act powers repealed	As in 1972, except: 1 at LA discretion for rented dwelling lacking standard amenities or for an owner-occupied dwelling where work could not be carried out to an adjoining dwelling 3 as outside special areas, with addition of Repair Grant 4 60% 5 90%	*Housing Action Areas (HAAs)* 1 as in GIAs 2 wide discretion of LA – for improvement, better management or well-being of residents 3 as in GIAs 4 75% and up to 90% in cases of undue hardship 5 as in GIAs 6 (a) maximum eligible expense: £50 per house, HMO or hostel for works on private land (b) CG contribution: 50%	*Priority Neighbourhoods (PNs)* As outside special areas, except: 2 as in HAAs

Key to area characteristics
1 compulsory improvement
2 compulsory acquisition
3 grant availability
4 grant rate
5 central government contribution to LA
6 environmental works subsidy from central government

References and notes

Chapter 1 Introduction

1 The figures here and elsewhere in the book are for England and Wales. No analysis is made of Scottish urban renewal policies or progress because of the complexities of differing legislation.
2 Text of address by Peter Shore, Secretary of State for the Environment, to *Save our Cities Conference* in Bristol, Department of Environment Press Notice 63 (1977), p. 8.
3 See, for instance, J. Q. Wilson, *Urban Renewal: The Record and Controversy* (MIT Press, 1966).
4 J. B. Cullingworth, *New Towns for Old: The Problems of Urban Renewal*, Fabian Research Series no. 229 (1962), p. 1.
5 For a summary of theoretical approaches see M. Goldsmith, *Politics, Planning and the City* (Hutchinson, 1980), especially Chapter 2.
See also K. Bassett and J. Short, *Housing and Residential Structure: Alternative Approaches* (Routledge and Kegan Paul, 1980), Chapters 8–11.
6 Community Development Project, *The Costs of Industrial Change* (1977), p. 5.

Chapter 2 The bulldozer to clear the slums

1 Department of the Environment (DoE), *Better Homes, the Next Priorities* (HMSO, 1973), Cmnd. 5339.
2 E. Gauldie, *Cruel Habitations: A History of Working-Class Housing 1780–1918* (Allen and Unwin, 1974).
3 G. Cherry, *Urban Change and Planning: A History of Urban Development in Britain* (Foulis, 1972), p. 26.
4 See, for example, A. Mearns, *The Bitter Cry of Outcast London: An Inquiry into the Conditions of the Abject Poor* (1883); and
A. Morrison, *A Child of Jago* (1896; Panther 1971), especially pp. 116–21 for the effects of the Boundary Street Improvement Scheme.
For a useful compilation of historical descriptions see D. Rubenstein, *Victorian Homes* (David and Charles, 1975).
5 F. Engels, *The Condition of the Working Class in England* (Panther, 1969), p. 93.
6 E. Gauldie, p. 145.
See also S. Merrett, *State Housing in Britain* (Routledge and Kegan Paul, 1979), pp. 3–30 for an account of nineteenth century reforms.
7 J. English and P. Norman, *One Hundred Years of Slum Clearance in England and Wales – Policies and Programmes 1868 to 1970*, Department of Social and

Economic Research, University of Glasgow (1975), Discussion Paper no. 1, p. 1.

8 E. Gauldie, p. 288.

9 A. S. Wohl, 'Unfit for human habitation', in H. J. Dyos and H. Wolff (eds.), *The Victorian City*, vol. 2 (Routledge and Kegan Paul, 1973), p. 613.

10 J. R. Kellett, *The Impact of the Railways on Victorian Cities* (Routledge and Kegan Paul, 1969).

11 J. N. Tarn, *Five Per Cent Philanthropy: An Account of Housing in Urban Areas between 1840 and 1914* (Cambridge UP, 1973).

12 A. Briggs, *Victorian Cities* (Penguin, 1968), p. 18.

13 F. Berry, *Housing: The Great British Failure* (Charles Knight, 1974), pp. 31–2.

14 P. Wilding, 'Towards Exchequer subsidies for housing', *Social and Economic Administration*, vol. 6, no. 1 (1972), pp. 3–18; and
L. F. Orbach, *Homes for Heroes: A Study of the Evolution of British Public Housing 1915–1921* (Seely, Service, 1977).

15 M. Bowley, *Housing and the State 1919–1944* (Allen and Unwin, 1945), pp. 11–12. For a history of policy development in the inter-war years see also S. Merrett, pp. 31–62.

16 J. English, R. Madigan and P. Norman, *Slum Clearance: The Social and Administrative Context in England and Wales* (Croom Helm, 1976), p. 19.

17 Ministry of Health, *Twelfth Annual Report 1930–31* (HMSO, 1931), Cmnd, 3937, p. 38 commented that the provision of new houses was critical in the 1920s and:

> it was considered that any direct and comprehensive plan to clear the slums and to meet the needs of the poorest workers must meanwhile be deferred. It was, however, hoped and expected that their conditions would be indirectly improved by a general process which has been described as 'filtering up'.

Reconditioning of slum properties was promoted as an alternative to clearance in these years, linked with the application of Octavia Hill housing management practices (see also Chapter 3) but vigorously attacked by some, particularly in the Labour Party, as an evasion of the need for more effective action.

18 See, for example, E. D. Simon, *How to Abolish the Slums* (Longman, 1929).

19 N. Branson and M. Heinemann, *Britain in the Nineteen Thirties* (Weidenfield and Nicholson, 1971).

20 For an analysis of the factors at work and the results of this process around one city see A. A. Jackson, *Semi-Detached London* (Allen and Unwin, 1973).

21 M. Bowley, p. 187.

22 D. V. Donnison, *The Government of Housing* (Penguin, 1967), p. 163.

23 M. Foot, *Aneurin Bevan 1945–60* (Paladin, 1973), pp. 92–5.

24 D. V. Donnison, p. 174.

25 A post-war government circular had commented:

> Because of the need to concentrate on the erection of new houses for families without a separate home of their own as much as possible of the labour and materials available for housing purposes, it will not be practicable to require the execution of works to existing houses which would make substantial calls on these resources or, save in exceptional circumstances, to set in motion procedures for the demolition of unfit houses which would involve the provision of new houses for persons who would be displaced.

Ministry of Health, *Circular 61/47: Standards of Fitness* (HMSO, 1947).

26 J. B. Cullingworth, *Housing Needs and Planning Policy* (Allen and Unwin, 1960), pp. 51–3.

27 L. Needleman, 'A long-term view of housing', *National Institute Economic Review*, no. 18 (1961), pp. 19–37.
28 R. Samuels, J. Kincaid and E. Slater, 'But nothing happens', *New Left Review*, no. 13 (1962), pp. 38–69.
29 F. T. Burnett and S. F. Scott, 'A survey of housing conditions in the urban areas of England and Wales, 1960', *Sociological Review*, New Series, vol. 10, no. 1 (1962), pp. 35–79 indicated obsolescence far in excess of the 850,000 dwellings reported as unfit; while P. G. Gray and P. Russell, *The Housing Situation in 1960* (Central Office of Information, 1962) estimated that nearly 2 million dwellings had less than fifteen years life, which would necessitate a clearance rate of 130,000 p.a. over the same period. The rate could be reduced to 81,000 if those properties capable of repair at reasonable expense were excluded.
30 D. V. Donnison, pp. 171–7, contains a full analysis of the trends leading up to this housing crisis.
31 J. B. Cullingworth. See also P. Hall *et al., The Containment of Urban England* (Allen and Unwin, 1973).
32 D. V. Donnison, p. 195.
33 The tenuous links between this particular landlord and the 'Profumo scandal' (which involved a Minister and call-girls) resulted in the exposure of his strong-arm tactics during the media's continuing search for revelations.
34 Ministry of Housing and Local Government (MoHLG), *The Housing Programme 1965–1970* (HMSO, 1965), Cmnd. 2835. This White Paper marked a shift in the Labour Party's thinking on housing: henceforth council housing was not for all, it was exceptional:

> The expansion of the public programme now proposed is to meet exceptional needs. It is borne partly of the conditions inherent in modern urban life. The expansion of building for owner-occupation however is normal: it reflects a long-term social advance which should gradually pervade every region.

See also Community Development Project, *Whatever Happened to Council Housing?* (1976), p. 22.
35 MoHLG, *Circular 92/69: Slum Clearance* (HMSO, 1969).
36 There are several other powers which a local authority could use to secure the demolition of older housing. Previously they could use Comprehensive Development Area powers, but, apart from in Birmingham (see Chapter 7), they were used more for central area commercial redevelopment. Far-reaching powers still exist under the Town and Country Planning Act, 1971 (Section 112) but similarly are more often used for other purposes than slum clearance. Part V of the Housing Act, 1957 provides wide powers for the provision of housing and has been used in London, where redevelopment has been justified to secure 'housing gain', i.e. more dwellings on a site. Often Part V has been used in areas of old but not necessarily unfit housing.
37 This section on the clearance and redevelopment process necessarily simplifies the legal powers and procedures used. A lawyer's summary of these powers and procedures is found in J. F. Garner, *Slum Clearance and Compensation* (Oyez, 1975);
J. English, R. Madigan and P. Norman, Chapter 3 give a comprehensive account; while Public Health Advisory Service, *Clearance and Redevelop-*

ment (1974), Practice Note 2, provides a basic guide for resident groups.

38 Prior to 1974 they had another option of making a 'clearance order' whereby the existing owners would be required to demolish and would retain the ownership of the land but this was little used in larger authorities.

39 Ministry of Health, Central Housing Advisory Committee, *Report of the Standards of Fitness for Habitation Sub-Committee* (Miles Mitchell Committee) (HMSO, 1946).

40 Central Housing Advisory Committee, *Our Older Homes: A Call for Action* (report of the Sub-Committee on Standards of Housing Fitness) (HMSO, 1966), para. 45.

41 MoHLG, *Circular 69/67: Housing Act, 1957: Slum Clearance* (HMSO, 1967).

42 R. Samuels *et. al.* p. 38.

43 J. English, R. Madigan and P. Norman, p. 63.

44 J. B. Cullingworth, *Housing and Local Government* (Allen and Unwin, 1966), pp. 194–202 contains an extract from an inspector's report on a clearance area Compulsory Purchase Order inquiry covering the arguments presented by the council and objectors.
B. Hudson, 'The Duke Street inquiry: professional conspiracy', *Community Action*, no. 13 (1974), pp. 26–8 reviews the proceedings of a public inquiry from the point of view of a community group opposing clearance.
Shelter Community Action Team, *Public Inquiries: Action Guide* (1974), mimeo, contains a guide for objections from community groups.

45 DoE, *Development and Compensation: Putting People First* (HMSO, 1972), Cmnd. 5124.

46 Central Housing Advisory Committee, *Council Housing: Purposes, Procedures and Priorities*, Ninth Report of the Housing Management Sub-Committee (HMSO, 1969), pp. 77–91.

47 For a discussion of the issue of interpretation as it affected coloured immigrants in the 1960s see E. Burney, *Housing on Trial: A Study of Immigrants and Local Government* (OUP, 1967), pp. 61–8.

48 P. Norman, 'Corporation town', *Official Architecture and Planning*, vol. 34, no. 5 (1971), pp. 360–2.

49 A. S, Wohl. After local government reorganization in 1974 the profession became known as Environmental Health Officers.

50 P. Norman.

51 J. English, R. Madigan and P. Norman, Chapters 4 and 5.

52 For a general discussion of allocation policies including 'grading' see Housing Services Advisory Group, *Allocation of Council Housing* (HMSO, 1978).
For critical views of this practice see S. Damer and R. Madigan, 'The housing investigator', *New Society* (25 July 1978), pp. 225–6;
F. Gray, 'Selection and allocation in council housing', *Transactions of the Institute of British Geographers*, New Series, vol. 1, no. 1 (1976), pp. 34–46; and
I. Christie and J. Musgrove, 'Degrading grading', *Built Environment Quarterly*, vol. 3, no. 1 (1977), p. 46.

53 D. M. Muchnick, *Urban Renewal in Liverpool: A Study of the Politics of Redevelopment* (Bell, 1970), Occasional Paper in Social Administration no. 33, p. 80.

54 S. Millward and S. M. Schofield, 'The Mechanics of Urban Renewal', *Official Architecture and Planning*, vol. 31, no. 1 (1968), pp. 58–61.

55 For a full discussion of the fluctuations in housebuilding performance in the nineteenth century see J. P. Lewis, *Building Cycles and Britain's Growth* (Macmillan, 1965).

56 A. Ravetz, 'From working-class tenement to modern flat: local authorities and multi-storey housing between the wars', in A. Sutcliffe (ed), *Multi-Storey Living: the British Working Class Experience* (Croom Helm, 1974), pp. 122–50.

57 C. Buchanan, 'Cities in crisis', *Journal of the Royal Town Planning Institute*, vol. 61, no. 7 (1965), p. 260.

58 W. Burns, *New Towns for Old* (Leonard Hill, 1963), p. 61.

59 E. W. Cooney, 'High flats in local authority housing in England and Wales since 1945', in A. Sutcliffe, pp. 151–80'; and
P. McCutcheon, 'High flats in Britain 1945 to 1971', in *Political Economy and the Housing Question* (1975), papers presented at the Housing Workshop of the *Conference of Socialist Economists*, pp. 92–103.

60 Community Development Project, p. 30.

61 J. Seabrook, *The Everlasting Feast* (Allen Lane, 1974), p. 223.

62 See for example, C. R. Harlin, *Slums and Slummers: A Sociological Treatise on the Housing Problem* (Baile Sons and Daniellson, 1935);
B. S. Townroe, *The Slum Problem* (Longman, 1928), p. 6.
For a withering attack on this philosophy, see F. Berry, pp. 158–60.
For a fictional account of upper-class attitudes to slum-dwellers at this time see also J. Galsworthy, *Swan Song* (Heinemann, 1928), pp. 133–62.

63 W. Burns, p. 93–4.

64 Much of the following review is based on the summary in R. Madigan and P. Norman, *Some Determinants of Housing Attitudes in Slum Clearance Areas*, Department of Social and Economic Research, University of Glasgow (1975), Discussion Paper no. 7.

65 P. Wilmott and M. Young, *Family and Kinship in East London* (Routledge and Kegan Paul, 1957; reprinted by Penguin, 1962).
See also J. Platt, *Social Research in Bethnal Green: An Evaluation of the Work of the Institute of Community Studies* (Macmillan, 1971).

66 P. Wilmott and M. Young, p. 42 (Penguin edition). The changed situation is encapsulated in the following quotation:

> Although any day you can see a large round mother standing with her slim and anxious daughter behind her at the counter of the Housing Department, in this sphere her voice cannot gain priority for her children. Kindly administrators do their best to see that members of families get rehoused close together. But it is much rarer for council tenants to be clustered in families, for the mother has none of the special influence with the local authorities that she does with the private rent collectors.

67 See J. H. Mogey, *Family and Neighbourhood* (Oxford UP, 1956), and H. Jennings, *Societies in the Making: A Study of Development and Redevelopment Within a County Borough* (Routledge and Kegan Paul, 1962).
A much later study of the effects of clearance in St. Ann's, Nottingham by tracing families some years after movement concluded that kinship ties had actually been strengthened. Many of those displaced were actually able to move into council housing closer to relatives, while a pride in their new homes encouraged visiting. See K. Coates and R. Silburn, *Beyond the Bulldozer*, Nottingham University Department of Adult Education (1980).

68 B. J. Parker, 'Some sociological implications of slum clearance programmes', in D. V. Donnison and D. Eversley (eds.), *London: Urban Patterns, Problems and Policies* (Heinemann, 1973), Chapter 8, pp. 248–73.

69 C. Vereker and J. B. Mays, *Urban Redevelopment and Social Change: A Study of Social Conditions in Central Liverpool, 1955–56* (Liverpool UP, 1961).

70 R. Wilkinson and E. Sigsworth, 'A survey of slum clearance areas – Leeds' *Yorkshire Bulletin of Social and Economic Research*, vol. 15, no. 1 (1963), pp. 25–51; and

R. Wilkinson and D. Merry, 'A statistical analysis of attitudes to moving' *Urban Studies*, vol. 2, no. 1 (1965), pp. 1–14.

71 J. Seabrook, p. 222.

72 R. Madigan and P. Norman, pp. 61–2.

73 N. Dennis, *People and Planning: The Sociology of Housing in Sunderland* (Faber, 1970), pp. 291–2.

74 Although increasing owner-occupation in older housing areas is an important factor in explaining growing opposition to clearance, it is important to recognize the different attitudes within tenure groups. In particular, the purchase of cheap property in advance of the clearance process, sometimes by rental purchase, can be deliberately chosen by some younger households as a step towards council rehousing. See J. English *et al.*, p. 194.

75 D. Gee, *Slum Clearance* (Shelter, 1975), p. 3.

76 A. Stones, 'Stop slum clearance – Now', *Built Environment*, vol. 35, no. 2 (1972), p. 108.

77 Department of the Environment/Department of Health and Social Security, *Circular 18/74: Homelessness* (HMSO, 1974), advocated that 'maximum use should be made of short-life property . . . with due attention paid to hazards of safety and public health'; but see

B. Widdowson, 'Short-life ghettos', *Roof*, vol. 2, no. 2 (1977), pp. 42–5.

Shelter was very critical of acquisition by councils prior to clearance inquiries being followed by bricking-up or demolition, thus pre-empting decisions and wasting housing resources – see Shelter, *Buy Up, Brick Up and Demolish: A Report on Prior Demolition* (1979).

For an economic analysis see J. Tate and N. Moreton, *Short-Life Dwellings: The Utilization of a Resource*, City of Birmingham Polytechnic, Department of Planning and Landscape (1978), Discussion Note no. 1.

78 J. English, R. Madigan and P. Norman, p. 125.

79 Central Housing Advisory Committee, *Moving From the Slums*. Seventh Report of the Housing Management Sub-Committee (HMSO, 1956).

80 Central Housing Advisory Committee, p. 28.

81 K. Coates and R. Silburn, *Poverty: The Forgotten Englishmen* (Penguin, 1970), p. 228.

82 For instance, C. Ungerson, *Moving Home: A Study of the Redevelopment Process in two London Boroughs* (Bell, 1975), Occasional Paper on Social Administration no. 44, p. 7, 'Between the slum and the new housing estate which takes its place are many years of work by the local authority and of confusion for the people who are affected'.

See also R. Guthrie, 'The new blitz', *New Society* (19 September 1968), pp. 397–8.

83 J. English, R. Madigan and P. Norman, Chapter 6.

84 D. G. Bull, 'Public relations in clearance areas: whose responsibility?', *Housing Review*, vol. 18, no. 2 (1969), pp. 63–70.
See also D. G. Bull, 'Rehousing from clearance areas: people's rights and local authority obligations', *Housing Review*, vol. 19, no. 1 (1970), pp. 26–30.

Chapter 3 Old houses into new homes

1 In 1967 it was observed that:

> The care of existing dwellings has for long been left to the Cinderellas of housing policy. Every now and then some step-children at the town hall or the ministry are told to tidy up the ashes as best they can, while the authors of redevelopment schemes, dressed in their fine plans, go off to the council chamber to receive the acclamations.

'Urban renewal in housing areas', *Housing Review*, vol. 16, no. 1 (1967), pp. 7–13.

2 Until 1977 official statistics usually refer to grants *approved* rather than *paid*, thus overstating progress. The significance of this factor is indicated by the statement in the 1977 Housing Green Paper that of the 629,000 standard grants approved for private owners to the end of 1970 only 500,000 were paid – Department of the Environment (DoE), *Housing Policy: A Consultative Document*, Technical Volume, Part 1 (HMSO, 1977), p. 34.

3 M. Bowley, *Housing and the State 1919–1944* (Allen and Unwin, 1945), p. 147. For a full discussion of the role of reconditioning in the inter-war years, the importance of which is often neglected in other accounts, see R. Moore, *Reconditioning the Slums: The Development and Role of Housing Rehabilitation*, Polytechnic of Central London, School of Environment (1980), Planning Studies no. 7.

4 A. D. Simon, *The Anti-Slum Clearance Campaign*, (Longman, 1935), p. 37, comments that the Act contained '. . . a quite new invention known as the Improvement Area'. Reconditioning was, by this time, not officially regarded as an alternative to clearance but rather as a supplementary activity to stop slum formation. Only 101 Improvement Areas were declared between 1930 and 1935 when the provisions were repealed. Formal or informal action to make owners undertake remedial action to houses outside Improvement Areas was much more significant.
See also R. Moore, pp. 43–52 and pp. 71–9 for a case study of Bradford, one city which eschewed extensive clearance in favour of reconditioning.

5 The relevant reports were: Ministry of Health, *Report of the Departmental Committee on Housing* (Moyne Report), (HMSO, 1933), Cmnd. 4397;
Central Housing Advisory Committee, *Conversion of Existing Houses* (Silkin Report), (HMSO, 1945); and
Central Housing Advisory Committee, *Reconditioning in Rural Areas* (Second Hobhouse Report) (HMSO, 1947).
See also J. B. Cullingworth, *Housing and Local Government* (Allen and Unwin, 1966), pp. 204–6.

6 In fact a limited municipalization programme had been launched immediately after the First World War, when local authorities had been given powers to acquire old houses by negotiation and recondition them. These provisions were seen mainly as a stop-gap solution to the need to provide units while the building

programme got under way and official advice on converting larger houses was produced. See Ministry of Health, *Manual on Conversion of Houses into Flats for the Working Classes* (HMSO, 1919).
The failure of the programme is discussed in S. Pepper, *Housing Improvement: Goals and Strategy* (Lund Humphries, 1971), Architectural Association Paper no. 8, p. 24.

7 J. B. Cullingworth, pp. 31–2. Other critics argued that the removal of rent control would, by restoring profitability, obviate the need for grants.

8 D. V. Donnison, *The Government of Housing* (Penguin, 1967), p. 165 quotes Aneurin Bevan's forceful comments on municipalization:

> It cannot and would not be done at the present time . . . if we tried to do that through the 1700 odd local authorities, it would be an operation compared with which the Italian campaign was one of the most simple ever carried out.

9 J. B. Cullingworth, p. 207.

10 Central Housing Advisory Committee, *Conversion of Existing Houses.*

11 Ministry of Health, *Circular 90/49: Housing Act, 1949* (HMSO, 1949).

12 Ibid.

13 Official publications set out the Government's view. For instance, Ministry of Housing and Local Government (MoHLG), *Grants for Improvements and Conversions* (HMSO, 1954), pp. 3–4, pointed out that:

> . . . the nation cannot afford to let something like a third of its total stock of houses decline into slums. There must be a concentrated effort to preserve them . . . if they could be brought up to standard, they would provide good houses for a generation or more.

14 D. V. Donnison, p. 170.

15 Again government publicity leaflets stressed the necessity for a tandem approach. See, for instance, MoHLG, *New Grants for Better Homes* (HMSO, 1959).

16 D. V. Donnison, Chapters 5 and 6.

17 MoHLG, *Housing* (HMSO, 1963), Cmnd. 2050.
For a critical discussion of this White Paper '. . . permeated with the optimism of affluence' see R. McKie, *Housing and the Whitehall Bulldozer*, Hobart Paper 52, Institute of Economic Affairs (1971), pp. 12–14.

18 MoHLG, *Housing*, p. 14, para. 69.

19 MoHLG, *Circular 53/64: Housing Act, 1964* (HMSO, 1964), para. 2.

20 During the debate on the 1949 Housing Bill, Bevan had earlier expressed the potential of comprehensive improvement thus:

> I can visualize a long street. I was brought up in the middle of a street of a hundred houses. They are still there, still structurally quite sound. The additions (of bathrooms etc.) would be all that would be required. Here and there for the purposes of getting rid of the monotony of the street and of giving back access, and in order that there might be a group of buildings organically suitable and attractive, one or two of the houses could be carved out here and there in the street, so that the whole street could be rescued from obsolescence and monotony, and would provide people with good houses for many years to come.

Quoted in J. T. Roberts, *General Improvement Areas* (Saxon House, 1976), pp. 5–6.
Government publicity material in the 1950s occasionally referred to area

improvement, e.g. T. L. C. Duncan, *Housing Improvement Policies in England and Wales*, University of Birmingham, Centre for Urban and Regional Studies, Research Memorandum, no. 28 (1974), p. 16, quotes the *New Homes for Old* booklet of 1954 which emphasizes the opportunities available for:

> local authorities and residents to play their full part in the general improvement of neighbourhoods, such as tidying up derelict open spaces, closing streets or parts of streets to form safe play areas for children and planting gardens with grass, flowers and trees.

21 For a discussion of the improvement provisions of the Housing Act, 1964 see J. B. Cullingworth, pp. 215–20.

22 F. Berry, *Housing: The Great British Failure* (Charles Knight, 1974), p. 59.

23 MoHLG, *Circular 53/64*, para. 5.

24 See C. Buchanan, *Traffic in Towns* (shortened ed. Penguin, 1963), pp. 65–7.

25 K. M. Spencer, 'Older urban areas and housing improvement policies', *Town Planning Review*, vol. 41, no. 3 (1970), pp. 250–62.

26 See R. Crossman, *The Diaries of a Cabinet Minister*, vol. 1 (Hamish Hamilton and Jonathan Cape, 1975). In November 1964 he was:

> . . . pretty clear what the long-term plan should be. . . . A Labour Minister should impose central leadership, large-scale state intervention in these blighted areas of cities, the twilight areas which were once genteelly respectable and are now rotting away, where Commonwealth immigrants settle and where there are racial problems. (p. 44)

In January after a visit to Manchester he wrote:

> I found myself impressed by the clearance, but depressed by the standard of houses with which they are filling it. (p. 25)

After a visit to Leeds the following week, he wrote:

> I soon discovered that Leeds is as proud of its policy of improving the old central areas, wherever possible, as Manchester is proud of its policy of total clearance. I must say here I am wholly on the side of Leeds. (p. 127)

27 Central Housing Advisory Committee, *Our Older Homes: A Call for Action* (HMSO, 1966).

28 Discussion in this chapter draws on the most useful analyses available to date:
F. Berry, Chapter 13;
Community Development Project, *The Poverty of the Improvement Programme* (revised ed., 1977), pp. 5–12;
T. L. C. Duncan, pp. 7–10;
T. Mason, 'Politics and planning of urban renewal in the private housing sector', in C. Jones (ed.), *Urban Deprivation and the Inner City* (Croom Helm, 1979), Chapter 6;
C. Paris, 'Policy change: ideological consensus and conflict', in M. Harloe (ed.), *Urban Change and Conflict*, Centre for Environmental Studies Conference Series no. 19 (1978), pp. 130–3;
S. Pepper, Chapters 2, 6 and 7;
T. J. Roberts, Chapters 1 and 2.

29 The Taylor Woodrow Group, *The Fulham Study* (1964), mimeo.

30 Hallmark Securities, *The Halliwell Report* (1966), mimeo.
A summary of this report and the Fulham Study was subsequently incorporated

in National Economic Development Office, *New Homes in the Cities. The Role of the Private Developer in Urban Renewal in England and Wales* (HMSO, 1971), Appendix 1, pp. 38–49.

31 R. McKie, pp. 30–1.

32 MoHLG, *The Deeplish Study – Improvement Possibilities in a District of Rochdale* (HMSO, 1966).
For a discussion of this and other studies in Barnsbury and Reading see K. M. Spencer and G. E. Cherry, *Residential Rehabilitation: A Review of Research*, University of Birmingham, Centre for Urban and Regional Studies (1970), Research Memorandum no. 5, pp. 7–18.

33 K. M. Spencer and G. E. Cherry, p. 7.

34 'The Deeplish experiment gets under way', *Architects Journal*, vol. 148, no. 48 (1968), pp. 1250–2.

35 M. Hook, 'Newton Exeter area improvement at an advanced stage', *Architects Journal*, vol. 151, no. 23 (1970), pp. 1468–70.

36 'Old back-to-backs now modern homes', *Surveyor*, vol. cxxxiii (1969), pp. 37–8.

37 G. Ashworth, 'Environmental recovery in Skelmersdale', *Town Planning Review*, vol. 41, no. 3 (1970), pp. 263–92.

38 See Chapter 8.

39 J. T. Roberts, p. 12.

40 Academic research also contributed several case studies of older housing areas. For a summary see K. M. Spencer and G. E. Cherry, pp. 19–28 and 49–62.
A detailed account of a study in Liverpool is given in F. M. Jones, 'A study in obsolescence', *Town Planning Review*, vol. 38, no. 3 (1967), pp. 187–201.

41 J. B. Cullingworth, *Housing in Transition: A Case Study of the City of Lancaster* (Heinemann, 1963), pp. 216–17.

42 J. T. Roberts, p. 12.

43 Central Housing Advisory Committee, *Our Older Homes*.
For a summary and discussion see E. Denington, 'Our older homes: a case for action', *Housing Review*, vol. 17, no. 3 (1968), pp. 85–9.

44 L. Needleman, *The Economics of Housing* (Staples Press, 1965), p. 201. Chapter 10 outlines the principles of this approach.
Its application to areas of older housing was discussed in L. Needleman, 'The comparative economics of improvement and new building', *Urban Studies*, vol. 6, no. 2 (1969), pp. 196–209.

45 See E. M. Sigsworth and R. K. Wilkinson, 'Rebuilding or renovation', *Urban Studies*, vol. 14, no. 2 (1967), pp. 109–20;
L. Needleman, 'Rebuilding or renovation? A reply', *Urban Studies*, vol. 5, no. 2 (1968), pp. 86–90; and
E. M. Sigsworth and R. K. Wilkinson, 'Rebuilding or renovation? A rejoinder', *Urban Studies*, vol. 7, no. 1 (1970), pp. 92–4.

46 These arguments were first presented in J. P. Lewis, *Building Cycles and Britain's Growth* (Macmillan, 1965).
See also J. P. Lewis, 'What kind of housing programme do we need?' *Housing Review*, vol. 16, no. 5 (1967), pp. 148–54;
J. P. Lewis, 'Urban renewal', *District Bank Review*, no. 166 (1968), pp. 3–20;
F. Medhurst and J. P. Lewis, *Urban Decay: An Analysis and Policy* (Macmillan, 1969), Chapter 6.

47 J. P. Lewis, 'What kind of housing programme do we need', p. 151.

48 For a graphic account of the economic problems facing the Labour Governments of 1964–70 and the way in which a dependence on loans from the International Monetary Fund constrained their economic and social policies see D. Coates, *The Labour Party and the Struggle for Socialism*, (Cambridge University Press, 1975), particularly Chapter 5.

49 R. Crossman, p. 626.

50 R. Mellish, 'Housing blight and stress in industrial towns', *Housing Review*, vol. 16, no. 4 (1967), pp. 117–18. Mellish was then Joint Parliamentary Secretary, MoHLG.

51 J. MacColl, 'Best use of our houses', *Housing Review*, vol. 16, no. 5 (1967), pp. 139–48. MacColl was then Joint Parliamentary Secretary, MoHLG. He emphasized the importance of a ministry sponsored study conference at Cambridge in June 1967 which 'drew together the threads of the review'.

52 'More houses than households by the early 1970s', *Guardian* (21 September 1967).

53 'Economics may halt growth in council building', *Guardian* (23 December 1967).

54 Quoted by F. Berry, p. 197.

55 Referring to the Ministry's recently completed assessment of housing needs he said 'In this reappraisal we are taking into account the social and economic case for shifting some of the emphasis to repairing and improving the many structurally sound old houses in our existing housing stock. The more we are successful in this, the less will be our future need for new building.' Quoted in 'Government abandons 1970 housing target', *Guardian* (19 January 1967).

56 R. Crossman, p. 340.

57 'Minister expects 1968 housing records', *Guardian* (23 January 1967).

58 MoHLG, *Old Houses into New Homes* (HMSO, 1968), Cmnd. 3602.

59 Ibid., p. 1, para. 1.

60 Ibid., p. 2, para. 6.

61 A. Greenwood, 'A New Year message from the Minister of Housing and Local Government', *Housing Review*, vol. 18, no. 1 (1969), p. 1.

62 MoHLG, *Circular 65/69: Housing Act, 1969: Area Improvement* (HMSO, 1969), para. 12.

63 See, for example, J. B. Thring, 'Housing backlog: the case for rehabilitation', *Official Architecture and Planning*, vol. 33, no. 11 (1969), pp. 1339–43; and P. A. Stone, 'Improve or build: economic realities', *Official Architecture and Planning*, vol. 33, no. 2 (1970), pp. 131–4.

64 'No housing problem after 1973?', *Housing Review*, vol. 18, no. 3 (1969), pp. 77–8. In 1969 a major review of council housing stated 'It is clear that we no longer have a single national housing problem: we have a large number of local problems of great variety', Central Housing Advisory Committee, *Council Housing Purposes, Procedures and Priorities* (Cullingworth Report) (HMSO, 1969), para. 448.

65 See F. Allaun, *No Place like Home* (Andre Deutsch, 1972), pp. 193–6, and F. Berry, pp. 191–3.

66 S. Pepper, pp. 102–3.

67 See, for example, D. Hall, 'Comments on the White Paper *Old Houses into New Homes*', *Town and Country Planning*, vol. 36, no. 9 (1968), pp. 388–92.

68 For a full discussion see S. Pepper, pp. 102–3.
For an analysis of the changes in Liverpool's policy see M. S. Gibson, *The Developing Role of the 1969 Act in the Changing Process of Urban Renewal*, (MSc thesis, Aston University, 1971), Chapter 4.

69 S. Pepper, p. 105.

70 Ibid., pp. 108–9, and L. Bilsby, 'Old houses into new homes?', *Town and Country Planning*, vol. 36, no. 12 (1968), pp. 527–8.

71 T. L. Blair, 'Rehabilitation: the social aspects', *Official Architecture and Planning*, vol. 33, no. 2 (1970), pp. 126–30.

72 Housing Centre Trust, 'The opportunity for improvement under the Housing Act 1969', *Housing Review*, vol. 18, no. 6 (1969), pp. 196–203.

73 The repeal of compulsory improvement powers was considered premature, particularly by the Association of Public Health Inspectors – see Housing Centre Trust, 'Housing Centre Trust memorandum on the Housing Bill', *Housing Review*, vol. 18, no. 4 (1969), pp. 115–16.
The Town and Country Planning Association were prominent in the lobby for a higher environmental subsidy – see D. Hall, pp. 391–2.

74 For example, J. G. Davies, 'Pollution by planning', *Official Architecture and Planning*, vol. 32, no. 6 (1969), pp. 687–91.

75 DoE, *Circular 63/71: Housing Act, 1971: House and Area Improvement in Development and Intermediate Areas* (HMSO, 1971), p. 2, para. 7. In this Circular the provisions were to apply for a limited period of two years only, from June 1971 to June 1973, but were later extended in the Housing (Amendment) Act, 1973 by a further year to work completed by June 1974.
See also J. Morton, 'Improving slowly', *New Society* (20 January 1972), pp. 118–19.

76 DoE, *Housing Policy: A Consultative Document*, Technical Volume, Part III (HMSO, 1977), p. 120.

77 Ibid., para. 39 and para. 56.

78 L. Gardiner, *Studies of Distribution of Improvement Grants 1972–3 and 1973–4* (DoE, 1974), p. 20, Table 111.

79 D. M. Muchnick, *Urban Renewal in Liverpool* (Bell, 1970), Occasional Papers on Social Administration no. 33, p. 22.

80 S. Pepper, p. 105, commented that 'the minimum period for a grant had only been a problem for those cities that actually believed their own clearance schedule', but most authorities tended to err on the side of caution.

81 For an example of an authority taking a more positive approach see the discussion of Bristol in J. Fleming, 'How should we use our houses?', *Housing Review*, vol. 16, no. 5 (1967), pp. 157–61.

82 K. M. Spencer and G. E. Cherry, pp. 38–48.

83 MoHLG, *Circular 63/69: Housing Act, 1969* (HMSO, 1969) and
MoHLG, *Circular 65/69*.

84 MoHLG, *Circular 65/69*, para. 14.

85 The results of various surveys in the early 1970s describe these developments in local strategies. See T. L. C. Duncan;
J. T. Roberts;
S. Adamson, 'The politics of improvement grants', *Town Planning Review*, vol. 45, no. 4 (1974), pp. 375–86; and

Royal Town Planning Institute, *House Improvement Grants* (1973), RTPI Planning Paper no. 1.

86 T. L. C. Duncan, pp. 45–52.

87 J. T. Roberts, pp. 46–51.

88 Ibid., pp. 34–6, T. L. C. Duncan, pp. 38–45.

89 J. B. Cullingworth, *Housing and Local Government*, p. 209.

90 Central Housing Advisory Committee, *Our Older Homes*, Chapter 4.

91 MoHLG, *Circular 64/69: Housing Act, 1969: House Improvement and Repair* (HMSO, 1969), para. 8.

92 The Denington Committee had pointed out that fifteen years is the length of a childhood and this extension of local authority discretion reflected the Committee's recommendation.

93 Central Housing Advisory Committee, *Our Older Homes* – see Cullingworth's 'Note of reservation', pp. 37–9, 'Over a large part of the country it (the grant system) has received less publicity than any soap manufacturer introducing a new line would consider to be an absolute minimum'.

94 See J. E. M'Kenzie-Hall, 'Improvement grants – action now', *Official Architecture and Planning*, vol. 33, no. 2 (1970), pp. 121–5.

95 DoE, *Circular 41/72: Government Contribution for Environmental Improvement in General Improvement Areas* (HMSO, 1972).

96 See D. F. Medhurst and J. P. Lewis, pp. 108–10 for a description of techniques developed in the preparation of the Teeside Survey and Plan.
Government advice on house condition surveys was eventually incorporated in DoE, *Sample House Condition Survey* (HMSO, 1971), Area Improvement Note 1; and
DoE, *House Condition Survey Within a Potential GIA* (HMSO, 1971), Area Improvement Note 2.

97 RTPI, p. 3.

98 The complex series of activities which have to be co-ordinated are illustrated in DoE *Networks for House and Area Improvement* (HMSO, 1977), Area Improvement Note 11.

99 J. T. Roberts, p. 111.

100 This classification is an adaptation of that devised by T. L. C. Duncan, pp. 33–8.

101 It was, however, abundantly clear to housing managers – see Institute of Housing Managers, *Improving and Modernizing Houses and Estates* (1969). Referring to the 1968 White Paper's emphasis on private housing the introduction to the manual pointed out:

> Privately owned accommodation coming within this category has been given considerable publicity, because much is multi-occupied and the cause of intense housing distress, but it is not perhaps generally realized that there are also many dwellings throughout the country built and owned by local authorities . . . which although occupied at an acceptably low level, lack amenities now considered a social necessity. These properties, some provided at a time when their standards were acceptable, others victims of the building restrictions caused by limited physical and financial resources and by fluctuating political policies, have been a matter of concern for some time, and some authorities have already embarked on programmes of improvement to a high standard.

102 For further details see Institute of Housing Managers, which illustrates the

improvement of purpose built council housing.
DoE, *House Improvement and Conversions* (HMSO, 1972), Area Improvement Note 4, illustrates the variety of old housing involved and different types of improvement and conversion.

103 This discussion drawn on information from L. Gardiner.

104 Larger firms were not attracted to private sector improvement because continuity of work could not be guaranteed. Many smaller firms had cash flow problems as a result of the way grants were paid. They often did several houses at the same time, resulting in long delays in the improvement of individual houses. In some cases builders simply did not complete the work: RTPI, pp. 3–5.

105 J. T. Roberts, p. 157.

106 For further discussion of environmental improvement see: DoE, *Improving the Environment* (HMSO, 1971), Area Improvement Note 3;
DoE, *Environmental Design in Four General Improvement Areas* (DoE, 1972), Area Improvement Note 5;
DoE, *Environmental Improvements* (DoE, 1976), Improvement Research Note 1–76, Housing Improvement Group H6.

107 J. B. Cullingworth, *Problems of an Urban Society: Volume 2, The Social Content of Planning* (Allen and Unwin, 1973), p. 86.

108 For a brief discussion of the salient features of the private sector see D. Eversley, 'The landlords' slow goodbye', *New Society* (16 January 1975), pp. 119–27.
For more detailed information see A. Murie, P. Niner and C. Watson, *Housing Policy and the Housing System* (Allen and Unwin, 1976), Chapter 6; and
DoE, *Housing Policy: A Consultative Document*, Technical Volume, Part III (HMSO, 1977), Chapter 8.

109 B. A. Elliot and D. McCrone, 'Property relations in the city: the fortunes of landlordism', in M. Harloe (ed.), *Urban Change and Conflict*, Centre for Environmental Studies Conference Paper 14 (1975), pp. 31–61.

110 Stereotypes of landlords have a long history:

> Ideally the worst type of slum landlord is a fat wicked man, preferably a bishop, who is drawing an immense income from extortionate rents. Actually it is a poor old woman who has invested her life's savings in three slum houses, inhabits one of them, and tries to live on the rent of the other two – never, in consequence, having any money for repairs.

G. Orwell, *The Road to Wigan Pier* (1937; Penguin ed., 1975), p. 50.
As Pepper (p. 113, fn. 89) pointed out, political debate tended to be couched in terms of extremes of 'the senile amiability of the Tory archetype and the malevolent Rachmen of the Labour left'.

111 Between 1961 and 1969 a 12½ per cent return was allowed. After setting aside a sum for depreciation, the net return on improvement investment over twenty-five years was reduced to 6 per cent (and the shorter life of the property, the lower the net return). This was an important factor in the low take-up of grants; see *Report of the Committee on Housing in Greater London* (The Milner Holland Report) (HMSO, 1965), Cmnd. 2605, pp. 37–9.

112 J. Greve, *Private Landlords in England* (Bell, 1965), Occasional Papers in Social Administration no. 15, indicated that over two thirds of the country's landlords were individuals. Most of them had not established a limited company, 80 per cent owned less than five tenancies, and 40 per cent only one. While there were

very few large landlords, mainly companies, they owned 15 per cent of all privately rented accommodation. Subsequent local studies include:
J. B. Cullingworth, *Housing in Transition* – Lancaster;
DoE, *Report of the Committee on the Rent Acts* (Francis Report) (HMSO, 1971), Cmnd. 4609 – Greater London and the West Midlands; and
M. Harloe *et al.*, – Lambeth and Sutton.

113 For a discussion of the practices of building societies in older areas see M. Harloe *et al.*, Chapter 4.

114 This simple classification was used by E. Gittus, 'Sociological aspects of urban decay', in F. Medhurst and J. P. Lewis, Chapter 3.
For further discussion see R. Mellor, 'Structure and processes in twilight areas', *Town Planning Review*, vol. 44, no. 1 (1973), pp. 54–70.

115 Property developers were making between £20,000 and £30,000 profit on the conversion of a single large house into flats. See
B. Kilroy, 'Improving profits', *New Society* (13 July 1972), p. 79;
B. Kilroy, 'Improvement grants threaten North Kensington', *Housing Review*, vol. 21, no. 3 (1972), pp. 79–81.
Abuses of the grant system were controversial during 1972 when they became good news copy – see L. Marks, 'Many housing grants going to speculators', *Observer* (16 April 1972).

116 D. Raynor, 'Improving Housing Without Destroying Communities', *Municipal Engineering Supplement* (30 March 1973). See also C. Hamnett, 'Improvement Grants as an Indicator of Gentrification in Inner London', *Area* (1973), vol. 5, no. 4, pp. 252–61, and P. N. Balchin, *Housing Improvement and Social Inequality* (Saxon House 1979).

117 P. Pearson and A. Henney, *Home Improvement – People or Profit?* (Shelter, 1972). This comprehensive analysis of the problem of gentrification estimated that in London only 14 per cent of existing tenants remained after improvement. An official DoE study of grants in London during 1972 found that over two thirds of grants had been preceded by household movement, most commonly related to house sale, and four fifths of the previous occupants had been tenants – see DoE, *Housing Policy: A Consultative Document*, Technical Volume, Part III (HMSO, 1977), p. 118.

118 See J. G. Davies, *The Evangelistic Bureaucrat* (Tavistock, 1972), for an account of the ill-fated Rye Hill project where nine years work produced only seven fully modernized houses.

119 Shelter Neighbourhood Action Project, *Another Chance For Cities: SNAP 69/72* (Shelter, 1972).

120 See R. M. Kirwan and D. B. Martin, *The Economics of Urban Residential Renewal*, Centre for Environmental Studies Working Paper 77 (1972).

121 Robert Matthew, Johnson Marshall and Partners, *New Life in Old Towns* (HMSO, 1971).

122 Ibid., p. 9. quotes a hypothetical example of the choice facing a typical landlord of a two-up, two-down terraced house in industrial towns of the North: the annual rental was £52, the outgoings £40 and thus profit before tax was £12; such a house had a market value of about £400 which, if invested at moderate risk, would have yielded a return three or four times as high as the profit from letting.

123 For a general discussion of the problems of these declining neighbourhoods

which argued for continuing clearance rather than switching to improvement as an alternative see A. Henney, 'Managing older housing areas', *Journal of the Royal Town Planning Institute*, vol. 59, no. 2 (1973), pp. 73–7.

124 MoHLG, *Circular 65/69*, para. 23.
As with most other aspects of area improvement more detailed guidance for local authorities took several years to materialize; see DoE, *Public Participation in GIAs* (HMSO, 1973), Area Improvement Note 8.

125 MoHLG, *A New Look For Your Neighbourhood* (HMSO, 1969).

126 J. T. Roberts, Chapters 9 and 10.
For an early discussion of the development of community action in the context of GIAs and critical comments on local authority attitudes see 'Action report: General Improvement Areas', *Community Action*, no. 2 (1972), pp. 11–30.

127 J. G. Davies, 'Pollution by planning', p. 691.

128 J. Ferris, *Participation in Urban Planning: The Barnsbury Case* (Bell, 1972), Occasional Papers on Social Administration no. 48.

129 For one example of the potential for residents involvement see R. Hackney, 'Black Road keeps it up', *Community Action*, no. 6 (1973), pp. 29–31; and R. Hackney, 'Black Road – self-help in Macclesfield', *Housing Review*, vol. 24, no. 5 (1975), pp. 130–1.
For an account of work set in the contrasting environment of Cambridge see R. Darlington, *Public Participation in Practice: Experience in a General Improvement Area in the Back Streets of Cambridge* (Cambridge City Council, 1975).

130 J. T. Roberts, p. 52.

Chapter 4 Gradual renewal

1 F. Horton and S. Pepper, 'Recent changes in housing legislation in the United Kingdom', *Journal of Architectural Research*, vol. 4, no. 2 (1975), pp. 55–8.

2 For an analysis of the 1970–4 period see S. Lansley and G. Fiegehen, *One Nation? Housing and Conservative Policy* (Fabian Society, 1974), Fabian Tract 432.

3 Department of the Environment (DoE), *Fair Deal for Housing* (HMSO, 1971), Cmnd. 4728. The paper outlined proposals designed to promote 'a decent house for every family at a price within their means, a fairer choice between owning a home and renting one, and fairness between one citizen and another in giving and receiving help towards housing costs'. Fairness is in the eye of the beholder and Berry's caustic comment on the Heath Government's attitude to state intervention bear repeating to illustrate the mood of politics in these years. After referring to the concern about homelessness and inadequate housing in the late 1960s stimulated by the television play *Cathy Come Home*, he remarked:

> In little more than three years a new government would come to power modelled on the concept of Selsdon Man, dedicated to ridding the country of its lame ducks and determined to root out the soggy morass of subsidized incompetence. Cathy could go hang.

F. Berry, *Housing: The Great British Failure* (Charles Knight, 1974), p. 63.
See also, though, P. Walker, 'Cabinet Ministering', *Roof*, vol. 3, no. 4 (1978), p. 128.

4 For a factual description of the Act see M. E. H. Smith, *Guide to Housing*

(Housing Centre Trust, 1977), pp. 30–2.

5 J. Morton, 'Vanishing housing lists', *New Society* (21 January 1971), pp. 99–103. See also M. Ash, 'Destiny of our cities', *Town and Country Planning*, vol. 38, no. 11 (1970), pp. 516–17.

6 B. R. Davidson, 'The effects of land speculation on the supply of housing in England and Wales', *Urban Studies*, vol. 12 (1975), pp. 91–9.

7 DoE, *Circular 112/73: Land Availability for Housing*, (HMSO, 1973). See also Community Development Project, *Profits Against Houses* (CDP Information and Intelligence Unit, 1976).

8 P. Ambrose and B. Colenutt, *The Property Machine* (Penguin, 1975).

9 *Housing Improvement Grants* (Tenth Report of the Expenditure Committee) (1973), House of Commons Paper 349, Session 1972–3, 3 vols.

10 Ibid., para. 14.

11 Ministry of Housing and Local Government (MoHLG), *Circular 65/69, Area Improvement* (HMSO, 1969), para. 37, commented:

> '. . . there are a limited number of areas, mainly in large cities, where problems of physical decay are combined with problems of overcrowding and multiple occupation and other severe and intractable problems. They have been called twilight areas and coincide in some cases with what have been called in another context areas of multiple deprivation. The social reasons for taking action in such areas may be imperative even if the economic prospects are doubtful.

12 For a case study see S. S. Duncan, 'Cosmetic planning or social engineering? Improvement grants and Improvement Areas in Huddersfield', *Area*, vol. 6, no. 4 (1974), pp. 259–71.

13 See, for instance, C. Holmes, *Tomorrow in Upper Holloway: A Study in Area Improvement* (North Islington Housing Rights Project, 1973).

14 DoE, *Report of the Committee on the Rent Acts* (Francis Report) (HMSO, 1971), Cmnd. 4609. See also H. E. Francis, 'Report of the Committee on the Rent Acts', *Housing Review*, vol. 20, no. 4 (1971), pp. 107–10.

15 B. Kilroy, 'Stress areas and the compulsory purchase blind spot', *Housing Review*, vol. 22, no. 1 (1973), pp. 18–21.

16 D. Munby, *The Rent Problem* (Fabian Society, 1952), Fabian Research Series 151; D. Eversley, *Rents and Social Policy* (Fabian Society, 1955), Fabian Research Series 174; and J. MacColl, *Plan for Rented Houses* (Fabian Society, 1957), Fabian Research Series 192.

17 M. Wicks, *Rented Housing and Social Ownership* (Fabian Society, 1973), Fabian Tract 421. See also Housing Group of the Society of Labour Lawyers, *The End of the Private Landlord* (Fabian Society, 1973), Fabian Research Series 312.

18 For an attack on this consensus see J. Swann, 'Housing associations: a socialist critique' in Conference of Socialist Economists, *Political Economy and the Housing Question* (1975), pp. 116–22.

19 MoHLG, *Report of the Committee on Housing in Greater London* (HMSO, 1965), Cmnd. 2605; and DoE, *Greater London Development Plan, Report of the Panel of Inquiry* (Layfield Report) vol. 1 (HMSO, 1973), pp. 199–200.

20 D. Frost and N. Sharman, 'Housing and community – based renewal', *Housing Review*, vol. 24, no. 6 (1975), pp. 157–9.
See also A. Barr and J. C. Urwin, *Phased Residential Redevelopment* (Oldham CDP, 1977).
21 M. Barnes, *The Slum: its Story and Solution* (P. J. King, 1931), p. 327.
22 MATAR, *The Meadows is Our Home: We Want the New Houses* (1974), mimeo.
23 'Urban redevelopment – the Byker experience', *Housing Review*, vol. 23, no. 6 (1974), pp. 149–56.
For an evaluation of the scheme, see P. Malpass, 'Byker: community-based renewal', *Roof*, vol. 2, no. 5 (1977), pp. 138–40; and
P. Malpass 'A reappraisal of Byker', *Architects Journal*, Part 1 (9 May 1979), pp. 961–9; Part 2 (16 May 1979), pp. 1011–21.
24 See D. Frost and N. Sharman, 'Participation in urban renewal: the Swinbrook project', *GLC Intelligence Unit Quarterly Bulletin*, no. 25 (1973), pp. 5–12; and R. U. Redpath and D. J. Chivers, 'Swinbrook: a community study applied', *Greater London Intelligence Quarterly*, no. 26 (1974), pp. 5–17.
25 G. Green, 'Politics, local government and the community', *Local Government Studies*, no. 8 (1974), p. 5.
26 Ibid. See also B. Hindess, *The Decline of Working Class Politics* (Paladin, 1971).
27 E. F. Derrick, *House and Area Improvement in Britain*, Centre for Urban and Regional Studies, University of Birmingham (1976), Research Memorandum 54, pp. 108–10.
28 D. Ward, 'Manchester's bulldozer stopped', *Community Action*, no. 16 (1974), pp. 33–4.
See also I. Robertson, *Community Self-Surveys in Urban Renewal* (1976), Monograph 4, Department of Adult Education, Manchester University.
29 'Action report: General Improvement Areas', *Community Action*, no. 2 (1972), p. 25.
30 R. McKie, *Housing and the Whitehall Bulldozer*, Hobart Paper 52, Institute of Economic Affairs (1971), p. 58.
31 N. Dennis, *People and Planning: The Sociology of Housing in Sunderland* (Faber, 1970); and
N. Dennis, *Public Participation and Planners' Blight* (Faber, 1971);
J. G. Davies, *The Evangelistic Bureaucrat: A Study of a Planning Exercise in Newcastle-upon-Tyne* (Tavistock, 1972).
32 J. G. Davies, p. 229.
But see North Tyneside CDP, *Some Housing and Town Planning Issues in North Tyneside* (1976), mimeo, pp. 12–13 for criticism of 'the North-Eastern school of political sociology' basing its arguments on the conflicting value systems of planners and residents rather than looking behind their roles at the operation of the property market.
33 R. McKie, 'Cellular renewal', *Town Planning Review*, vol. 45, no. 3 (1974), p. 276.
34 R. McKie, *Housing and the Whitehall Bulldozer*, p. 36.
35 Quoted in G. M. Lomas, 'The contribution of the Skeffington Report to the discussions on citizen participation in planning', *Town and Country Planning Summer School, Report of Proceedings* (1970), pp. 18–20.
36 Hancock, Hawkes, *Greater Peterborough Draft Basic Plan* (1967).
37 See, for instance, R. Moore, 'Progressive redevelopment', *Official Architecture and Planning*, vol. 34, no. 10 (1971), pp. 775–7; and

M. McEvoy, 'Gradual redevelopment', *Built Environment*, vol. 2, no. 10 (1973), pp. 574–81.

38 R. Moore, 'Gradual renewal', *Architects Journal* (5 February 1975) pp. 275–78. This was reprinted in DoE, *Gradual Renewal* (1975), Area Improvement Occasional Paper 2–75.

39 DoE, *Circular 50/72: Slums and Older Housing: An Overall Strategy* (HMSO, 1972).

40 Ibid., para. 9.

41 Ibid., Annex B, Speech by Julian Amery, Minister for Housing and Construction.

42 DoE, *Circular 115/72: Improvement of Tenanted Dwellings* (HMSO, 1972), briefly noted emerging problems of illegal evictions and suggested that tenants be informed of their rights and that local authorities might prosecute.
However, Amery was quoted as commenting 'improvement is the name of the game' on a television programme in 1972 when replying to criticisms of the effects of the 1969 legislation. See Counter Information Services, *The Recurrent Crisis of London* (1973), p. 41.

43 DoE, *Better Homes: the Next Priorities* (HMSO, 1973), Cmnd. 5339.

44 DoE, *Widening the Choice: the Next Steps in Housing* (HMSO, 1973), Cmnd. 5280, para. 37.
See also J. R. Dykes, 'The development and role of housing associations', in S. Millward (ed.), *Urban Harvest: Urban Renewal in Retrospect and Prospect* (Geographical Publications, 1977), pp. 133–50.

45 DoE, *Better Homes*, para. 15.

46 DoE, *Circular 70/74: Local Authority Housing Programmes* (HMSO, 1974), para. 5.

47 M. Cutting, *Landlord: Private or Public? (A Study of the Rent Act 1974)*, Occasional Paper 4, Catholic Housing Aid Society (1977).

48 Crosland said during the second reading: 'Had we been able to take more time over the preparation of the Bill we should now be debating a much more radical and comprehensive measure'. *Hansard* (6 May 1974), col. 45.

49 DoE, *Circular 13/75: Housing Act 1974: Renewal Strategies* (HMSO, 1975), para. 5.

50 Ibid., para. 10. All quotes which follow are from this section of the circular.

51 Ibid., para. 23.

52 DoE, *Circular 14/75: Housing Act 1974: Parts IV, V, VI, Housing Action Areas, Priority Neighbourhoods, General Improvement Area* (HMSO, 1975).

53 Ibid., Memorandum A, para. 1.

54 Section 36(2) of the Housing Act, 1974.

55 DoE, *Circular 14/75*, Memorandum A, para. 19.

56 D. Pickup, 'The provisions of the Housing Act, 1974' *Housing Review*, vol. 24, no. 2 (1975), p. 55.

57 DoE, *The Use of Indicators for Area Action, Housing Act, 1974* (HMSO, 1975), Area Improvement Note 10.

58 DoE, *Circular 160/74: Housing Act, 1974: Improvement of Older Housing* (HMSO, 1974).

59 DoE, *Circular 170/74: Housing Corporation and Housing Associations* (HMSO, 1974).
See also C. Baker, 'Housing Associations', *Estates Gazette* (1976).

60 J. Hands, *Housing Co-operatives*, Society for Co-operative Dwellings (1975).

61 DoE, *Final Report of the Working Party on Housing Co-operatives* (Campbell Committee) (HMSO, 1976); and
DoE, *Circular 8/76: Housing Co-operatives* (HMSO, 1976).

62 R. McKie, 'Gradual renewal: a quiet revolution', *Architects Journal* (19 February 1975), p. 392.

63 Ibid.

64 M. Fleetwood, 'What gradual renewal means', *Architects Journal* (5 February 1975), pp. 283–4.

65 Welsh Office, *Circular 4/75: Housing Act, 1974: Renewal Strategies* (HMSO, 1975), para. 12.

66 K. Gould, 'The changing role of local authority housing', *Housing Review*, vol. 24, no. 5 (1975), pp. 126–8.

67 R. Pahl, 'Housing action', *New Society* (14 June, 1973), p. 623.

68 T. Mason, 'Intention and implication in housing policy: A study of recent developments in urban renewal', *Journal of Social Policy*, vol. 6, no. 1 (1977), pp. 17–30.

69 North Islington Housing Rights Project, *Priorities for Housing Action*, (Shelter, 1973).

70 R. McKie, 'Gradual renewal'.

71 B. Kilroy, 'Housing associations in Housing Action Areas', paper given at the *National Federation of Housing Societies Conference* (1973).

72 DoE, *Housing Policy: A Consultative Document*, Technical Volume, Part III (HMSO, 1977), p. 120.

73 DoE, *Housing Action Areas: A Detailed Examination of Declaration Reports* (DoE, 1976), Improvement Research Note 2–76.

74 Ibid., para. 3.5.

75 DoE, *Housing Policy: A Consultative Document*, Table X31, p. 124; and
J. Wintour and S. Van Dyke, 'Housing Action Areas but where's the action?', *Roof*, vol. 2, no. 4 (1977), pp. 113–15.
See also K. Bassett and J. Short, 'Housing improvement in the inner city', *Urban Studies*, vol. 15, no. 3 (1978), pp. 333–42.

76 This section draws on M. Gibson and M. Langstaff, 'Policies and strategy in gradual renewal', *The Planner*, vol. 63, no. 3 (1977), pp. 35–8.

77 DoE, *Circular 13/75*, para. 6.

78 An indication of what this official advice would eventually contain was given in L. Isaacson, 'Choosing renewal options', *Housing Review*, vol. 25, no. 1 (1976), pp. 7–11; and
P. Marsh, 'Knock them down or tart them up?', *New Scientist* (4 August 1977), pp. 300–2; and eventually was published in DoE, *The Economic Assessment of Renewal Options* (DoE, 1978), Improvement Research Note 4–78.
See E. Howes, 'Housing renewal: how to evaluate the options', *CES Review*, no. 8 (1980), pp. 13–19, for an application of its methodology to one HAA in Leicester.

79 Several London boroughs were uncomfortably reminded of the new climate when the Secretary of State turned down their CPO applications for clearance under Part V of the 1957 Act. The Court of Appeal quashed a London Borough of Southwark confirmed CPO under Part III powers on the grounds that the

issues of alternative accommodation, adequate resources and comparative costs of improvement had not been properly considered. See Times Law Report, 'Compulsory Purchase Order quashed', *The Times* (28 June 1977).

80 DoE, *Environmental Improvements* (DoE, 1976), Improvement Research Note 1-76.

81 For two general reviews of their progress and problems see
C. Paris, 'Housing Action Areas', *Roof*, vol. 2, no. 1 (1977), pp. 9–14; and
P. Lawless, 'HAAs: powerful attack or financial fiasco?', *The Planner*, vol. 63, no. 3 (1977), pp. 39–42.

82 Haringey LB, *First Steps Towards a Housing Action Area* (1975).

83 P. Lawless.
See also National Building Agency, *Organisation and Staff Resources for Area Improvement, Part 1: The General Approach* (NBA, 1977).

84 J. Wintour and S. Van Dyke.
See also J. Cameron, 'Landlords in Housing Action Areas', *Housing Review*, vol. 27, no. 6 (1978), pp. 144–6.

85 North Islington Housing Rights Project, *Street by Street: Improvement and Tenant Control in Islington* (Shelter, 1976);
C. Holmes, 'Islington's tough approach works', *Roof*, vol. 2, no. 3 (1977), pp. 81–3; and
T. Hadden, *Compulsory Repair and Improvement*, Research Study 1, Centre for Socio-Legal Studies, Oxford University (1978), Appendix D.

86 G. Lomas and E. Howes, 'Private improvement in Leicester', *CES Review*, no. 6 (1979), pp. 50–5 outlines the methods used in one area to stimulate grant take-up. See also J. Young, 'Newport wraps up improvement package', *Roof*, vol. 4, no. 4 (1979), pp. 116–17.

87 A. Thompson, *The Role of Housing Associations in Major Urban Areas: A Case Study of Merseyside Improved Houses*, University of Birmingham, Centre for Urban and Regional Studies (1977), Research Memorandum no. 60;
Housing Corporation, *Circular 3/78: In the Public Eye* (1978); and
C. Holmes, 'The elusive panacea', *Roof*, vol. 3, no. 4 (1978), pp. 110–12.

88 C. Holmes, 'Islington's tough approach works'.

89 S. Weir, 'Tenants take over: reality or myth', *Roof*, vol. 1, no. 2 (1976), pp. 54–7. See also A. Power, *Holloway Tenant Co-operative: Five Years On*, Holloway Tenant Co-operative (1977).

90 See C. Holmes, 'The party's over: the Government retreats from its housing strategy', *Roof* (October 1975), pp. 15–19; and
NUPE/SCAT, *Up against a Brick Wall: The Dead End in Housing Policy* (1978).

91 Tenth Report of the Expenditure Committee, *House Improvement Grants*, para. 55.

92 Mr Armstrong (Under-Secretary of State for the Environment) commented that

'. . . over the past few years too large a proportion of the resources available for the improvement of the nation's older housing has been devoted to purpose-built, inter-war, council estates, many of which were already in a relatively satisfactory condition, certainly when compared with the bulk of the substandard houses remaining in the hands of private landlords'. *Hansard* (7 August, 1975), col. 794.

93 See D. A. Kirby, 'The inter-war council dwelling: A study of residential obsolescence and decay', *Town Planning Review*, vol. 42, no. 3 (1971), 250–68.

94 DoE, *Circular 64/75: Housing Expenditure Changes* (HMSO, 1975).

95 G. Lomas and E. Howes, 'Private sector improvement since the 1974 Act: some facts and figures', *CES Review*, no. 2 (1977), pp. 109–12.
See also National Home Improvement Council, *Improvement in United Kingdom Housing – A Reappraisal* (1976).

96 DoE, *Circular 38/77: House Renovation Grants* (HMSO), called upon local authorities to relax repayment provisions in the case of owner-occupiers moving home in most circumstances, not to exact repayment in the case of mortgage default, and to provide guarantees of grants in connection with building society mortgages for unimproved properties.
However, many problems remained. See J. Wintour, 'Are Improvement grants tied up in the town halls?' *Roof*, vol. 3, no. 3 (1978), pp. 81–3.
Comprehensive studies of grant take-up and local discretion and of administration are found in National Home Improvement Council, *The Take-Up of Private Sector Improvement Grants* (1979); and
National Building Agency, *Improvement Grant Administration* (1979).

97 S. Weir, 'Red-line districts', *Roof*, vol. 1, no. 4 (1976), pp. 109–14;
V. Karn, 'Housing policies which handicap inner cities', *New Society*, (11 May 1978), pp. 301–3.

98 For a full discussion of building societies see M. Boddy, *The Building Societies*, (Macmillan, 1980).
See also 'The irrestible rise of building societies', *Roof*, vol. 1, no. 4 (1976), pp. 105–8.
For a discussion of 'exchange professionals' see P. Williams, *The Role of Financial Institutions and Estate Agents in the Private Housing Market*, University of Birmingham, Centre for Urban and Regional Studies (1976), Working Paper 39; and
J. Ford, 'The role of the building society manager in the urban stratification system: autonomy versus constraint', *Urban Studies*, vol. 12, no. 3 (1975), pp. 295–302.

99 DoE, *Circular 80/76: Local Authority Housebuilding, Local Authority Mortgage Lending* (HMSO, 1976).
See also *Shelter's Case Against the Housing Cuts*, (Shelter, 1976).

100 The cuts were accompanied by a tortuous exercise in self-justification; 'Although I very much regret the constraint on housing expenditure I do not regret introducing controls over the total level of new building expenditure by local authorities, for it was an absurdity that we should have controlled through Section 105 that which we sought to encourage – rehabilitation – while failing to control that which we were seeking to discourage – namely demolition of property where rehabilitation was a reasonable alternative.' P. Shore, *Speech by the Secretary of State for the Environment on Housing Finance at Birmingham* (16 September 1976).

101 D. Nicholas, 'Government by circular, telephone and "leak" ', *Roof*, (October 1975), pp. 19–20.

102 DoE, *First Report of the Study Group on Programmes of Social Ownership and*

Renovation of Council Dwellings (DoE, 1976).

103 D. Bebb, G. Filkin and C. Meredith, *Unfair Shares* (1977), mimeo.

104 A. Roberts, 'The bulldozers must come back', *Labour Weekly* (14 January 1977).

105 Community Development Project, *The Poverty of the Improvement Programme* (revised ed. 1977), p. 4.

106 M. E. H. Smith, p. 198.

107 E. Craven, 'Housing', in R. Klein (ed.), *Social Policy and Public Expenditure 1975; Inflation and Priorities*, Centre for Studies in Social Policy (1975).

108 See, for instance, C. Trinder, 'Housing expenditure: who benefits most?', *Roof*, vol. 1, no. 3 (1976), pp. 81–4.

109 A. Crosland, *Towards a Labour Housing Policy* (1971), Fabian Tract 410.

110 A. Crosland, 'The finance of housing', *Housing Review*, vol. 24, no. 5 (1975), pp. 128–30.

111 See, for instance, F. Berry, p. 163. 'For whatever may have been in the minds of those responsible for bringing forward these complicated provisions, there can be little doubt that those who voted for them in Parliament felt a distaste for local authority housing, that council tenants were on the whole worthless parasites who had had it easy for far too long and who ought to be clobbered hard enough to drive them out of rented housing altogether, wherever possible'.

112 For an overall review of this evidence see H. Aughton, 'Something to think about', *Housing and Planning Review*, vol. 32, no. 2 (1976), pp. 4–6.

113 DoE, *Housing Policy: A Consultative Document*, foreword by the Secretary of State for the Environment and the Secretary of State for Wales.

114 This review of the Green Paper is largely based on M. Harloe, 'Will the Green Paper mean better housing', *Roof*, vol. 2, no. 5 (1977), pp. 143–8.
See also S. Lansley, *Housing and Public Policy* (Croom Helm, 1979), Chapter 7, for a critique of the review as 'almost a non-event in terms of its policy recommendations.'

115 DoE, *Housing Policy: A Consultative Document*, Technical Volume, Part 1, p. 110.

116 See, for instance, Housing Centre Trust, *Housing Finance Review* (1975).
See also B. Kilroy, *Housing Finance – Organic Reform?*, Labour Economic, Finance and Taxation Association (1978).

117 J. B. Cullingworth, 'Housing priorities and inflation', *Housing Review*, vol. 24, no. 1 (1976), p. 6.

118 P. Shore.

119 For an analysis of the implications and operation of HIPs see C. Watson, 'Housing Investment Programmes', *Housing Review*, vol. 26, no. 4 (1977), pp. 80–2; and
A. Murie and P. Leather, 'Developments in housing strategies', *The Planner*, vol. 63, no. 6 (1977), pp. 167–9.

120 DoE, *Circular 18/77: Housing Capital Expenditure* (HMSO, 1977).

121 DoE, *Circular 63/77: Housing Strategies and Investment Programmes* (HMSO, 1977).
See also DoE, *Circular 38/78: Housing Strategies and Investment Programmes for Local Authorities in England; Arrangements for 1979/80* (HMSO, 1978).

122 B. Crofton, 'Housey, housey', *New Society*, (23 February 1978), pp. 428–9.

For overall reviews of HIPs see RTPI Housing Working Party, *Housing Investment Programmes: The Role of Central Government* (RTPI, 1980); and J. Morris, 'The rise and fall of local housing strategies', *Housing Review*, vol. 29, no. 2 (1980), pp. 50–3.

123 DoE, Statement by Peter Shore, Secretary of State for the Environment at a Press Conference on 22 March (DoE, 1979), Press Notice 134.

124 For a critical review of the consultation papers leading up to the Bill see 'The Housing Bill: what's left of it', *Roof*, vol. 3, no. 6 (1978), pp. 173–6.

125 DoE, *Housing Repair and Improvement: Proposed Legislation and Other Changes* (1978), mimeo.

126 See DoE, *Housing Policy: A Consultative Document*, Technical Volume, Part III, pp. 129–57, for details of the 1971 survey in England and Wales and the separate surveys for the two countries in 1976.

127 Ibid., p. 94.

128 DoE, *Housing Repair and Improvement*, p. 3.

129 Ibid., p. 1.

130 M. Gibson, 'Improving improvement?', *Housing Review*, vol. 28, no. 2 (1979), pp. 179–80.

131 Association of Metropolitan Authorities, *Policies for Improvement: A Report on Housing Repair and Renovation* (1978), mimeo, p. 16.

132 This joint letter was from thirteen organizations, including local authority bodies, professional institutes and pressure groups. It stated '. . . the proposals for inclusion in the Housing Bill will have little effect in increasing grant up-take, and in some cases will be counter-productive. The need to reverse the decline in living conditions in areas of older housing is an urgent one and cannot wait for the next Housing Act'.

133 See, for instance, Royal Town Planning Institute Housing Working Party, *Housing Renewal Policy: Will it work?* (RTPI, 1979).

134 DoE, *Housing Action Areas: An Analysis of Annual Progress Reports for 1977* (DoE, 1979), Improvement Research Note 5/78. See also 'Housing in Action Areas', *Roof*, vol. 4, no. 5 (1979), pp. 151–3.

135 Community Development Project, p. 12.

136 Official advice to housing associations stresses the need to consider cost savings and postpone repair work. For a discussion of these issues see D. Levitt, 'A Thirty-year Life for Rehabilitation – fact or fiction?', *Housing Review*, vol. 26, no. 4 (1977), pp. 94–6; and Housing Centre Trust, 'Recommended standards for the rehabilitation of older houses', report of a joint HCT/NFHA seminar, *Housing Review*, vol. 29, no. 4 (1980), pp. 127–35.

137 More detailed information on changes in HAAs began to emerge in 1979 when the first results of DoE sponsored monitoring studies were published. See, for instance, A. D. Thomas, *Area Based Renewal: Three Years in the Life of a Housing Action Area*, Centre for Urban and Regional Studies, University of Birmingham (1979), Research Memorandum no. 72.

138 Both quotes are from A. Ravetz, *The Housing Poor: A New Appraisal*, Catholic Housing Aid Society, Occasional Paper no. 3 (1976), p. 14 and p. 15.

139 One authority which adopted this approach was Blackburn; see J. T. Roberts, 'Blackburn's housing renewal strategy', *Housing Review*, vol. 29, no. 3 (1980),

pp. 84–6.

140 R. McKie, 'The strange death of gradual renewal', *District Council Review* (March 1977), p. 56.

141 See J. M. McKean, 'Cellular renewal in Southwark', *Architects Journal*, (17 November 1976), pp. 925–30;
and for an attempt to refute criticism based on 'the hollow ring of prejudice' see M. Hook, 'Microfact, macroview', *Roof*, vol. 3, no. 5 (1978), p. 160.

142 J. T. Roberts, 'Housing renewal policy', paper presented to the *Annual Conference of the Institution of Municipal Engineers* (1979).

143 Benwell CDP, *Slums on the Drawing Board* (1978), Final Report Series no. 4, Benwell Community Project.

144 D. Parish, 'Bring back the bulldozers', *Environmental Health* (August 1978), pp. 180–1 attacks a fashionable emphasis on rehabilitation and comments on the myth of a community spirit in older areas: 'Civil servants seem to have gleaned this community spirit factor when sitting in their detached houses in Henley-on-Thames watching Coronation Street on television and have decided that this idyll is universal and should be enshrined in HAAs!'

145 D. Levitt and A. Burrough, 'Rehab at all costs', *Architects Journal*, (4 July 1979), p. 17.

146 D. Webster, 'Housing', in N. Bosanquet and P. Townsend (eds.), *Labour and Equality: A Fabian Study of Labour in Power, 1974–9* (Fabian Society, 1980), pp. 244–63.

Chapter 5 The Poverty Programme

1 K. Coates and R. Silburn, *Poverty: the Forgotten Englishman*, (Penguin, 1970), p. 13 commented that:

> During the 1950s . . . the period since the end of the Second World War was interpreted as one of more or less uninterrupted and continuing economic growth, with the new wealth being distributed increasingly equitably throughout the population. The age-old malaise of poverty, far from being an endemic problem facing a mass of the population, was felt to be a slight social hangover: a problem affecting tiny groups of people who, through their incompetence or fecklessness, were failing to share in the new affluence. Increasingly the problems of affluence commanded public attention. . . .

2 For a succinct and extensively referenced assessment of the state of knowledge about the poor in the late 1960s see A. Sinfield, 'Poverty rediscovered' *Race*, vol. X, no. 3 (1968), pp. 202–9, reprinted in revised form in J. B. Cullingworth (ed.), *Problems of an Urban Society. Volume 3: Planning for Change* (Allen and Unwin, 1973), Chapter 7.
For a more detailed discussion see D. Wedderburn (ed.), *Poverty, Inequality and Class Structure* (CUP, 1974), a collection of essays which are mainly revised versions of papers originally written in 1969;
R. Holman, *Poverty: Explanations of Social Deprivation* (Martin Robertson, 1978), provides a detailed analysis of the definitions and explanations of poverty which have informed post-war social policy.

3 P. Townsend, 'The meaning of poverty', *British Journal of Sociology*, vol. XIII, no. 3 (1962), p. 225.
See also P. Townsend, 'Poverty as relative deprivation', in D. Wedderburn (ed.), Chapter 1.

4 See F. Lafite, 'Income deprivation', in R. Holman (ed.), *Socially Deprived Families in Britain* (Bedford Square Press, 1970), Chapter 1; and
A. B. Atkinson, 'Poverty and income inequality in Britain', in D. Wedderburn (ed.), Chapter 2.

5 B. Abel Smith and P. Townsend, *The Poor and the Poorest* (Bell, 1965), Occasional Papers on Social Administration no. 17; in fact the 'poverty line' adopted was 140 per cent of basic national assistance rates, i.e. those whose resources amounted to less than 40 per cent above these scales – see pp. 16–20 for a discussion of the reasons.

6 J. Westergaard and H. Resler, *Class in a Capitalist Society* (Penguin, 1975), p. 51. Part 2, Section 2, 'Trends in income inequality' incorporates the results of much of the research of the late 1950s and early 1960s.

7 A. B. Atkinson, *Unequal Shares* (revised ed., Penguin, 1974), Chapters 1 and 3.

8 R. Holman, 'Combating social deprivation', in R. Holman (ed.), *Socially Deprived Families*, pp. 140–4.

9 A. Sinfield, p. 132.

10 R. Holman, *Socially Deprived Families*, pp. 154–7 summarizes the limited research on deprived areas in the 1960s.

11 This phrase characterizing conventional explanations of the persistence of poverty was coined by W. Ryan, *Blaming the Victim*, (Orbach and Chambers, 1971).

12 For a brief discussion see A. Sinfield.
K. Coates and R. Silburn, Chapters 7, 8 and 9 relate different explanations of poverty to their study of St Ann's in Nottingham.
J. Higgins, *The Poverty Business: Britain and America* (Basil Blackwell, 1978), pp. 100–8 compares the relative significance of explanations of poverty in Britain and the USA.

13 A. Sinfield, p. 132.

14 D. Donnison, 'Policies for priority areas', *Journal of Social Policy*, vol. 3, no. 2 (1974) pp. 127–35. For a full discussion of the development and limitations of social policy in the 1960s see R. Titmuss, *Commitment to Welfare* (Allen and Unwin, 1968).

15 For the origins and development of the Poverty Programme see N. Flynn, 'Urban Experiments Limited: Lessons from CDP and the Inner Area Study', paper presented to *CES Conference on Urban Change and Conflict*, University of York (4–7 January 1977);
Community Development Project, *Gilding the Ghetto* (CDP, 1977);
J. Edwards and R. Batley, *The Politics of Positive Discrimination: An Evaluation of the Urban Programme 1967–77* (Tavistock, 1978), Chapter 2;
J. Higgins, Chapter 3;
D. McKay and A. Cox, 'Confusion and reality in public policy: the case of the British Urban Programme', *Political Studies*, vol. XXVI, no. 4 (1978), pp. 491–506;
and

D. McKay and A. Cox, *The Politics of Urban Change* (Croom Helm, 1979), pp. 234–48.

16 Central Advisory Council for Education, *Children and their Primary Schools* (Plowden Report) (HMSO, 1967), para. 132.

17 Ibid.

18 Ibid., para. 15, commented:

> We ask for 'positive discrimination' in favour of such schools and the children in them, going well beyond an attempt to equalize resources. . . . The justification is that the homes and neighbourhoods from which many of their children come provide little support and stimulus for learning. The schools must supply a compensating environment.

19 Secretary of State for the Home Department, *et al.*, *Report of the Committee on Local Authority and Allied Personal Social Services* (Seebohm Report) (HMSO, 1968).

20 Ibid., para. 141.

21 Ibid., para. 477.

22 Ibid., para. 480.

23 Ibid., para. 487 concluded that 'concentration upon priority areas is not . . . an alternative to extra resources – it assumes their existence'.

24 Planning Advisory Group, *The Future of Development Plans* (HMSO, 1965)

25 Ministry of Housing and Local Government (MoHLG), *People and Planning* (Skeffington Report) (HMSO, 1969).

26 MoHLG, *Report of the Committee on Housing in Greater London* (Milner Holland Report) (HMSO, 1965), p. 122.

27 MoHLG, *Report of the Committee on the Management of Local Government* (Maud Report) (HMSO, 1965).

28 R. Hambleton, *Policy Planning and Local Government* (Hutchinson, 1978), p. 45.

29 National Committee for Commonwealth Immigrants, *Areas of Special Housing Need* (NCCI, 1967).
See also E. J. B. Rose *et al.*, *Colour and Citizenship: A Report on British Race Relations* (OUP, 1969).

30 For a general account of American experience see P. Marris and M. Rein, *Dilemmas of Social Reform* (Routledge and Kegan Paul, 1971).
See also D. Moynihan, *Maximum Feasible Misunderstanding* (Free Press, 1969).
Halsey later described 'ideas drifting casually across the Atlantic, soggy on arrival and of dubious utility': A. H. Halsey, *Times Educational Supplement* (9 February 1973).

31 M. Mayo, 'The history and early development of CDP', in R. Lees and G. Smith (eds.), *Action – Research on Community Development* (Routledge and Kegan Paul, 1975), p. 7.

32 The reaction of the then Home Secretary, Callaghan, was 'we must stop all this bloody religious nonsense' – see R. Crossman, *Diaries of a Cabinet Minister*, Vol. III (Hamish Hamilton and Jonathan Cape, 1978), p. 139.
There is general agreement that Morell was very influential in the development of area-selective approaches to deprivation – see, for example, J. Higgins, pp. 41–2; and
M. Mayo, p. 8.

33 For a brief summary of the Urban Programme see R. Batley and J. Edwards,

'CDP and the Urban Programme', in R. Lees and G. Smith (eds.), Chapter 17. For the definitive study based on research within the Home Office alongside the Civil Servants responsible, see J. Edwards and R. Batley, Chapters 3–7.

34 Ibid., Chapter 3 gives an account of events in Whitehall following Wilson's announcement.

35 *Hansard* (23 July 1968), col. 40.

36 Home Office, *Urban Programme Circular No. 1* (4 October 1968).

37 Home Office notes on the Urban Programme quoted by M. Meacher, 'The politics of positive discrimination', in H. Glennester and S. Hatch (eds.), *Positive Discrimination and Inequality* (Fabian Society, 1974), Fabian Research Series no. 314, p. 4.

38 Home Secretary's announcement in Parliament quoted in CDP Information and Intelligence Unit, *The National Community Development Project: Inter-Project Report* (CDP, 1974), p. 1.

39 'Government opening campaign against urban poverty', *Guardian* (15 January 1969).

40 Quotes from a Home Office paper (1971), published in R. Lees and G. Smith, Chapter 1.

41 The Plowden Committee's recommendations for experimental action research were being implemented in 5 EPAs in inner urban areas. They involved the injection of additional resources into their schools to raise educational standards, and monitoring to establish the best methods for incorporation in a long-term programme for improving primary education.

For a discussion see P. Lawless, *Urban Deprivation and Government Initiative* (Faber and Faber, 1979), Chapter 3.

42 See, for example, T. and G. Smith, 'Urban first aid', *New Society*, (30 December 1971), pp. 1277–80;

M. Gibson and C. Paris (eds.), 'The Urban Programme', *West Midlands Grassroots* no. 3 (1972), pp. 3–10, part of which was reprinted as J. Edwards, 'The Urban Programme', in E. Butterworth and R. Holman (eds.), *Social Welfare in Modern Britain* (Fontana, 1975), pp. 329–33; and

Community Action, 'Action Report: The Urban Aid Programme', *Community Action*, no. 3 (1972), pp. 17–26.

43 Shelter Neighbourhood Action Project, *Another Chance for Cities: SNAP 69/72* (Shelter, 1972), p. 5.

For a summary by the project's director see D. McConaghy, 'SNAP – An Urban Programme', in J. Brand and M. Cox (eds.), pp. 33–8.

For critical reviews see H. Rose and T. Puckett, 'Blueprint for bureaucrats', *Royal Institute of British Architects Journal* (June 1973), pp. 277–81; and Community Action, 'Inner city: dream and reality', *Community Action*, no. 8 (1973), pp. 13–16.

44 Quoted in Community Action, 'Inner city: dream and reality', p. 13.

45 Birmingham IAS, *Project Report*, IAS/B/1 (DoE, 1974), p. 4.

46 Quoted in CDP, *Gilding the Ghetto*, p. 14; Part I of this publication gives a brief summary of all the Poverty Programme projects;

For an assessment of the minor Conservative initiatives see P. Lawless, Chapters 4 and 5.

47 Quoted in CDP, *Gilding the Ghetto*, p. 15: the Home Office did not, however, give a high priority to urban deprivation and the CCP initiative 'fizzled out' – for an account of 'the three wasted years' 1974–7 see M. Wicks, in N. Bosanquet and P. Townsend (eds.), *Labour and Inequality* (Heinemann, 1980).

48 CDP Information and Intelligence Unit, *Inter-Project Report* (1974).

49 Coventry CDP, *CDP Final Report: Part 1: Coventry and Hillfields: Prosperity and the Persistence of Inequality* (CDP Information and Intelligence Unit 1975), p. 40.

50 CDP Information and Intelligence Unit, *Inter-Project Report*, p. 53.

51 Although this brief outline conveys the generality of the shifting perspectives within CDP it should be noted that the twelve teams did not embrace the emerging radical perspectives to the same extent or in the same ways – see P. Lawless, Chapter 6.
The evolution of CDP is best described in the Coventry CDP Final Report – see also J. Bennington, 'The flaw in the pluralist heaven: changing strategies in the Coventry CDP', in R. Lees and G. Smith (eds.), Chapter 19.
For an outline of the work proposed within this changed perspective see CDP, *Forward Plan 1975–6* (CDP Information and Intelligence Unit, 1975).

52 P. Walding, Director of Birmingham IAS, quoted in N. Flynn, p. 14. The Liverpool IAS were thinking on similar lines:

> . . . to a great extent this poverty is a reflection of inequalities in society as a whole. Clearly the scale and character of the problem is too great for policies concerned solely and specifically with inner areas to be effective. Any fundamental change must come through policies concerned with the distribution of wealth and the allocation of resources.

Liverpool IAS, *Third Study Review*, IAS/L1/6 (DoE, 1974), p. 10.

53 Coventry CDP.
These proposals attracted widespread publicity, see for example the full-page treatment 'Coventry's pride and prejudice', *Guardian* (June 24 1975).

54 'CDPs writ larger', *New Society* (17 July 1975), p. 122.
See also 'Massacre by the Mersey', *Sunday Times* (6 February 1977).

55 For a polemical analysis see M. Gibson and N. Flynn, 'Urban Experiments Ltd. 1: The sham of the poverty programme', *West Midlands Grassroots*, no. 15 (1974), pp. 7–15.
This analysis was criticized on the grounds that the Poverty Programme was not mere tokenism but 'an integral part of a co-ordinated and centralized programme of internal control and repression' – L. Bridges, 'The Ministry of Internal Security: British Urban Social Policy 1968–74', *Race and Class*, vol. XVI, no. 4 (1975), pp. 375–86.

56 M. Meacher, pp. 7–8.

57 For a development of this argument see P. Townsend, 'Area deprivation policies', *New Statesman* (6 August 1976), pp. 168–71.

58 This argument is extended in reply to Townsend's points in N. Deakin, 'Inner area problems: positive discrimination revisited', *Greater London Intelligence Journal*, no. 37 (1977), pp. 4–8.
See also S. Holtermann, 'The welfare economics of priority area approaches', *Journal of Social Policy*, vol. 7, no. 1 (1978), pp. 23–40.

59 For a discussion see H. Glennerster and S. Hatch.

Chapter 6 Saving cities

1 Department of the Environment (DoE), *Policy for the Inner Cities* (HMSO, 1977), Cmnd. 6845.

2 DoE, 'Inner urban policy', Press Notice 835 (17 September 1976) provides the text of the speech.
It was dubbed memorable in *Inner Cities 'A Memorable Speech' Commitment to Action* (1977) a submission by the cities of Birmingham, Leeds, Liverpool, Manchester, Newcastle and Sheffield.

3 DoE, 'Inner urban policy', p. 4.

4 Ibid., p. 5.

5 Ibid., p. 8.

6 For a discussion of the planning background to post-war urban renewal see G. E. Cherry, 'Aspects of urban renewal', in T. Hancock (ed.), *Growth and Change in the Future City Region* (Leonard Hill, 1976), Chapter 4.

7 The implications of changing assessments of housing needs for strategic planning policies were brought sharply into focus in J. B. Cullingworth, *Housing Needs and Planning Policy* (Routledge and Kegan Paul, 1960).

8 D. Eversley, *Planning Without Growth* (Fabian Society, 1975), Fabian Research Series 321, p. 5.

9 J. B. Cullingworth, 'Social problems of cities (2)', in RTPI *The Urban Crisis: Social Problems and Planning* (1974), p. 12.

10 See *Inner Cities 'A Memorable Speech' Commitment to Action*, p. 1.

11 Royal Town Planning Institute, *Land Values and Planning in the Inner Areas* (RTPI 1978). Consultation Document, p. 1.

12 P. Townsend and N. Bosanquet (eds.), *Labour and Inequality* (Fabian Society, 1972).

13 Prominent contributions included R. E. Pahl, *Whose City?* (Longman, 1970); D. Harvey, *Social Justice and the City* (Edward Arnold, 1973); and J. M. Simmie, *Citizens in Conflict: the Sociology of Town Planning* (Hutchinson, 1974).

14 See P. Hall *et al.*, *The Containment of Urban England. Volume Two: The Planning System: Objectives, Operations, Impact* (Allen and Unwin, 1973), especially Chapters 11, 12 and 13:

> Overall the idealized system obviously had a strong element of planning for the least fortunate; urban containment and the creation of self-contained and balanced communities were supposed specifically to help the less advantaged members of society. But in practice, the system seems almost systematically to have had the reverse effect: it is the most fortunate who have gained the most benefit from the operation of the system while the least fortunate have gained very little. (p. 409)

15 See J. D. Stewart, 'Corporate planning', in M. J. Bruton (ed.), *The Spirit and Purpose of Planning* (Hutchinson, 1974), Chapter 8.

16 For an assessment of corporate planning practice in the mid-1970s see R. Hambleton, *Policy Planning and Local Government* (Hutchinson, 1978), pp. 57–8.

17 Shelter Neighbourhood Action Project, *Another Chance for Cities: SNAP 69/72* (Shelter, 1972), p. 17.

18 A substantial critique of corporate planning, highlighting its tendency to ignore or obscure distributional questions, was developed by the Coventry CDP – see

J. Bennington and P. Skelton, 'Public participation in decision making by governments', in *Government and Programme Budgeting* (Institute of Municipal Treasurers and Accountants, 1973).

19 See R. Hambleton, Chapter 3.

20 See J. Stewart *et al.*, *Local Government: Approaches to Urban Deprivation* (Home Office Deprivation Unit, 1976), a report of a study undertaken by the Institute of Local Government Studies (INLOGOV), University of Birmingham.

21 Ibid., p. 16.

22 See, for example, E. Brooks, 'Development problems of the inner city', *Geographical Journal*, vol. 141, no. 3 (1975), pp. 355–62.

25 For an overview see R. Holman, *Poverty: Explanation of Social Deprivation* (Martin Robertson, 1978), pp. 260–76.
See also D. Donnison, 'Micro-politics of the city', in D. Donnison and D. Eversley (eds.), *London: Urban Patterns, Problems and Politics* (Heinemann, 1973), Chapter 12.

24 See S. Baine, *Community Action and Local Government* (Bell, 1975), Occasional Papers on Social Administration no. 59. Awareness of the contradiction between the intractable housing problems of Notting Hill and the moribund local Labour Party's preoccupation with narrow electoral politics meant that for the author:

> . . . from then on, the Labour Party was dead as a possible organizational form. The same was true of hundreds of other young, and not so young, people who turned to the ideas of community action as a basis for their political life. (p. 10)

25 See J. Allen and J. Palmer, 'Community planning: ideology as a positive reason for action', in *Ideologies in Planning*, Kingston Polytechnic, Planning Workshop Paper no. 2 (1973); and
M. E. Taylor, 'The contribution of the professional to community education and action', paper presented to the *PTRC Summer Annual Meeting*, University of Warwick (12–16 July 1976).

26 Other housing issues frequently taken up included exposures of exploitative landlords and the existence of empty properties whilst many families were homeless – see R. Bailey, *The Squatters* (Penguin 1973); and
R. Bailey *The Homeless and the Empty Houses* (Penguin, 1977).

27 D. Eversley, p. 9.

28 See D. Eversley, 'Old cities, falling populations and rising costs', *GLC Intelligence Unit Quarterly Bulletin*, no. 18 (March 1972), pp. 5–17; and
D. Eversley, 'Who will rescue our cities', *Built Environment Quarterly*, vol. 1, no. 3 (1975), pp. 194–8.

29 N. Falk and H. Martinos, *Inner City: Local Government and Economic Renewal* (Fabian Society, 1975), Fabian Research Series 320, p. 2.

30 G. Lomas, *The Inner City*, London Council of Social Service (1974).

31 D. Eversley, *Planning Without Growth*, p. 27.

32 See, for example, D. Senior, 'Ebenezer's other half', *Built Environment Quarterly*, vol. 1, no. 3 (1975), pp. 199–202; and
M. Ash, 'Planning, growth and change: the new towns versus inner cities fallacy', *Town and Country Planning*, vol. 44, no. 2 (1976), pp. 55–61;
For a detailed analysis of the debate as it had developed by early 1976, see R. Coursey, *The Debate on Urban Policy*, Retailing and Planning Associates (1977).

33 G. H. Peters, 'In defence of SPNW', *Town and Country Planning*, vol. 43, no. 3 (1975), pp. 171–5.

34 M. Myers, 'Urban deprivation and the GLC', in *Greater London Intelligence Quarterly*, no. 31 (1975), pp. 25–30.

35 J. Hillman, 'Council admits blame for lost jobs', *Guardian* (12 October 1976) – a report of the Wandsworth Council Study which revealed that its redevelopment schemes had in the past ten years displaced 250 firms, only thirteen of which had been relocated.

36 See R. Hargreave, 'An experimental industrial GIA', *Town and Country Planning*, vol. 44, no. 1 (1976), pp. 36–9; and
P. B. Rogers and C. R. Smith, 'The local authority's role in economic development' *Regional Studies*, vol. 11, no. 3 (1977), pp. 153–64.

37 For a general discussion see J. D. Stewart, *Management in an Era of Restraint, and Central and Local Government Relationships*, The Municipal Group (1977).

38 For a useful chronological summary of the debate see M. J. Allen, 'The development of the inner city initiative', paper presented to the PTRC Conference *The Inner City Initiative: Action and Interaction* (1–3 November 1978).

39 Notably the *Save Our Cities* Conference at Bristol University in February 1977, sponsored by the Calouste Gulbenkian Foundation and the *Sunday Times* – see R. Righter, *Save Our Cities*, Calouste Gulbenkian Foundation (1977).

40 See the three-part feature 'Save our cities', *The Sunday Times Magazine*, 28 November, 5 December and 12 December 1976.

41 Community Development Project (CDP), *Gilding the Ghetto* (1977); and CDP, *The Costs of Industrial Change* (1977).

42 DoE, *Inner Area Studies: Summaries of Consultant's Final Reports* (HMSO, 1977).
The rapid transformation in the fortunes of IAS is indicated by the comment of the director of the Liverpool project:

> We have now had a policy for the inner city for 12 months. . . . Yet only two years ago, we in the Liverpool study team were wondering whether our work might live up to its terms of reference by drawing lessons for government about the problems of inner city areas. At the time we had very little evidence that government was looking for such lessons and were sustained only by the enthusiasm of Reg Freeson, chairman of our steering committee in Liverpool.

L. Davies, 'Evolution of policy', *Architects Journal* (5 July 1978), p. 16.

43 See, for example, Association of Metropolitan Authorities, *Report on the Problems of the Old Industrial Cores of the Metropolitan Areas* (AMA, 1976).
Inner City Working Group of the Joint Centre for Regional, Urban and Local Government Studies, *Inner Area Studies: A Contribution to the Debate*, University of Birmingham (1977);
Town and Country Planning Association, 'Inner cities of tomorrow: a TCPA policy statement', *Town and Country Planning*, vol. 45, no. 5 (1977), pp. 265–77;
Southwark Trades Council, *Employment in Southwark: A Strategy for the Future* (1976).

44 Lambeth IAS, *Inner London – Policies for Dispersal and Balance* (HMSO, 1977);
Birmingham IAS, *Unequal City* (HMSO, 1977);
Liverpool IAS, *Change or Decay* (HMSO, 1977).

45 P. Hall, 'The inner cities dilemma', *New Society* (3 February 1977), pp. 223–4.

46 DoE, *Inner Area Studies: Summaries*, p. 3.

47 A. Kirby, *The Inner City: Causes and Effects*, Retailing and Planning Associates (1978), p. 3.

48 DoE, *Inner Area Studies: Summaries*, pp. 20–1;
For a full discussion see Birmingham IAS, *Unequal City*, Chapter 2.

49 'Concentrations of unemployed, such as we have now in collectively deprived inner areas, are potentially explosive, especially where the population is racially mixed' – P. Walding, 'Urban deprivation and jobs: some considerations for strategy', in Polytechnic of the South Bank, *Homes and Jobs in Inner Cities*, Proceedings of National Conference (14–15 September 1977), Department of Town Planning, p. 20.

50 DoE, *Inner Area Studies: Summaries*, p. 8.

51 Ibid., p. 3.

52 P. Hall, 'The inner cities dilemma', p. 224.

53 For a review see C. Jones, 'Population decline in cities', in C. Jones (ed.), *Urban Deprivation and the Inner City* (Croom Helm, 1979).
For a detailed examination and evaluation of the available evidence see D. Eversley and L. Bonnerjea, *The Inner City in Context 2: Changes in the Resident Populations of Inner Areas* (Social Science Research Council, 1980).

54 See K. Young and J. Kramer, *Strategy and Conflict in Metropolitan Housing: Suburbia versus the Greater London Council, 1965–75* (Heinemann, 1978).

55 See G. Shankland, P. Willmott and D. Jordan, *Inner London: Policies for Dispersal and Balance: Final Report of the Lambeth Inner Area Study* (HMSO, 1977), Chapter 6.

56 For an overview of the subject, based on a paper presented at a series of seminars and a conference sponsored by CES in 1975 and 1976, see A. Evans and D. Eversley (eds.), *The Inner City: Employment and Industry*, (Heinemann, 1980).
G. Bramley, 'The inner city labour market', in C. Jones (ed.), Chapter 3, provides a useful summary discussion; and
G. Bramley, 'Employment problems in Lambeth', in A. Evans and D. Eversley (eds.), summarizes the findings of the Lambeth IAS.

57 See, for example, J. Corkindale, 'The decline of employment in metropolitan areas', *Department of Employment Gazette* (November 1977), p. 1202; also
D. Metcalf and R. Richardson, 'Unemployment in London', in A. Evans and D. Eversley (eds.), Chapter 8.

58 CDP, *Costs of Industrial Change*, pp. 73–5.

59 See R. Berthoud, 'Employment in a changing labour market', in A. Evans and D. Eversley (eds.), Chapter 10; and
R. Nabarro, 'The impact on workers from the inner city of Liverpool's economic decline', ibid., Chapter 13.

60 See R. Nabarro, 'New jobs in old cities?', *Built Environment Quarterly*, vol. 2, no. 4 (1976), pp. 284–7.
Similarly in South-East Inner London during the period 1966–74 only twenty enterprises with more than twenty employees opened, creating less than 900 jobs, compared with 231 establishment closures accounting for the loss of 39,000 jobs – see P. Gripaios, 'The end of decentralization policy in London: some comments', *Town and Country Planning*, vol. 44, no. 10 (1976), pp. 426–8.

61 See B. M. D. Smith, 'Employment in inner city areas: a case study of the position in Small Heath, Birmingham, 1974', in A. Evans and D. Eversley (eds.), Chapter 14; and

R. Dennis, 'The decline of manufacturing employment in Greater London: 1966–74', *Urban Studies*, vol. 15 (1978), pp. 63–73 (also ibid., Chapter 2).

62 See G. Cameron, 'Economic renewal in the inner city: Glasgow', *Architects Journal* (2 February 1977), pp. 215–17.

63 R. Nabarro, p. 286.

64 CDP, *Costs of Industrial Change*, pp. 34–37.

65 Ibid., p. 37.

66 One such explanation is the operation of negative multiplier effects: the cumulative consequences of firms moving out in the 1950s and 1960s which had adversely affected the viability of remaining firms through reduced inter-industry demand – see P. Gripaios, 'The closure of firms in the inner city: the South-East London Case 1970–5', *Regional Studies*, vol. 11, no. 1 (1977), pp. 1–6; and

P. Gripaios, 'Economic decline in S. E. London', in A. Evans and D. Eversley, Chapter 3.

67 R. Nabarro, p. 284.

68 D. B. Massey and R. A. Meegan, 'Industrial restructuring versus the cities', *Urban Studies*, vol. 15, no. 4 (1978), pp. 273–88 (also in A. Evans and D. Eversley (eds.), Chapter 4).

69 CDP, *Costs of Industrial Change*, p. 64.

70 See P. Dicken and P. E. Lloyd, 'The corporate dimension of employment change in the inner city', in C. Jones (ed.), Chapter 2; and

D. Keeble, 'Industrial decline in the inner city and conurbation', in A. Evans and D. Eversley (eds.), Chapter 5.

71 Ibid., p. 72; see also

I. Harford, 'The inner city – whose urban crisis?', *The Planner*, vol. 63, no. 4 (1977), pp. 99–101.

72 CDP, *Costs of Industrial Change*, p. 72.

73 Ibid., p. 96.

74 D. B. Massey and R. A. Meegan.

75 Ibid., p. 288.

76 'Callaghan attacks planners who wreck inner cities', *Sunday Times* (30 January 1977).

77 See, for example, M. S. Allan, 'How L.A.s can help the small firm back to the inner city', *Surveyor* (24 November 1977), pp. 11–17.

78 N. Flynn and K. Thomas, 'Employment and housing in the inner city', *Planning*, no. 210 (1977), pp. 6–7; and

K. Thomas, 'The impact of renewal on small firms', *The Planner*, vol. 63, no. 2 (1977), pp. 48–9.

79 See N. Falk and H. Martinos, pp. 9–14.

80 P. Gripaios, 'The closure of firms in the inner city', p. 4; and

D. B. Massey and R. A. Meegan, p. 281.

81 See D. Massey and R. Meegan, *The Inner City and the International Competitiveness of British Industry; the Employment Implications of the Industrial Reorganisation Corporation*, Centre for Environmental Studies, Working Note 437 (1976);

also
CDP, Costs of Industrial Change, pp. 76-92.

82 DoE, *Inner Area Studies: Summaries*, pp. 4 and 41.

83 For a brief outline of the spectrum by the Director of the Birmingham IAS, see P. Walding, pp. 19–20.

84 Except where otherwise indicated the quotations in this section are from the 1977 White Paper.

85 For a brief outline see G. Nethersall, 'Local government finance', *The Planner*, vol. 63, no. 5 (1977), pp. 140–1. For a discussion of the implications of local government finance see S. Kennett, *The Inner City in Context 6: Local Government Fiscal Problems: A Context for Inner Cities* (SSRC, 1980).

86 Transport Policies and Programmes (TPPs) were introduced in 1973 and were the model on which the HIP system was based. Each year county councils are required to submit their TPP, setting out the strategy, objectives and priorities of a five-year rolling programme of expenditure. On this basis the Transport Supplementary Grant is allocated.

87 DoE, *Circular 61/78: Urban Programme Circular No. 18, Capital and Non-Capital Projects Starting in 1979–80 (England)* (HMSO, 1978).

88 The provisions of the Act are summarized in DoE, *Circular 68/78: Inner Urban Areas Act, 1978* (HMSO, 1978).

89 G. Barnett, 'The government initiative', *The Planner*, vol. 64, no. 3 (1978), p. 75.

90 See DoE, *Inner City Needs Indicators Published*, Press Notice 334 (13 June 1978).

91 DoE, *Circular 71/77: Local Government and the Industrial Strategy* (HMSO, 1977).

92 DoE, *Circular 68/78*, para. 15.

93 Ibid., Annex 5, para. 1.

94 See National Building Agency, *Inner Area Programmes: A Study of Approaches to their Preparation* (NBA, 1979).

95 For a perceptive discussion see A. J. Harrison and C. M. E. Whitehead, 'Is there an inner city problem?' *Westminster Bank Review* (1978), pp. 31–46.

96 For an example of the former see M. Loney, 'Radical reconstruction', in M. Loney and M. Allen (eds.), *The Crisis of the Inner City* (MacMillan Press, 1979). For the latter see G. Bailey *et al.*, *Saving Our Cities: Freeing Enterprise in the Inner Areas* (Bow Group Publications, 1978).

97 See Town and Country Planning Association, 'TCPA policy statement the inner cities', *Town and Country Planning*, vol. 48, no. 1 (1979), pp. 30–4.

98 This line of argument was presented by R. E. Pahl, 'Will the inner city problem ever go away?', *New Society* (28 September 1978), pp. 678–81.
See also C. Ward, 'Into the Enterprise Zone', *New Society* (22 March 1979), pp. 684–5; and
C. Ward, 'Professor Pahl's conversion', *Town and Country Planning*, vol. 48, no. 1 (1979), pp. 21–2.

99 *Hansard*, (9 February 1978), cols. 1717–19. For an elaboration of this version of a 'middle ground' approach see P. Walker, 'Our inner cities', Chapter 7 in *The Ascent of Britain* (1977), pp. 124–146.

100 See H. Brown, 'Inner areas: the light of experience', *Municipal Journal* (6 June 1980), pp. 710–1.

101 *Hansard* (9 February 1978), col. 1722.

102 See, for example, the comments of T. Litterick MP, ibid., cols. 1741–6, and A. Steen MP, cols. 1754–61.

103 M. Thomas MP, ibid., col. 1769 – 'the Henley description' refers to an earlier contribution by M. Heseltine, MP for Henley.

104 See R. Hambleton, 'Expenditure planning for the inner areas', *Municipal and Public Services Journal* (31 August 1979), pp. 919–21; and
P. Lawless, 'Partnerships: a critical evaluation', *Local Government Studies*, vol. 6, no. 3 (1980), pp. 21–39.

105 1977 prices – quoted by R. Nabarro, 'The urban programme: will it really help the inner city', *The Planner*, vol. 64, no. 6 (1978), pp. 171–3.

106 See R. Simpson, 'For richer for poorer', *New Society* (10 November 1977), pp. 299–301;
T. Travers, *Rate Support Grant: Changes and Consequences 1974–5/1977–8*, Centre for Institutional Studies, North East London Polytechnic (1979), Commentary Series C9; and
S. Kennett, pp. 47–50.

107 For a discussion of Newcastle's efforts see J. Beecham, 'Problems and opportunities of partnership: a political perspective', in T. A. Broadbent (ed.), *Inner Area Partnerships and Programmes: The First Year's Experience*, Centre for Environmental Studies, Policy Series 8 (1979).

108 P. Hall, 'Spending priorities in the inner city', *New Society* (21/28 December 1978), pp. 698–9.

109 A typical ministerial overstatement was made by Freeson during the passage of the Inner Urban Area Bill:

> I cannot stress enough the words 'co-ordination' and 'integration', because in my view the chief practical obstacle to advance in the inner urban areas is compartmental and fragmented central and local government policies, programmes and budgets.

Hansard, (9 February 1978), col. 1807.

110 See E. Sharp, 'Inner cities in decay: problems, priorities and possibilities', *Chartered Surveyor* (November 1978), pp. 99–102; and
S. Marks, 'Inner city partnerships: one year left to prove themselves', *Municipal and Public Services Journal*, vol. 87, no. 12 (1979), p. 299.

111 For a discussion which focusses on commercial revitalization – retailing, warehousing, leisure and mixed use property – see R. Hambleton, *Inner Cities: Engaging the Private Sector*, Working Paper 10, School for Advanced Urban Studies, University of Bristol (1980).

112 See, for example, C. Leicester, 'Future employment trends', *The Planner*, vol. 64, no. 4 (1978), pp. 103–5; and
'Mass unemployment into the eighties', *New Society* (1 February 1979), p. 252.
For a summary of the 'great chips debate' see T. Forester, 'The micro-electronic revolution', *New Society* (9 November 1978), pp. 330–2; and
T. Forester, 'Society with chips and without jobs', ibid. (16 November 1978), pp. 387–8.
For a detailed analysis see J. B. Goddard and A. T. Thwaites, *The Inner City in Context 4: Technological Change and the Inner City* (Social Science Research Council 1980).

113 See J. Hughes, 'Recent measures to combat unemployment', *The Planner*, vol.

64, no. 4 (1978), pp. 108–9.

114 N. Falk, *Think Small: Enterprise and the Economy* (Fabian Society, 1978), Fabian Tract 453; and
N. Falk, 'Finding a place for small enterprise in the inner city', in A. Evans and D. Eversley (eds.), Chapter 16.

115 N. Hildyard, 'Small trades or small industries', *New Ecologist*, no. 1 (1978), p. 9. For discussions of the limited role and potential of small firms see N. Flynn and K. Thomas, and I Harford.

116 N. Hildyard, p. 9.
For a discussion of 'the workshop approach' based on experience in Clerkenwell see M. Franks, 'Teeming with life: how to re-establish our shattered communities', *New Ecologist*, no. 3 (May/June 1978), pp. 88–90.

117 J. Curran and J. Stanworth, 'Some reasons why small is not always beautiful' *New Society* (14 December 1978), pp. 627–9.

118 Department of Employment, 'Small firms subsidy extended', *Department of Employment Gazette* (November 1977), p. 1270, quotes the then Secretary of State for Employment:

> This is not a crutch for limping firms – it is hard cash encouragement for lusty industrial infants who want to grow – and grow now.

119 DoE, *Circular 71/77*.

120 See, for example Royal Town Planning Institute, *Employment Planning: A Consultation Document, Report of the Working Party* (RTPI, 1979), p. 35.

121 For a discussion of general principles see P. M. Townroe, 'The design of local economic development policies', *Town Planning Review*, vol. 50, no. 2 (1979), pp. 148–63.
For their application on Merseyside see W. A. K. Struthers and C. B. Williamson, 'Local economic development: integrated policy planning and implementation on Merseyside', ibid., pp. 164–83.

122 See Royal Town Planning Institute, *Employment Planning*;
G. Bramley, M. Stewart and J. Underwood, 'Local economic initiatives: a review', *Town Planning Review*, vol. 50, no. 2 (1979), pp. 137–47;
K. Young, C. Mason and E. Mills, *The Inner City in Context 11: Urban Government and Economic Change* (Social Science Research Council, 1980); P. Lawless, 'New approaches to local authority economic intervention', *Local Government Studies*, vol. 6, no. 1 (1980), pp. 17–31;
T. Davies, *Inner Cities: Building Bridges: Linking Economic Regeneration to Inner City Employment Problems*, University of Bristol, School for Advanced Urban Studies (1980), Working Paper 8.

123 For a discussion of the work of the MSC see G. L. Reid, 'Manpower policy and the inner cities', in A. Evans and D. Eversley (eds.), Chapter 18.

124 For a range of views on this issue see N. Falk, *Think Small* and 'Finding a place'; D. Keeble;
G. Cameron, 'The inner city: new plant incubator?' in A. Evans and D. Eversley, Chapter 15; and
J. J. Fagg, 'A re-examination of the incubator hypothesis: a case study of Greater Leicester', *Urban Studies*, vol. 17 (1980), pp. 173–94.

125 For a discussion which contrasts the prospects of inner Liverpool and inner Manchester in these terms see P. Dicken and P. E. Lloyd, 'Inner metropolitan

industrial change, enterprise structures and policy issues: case studies of Manchester and Merseyside', *Regional Studies*, vol. 12 (1978), pp. 181–97.

126 For a discussion of these issues see M. Stewart, 'Inner city employment and the built stock', *Built Environment Quarterly*, vol. 4, no. 3 (1978), pp. 222–8.

127 See I. McDonald, F. Stafford, and M. Franklin, 'Use of redundant buildings for small enterprises', *Architects Journal* (20 June 1979), pp. 1279–85 for a general discussion of IIAs; and
I. McDonald, F. Stafford and M. Franklin, 'Rochdale fights back', ibid. (18 July 1979), pp. 137–57 for an evaluation of Crawford Street IIA.
See also Roger Tym and Partners *et al.*, *Time for Industry: Evaluation of the Rochdale Improvement Area* (HMSO, 1979).

128 See R. Minns and J. Thornley, *State Shareholding and the Role of Local and Regional Authorities* (Macmillan, 1978).

129 For example, P. E. Lloyd, 'The components of industrial change for Merseyside inner area 1966–75', *Urban Studies*, vol. 16, (1979), pp. 45–60; and
C. M. Mason, 'Industrial decline in Greater Manchester 1966–75: a component of change approach', *Urban Studies*, vol. 17 (1980), pp. 173–84.

130 This point is elaborated in P. Cheshire, 'Inner areas as spatial labour markets: a critique of the Inner Area Studies', *Urban Studies*, vol. 16, no. 1 (1979), pp. 29–43.

131 N. Sharman, 'Double think in inner city investment policies', *New Society* (1 February 1979), p. 246.
See also various papers in T. A. Broadbent (ed.).

132 See D. Senior.

133 See J. Burrows, 'Vacant land: a continuing crisis', *The Planner*, vol. 64, no. 1 (1978), pp. 7–9;
T. Cantell, 'Britain's idle acres', *Built Environment Quarterly*, vol. 3, no. 3 (1977) pp. 238–40; and
Civic Trust, *Urban Wastelands* (Civic Trust 1977).

134 R. Colenutt, 'Are inner city land values a problem?', *Architects Journal* (9 July 1978), pp. 20–1.

135 Royal Town Planning Institute, *Land Values and Planning in the Inner Areas. Final Report of the Working Party* (RTPI, 1979).
For a summary see G. Smart and R. Nabarro, 'Land values and the inner city', *The Planner*, vol. 64, no. 3 (1978), pp. 78–9.

136 M. Edwards, 'Vagaries of the inner city land market', *Architects Journal* (2 February 1977), pp. 206–7.

137 For a discussion of different explanations of the workings of the land market and its implications for inner areas see M. Edwards and D. Lovatt, *The Inner Cities in Context 1: Understanding Urban Land Values: A review* (Social Science Research Council, 1980).

138 For a critical analysis see A. Stones, 'Liverpool now: inner city wasteland', *Built Environment Quarterly*, vol. 3, no. 1 (1977), pp. 47–50.
See also Liverpool Inner Area Study, *Vacant Land* (DoE, 1976).

139 See R. Colenutt; also
R. Nabarro and G. Smart, 'High cost and low values in urban land', *Built Environment Quarterly*, vol. 4, no. 3 (1978), pp. 229–36.

140 For a comprehensive analysis of the problems of vacant and underused land and buildings, focussing on the London Borough of Tower Hamlets, see R. Nabarro

and D. Richards, *Wasteland: A Thames Television Report*, Thames Television Ltd (1980).
See also Royal Society of Arts, 'Urban wasteland', *The Royal Society of Arts Journal*, vol. cxxviii, no. 5292 (1980), pp. 840–53.

141 For example P. Shore, 'Private investment needed in inner cities', *Chartered Surveyor* (November 1978), pp. 97–8.

142 Wirral MBC is one authority which has developed its local plans to provide a framework for its IAP – see B. Adcock, 'Case study: the Wirral Inner Area Programme', in T. A. Broadbent (ed.).

143 For a substantial examination of emerging practices in IAPs see J. Bishop and J. Underwood, *Inner Cities: Improving the Physical Environment*, School for Advanced Urban Studies, University of Bristol (1980), Working Paper 9.

144 DoE, *Policy for the Inner Cities*, paras 34 and 35.

145 For an overview, see National Council of Social Service, *The Inner Cities Programme 1: Community Involvement* (NCSS, 1979).
For a detailed study of the Birmingham, Liverpool and Manchester Partnerships see M. Loughran, *Public Participation in the Inner City Partnerships* (Unpublished Dip.TP dissertation, City of Birmingham Polytechnic, Department of Planning and Landscape, 1979).

146 For a community worker's analysis of public involvement see H. Simmons, '*Community involvement: one perspective*', paper presented at PTRC 'The Inner City Initiatives: Action and Interaction (1–3 November 1978).

147 DoE, *Policy for the Inner Cities*, para. 37.

148 Ibid., para. 18.

149 C. Cross, *Ethnic Minorities in the Inner City: The Ethnic Dimension in Urban Deprivation in England*, Commission for Racial Equality (1978), p. 29.

150 Quoted from the Manpower Services Commission Review and Plan 1977 in H. McKay and A. Cox, *The Politics of Urban Change* (Croom Helm, 1979), p. 255.

151 The Birmingham IAS had commented that a greater Asian concentration in Small Heath could result 'in a more stable, mostly home-owning and self-reliant community with its own culture and identity' – see DoE, *Inner Area Studies: Summaries*, p. 34;
P. Hall, *Inner Cities Dilemma*, took the argument further by suggesting the encouragement of more immigration of those with entrepreneurial talents to generate spontaneous economic revival.

152 See D. J. Smith, *Racial Disadvantage in Britain* (Pelican, 1977).

153 Statement by Shore, the then Secretary of State, DoE, Press Notice 835, p. 8.

Chapter 7 Birmingham: second city first

1 M. B. Steadman and P. A. Wood, 'Urban renewal in Birmingham: an interim report', *Geography*, vol. L, no. 1 (1965), pp. 1–17.

2 For a summary of the inquiry's findings and recommendations see Bournville Village Trust, *When We Build Again* (George Allen and Unwin, 1941), pp. 12–23.

3 For a general account of the growth of Birmingham see M. J. Wise and P. O. N' Thorpe, 'The growth of Birmingham 1800–1950', in British Association for the Advancement of Science, *Birmingham in its Regional Setting* (1950), pp. 213–38.

4 For a description of this environment see Bournville Village Trust.

5 *The Report from the Select Committee on the Health of Towns* (1840) commented on the above average quality of housing provision in Birmingham. This was a function of the relatively high proportion of well-paid skilled workers. During the 1860s and 1870s accelerated immigration of unskilled workers resulted in increasing densities (by infilling) and overcrowding. Conditions in the inner ring rapidly became more typical of Victorian cities – M. J. Wise and P. O. N'Thorpe.

6 A. Briggs, *Victorian Cities* (Penguin, 1968), p. 184: key services were municipalized and Birmingham was dubbed 'the best governed city in the world'. See also E. P. Hennock, *Fit and Proper Persons* (Edward Arnold, 1973), pp. 104–30.

7 E. P. Hennock, p. 126.

8 Bourneville Village Trust, p. 17: the population was increasing at the rate of 8,000 p.a. During 1910–13 only 1400 new houses were built annually, and significant numbers were being cleared for road works, factory extensions etc.

9 A. Sutcliffe, 'A century of flats in Birmingham', in A. Sutcliffe (ed.), *Multi-Storey Living: The British Working-Class Experience* (Croom Helm, 1974), p. 182.

10 Quoted in E. P. Hennock, p. 125.

11 See A. Briggs, pp. 226–31;
E. P. Hennock, pp. 125–30; and
E. Gauldie, *Cruel Habitations* (Allen and Unwin, 1974), pp. 151 and 278–81.

12 Quoted in A. Sutcliffe, p. 183.

13 See G. E. Cherry, *Factors in the Origins of Town Planning in Britain: The Example of Birmingham*, University of Birmingham, Centre for Urban and Regional Studies (1975), Working Paper 36.
Nettlefold was a prominent Edwardian housing reformer who developed the work of the Cadburys who had built Bournville garden suburb. However as A. Sutcliffe, p. 189, pointed out, '. . . this sylvan ideal, municipalized by the council's enthusiastic ventures into suburban planning, obscured the survival of the central slums'.

14 See J. S. Nettlefold, *Practical Housing* (Garden City Press Ltd, 1908), for details of this strategy.
S. Chapman and J. N. Bartlett, in S. D. Chapman (ed.), *The History of Working Class Housing* (David and Charles, 1971), commented: 'Nettlefold courts can still be seen in the twilight zones of the city, gaping monuments to a panic policy that could do no more than alleviate the stench of urban poverty'. (p. 232)

15 A. Sutcliffe, p. 189–90.

16 Bournville Village Trust, pp. 41–50.

17 Ibid., p. 26.

18 See J. L. Macmorran, *Municipal Public Works and Planning in Birmingham, 1852–1972*, City of Birmingham (1973), pp. 65–8 and Bournville Village Trust, pp. 10–11 and 29–33.

19 A. Sutcliffe, p. 190–2.

20 It was estimated that the weekly cost of living of the average working class family in the suburbs was 10–15 per cent higher than that of a similar family living in the inner ring slum – Bournville Village Trust, pp. 87–8.

21 A. Sutcliffe, p. 193 argued that '. . . it came to be agreed in the 1930s by those who

governed the city, that Birmingham was already big enough, and that those whom slum clearance would consign to the suburbs were the least able and willing to live in them'.

22 S. Schifferes, *Tenants Struggles in the 1930s* (Thesis presented for MA in Labour History, University of Warwick, 1975), Chapter 5: 'The Birmingham municipal tenants strike'.

23 A. Sutcliffe, p. 193.

24 Ibid., pp. 193–8.

25 S. Schifferes, 'Council tenants and housing policy in the 1930s: the contradictions of state intervention', in *Housing And Class in Britain*, papers presented at the *Political Economy of Housing Workshop* of the Conference of Socialist Economists (1976), p. 67.

26 The management and allocation of council houses in the 1930s was the responsibility of the City Estates Department, whose general manager described the allocation process for slum clearance families thus:

> . . . so concerned was I, years ago, at the class of tenants put into new houses, that I recommended purchasing investment properties in the open market with the object of effecting exchanges. Some hundreds of houses were purchased without loss to the ratepayers, and the better-class tenants occupying them were approached with the object of their removal to an estate house, and the lower standard houses thus vacated became the training ground of the less desirable applicant.

W. Smith, 'The management of municipal housing estates', *Transactions of the Royal Sanitary Institute*, no. 5 (1946), p. 528.

27 Sir H. J. Manzoni, 'Redevelopment of blighted areas in Birmingham', *Journal of the Town Planning Institute*, vol. 41, no. 3 (1955), p. 92.

28 Ibid.

29 Bournville Village Trust, p. 33.

30 S. Schifferes, *Tenants Struggles*, and 'Council tenants'.

31 Sir H. L. Manzoni, p. 91.

32 P. Abercrombie and H. Jackson, *The West Midlands Plan* (Ministry of Town and Country Planning, 1948).

33 For a brief analysis of the evolution of post-war planning strategies see D. Saunders, 'Changing planning framework', in F. Joyce (ed.), *Metropolitan Development and Change. The West Midlands: A Policy Review*, (Saxon House, 1977), pp. 36–49.
For a detailed account see P. Hall, 'The West Midlands: Birmingham, Coventry and the Counties', in P. Hall *et al.*, *The Containment of Urban England*, vol. 2 (Allen and Unwin, 1973).

34 A. Sutcliffe and R. Smith, *History of Birmingham, Volume III, Birmingham 1939–70* (1974), pp. 225–8.
For a general account of post-war renewal policy see M. Archer, 'Housing – redevelopment and renewal', in F. Joyce (ed.), pp. 217–30.

35 *Birmingham City Council Minutes* Report of Housing Management Committee (13 October 1953), pp. 482–4.

36 P. Hall *et al.*, pp. 525–8.

37 A. Sutcliffe and R. Smith, pp. 437–8.
For a full analysis of changes in the middle ring during the 1950s and 1960s see C.

Paris and B. Blackaby, *Not Much Improvement: Urban Renewal Policy in Birmingham* (Heinemann, 1979), Chapter 3.

38 Ibid., p. 232.

39 Bournville Village Trust, p. 20.

40 A detailed analysis of demographic changes in the 1950s and 1960s is provided in A. Sutcliffe and R. Smith, Chapter VI.

41 For early analyses of the patterns and processes of immigrant settlement in the middle ring see J. Rex and R. Moore, *Race, Community and Conflict*, (OUP, 1967); and the critical comments by V. A. Karn, 'A note on race, community and conflict: a study of Sparkbrook' *Race*, vol. IX, no. 1 (1968), pp. 100–7. See also P. N. Jones, 'Ethnic areas in British cities', in D. T. Herbert and D. M. Smith (eds.), *Social Problems and the City* (OUP 1979).

42 A five-year residential qualification was introduced in 1949 when the waiting list was increasing very rapidly. It stipulated that, although people could register on arrival in the city and start accumulating points, they had to wait a minimum of five years before being allocated a house. For a discussion of allocation policies see J. Lambert, C. Paris and B. Blackaby, *Housing Policy and the State: Allocation, Access and Control* (Macmillan, 1978), Chapter 3.

43 V. A. Karn, *Priorities for Local Authority Mortgage Lending: A Case Study of Birmingham*, Research Memorandum 52, Centre for Urban and Regional Studies, University of Birmingham (1976), p. 15: by mid-1974 9235 loans for house purchase (88 per cent of the total) had been given on pre-1919 properties.

44 N. Deakin *et al.*, *Colour, Citizenship and British Society* (IRR, 1970), pp. 82–7.

45 V. A. Karn, 'A note on race', p. 102–3.

46 J. Rex and R. Moore, p. 31.

47 Ibid., p. 279.

48 *Birmingham City Council Minutes*, Report of General Purposes Committee, (6 December 1960).

49 For an analysis of policy in the middle ring in the 1950s and 1960s see M. J. Langstaff, *Housing Improvement and Community Action in Birmingham: A Study Based on Institutional Urban Theory* (M.Soc.Sci. thesis, Centre for Urban and Regional Studies, University of Birmingham, 1972), Chapter 6.

50 A. Sutcliffe and R. Smith, pp. 377–81.

51 For a discussion of the impact of multi-occupation policy on immigrant settlement see E. Burney, *Housing on Trial* (OUP, 1967), pp. 25–31.

52 M. J. Langstaff, pp. 135–7.

53 For a description of this work by the then Chief Public Health and Housing Inspector see E. Wakelin, 'Improvement techniques in practice', in S. Millward (ed.), *Urban Renewal*, papers presented at a symposium at the University of Salford (1969).

54 See M. J. Langstaff, pp. 136–45.

55 A description of the scheme by the then City Engineer, Surveyor and Planning Officer is given in N. Borg, 'Summerfield Improvement Area', *Architecture West Midlands*, no. 7 (1971).

56 *Birmingham City Council Minutes*, Report of the Health Committee, (2 November 1971).

57 M. Gibson and M. Langstaff, 'Community action and housing policy:

possibilities in Birmingham', *Community Action*, no. 2 (1972), pp. 17–19.

58 The buffer policy was most clearly articulated in the north-west suburbs where a line of GIAs separated Handsworth, an area of Victorian housing and immigrant settlement, from the middle-class inter-war suburb of Handsworth Wood.

59 Their pessimism was most marked in areas of HMOs:

> . . . you've only got to get multi-occupation in any district and it drops straight away. In two years it can go from good housing to that requiring clearance action. You'd never get people prepared to spend £1000 or so in an area of that sort. . . .

quoted in M. J. Langstaff (1972), pp. 136–7.
The city's Chief Public Health Inspector addressed a conference thus:

> May I again stress compulsion. I am saying this for the benefit of ministry representatives present, and I hope they are listening because the idea of persuasion I am afraid is not going to work.

E. Wakelin, p. 120.

60 For residents' attitudes see M. Gibson, 'A consumer's eye view of Handsworth No. 1 GIA', *West Midlands Grass Roots*, no. 2 (1972), pp. 5–6.
For the views of the then Chairman of the Health Committee see Cllr, J. Bryant, 'Birmingham's GIA policy', *West Midlands Grass Roots*, no. 3 (1972), p. 3.

61 There had been sporadic protest about the implementation of Phase I; see J. Norris, *Human Aspects of Redevelopment*, Studies in Housing and Industrial Location No. 2, Midlands New Towns Society (1960); and
N. S. Power, *The Forgotten People* (Arthur James, 1965).
Discontent about 'reconditioned' slums eventually exploded in a rent strike in Balsall Heath – 'We'll burn them down, tenants threaten', *Evening Mail* (2 April 1970).

62 For an analysis of Sparkbrook West I see J. Lambert, 'Housing class and community action in a redevelopment area', in C. Lambert and D. Weir (eds.), *Cities in Modern Britain* (Fontana, 1975), pp. 415–24; and
J. Lambert *et al.*, Chapter 4.

63 See J. Lambert *et al.*, p. 66.

64 See W. Smith for the origins of this practice of grading tenants according to their suitability for different types of council accommodation.
R. Means, *Social Work and the 'Undeserving Poor'*, University of Birmingham Centre for Urban and Regional Studies, Occasional Paper no. 37 (1977), provides a detailed analysis of the effect of allocation practices on the lives of the so-called 'problem families'. See also J. Lambert *et al.*, pp. 50–2.

65 M. Archer, p. 224 states the official version of events:

> With regard to the areas to which families were moved there was no explicit restriction of choice. In reality, however, choice was controlled by the availability of dwellings at any one time. These limitations applied to location and type. . . . A very large proportion of families did, however, move locally to an area earlier in the clearance programme or to the first houses completed in their own area.

There is no published evidence to support this claim or to refute evidence from unofficial sources which suggests that 'a very large proportion' is a considerable overestimate – see, for example, Rev. W. S. Dixon, *Small Heath. A Survey of a Redevelopment Area*, Small Heath Baptist Chuch (1974).

66 Cllr. B. Shuttleworth, 'Redevelopment and people', *West Midlands Grass Roots*, no. 2 (1972), pp. 13–14;
C. Dix, 'Problems are human', *Guardian* (5 April 1972).

67 '. . . if redevelopment had been quick, well managed, and had produced well appointed housing at reasonable rents then the entire structure of local debate would have been different', C. Paris and B. Blackaby, p. 77, – Chapter 4 analyses the emergence of the new policy in 1972.

68 These informal plans were prepared with staff and students of the City of Birmingham Polytechnic, School of Planning and Landscape: for a personal view of this work see A. J. Edgar, 'Public participation or community plan', *Housing Review*, vol. 23, no. 4 (1974), pp. 95–7.

69 For a study of housing associations in Birmingham in the early 1970s see A. Pickford, *Housing Associations and the Urban Environment* (Unpublished Dip TP dissertation, City of Birmingham Polytechnic, 1973).

70 M. J. Langstaff (ed.), 'The Sparkbrook West story', *West Midlands Grass Roots*, no. 12 (1974), pp. 7–14; and
J. Lambert *et al.*, Chapter 6.

71 In the controversy over the rent strike in Balsall Heath an official stated 'We do not need anybody to tell us we have a slum clearance problem. We do need someone to tell us where we are going to get the money to solve it' – 'The end of the slums' *Evening Mail* (2 April 1970).

72 Cllr. B. Shuttleworth, 'Our plan for housing', *Evening Mail* (27 April 1972). There was some dissent from this general view. Some Conservative and Labour councillors felt that improvement was a 'second best' solution.

73 City of Birmingham Urban Renewal Conference, *Urban Renewal Policy* (1973).

74 Ibid., p. 5.

75 M. Gibson and C. Paris, 'Unresolved problem of urban renewal', *West Midlands Grass Roots*, no. 8 (1973), p. 2.

76 Standing Conference on Urban Preservation and Renewal, *Report to the General Purposes Committee* (9 October 1972). For perceptions of inner area problems at the time see P. Smith, 'Knocking down is not solving problems' *Municipal Review*, no. 514 (1972), pp. 290–93.

77 During August 1973 over a dozen substantial articles in the local press (illustrated by maps) listed clearance and retention properties in the renewal areas, e.g. 'Spotlight on the future of city homes', *Evening Mail* (7 August 1973). While some residents welcomed the prospect of clearance and rehousing, others were outraged – 'City house owners to fight demolition', *Evening Mail* (9 August 1973).

78 *Birmingham City Council Minutes*, Report of Performance Review Committee (January 1975):

> On the one hand the Urban Renewal representatives maintained that the programme was realistic, up-to-date and capable of being maintained so far as Renewal and Improvement Areas were concerned, while at the other extreme some chief officers identified various specific delays or suggested that no programmes existed.

79 For critical analyses see Birmingham Inner Area Study, *The Management of*

Urban Renewal, IAS/B/10 (DoE, 1976); and
C. Paris and B. Blackaby, Chapter 5.

80 For discussions of HAA selection see Birmingham Inner Area Study, *Little Green: A Case Study in Urban Renewal*, IAS/B/7 (DoE, 1975); and
C. Paris, 'Birmingham: a Case Study in Urban Renewal' *CES Review*, no. 1 (1977), pp. 54–61.

81 B. Young, 'Environmental improvement in Housing Action and General Improvement Areas', in Environmental Health Officers Association Midland Centre, *A Practical Approach to Urban Renewal*, Proceedings of a One Day Seminar (1976).

82 See J. Tate and N. Moreton, 'Too many empty houses?', *Housing Review*, vol. 24, no. 4 (1975), pp. 102–4.

83 The limited effect of enforcement action exacerbated the problems of many private tenants. Landlords in Saltley, for example, were failing to comply with disrepair notices and some were harassing tenants in order to obtain vacant possession and sell – Birmingham CDP, *Property Speculation in Havelock Road* (1974). The Performance Review Committee had noted 'a lack of total commitment at committee level', while differences of opinion between the Environmental Health Department (favouring the service of statutory notices) and the Housing Department (favouring compulsory purchase) further delayed the resolution of a firm policy.

84 For a detailed assessment of Birmingham's compulsory repair and improvement policy see T. Hadden, *Compulsory Repair and Improvement*, Centre for Socio-Legal Studies, Wolfson College (1978), Oxford Research Study no. 1., Social Science Research Council – Appendix B: Birmingham, pp. 76–89.

85 T. Hadden, pp. 88–9.

86 For analyses of the problems of implementation see M. Gibson, 'Housing cuts from the top down', *West Midlands Grass Roots*, no. 19 (1975), pp. 6–12;
J. Freeman, 'Small Heath: lessons from the inner area study', *The Planner*, vol. 63, no. 2 (1977), pp. 46–7;
Llewelyn-Davies, Weeks, Forestier-Walker and Bor, *Unequal City: Final Report of the Birmingham Inner Area Study* (HMSO, 1977), Chapter 5;
C. Paris, 'Birmingham'; and
R. Watkins and J. Shutt, *From Failure to Facelift: Birmingham Community Development Project Final Report, No. 6, Urban Renewal*, Birmingham CDP (1980).

87 For an account of the early experience of one of the project teams by the team leader see P. Archer, 'Policy and practice – Housing Action Areas', in Environmental Health Officers Association.

88 J. Freeman, p. 47 refers to a survey suggesting that only 28 per cent of owners in Small Heath thought that major repairs were necessary.

89 For an analysis of building societies' local practice see C. Lambert, *Building Societies, Surveyors and the Older Areas of Birmingham*, Working Paper 38, Centre for Urban and Regional Studies, University of Birmingham (1976).

90 For example, in Saltley the average monthly payments on conventional loans were about £20 in 1972–3 compared with £34 for clearing bank loans and £47 for fringe bank loans, despite the fact that the latter categories were smaller loans – V. A. Karn, *Priorities for Local Authority Mortgage Lending*, p. 19.

91 'Home-loan bid to beat the sharks', *Evening Mail* (14 March 1975).

92 See G. Green, *Leasehold Loopholes: Birmingham Community Development Project Final Report No. 5*, Birmingham CDP Research Team, Oxford University (1979).

93 For a study of landlords' attitudes to improvement see Birmingham Inner Area Study, *Little Green*, pp. 49–53;
see also R. Watkins and J. Shutt, Chapter 4.

94 Empty houses awaiting improvement attracted adverse publicity, e.g. 'City houses that stand empty a long time', *Evening Mail* (30 January 1976).

95 See B. Young.

96 The IAS argued that a major problem was the division between the Environmental Department (responsible for GIA and HAA declarations) and the Housing Department (responsible for most of the relevant capital expenditure) – Birmingham Inner Area Study, *The Management of Urban Renewal.*

97 Birmingham Inner Area Study, pp. 150–1.

98 Ibid., p. 202.

99 R. Groves, *Urban Renewal: A View from the Grass Roots*, paper presented to John Hopkins International Seminar, University of Birmingham, Centre for Urban and Regional Studies (1975).

100 Ibid., p. 8.

101 City of Birmingham, *Housing Strategy and Investment Programme* (1980), pp. 12–13.

102 See M. Gibson, 'From redevelopment to envelopment? Housing Action Areas in Birmingham', *Housing Review*, vol. 28, no. 2 (1979), pp. 35–9.

103 Birmingham Inner City Partnership, *Inner City Partnership Programme 1979–82* (1978), pp. 59–71.

104 T. J. Brunt, 'Where do we go from here – there is a better way', in Environmental Health Officers Association *Rehabilitation or Renewal*, Proceedings of *Twelfth Annual Lancaster Symposium* (1979).

105 See Community Forum, *Building Standards and Home Improvement: Report of a 'Public Inquiry'* (1979);
Community Forum, *Improve or Bust: the Prospects for Home Improvement in the 1980s* (1980); and
Community Forum, *Manifesto 1980* (1980).

106 R. Watkins and J. Shutt.

107 See, for example, A. Cochrane and R. Dicker, *Workers on the Scrap Heap: Birmingham Community Development Project Final Report No. 2: Employment*, Birmingham CDP Research Unit, Oxford University (1980); and
West Midlands County Council, *County Structure Plan Report of Survey: Inner Areas* (WMCC, 1978).

108 Birmingham Inner City Partnership, p. 11.

109 Birmingham Inner City Partnership, *Inner City Partnership Programme 1980–3* (1979), p. 26.

110 Joint Unit for Research on the Urban Environment, University of Aston, *Industrial Renewal in the Inner City: An Assessment of Potential and Problems* (DoE, 1980), Inner Cities Research Report no. 2.
For a summary see H. Williams and N. Bozeat, 'Industry muddle in the second city', *Planning*, 384 (1980), pp. 6–7.

111 Birmingham Inner City Partnership, *Vacant Land in the Core Area 1980* (1980).

112 For critical comments on participation procedures see G. Green, 'Birmingham's partnership: participation excluded', *The Planner*, vol. 64, no. 3 (1978), p. 76. Birmingham Voluntary Service Council, *Priorities in the Inner City 3* (1979) provides a summary of the views of voluntary organizations on inner city issues and policy.
For elaborations of the case for a stronger locality base for the ICPP see Community Forum, *Area Committees in the Inner City* (1978); and
BVSC Inner City Unit, *Inner City Money and Voluntary Groups: A Discussion Paper* (1980).

113 For discussion of the ICPP by officers heavily involved see T. J. Brunt, 'Housing and the inner city partnership', *Housing Review*, vol. 28, no. 1 (1979), pp. 21–3; and
G. Shaylor, 'Stabilizing the centre', in *The West Midlands RTPI Annual Conference Handbook* (1979).

Chapter 8 Leeds leads

1 Final Report of the National Unhealthy Areas Committee, quoted in the *Weekly Citizen* (1934), 'Decent houses for all' being the minority report with some additional notes and a preface by Ald. A. J. Dobbs.

2 A. J. Taylor, 'Leeds and the Victorian economy', in *The University of Leeds Review*, vol. 17, no. 2 (1975), pp. 286–304. The author notes that expansion was relatively continuous and even, and of the growing population much the greater proportion was born in Leeds and the surrounding county area. Two groups of immigrants gave variety – the Irish in the middle of the century and then later the Jews fleeing from the pogroms of Eastern Europe.

3 See E. Gauldie, *Cruel Habitations: A History of Working-Class Housing 1780–1914* (Unwin, 1974). See p. 74 and p. 110 for two telling quotes from the Minutes of Evidence to the Select Committee on the Health of Towns, 1840.
See also J. N. Tarn, *Working-Class Housing in 19th-Century Britain*, Architectural Association Paper No. 7 (Lund Humphries, 1971), pp. 13–14 for a description of conditions in the middle part of the century and limited philanthropic reforms; and
J. Hole, *The Homes of the Working Classes with Suggestions for their Improvement* (1866).

4 M. W. Beresford, 'The back-to-back house in Leeds 1787–1937', in S. D. Chapman (ed.), *The History of Working Class Housing: A Symposium* (David & Charles, 1971), p. 105.

5 J. Clayton, 'Housing of the poor', in A. T. Marles (ed.), *Hypnotic Leeds* (1894), pp. 15–16.

6 F. M. Lupton, *Housing Improvement: a summary of Ten Years' Work in Leeds* (Jowett and Sowry, 1906).
For a full discussion of local politics in the last century see also E. P. Hencock, *Fit and Proper Persons: Ideal and Reality in Nineteenth-Century Urban Government* (Edward Arnold, 1973), pp. 179–291.

7 The development of back-to-back housing by small speculators in the nineteenth

century was reflected in the curious pattern of street-naming which dominated See D. McKie, 'Motorway city of the seventies', *Guardian* (17 April 1971):

> Often they named the streets after their children: Bertha Grove, Bertha View, Bertha Place, Bertha Crescent, Bertha Mount, Bertha Street. (The Crescents are no less straight than the rest of them, the Mounts no less flat: catch a speculator in a hurry wondering over details like that.) Sometimes they evoked the abstract virtues (Education Road, Providence Terrace, Perseverance Street); sometimes using names borrowed or vaguely recollected, they tried to give a sound of style where no style existed (Bayswater, Clifton, Luxor and Lascelles). And here and there they sought to summon up thoughts of rest and contentment which the physical circumstances of the place totally deny: Hopeful View; Humane Place; Balm Lane; Easy Road.

8 E. Gauldie, pp. 201–2.

9 City of Leeds, *A Short History of Civic Housing* (Jowett and Sowry, 1954), p. 26. The plan involved the demolition of 2000 houses, the repair of 9000 and the building of 9000 new houses over five years.

10 Ibid., p. 47.

11 Leeds City Council, *Report of the Sub-Improvements (Housing) Committee on the Present Position and Future Policy in the City of Leeds* (1932).

12 F. Barraclough, F. H. O'Donnell and C. Jenkinson, *Housing Policy in the City of Leeds, being a Minority Report of a Sub-Committee of the Improvements Committee* (1933).

13 Ibid., p. 40.

14 For fuller accounts of the inter-war period see R. Finnigan, 'Housing policy in Leeds between the wars', in J. Melling (ed.), *Housing, Social Policy and the State* (Croom Helm, 1980), pp. 113–38; and
A. Ravetz, *Model Estate: Planned Housing at Quarry Hill, Leeds* (Croom Helm, 1974), Chapter 2.

15 H. J. Hammerton, *This Turbulent Priest: the story of Jenkinson, parish priest and housing reformer* (Lutterworth Press, 1952).

16 'Full clearance plans announced in Leeds', *Yorkshire Post* (12 July 1934).

17 Ibid.

18 A. Ravetz, pp. 30–8.

19 R. C. Davies, 'A policy of communal socialism', *Yorkshire Post* (19 March 1934).

20 *Yorkshire Post* (8 February 1935).

21 A. Ravetz, pp. 34–5. The issue came to a head when proposals for building a self-contained 'satellite town' at Moortown for 10,000 people were passed by one vote amidst such comments as 'sending tenants to a foreign country', and 'a deliberate attack on property owners'. After later being cancelled by the Conservatives the following comment was made by the Communist Party: 'The real reason why the Tories scrapped the Moortown scheme was because their rich pals did not want the working class as their neighbours' – see Leeds Branch of the Communist Party, *Leeds has a Plan for Health and Happiness* (1938).

22 'Leeds "city of slums" charge denied', *Yorkshire Post* (11 April 1934).

23 'Slum clearance hardship of property owners', *Yorkshire Post*, (28 June 1934). The Leeds experience led to some argument within the Conservative Party and the Leeds delegate, Ald. Davies, carried a motion at their 1934 conference

against the platform (and Sir Hilton Young) calling for changes in legislation; see *Yorkshire Post* (5 October 1934).

24 N. C. Rodgers, *The Socialist Housing Schemes and a Non-Socialist Alternative* (1934), mimeo.

25 G. Morris, *Democracy or Dictatorship: A Searching Criticism of the Socialist Housing Scheme* (1934), p. 5.

26 A. Ravetz, pp. 36–8.

27 'Clearance and rehousing in Leeds', *Yorkshire Post* (18 July 1936).

28 The Housing Director, Livett, was a persuasive advocate of flats in this period. He produced several articles, e.g. R. A. H. Livett, 'Housing and slum clearance in Leeds', *Journal of the Royal Institute of British Architects* (June 1937), pp. 765–78.

29 Local rehousing in flats was in fact proposed for Camp Field, an area where the Catholic church led opposition in 1934 to the dispersal of residents. This was opposed by Jenkinson as merely replacing old slums with new slums. When plans were resurrected in 1936 they had to be scrapped since the Minister pronounced the site unsuitable.

30 For a full history of the Quarry Hill Estate see A. Ravetz; and A. Ravetz, 'The history of a housing estate', *New Society* (27 May 1971), pp. 907–10.

31 Leeds City Council, *Annual Report of the Housing Committee to the Council* (1952), p. 30.

32 Leeds City Council, *First Review of City Development Plan* (Written Analysis) (1968), p. 39.

33 Ibid., p. 39.

34 Leeds City Council, *Older Housing In Leeds: An Assessment of Redevelopment Potential and Priorities 1971–1991, vol. 1* (1971), p. 17.

35 See C. Buchanan, *Traffic in Towns* (shortened ed., Penguin, 1963), pp. 111–40; and
Leeds City Council, MoT and MoHLG, *Planning and Transport: The Leeds Approach* (HMSO, 1969).

36 The report is discussed in City of Leeds, *A Short History of Civic Housing*, pp. 47–52.

37 Ministry of Housing and Local Government (MoHLG), *Families Living at High Density: A Study of Estates in Leeds, Liverpool and London* (HMSO, 1970), Design Bulletin 21.

38 Leeds City Council, *Older Housing in Leeds*, vol. 1, p. 15.

39 For a full discussion of Leeds' use of conversion areas and improvement grant areas and of implementation by the 'Leeds method' see S. Pepper, *Housing Improvement: Goals and Strategy*, Architectural Association paper No. 8, (Lund Humphries, 1971), pp. 67–75.

40 'Unwanted houses problem' *Yorkshire Post* (6 January 1938).

41 City of Leeds, *A Short History of Civic Housing*, p. 68.

42 Leeds City Council, *Annual Report of the Housing Committee to the Council* (1956), p. 30.

> On acquisition the dwellings are generally fully occupied and in many cases there are furnished lettings with which to contend. In these latter cases arrangements have been made with some previous owners to continue hiring the furnishings to the existing tenants

until the Committee are in a position to rehouse the occupants and proceed with conversion into self-contained units.

43 C. Duke, *Colour and Rehousing: A Study of Redevelopment in Leeds*, (Institute of Race Relations, 1970), p. 12.

44 J. Goodfellow, *Leeds House Improvements, Heating Efficiency and Clean Air*, (Malcolm Page, 1964), p. 23. The booklet explains the aims of the 'Leeds method' and the procedures used.
For a discussion of the resolution of ventilation problems in back-to-backs see I. G. Davies, 'The improvement of back-to-back houses with special reference to ventilation', in *Medical Officer of Health Annual Report* (City of Leeds, 1955).

45 S. Pepper, p. 70.
See also Central Housing Advisory Committee, *Our Older Homes: A Call for Action* (HMSO, 1966), Appendix 4: Housing improvement in Leeds.

46 R. Crossman, *The Diaries of a Cabinet Minister*, vol. 1 (Hamish Hamilton and Jonathan Cape, 1975), p. 127 talks of 'another strong personality controlling Leeds housing' (the first being Jenkinson) and of Cohen running the housing committee as if it were his personal possession (see also pp. 541–2).

47 Central Housing Advisory Committee.

48 For a review of the land-use and townscape changes brought about by slum clearance see G. C. Dickinson and M. G. Shaw, 'Coronation Street moves out of town', *Geographical Magazine*, (February 1979), pp. 286–91.

49 R. Wilkinson and E. M. Sigsworth, 'A survey of slum clearance areas – Leeds', *Yorkshire Bulletin of Social and Economic Research*, vol. 15, no. 1 (1963), pp. 25–51. See also R. Wilkinson, 'A statistical analysis of attitudes to moving', *Urban Studies*, vol. 2, no. 1 (1965), pp. 1–14.

50 R. Wilkinson and E. M. Sigsworth, p. 47.

51 S. I. Benson, 'The problems, programmes and progress in the provinces with special reference to Leeds', *Housing Review*, vol. 16, no. 4 (1967), p. 133.

52 For a full discussion of the logic of this pursuance of tandem policies leading up to the tension which developed and Strategy D see M. S. Gibson, *The Developing Role of the 1969 Act in the Changing Process of Urban Renewal*, (M.Sc.Thesis, Aston University, 1971), Chapter 5: 'The Leeds situation'.

53 See A. M. Townsend, 'Improvement techniques in practice', in S. Millward (ed.), *Urban Renewal*, papers presented at a symposium at the University of Salford (1969), pp. 124–33.
For a critical view see M. Hook, 'Burley Lodge, Leeds: indiscriminate housing rehabilitation plus belated traffic management and environmental improvement', *Architects Journal*, vol. 15, no. 23 (1970), pp. 1464–7.

54 'Garden city plan for suburb', *Evening Post* (4 October 1966).

55 Leeds City Council, *Housing Redevelopment Potential and Priorities 1971–91: Report to the Finance and Planning Committee* (1971), p. 6.

56 Leeds City Council, *Older Housing in Leeds*, vols 1–6.

57 A. Ravetz, 'Housing for the poor', *New Society* (10 April 1975), p. 71.

58 'The bombshell that hit Burley Lodge', *Evening Post* (7 November 1972).
A. Ravetz, 'The hopes and dreams that went up in smoke', *Yorkshire Post* (8 December 1972).

59 T. Hancock, R. McKie and M. Hook, *Neighbourhood Study: Burley Lodge Road*, Leeds Civic Trust (1973)
J. Bratt, 'Triumph to disaster in Leeds', *Architects Journal* (28 April 1973), p. 963.

60 Leeds City Council, *Leeds Housing Strategy*, 1975.

61 This included 300 properties p.a. affected by highway proposals, planning projects and the demolition of the Quarry Hill flat complex.

62 J. English, R. Madigan and ·P. Norman, *Slum Clearance: The Social and Administrative Context in England and Wales* (Croom Helm, 1976), Chapter 5.

63 Leeds City Council, *The Clearance Process and You* (1975) begins with the comment: 'What is this booklet for? It is designed to help you understand the clearance process which can often be confusing and upsetting. . . . It deals with the steps involved, your rights to object if you disagree with the proposals and how residents and the city council can together minimize some of the problems which can arise'. Written information is backed up by cartoons.

64 Leeds City Council, *Clearance Programme and Local Rehousing* (1975), p. 1.

65 Hunslet was the setting for Hoggart's rich analysis of working-class culture in R. Hoggart, *The Uses of Literacy* (Penguin edition, 1958). See p. 41 for his description of the physical environment, e.g. 'The houses are fitted into the dark and towering canyons between the giant factories and services which attend them'.

66 For the impact of comprehensive redevelopment and more recent refinements to the clearance process in Hunslet see B. Craig, *Hunslet's Housing* (1976), mimeo; and
Leeds City Council, Department of Planning, *Hunslet Appraisal: Current Position* (1976). The first major redevelopment scheme was the massive deck access, system-built complex of Hunslet Grange (Leek Street flats), the focus of much recent controversy and remedial programmes. See Hunslet Grange Heating Action Group, *Hunslet Grange: An Experiment and its Victims* (1976), mimeo.

67 Rocheford Tenants Association (1976). The following quote summarizes their reaction:

> Everyone feels that the pre-allocation scheme has worked and that it has very many advantages. That is not to say there have been no problems, however the problems that there have been have almost entirely been linked to the question of house and estate design. The actual decision to allocate the houses in advance we feel has been an unqualified success.

68 Leeds City Council, *Area Improvement Programme* (1975)

69 A. Chippendale, *Housing For Single Young People: A Survey of Single Young People Living in Multi-Occupied Houses*, Research Paper 11, Institute of Advanced Architectural Studies, University of York (1976).

70 Cohen was chairman of a government committee considering the future of housing associations at this time. The committee disagreed over whether the voluntary housing movement had a useful role to play and did not complete its work. The evidence presented to it was later summarized in DoE, *Housing Associations* (HMSO, 1971).

71 S. Billcliffe, 'Twist the lion's tail', *Roof*, vol. 4, no. 2 (1979), p. 54; and
Leeds Trades Council, *Which Way Home? A Report on Housing in Leeds* Trades Council (1978).

72 By March 1980 3227 houses had been sold. The policy was the subject of some controversy when its financial premises were attacked in an article by B. Kilroy, 'No jackpot from council house sales', *Roof*, vol. 2, no 3 (1977), pp. 74–80. See also A. Friend, *A Giant Step Backwards: Council House Sales and Housing Policy*, Catholic Housing Aid Society (1980), pp. 7–12.

73 'Council to sell building land', *Evening Post* (2 July 1976).

74 The waiting list had subsequently climbed again to 22,000 by 1979.

75 Completed grant-aided works fell from a peak of 2739 in 1974–5 to 485 by 1979–80.

76 Acquisitions fell from a peak of 714 in 1975–6 (reflecting commitments entered into in the previous two years) to 163 in 1979–80. The improvement of houses on council estates fell from 1311 in 1974–5 to 443 in 1975–6, thereafter to rise again to between these levels. However, there was no major shift to improving acquired houses and in 1979–80 only eighty-two were completed. A major part of the Section 105 allocation went on remedial programmes for 1960s system-built houses and flats in these years.

77 M. L. Harrison, *Local Authority Mortgages in Leeds after Local Government Reorganization*, Housing Research Working Paper 2, Department of Social Policy and Administration, University of Leeds (1977).

78 'Home-loan queues in the rain at 6 a.m.', *Evening Post* (1 October 1976).

79 S. Weir, 'Red Line districts', *Roof*, vol. 1, no. 4 (1976), pp. 109–14. North Hyde Park Residents' Association and South Headingley Community Association, *Evidence to the DoE Housing Finance Review* (1976), unpublished.

80 M. L. Harrison, *The Local Authorities/Building Societies Support Scheme in Leeds*, Housing Research Working Paper 3, Department of Social Policy and Administration, University of Leeds (1977).

81 Department of the Environment, (DoE), *Application for the Confirmation of the City of Leeds, Oldfield Lane (Colmore Street) Clearance Areas Nos. 1 and 2 CPO*, Report of the Inspector (1975). The report also comments 'At a cost the dampness could be eradicated, an internal w.c. and bathroom formed at the expense of losing one of the bedrooms, and the attic bedroom could be made satisfactory by cutting a large dormer window into the roof. However, were all this to be done, the result would still be a lot of very small back-to-back houses entered directly from the pavement, and with steep, dark and winding stairs. . . .'

82 This section deemed back-to-backs built after 1909, i.e. the best back-to-backs as unfit. Although Leeds uses Section 4 criteria (see Chapter 2) to justify clearance, the parallel legislation of Section 5 was confusing. It was eventually repealed in the Housing Act, 1980 but only after some impassioned debate in the Standing Committee about the evils of such housing, with frequent references to conditions in Leeds. See *Hansard*, Standing Committee on the Housing Bill (30 April 1980), cols. 2587–2600.

83 'Cash row over back-to-backs', *Yorkshire Evening Post* (1977).

84 Community Housing Working Party, *Gradual Renewal in Leeds* (1976).

85 W. E. Dyson, *Press release from Belle Vue and Burley Community Association* (1975).

86 In early 1977 Leeds Civic Trust organized a public meeting on housing renewal at which the main theoretical proponents of cellular renewal (R. McKie, R. Moore and M. Hook) spoke; see Leeds Civic Trust, *Outlook*, no. 15 (1977).

McKie was reported as predicting 'dire consequences' if present renewal policies continued: 'Ulster-type violence in our cities – claim', *Yorkshire Evening Post* (18 February 1977).

87 The inquiry was unusual in two respects. First, it lasted for two weeks, much longer than any clearance inquiry held since the 1930s; second, it was held initially in the local working men's club, rather than the more formal setting of the civic hall. DoE, *Application for the Confirmation of the City of Leeds Tong Road (Fitzarthur Street) Clearance Area CPO*, Report of the Inspector (1978).

88 DoE, *Application for the Confirmation of the Hill Street (Lincoln Road) Clearance Area No. 1 CPO*, Report of the Inspector (1978).

89 Leeds City Council, *Gradual Renewal and its Application to Woodhouse* (1978).

90 Ibid., p. 4.

91 Community Housing Working Party, *The Better Way: An Approach to Gradual Renewal in Leeds* (1978).

92 R. Weiner, *the Economic Base of Leeds*, Workers Educational Association (1978).
See also J. M. Allen and M. Campbell, *Employment Performance and the Structure of Industry in Leeds 1948–73*, Paper presented at the Regional Studies Association conference on *The Economic Crisis and Local Manufacturing Employment* (1976)

93 R. Weiner, *The Engineering Industry in Leeds* Workers Educational Association (1976).

94 Leeds City Council, *Leeds Inner City Action: First Urban Programme Report* (1978), p. 7.

95 A research study has shown that the effect of displacement on small firms, brought about by the construction of the M1 through South Leeds and the inner ring road, was far from disastrous, however. In many cases it provided an 'assisted passage' to better premises. See B. Chalkley, *Urban Policy and Small Firms in the Inner City: A Case Study of Redevelopment in Leeds*, Department of Town Planning, Leeds Polytechnic (1979), Paper No. 13.

96 West Yorkshire Metropolitan County Council, *Structure Plan Written Statement* (1978), pp. 14–22.

97 T. Shelton, G. Jones and D. Titterington, 'Five years of local plans – the Leeds experience', *The Planner*, vol. 63, no. 4 (1979), pp. 112–14.

98 Leeds City Council, *Chapeltown Local Plan* (1975). The production of this local plan followed an ambitious social survey of the areas 3000 households. Though successful in its main objective – the reappraisal of previous conversion area policy and the definition of clearance areas and areas for re-improvement – the plan was unable to propose any other initiatives to counteract unemployment, racial disadvantage or environmental decay in the 'problem area' of Leeds.
See also Chapeltown News, *Planning to Deceive* (1975); and
D. Clark, 'Participation', *New Society* (24 July 1975), pp. 196–7.
By 1980 the failure of the local plan to significantly improve conditions in the area was being criticized in a series of articles dealing with unemployment, poor housing and racial tension in the area. See P. Lazenby, 'Anger, despair and plain bitterness', *Evening Post* (2 June 1980).

99 Of those cities contributing to the joint submission to the government in 1977, Leeds was one of two authorities not made a Partnership Authority (the other

being Sheffield). See submission by the cities of Birmingham, Leeds, Liverpool, Manchester, Newcastle and Sheffield, *Inner Cities, 'A Memorable Speech': Commitment to Action* (1977), mimeo.

100 The reduction is brought about by the continuing funding of previous Urban Programme projects.

101 'Scathing attack on Leeds Poverty Report', *Evening Post* (19 July 1978).

102 Leeds City Council, *Second Urban Programme Report* (1979)

103 See 'Third division Leeds: inner city problems demand government and district action' *Weekly Citizen* (6 January 1978); and
R. Jackman and M. Sellars, 'Why rate poundages differ: The case of metropolitan districts, *CES Review*, no. 2 (1977), pp. 26–32.

104 Leeds Branch of NALGO, *Leeds Leads From Behind* (1980).

Chapter 9 Unequal cities in an unequal society

1 For a full account of inter-war reconditioning programmes see R. Moore, *Reconditioning the Slums*, Polytechnic of Central London, School of Environment Planning Unit (1980), Planning Studies no. 7, Chapter 2.

2 H. Barnes, *The Slum: its Story and Solution* (P. S. King, 1931), p. 285.

3 Department of the Environment (DoE), *As Good as New: Housing and Area Improvement Policy in the United Kingdom*, paper for the *UN Habitat Conference*, Vancover (1976), para. 19.

4 G. Cherry, 'New towns and inner-city blight', *New Society* (8 February 1979), p. 296.

5 I. Gough, *The Political Economy of the Welfare State* (Macmillan, 1979).

6 For a collection of essays which have contributed to the development of the new theoretical perspective in urban sociology see C. G. Pickvance (ed.), *Urban Sociology: Critical Essays* (Tavistock Publications, 1979).
For an evaluation of the new urban theory see P. Saunders, *Urban Politics: A Sociological Interpretation* (Penguin, 1980), pp. 103–36.

7 S. Merrett, *State Housing in Britain* (Routledge and Kegan Paul, 1979), pp. 110–13.

8 D. M. Muchnick, *Urban Renewal in Liverpool* (Bell, 1970), Occasional Papers in Social Administration no. 33, p. 113.

9 J. Lambert, C. Paris and B. Blackaby, *Housing and the State: Allocation, Access and Control* (Macmillan, 1978), p. 141.

10 R. E. Pahl, 'Will the inner city problem ever go away?' *New Society* (28 September 1978), p. 678.

11 P. Waddington, 'Looking ahead – community work into the 1980s', *Community Development Journal*, vol. 14, no. 3 (1979), pp. 224–34.

12 See G. Craig, M. Mayo and N. Sharman, *Jobs and Community Action* (Routledge and Kegan Paul, 1979).

13 See B. Crofton, 'Hard core mythology', *Roof*, vol. 4, no. 2 (1979), pp. 51–4.

14 For an overall review of the literature see D. Kirby, *Slum Housing and Residential Renewal: The Case in Urban Britain* (Longman, 1979), Chapter 3.

15 For a general discussion of the rise of owner-occupation see M. Pawley, *Home Ownership* (Architectural Press, 1978).

For a comprehensive analysis of the growth and contradictions of owner-occupation in older housing see Benwell CDP, *Private Housing and the Working Class*, Final Report Series, no. 3 (1980).
See also V. Karn, 'Pity the poor home owner', *Roof*, vol. 4, no. 1 (1979), pp. 10–14.

16 See J. J. Attenburrow *et al.*, *The Problems of Some Large Local Authority Estates – An Exploratory Study* (Building Research Establishment, 1978);
S. Wilson and M. Burbidge, 'An investigation of difficult to let housing', *Housing Review*, vol. 27, no. 4 (1978), pp. 100–4; and
Benwell CDP, *Slums on the Drawing Board*, Final Report Series no. 4 (1978).

17 J. Wintour, 'Late news on housing crisis', *Roof*, vol. 4, no. 4 (1979), p. 110.

18 For a brief discussion see L. Burghes, 'More people poor now' *New Society* (5 October 1978), p. 20.
For a review of DHSS statistics see F. Field, *One in Eight: A Report on Britain's Poor* (Low Pay Unit, 1979).

19 P. Townsend, *Poverty in the United Kingdom: A Survey of Household Resources and Standards of Living* (Pelican, 1979), p. 31.

20 G. Norris, 'Defining urban deprivation', in C. Jones (ed.), *Urban Deprivation and the Inner City* (Croom Helm 1979), Chapter 1.

21 R. Forrest *et al.*, *The Inner City: In Search of the Problem*, University of Birmingham, Centre for Urban Regional Studies (1978), Working Paper no. 64, p. 6.

22 DoE, *Housing Survey Report No. 11, English House Condition Survey 1976. Part 2 Report of Social Survey* (HMSO, 1979).

23 For an exposition of the political philosophy of the new government see M. Thatcher, *Let Our Children Grow Tall, Selected Speeches 1975–77* (Centre for Policy Studies, 1977):

> A vital new debate is beginning, or perhaps an old debate is being renewed, about the proper role of government, the Welfare State and the attitudes on which it rests. . . . (p. 1)

> The fact about economic equality (as opposed to the myth) is that the rich are getting poorer and the poor are getting richer. . . . (p. 3)

> What is it that impels the powerful and vocal lobby in Britain to press for greater equality – for total equality even – when there is little evidence to show that ordinary people want it? Undoubtedly one important pressure is the *simpliste* desire to help the under-privileged. But more often the reasons boil down to an undistinguished combination of envy and what might be called 'bourgeois guilt'. (p. 4)

24 *The Government's Expenditure Plans 1980–1 to 1983–4* (HMSO, 1980), Cmnd. 7841, p. 3.

25 Ibid., p. 78.

26 Statement by Heseltine quoted in 'Michael Heseltine: inner city initiatives', *Architects Journal* (9 July 1980), p. 64.

27 Extract from DoE's letter to local authorities announcing the EZ initiative, quoted in P. Swann, 'Howe's budget and the new cuts', *Planning*, 362 (1980), p. 8.

28 DoE, *Circular 21/80: Housing Acts 1974 and 1980: Improvement of Older Housing* (HMSO, 1980).
See also DoE, *Circular 20/80: Local Authority Improvement For Sale Schemes and Sale of Unimproved Homes For Improvement by Purchase – Homesteading* (HMSO, 1980).

29 *The Government's Expenditure Plans 1980–1* (HMSO, 1979), Cmnd. 7746, p. 3.

30 H. Aughton, 'Demolition job planned on housing expenditure', *Roof*, vol. 5, no. 3 (1980), pp. 75–6.

31 See S. Lansley, 'Is this the end of local democracy?', *New Society*, (11 December 1980), pp. 510–11; and
T. Burgess and T. Travers, *Ten Billion Pounds: Whitehall's Takeover of the Town Halls* (Grant McIntyre, 1980).

32 P. Walker MP, *Hansard* (9 February 1978), col. 1717.

33 Property Advisory Group, *Structure and Activity of the Development Industry* (HMSO, 1980), p. 23.

34 See P. Chapman, 'New town for docklands', *Architects Journal* (21 November 1979), pp. 1082–4.
For a counter view see D. McConaghy, 'UDCs in the dock', *Local Government News*, (April 1980), pp. 18–19.
Opinions within the Property Advisory Group differed as to whether UDCs were a justifiable departure from normal democratic control, and the Group pointed out that while UDCs will have attractions for private investment

> . . . they cannot change fundamentally the attitude of the private sector towards investment in areas which are either unattractive or where there is little prospect of them becoming attractive and thereby stimulating demand. Until new environments have been created in these areas, the Corporations will only be able to act as catalysts.

Property Advisory Group, p. 30.

35 D. L. Birch, *The Job Generation Process*, MIT Program on Neighbourhood and Regional Change, Cambridge, Massachusetts, USA (1979).
The following discussion draws on S. Fothergill and G. Gudgin, *The Job Generation Process in Britain*, CES Research Series no. 32 (1979); and
D. Storey, *Job Generation and Small Firms Policy in Britain*, CES Policy Series 11 (1980).

36 For a critical discussion of EZs see J. Anderson, 'Back to the 19th century', *New Statesman* (11 July 1980), pp. 42–3.

37 House of Commons Environment Committee, *Enquiry into the Implications of the Government's Expenditure Plans 1980–1 to 1983–4 for the Housing Policies of the Department of the Environment* (HMSO, 1980).

38 Association of Metropolitan Authorities, *Housing in the Eighties: Prospects in the Public and Private Sectors* (AMA, 1980).
See also London Boroughs Association, *The Future of London's Housing* (LBA, 1980).

39 Shelter, *And I'll Blow Your House Down: Housing Need in Britain: Present and Future* (Shelter, 1980).

40 R. Best, *The Contraction of the Housing Association Movement* (National Federation of Housing Associations, 1980), mimeo.

41 V. Karn, 'How can we liberate council tenants?', *New Society*, (29 March 1979), p. 738.

42 Quoted in Editorial, 'Mr King washes his hands' *Town and Country Planning*, vol. 49, no. 11 (1980), p. 397.
For a discussion of the various themes of the Urban Renaissance Campaign see

'Urban Renaissance Year', *Planning*, no. 390 (17 October 1980), pp. 5–7.

43 For the summary report see H. W. E. Davies, *International Transfer and the Inner City*, Occasional Papers 0P5, School of Planning Studies, University of Reading (1980).
For topic reports see D. A. Hart, *Urban Economic Development*, Occasional Papers 0P2 (1980).
R. Newnham, *Community Enterprise*, Occasional Papers 0P3 (1980); and
J. Huntley, *Neighbourhood Revitalisation*, Occasional Papers 0P4 (1980).

44 See 'Neighbourhood revitalization: scheme reviewed', *NHIC Progress* (Autumn 1980), National Home Improvement Council.

45 R. Kirwan, *The Inner City in Context 8: The Inner City in the United States* (SSRC, 1980), p. 65.

46 See Cullingworth's comments on the continuous evolution of policies: 'The search for the holy grail should be abandoned in favour of a much more humble quest'. J. B. Cullingworth, *Essays on Housing Policy: The British Scene* (Allen and Unwin, 1979), p. 166.

47 An interesting variation on bald statements in the 'nothing can change until everything changes' vein is found in S. Merrett, Chapter 11, which outlines a housing strategy for the future after 'huge political advances have been made by the left'. (p. 283)

48 Some of these suggestions can be found in a more detailed form in Association of Metropolitan Authorities, *Policies for Improvement: A Report on Housing Repair and Renovation* (1978); and
SHAC, *Good Housekeeping: An Examination of Housing Repair and Improvement Policy* (SHAC, 1980).
Both authors are members of the RTPI Housing Working Party, which is to publish a report in Summer 1981 entitled *Renewal of Older Housing Areas: Into the Eighties.*

49 For a brief discussion see S. Holland and P. Ormerod, 'Why we must increase public spending', *New Society* (25 January 1979), pp. 193–4, and, for the development of the argument, D. Blake and P. Ormerod, *The Economics of Prosperity: Social Priorities in the Eighties* (Grant McIntyre, 1980).

50 For these arguments see B. Kilroy, *Housing Finance – Organic Reform?* Labour Economic Finance and Taxation Association (1978).

51 A. Broadbent, *Planning and Profit in the Urban Economy* (Methuen, 1977), p. 246.

52 R. E. Pahl.

Index

For Product Safety Concerns and Information please contact our EU representative GPSR@taylorandfrancis.com
Taylor & Francis Verlag GmbH, Kaufingerstraße 24, 80331 München, Germany

www.ingramcontent.com/pod-product-compliance
Lightning Source LLC
LaVergne TN
LVHW020002031026
849161LV00023B/817

* 9 7 8 1 0 4 1 1 2 7 5 1 2 *